Springer Series on Cultural Computing

Cultural Computing is an exciting, emerging field of Human Computer Interaction, which covers the cultural impact of computing and the technological influences and requirements for the support of cultural innovation. Using support technologies such as artificial intelligence, machine learning, location-based systems, mixed/virtual/augmented reality, cloud computing, pervasive technologies and human-data interaction, researchers can explore the differences across a variety of cultures and cultural production to provide the knowledge and skills necessary to overcome cultural issues and expand human creativity.

This series presents monographs, edited collections and advanced textbooks on the current research and knowledge of a broad range of topics including creativity support systems, creative computing, digital communities, the interactive arts, cultural heritage, digital culture and intercultural collaboration.

This Series is abstracted/indexed in Scopus.

Licia Calvi · Arnold Vermeeren · Amalia Sabiescu
Editors

Transformative Museum Experiences

Springer

Editors
Licia Calvi
Breda University of Applied Sciences
Breda, The Netherlands

Arnold Vermeeren
Delft University of Technology
Delft, The Netherlands

Amalia Sabiescu
Loughborough University
London, UK

ISSN 2195-9056 ISSN 2195-9064 (electronic)
Springer Series on Cultural Computing
ISBN 978-3-031-89520-3 ISBN 978-3-031-89521-0 (eBook)
https://doi.org/10.1007/978-3-031-89521-0

This Springer imprint is published by the registered company Springer Nature Switzerland AG
The registered company address is: Gewerbestrasse 11, 6330 Cham, Switzerland

Contents

Editors and Contributors

About the Editors

Licia Calvi is a senior lecturer at the Breda University of Applied Sciences, the Netherlands, specialising in the digital transformation of museums, and an adjunct professor in Museum Communication Studies at the University of Bergamo, in Italy. A digital humanist, she investigates how digital technology is used in museums beyond enhancing the visitor experience, to shape (new) museum practices and the role storytelling plays in them.

Arnold Vermeeren is Associate Professor at TU Delft, Faculty of Industrial Design Engineering and Director of the Faculty's MuseumFutures Lab. He was educated as an industrial designer and has been involved in various EU-funded projects on User Experience (UX) as well as a large variety of museum experience-related projects. His current research focuses on designing transformative museum experiences related to societal changes.

Amalia Sabiescu is a senior lecturer in Media and Creative Industries at Loughborough University London. A media and communications scholar with an interdisciplinary research agenda, Dr. Sabiescu employs ecological frameworks to study the nexus between social, cultural and digital change. Her research investigates this dynamic in communities, museums and the heritage sector, examining processes of digital transformation and the evolving social and educational roles of museums.

Contributors

Christianne K. J. Blijleven VU University Amsterdam, Amsterdam, The Netherlands

Kathryn Brown Loughborough University, Loughborough, UK

Licia Calvi Breda University of Applied Sciences, Breda, The Netherlands

Nicholas J. Clarke Department of Architecture, University of Pretoria, Pretoria, South Africa

Pieter M. A. Desmet Delft University of Technology, Delft, The Netherlands

Matthias Freiberger University of Copenhagen, Copenhagen, Denmark

Andrea Gaggioli Università Cattolica del Sacro Cuore, Milan, Italy

Tammy Hodgskiss Origins Centre, University of the Witwatersrand, Johannesburg, South Africa

Peter Kun IT University of Copenhagen, Copenhagen, Denmark

Johan Liedgren Independent Researcher, Seattle, WA, USA

Anders Sundnes Løvlie IT University of Copenhagen, Copenhagen, Denmark

Lora Markova Loughborough University, London, UK

Julian McDougall Bournemouth University, Bournemouth, UK

Louie Søs Meyer IT University of Copenhagen, Copenhagen, Denmark

Alessandra Miano Department of Architecture and Industrial Design, University of Campania "Luigi Vanvitelli", Aversa, Caserta, Italy

Silvia Naldini Heritage and Architecture, Faculty of Architecture and the Built Environment, Delft University of Technology, Delft, The Netherlands

Sebastian Risi IT University of Copenhagen, Copenhagen, Denmark

Amalia Sabiescu Loughborough University, London, UK

Emilie Sitzia University of Amsterdam, Amsterdam, The Netherlands; Maastricht University, Maastricht, The Netherlands

Christian Sivertsen IT University of Copenhagen, Copenhagen, Denmark

Linda Stoltze IT University of Copenhagen, Copenhagen, Denmark

Anders Sundnes Løvlie IT University of Copenhagen, Copenhagen, Denmark

Marjoleine G. van der Meij VU University Amsterdam, Amsterdam, The Netherlands

Arnold Vermeeren Delft University of Technology, Delft, The Netherlands

Timothy Wray IT University of Copenhagen, Copenhagen, Denmark

Noémi Zajzon Loughborough University, London, UK

Chapter 1
Introduction: Transformative Museum Experiences at a Time of Transformation

Amalia Sabiescu, Licia Calvi, and Arnold Vermeeren

Abstract This introductory chapter contextualises and reflects critically on the emerging trends characterising the evolving social role advocated by museums in society, with an emphasis on museum experiences as vehicles for change or transformation. It looks at transformation by adopting a systemic perspective, anchored in the transformative potential of the experiences that museums offer to visitors, and then zooming out to turn attention towards the way recent changes in the socio-political and cultural context reverberated in structural and functional changes inside the museum and connected institutions and communities. The chapter is structured along a series of questions, starting by unpacking a rationale for transformative experiences and why they are worthy of attention at this particular moment (Why), then focusing on what we mean by transformative experiences in the context of museums (What), on particularities of design approaches and supporting technologies for crafting transformative experiences (How), and closing with reflections on the meaning and significance of it all, for the museum, the visitor, diverse audience groups and society as a whole (For whom and For what). The final part of the Introduction then reviews these themes once again, narrating how they are woven in the book narrative.

Keywords Digital transformation · Museum ecosystems · Museum experience design · Museum learning · Social role of museums · Transformative museum experiences

In 2018, our jointly edited book *Museum Experience Design* captured a series of trends shaping the museum world and the experiences offered within, all subsumed

---

A. Sabiescu (✉)
Loughborough University, London, UK
e-mail: a.g.sabiescu@lboro.ac.uk

L. Calvi
Breda University of Applied Sciences, Breda, The Netherlands

A. Vermeeren
Delft University of Technology, Delft, The Netherlands

L. Calvi et al. (eds.), *Transformative Museum Experiences*, Springer Series on Cultural Computing, https://doi.org/10.1007/978-3-031-89521-0_1

to the pivotal change in the role and function of the museum, from being collection-centred to being audience-oriented and community-centred. This shift was instantiated by a series of movements affecting not only museums, but society as a whole, from the rapid evolution of technological opportunities for experience design to new ways of acknowledging and involving the public—ranging from crowdsourcing, adopted on a large scale by various cultural and social organisations (van der Lans et al. 2018; Wrigglesworth and Watts 2018) to initiatives recognising the role of and engaging local communities. These shifts, we proposed, also set in motion structural changes inside the museum (Sabiescu 2018; Sabiescu and Charatzopoulou 2018) and outside, integrating museums in interconnected ecosystems alongside other social, educational but also private technology organisations that expanded exponentially the realms of what is possible to offer as a 'museum experience' (Calvi and Hover 2018; Vermeeren et al. 2018a; Rozendaal et al. 2018).

Since 2018, this vortex of change has continued, partly accelerated by the COVID-19 pandemic and partly triggered by shifts and movements within the museum world itself as reflected by the recently adopted new ICOM definition (https://icom.museum/en/resources/standards-guidelines/museum-definition/) of what a museum is. Beyond definitions, local museum strategies see the museum shape shifting to position itself distinctively as a "start-up hub" (Murphy 2018), an "activist museum" (Bergevin 2018), a "social agora" (Baggesen 2014) or an educational centre hosting a diversity of experiences from creative entrepreneurship to place-making and locality, experientiality and transformations (Garner et al. 2016).

With this new book, we aim to acknowledge these changes and to reflect critically on the emerging trends, especially those related to the new role advocated by museums in society and its emphasis on experiences as vehicles for change. Thus, the central focus of this new volume on museum experience design is on change and transformation, analysed through a systemic perspective, anchored in the experiences that museums offer to visitors. One facet of our exploration regards the museum experience itself as an instrument for change, and at this level we conceptualise what we mean by a *transformative experience* and look at design approaches specifically geared towards inducing transformation. We then turn attention towards the way recent changes in the socio-political and cultural context reverberated in structural and functional changes inside the museum and connected institutions and communities, with shifting museum identities and social roles and new connections, forms of cooperation and partnerships emerging (Sabiescu and Zajzon 2023). Finally, we zoom in on the role of mediation and technology in the making of transformative museum experiences, looking at opportunities and affordances but also calling for an approach to integration of new technologies such as Artificial Intelligence informed by ethical considerations mindful of long-term consequences (in this volume, Chap. 12 by Anders Løvlie et al. and Chap. 13 by Kathryn Brown).

The remainder of this introductory chapter proceeds by unpacking a rationale for transformative experiences and why they are worthy of attention at this particular moment (*Why*), then focuses on what we mean by *transformative experiences* in the context of museums (*What*), on particularities of design approaches and supporting technologies for crafting transformative experiences (*How*), closing with reflections on the meaning and significance of it all, for the museum, the visitor, diverse audience groups and society as a whole (*For whom* and *For what*).

The final part of the Introduction then reviews these themes once again, narrating how they are woven in the book narrative, throughout the following 12 chapters.

1.1 Why Transformative Museum Experiences?

In her book, *Museum metamorphosis*, US-based arts consultant and educator Nico Wheadon argues that not only isolated museums, but rather the entire "museum industrial complex is at a critical juncture", an ecosystem being put in the position to change amidst the rising uncertainty and instability affecting the global socio-political system and tensions experienced locally (Wheadon 2022, p. 1). Similar ideas are echoed by other museum researchers and professionals, in dynamic dialogue with increasingly bold, transformative practices and missions assumed by museums both large and small, as they come to acknowledge the weight of their role as social, community, cultural institutions with a responsibility to carry forth agendas of equity, diversity and social justice (e.g., collection of case studies in Samis and Michaelson 2016; special issue on museums and change by Mac Devitt 2016; special issue by Altayli and Viau-Courville 2018a). In the present book, we focus on this agenda for change and zoom in on the centrepiece of the museum offering for visitors and society: the *experience*. In our view, the pinnacle of the changing role of museums in society resides in the transformative experiences they offer: museums are changing themselves and increasingly engage in dialogues that affect social perceptions, beliefs, attitudes and behaviour (e.g., Bull 2020; Lynch 2017; Mac Devitt 2016). While in the next section of this introductory chapter we will elaborate at length on what we mean by and how we conceptualise *transformative museum experiences*, in this part we start by examining how museums approach issues of transformation and change in their practices and how these reflect their foundational missions and agendas. By looking at some high-profile cases, our aim in this section is to sketch a rationale for museums to include transformative museum experiences in their agendas, in other words, to engage in visitor transformation. As we shall argue further, there is a thin boundary between having an implicit or an explicit agenda for transformation and it all comes down to how we define it. For instance, the International Council of Museums (ICOM)'s newest definition of museums (https://icom.museum/en/resources/standards-guidelines/museum-definition/) outlines their social and ethical responsibility, stating that museums should be "accessible and inclusive" and "foster diversity and sustainability". The definition also captures the centrepiece museum function of offering "experiences for education, enjoyment, reflection and knowledge sharing" (https://icom.museum/en/resources/standards-guidelines/museum-definition/). Thus, an agenda for playing an active social role potentially related to transformation might be implicit, though not explicitly spelled out in the ICOM definition. If we take this definition as a baseline, then by their foundational mission museums should become hubs for diversity, inclusivity and accessibility and offer experiences that build knowledge and encourage reflexivity. But is there a threshold by which museums adopt transformative agendas explicitly in their mission statements or for special projects and exhibitions, actively engaging with visitor transformation or more broadly with issues of social justice and social change?

Scholarly and practitioner literatures abound in examples that capture the manifold ways by which museum experiences may become transformative, and why museums are specifically including transformation in their strategic agendas. Peter Samis and Mimi Michaelson's book (2016) is an excellent compendium of case studies of community-oriented actions spearheaded by museums in the UK and the US, subsumed to an ethos and overarching frame of visitor-centeredness. The *Museum International* special issue on *Museums and Contested Histories* (2018b) shows how, when involved in the (re-)interpretation and negotiation of contested historical narratives, museums might go one step further, not limiting themselves to being exegesis arbiters, but actually stepping out in the arena to provide new platforms for silenced voices, offer experiences that challenge preconceptions and support dialogues to overcome fractured social and ethnic relationships. The articles in the collection unpack cases with a local scope, yet with echoes that connect to global realities. For instance, Albert's article (2018) looks at how the Museu d'Història de Barcelona's (MUHBA) contributed to re-writing the urban history of the city of Barcelona by including a previously ignored narrative, that of the informal settlement of Turó de la Rovira, located in the outskirts of the city for more than 50 years, until the 1990s. MUHBA's exhibition *Barraques, la ciutat informal*, held at *Casa Padellàs* in 2008 offered a platform for communicating for the first time in a coherent narrative the story of the settlement and its community battles and achievements. Locally, it inspired several projects and citizen initiatives around the history of shanty towns. The case reported in Albert's article is just one example of the local instantiation of a social issue experienced globally—the invisibility of marginalised communities and peripheral informal settlements. In this Barcelona-based case, the MUHBA made a poignant statement about how museums can step in and contribute to fostering inclusivity in urban historical narratives by organising exhibitions as vehicles for community voices and narratives that would otherwise be erased or forgotten from contemporary urban memory. In the present edited volume, Emilie Sitzia's chapter *Exhibiting Conflict as a Transformative Strategy* engages with similar issues, providing a vivid example of the role that museums can play in making otherwise hidden (even traumatic) local stories visible, and thus opening spaces for dialogue, understanding, and eventually transformation of social selves and social relationships.

In the same special issue of *Museum International* (2018), Mouliou's article reports on a project with refugee teenagers in Greece, a participatory, engaged process in which young people in the refugee camp were invited to discover the culture of Athens while expressing and reflecting on their own (Mouliou 2018). The work process described by Mouliou involved the creation of a safe space for discovery and self-expression by the young refugees. It resulted in the design and development of an exhibition in a pop-up museum in the camp, themed on *Discovery*. The design process and its outcomes were underpinned by a joint statement that read:

"A museum is a space of wonder, hope, creativity and discovery. This little museum corner is about us, our discoveries and hopes" (Mouliou 2018, p. 128). These themes are reflected as well in this volume by Julian McDougall's chapter on *Third Space Literacies and Museum Learning*, which explores the curatorial and engagement strategies employed by the London-based Museum of Homelessness to advance its social justice agenda and support the homeless community by including in its exhibiting practices 'object stories'—live performances coming from people with a direct experience of homelessness.

The examples above illustrate situated museum interventions that help us envision what might be some of the key reasons for museums engaging with change, a possible response to the question in the title of this section. Why (should museums aim to offer) transformative museum experiences? Quite simply, as stated by Lynch (2017—see also Altayli and Viau-Courville 2018a), because of the role they have been entrusted with, as socio-cultural institutions with a mandate to collect, store, curate, interpret, communicate and preserve culture and memory. For many museums, active engagement with issues of social justice and social change aligns naturally with their policies and missions, it is a foundational goal.

There is a thin boundary in these practices and the narratives that surround them, between mediation and activism. Or, should we say rather, an underlying dynamic alternating between speech and action, between ground for (re)interpretation/voice and grounds for interventions that seek changing the status-quo. As the editors Altayli and Viau-Courville argue about how museums might engage with contested histories in their special issue, museums might "address topics that divide public opinion as well as the ways in which they empower their communities to take a stand and make sure their voices are heard" (2018b, n.p.). On the one hand, we can see these museum actions as expressions of their knowledge dissemination and educational agendas, fulfilled by surfacing erased or forgotten histories and by offering new, sometimes unexpected and unconventional interpretations. A different dynamic plays out when museums act on a defined agenda for change that may take forms such as empowering previously marginalised communities to have a voice and create platforms for exercising that voice, or seeking to redress unequal stakes in the curation and communication of history in multicultural societies. The transformational potential of such practices is evident not only for the communities engaged, such as refugees in the host countries, or marginalised populations in the outskirts of metropoles such as Barcelona, as reported above. But also, if we take an ecological perspective (Vermeeren et al. 2018b; Sabiescu and Charatzopoulou 2018) as endorsed in this book, these actions unavoidably contribute to changing the balance of power, representation and visibility in societies. Oftentimes it might be a small ripple, nevertheless, its echoes might still go beyond the museum's exhibiting spaces and even the local boundaries, as illustrated for instance in Albert's article (2018), where MUHBA's exhibition about a shanty town inspired further projects and citizen initiatives on the same topic.

Discussions on museum impacts and social change have lately been framed in ways that put forth this active agenda of change in unambiguous terms by speaking about "the activist museum" (Bergevin 2018) or "the disobedient museum" (Message

2018). For Bergevin, the term frames museum impacts in a way that values visitors' own understandings and sees them as the active makers rather than the passive recipients of experiences staged for them: "an activist museum practice refers to an approach to museum work which advocates for positive socio-political change including the advancement of civil and human rights" (2018, p. ii). Similar to the stance endorsed in this book, transformative experiences are the cornerstone of activist museum practices, which Bergevin sees embedded in narratives of transformation that surround the visiting experience (an argument that we will come back to later in this introductory chapter).

1.2 What Do We Mean by "Transformative Museum Experiences"?

While in the previous section we have examined why museums might engage with social and visitor change and transformation, we now seek to bring clarity to the notion of *transformative museum experiences* and attempt to better outline the porous boundaries between these and other types of experiences that museums have traditionally offered and continue to offer. Traditionally, museums are used to researching, anticipating and leveraging visitors' background, beliefs and goals to promote meaningful experiences and learning (Garner et al. 2016). As we have argued above and as stated in the newest ICOM definition of museums, the value of museum experiences is associated with the potential to affect the visitor in some ways, and therefore to result in some type of change or transformation. This may take very different forms, from enhanced understanding and retention of cultural content in an educational experience, to potential for immersion and cutting off the visitor from the ordinary vibes of the everyday world, for an exhibition visitor. If museums have been offering *meaningful* experiences all along, what does it mean for a museum to cater for *transformative* experiences?

To elucidate this, the notion of "transformative experience" can be approached from several angles, framed by scholarship associated with different disciplines and research areas, from sociology to leisure studies. Before we unpack some of these, it is worth clarifying that we have in mind experiences that are designed and offered or staged with a clear purpose or intention. Duerden and colleagues (2015) argue that this sets apart designed or structured experiences from other spontaneous ones, as the nature of the experience and the outcomes for the visitor all occur within "provider manipulated frameworks", with examples ranging from the experience of dining in a restaurant to attending a concert or an exhibition (p. 603). We also use "transformative" and "transformational" experiences as synonyms.

An extremely well outlined, systematic theorisation of transformative experiences comes from leisure studies, in the work of Duerden et al. (2018) who outline a framework for designing "structured experiences", focussing on extraordinary types of experiences, those not typically experienced in everyday life. Duerden and colleagues distinguish between three types of extraordinary experiences: memorable, meaningful and transformational. The distinction between these is given by the degree of intensity of three possible subjective reactions that are quintessential for extraordinary experiences: emotion, discovery, and change (p. 202). Thus, memorable experiences are those where the subjective reaction to the experience is strong emotion; in meaningful ones the subjective reaction involves "strong emotions and the discovery of significant and personally relevant insights" (p. 206); while transformational experiences trigger all three reactions, being defined by the authors as:

> An experience where the objective elements engage an individual's attention and produce subjective reactions involving strong emotions, the discovery of significant and personally relevant insights, and personal changes in values, beliefs, intentions, or self-perceptions. Most often transformative experiences are characterized by intrinsically motivated, enduring changes in self-perception and behavior. (Duerden et al. 2018, p. 208)

The importance of emotional engagement is evident in Duerden's definition of transformative experiences, as is the fact that it is "personal", it is a reaction subjectively experienced by the person to whom the staged experience has been targeted. These are qualities mentioned as well in the still emerging literature on museums and change specifically focussed on transformative experiences (e.g., Bergevin 2018; Garner et al. 2016) and a larger body of literature on museums, emotional engagement and empathy (e.g., Gokcigdem 2016; Simon 2014; Wildt 2018), some of which hint at the transformative potential of empathetic and/or emotionally charged experiences. The edited volume on *Fostering empathy in museums* (Gokcigdem 2016) makes a direct connection between the degree of emotional and empathetic engagement and transformative experiences. In her 2018 article on museums and empathy, Dutch museum professional Annemarie de Wildt provides a few poignant examples of museum exhibitions that sought to employ empathy as an engagement device, to tell often difficult stories of conflict, trauma and violence. An example is the *Museum of Broken Relationships*, which narrates the experiences of the Balkan wars from the perspective of the people affected by the conflicts. Narrative and storytelling are central to de Wildt's analysis of empathetic museum spaces and experiences. For de Wildt, exhibiting personal stories is a means to create connectedness to visitors' personal emotions and thus trigger a sense of empathy, especially when these stories ask people to endorse a point of view embedded in a "performative space" (p. 81). Adopting somebody else's point of view is a powerful device for affording experiential engagements with difficult issues, from conflict and collective trauma to sex work and stigma. We find similar ideas in the work of Bergevin (2018), who looks at how storytelling and narrative contribute to creating "affective connectedness"—ways of engaging in the museum space characterised by intense emotion and empathy (2019). For Bergevin, affective connectedness is the cornerstone of transformation in the museum space.

Besides emotion, Duerden et al.'s definition (2018) emphasises two other aspects of *transformative museum experiences*—discovery and change. One of the best articulated frameworks on (designed) transformative experiences that captures these two dimensions comes from the work of Gaggioli (2016). While we will come back to Gaggioli's design framework in the next section, here we report on the theory around transformative museum experiences that underpins his design approach. These are, for Gaggioli, "self-actualization experiences" (2016, p. 97) that bear three characteristics: First, change is experienced as a sudden and intense rupture from previously held beliefs, ideas and even identity. Just like in other scholarly definitions of extraordinary experiences, these experiences are sudden and intense (Duerden et al. 2018), and "potentially life altering in that they may contribute to personal growth or renewal" (Jefferies and Lepp 2012, p. 38). Second, for Gaggioli, the change affects not only the contents of an individual's inventory (beliefs, ideas, values) but also their worldview, the experience of being oneself and engaging with the world. Thus, transformation is not merely small-scale change, it involves "epistemic expansion". Third, Gaggioli draws on dynamic systems theory to look at the mechanisms of change. A systems perspective enables the identification of multiple triggers and trajectories of change that culminate in the moment when the transformation is being experienced as a sudden event. Thus, even if perceived as instantaneous, the transformation is emergent, the result of complex mechanisms of self-organisation and multi-scaled changes that culminate in that critical moment of transformation as acknowledged by the agent.

Another analytical angle worth exploring regards the dynamics between the individual and the collective when analysing transformative museum experiences. Several recent works on museums and change take a collective stance, they focus on issues experienced collectively by social groups, communities or urban collectives and speak of outcomes such as community empowerment and collective agency (Altayli and Viau-Courville 2018a). Personal experiences are inherent in collective discourses and practices, as after all collective experiences can always be analysed from the angle of the individual person and the way their impact was subjectively felt. However, the analytical lens focussed on the individual tends to be rather associated with mechanisms and outcomes that emphasise emotion and empathy experienced personally, subjectively as outlined above and in the work of Bergevin (2018), de Wildt (2018) and the edited volume by Gokcigdem (2016). To make sense of transformative experiences for groups and collectives, other lenses on transformative experiences are useful, which put emphasis on relationships, connectedness and sense of community. One such theory comes from the work of performance studies scholar Victor Turner and his theory of anti-structure (2008). Turner characterises experiences that break the routine of everyday life and enable people to experience a sense of community, what he calls "communitas". These experiences are facilitated by special rituals and shared purposes that free participants of their everyday constraints and identities and open up novel ways of perceiving, activating their potential and connectedness to the others. These are highly unique, evanescent events that generate what sociologist Émile Durkheim calls "collective effervescence" (Durkheim 1912/1995). The focus in both Durkheim's and Turner's work is on the break-out nature of the experience and its being collective, shared, generating a sense of communion and solidarity that may also be felt as renewing and transformational for the self.

To adequately position the role of museums and their engagement with important social issues seeking transformation at individual and collective levels, it is useful to broaden the perspective to a systemic one, which locates the museum in ecosystems of social, cultural, economic and educational actors (Vermeeren et al. 2018b; Sabiescu and Charatzopoulou 2018). As Bergevin (2018) argues, to understand and appreciate the museum visit as transformative practice, we have to contextualise the museum experience within constellations of personal experiences that together may shift attitudes, assumptions, perspectives and even behaviour in visitors.

1.3 How Can We Design Transformative Experiences in Museums?

How can we design museum activities and exhibits that lead to transformative experiences, given the fact that the outcomes of transformative experiences are inherently subjective and therefore not predictable (e.g., Gaggioli 2016)?

In his focus on museum digital transformation, Mason (2022) proposes to adopt a design thinking approach, which he sees as a human-centred design practice. According to Mason (2022), design thinking approaches have four main principles in common: they are (1) people-centred, starting by gaining an understanding of people's needs, behaviours, and motivations by employing empathic, ethnographic methods; (2) problem-framing instead of problem-solving, re-framing the problem in human-centric ways; (3) highly collaborative, co-creative and visual processes involving members of interdisciplinary teams, as well as visitors and communities; (4) highly iterative creative processes based on a set of different prototype methods (to "make and experiment" and test towards the final design solution).

Gaggioli (2016) suggests that we should think in terms of designing transformational affordances, which, he argues, can be defined as theoretically-based design guidelines for inviting, eliciting or facilitating a transformative experience. He illustrates this by discussing four interrelated aspects of transformative experience design: (i) transformative medium, e.g., plays, storytelling, imagery, music, films and paintings; (ii) transformative content, referring to the content or subject and structure of an experience, which include epistemic and emotional affordances; (iii) transformative form, which concerns the style rather than the subject of the experience that is represented; (iv) transformative purpose, for which he suggests to think in terms of transformative processes rather than in terms of the transformative outcome and to consider interactive experiences as spaces for transformative possibilities.

The notion of liminal spaces is often brought up in this context. Liedgren et al. (2023) state that "In liminality, we know that what we see is not our existing world, yet we experience an immediate feeling of something very real" and that "Designing liminal spaces also means helping people to explore new 'spaces of the self'" (p. 2). Based on four assumptions about the nature of liminal spaces, Liedgren et al. (2023)

propose a conceptual framework and a three-step approach for developing technology that delivers transcendence and deeper experiences. According to the authors, "Putting on hold some beliefs from our existing narrative and entering a liminal space allows us to safely test, play with and consider alternative narratives" (Liedgren et al. 2023, p. 2).

The three-step process identified by Liedgren and colleagues (2023), referenced as well in the present volume (Chap. 2: *Juxtaposition and the Liminal Exhibit*) is in line with various phases that can be identified in models of transformative learning processes (e.g., Mezirow 1978; Nohl 2015). Such models generally start with some event that catalyses in the agent a need or desire for transformation, which is later followed by a process of gaining deeper understandings, experimental and undirected inquiry, exploring new attitudes and behaviour, until finally the new attitudes or behaviour become an integral part of one's life. Bergevin's study (2018) on roles that museums can play in visitors' narratives of transformation, suggests that museums can engage in various phases of a person's transformative process: either in a single phase, or in multiple phases. For example, a museum may "raise awareness" or "remind us" of a specific issue and thus instil in people a desire for transformation, it may help people "foster a deeper understanding" on a certain topic, or "may inspire action" (Bergevin 2018) by providing a liminal space in which visitors can explore new practices.

Any element of a museum's collection may potentially be used to build a transformative experience around it. Chisolm et al. (2020), for example, provide illustrative cases of how exhibits in an art museum were used for transformative learning of clinically-relevant skills in healthcare. Soren (2009) provides ten triggers for transformation in museums, and explains how a museum's collection contributed to the transformative experiences. For example, in the Canadian War museum the permanent collection is exhibited in spaces that "evoke the atmosphere of war, physically situate visitors in the trenches and battle grounds, and overwhelm" (Soren 2009, p. 236). In another example featuring an artwork by a former resident of a First Nations residential school, the resident's images "showed how devastating and monstrous his life was" (p. 237). Messages in the comment book by visitors who had personal experience with residential schools helped a visitor "understand how she deals with suffering and painful moments in history" (Soren 2009, p. 237). Another person at the Hagia Sophia museum in Istanbul, felt "completely immersed in the history because of the reality of the building, and the authenticity of the objects and the mosaics". For her, the experience "was a culmination of everything she had learned and seen related to this masterpiece of Byzantine architecture" (p. 236). As these examples illustrate, any collection item may be used for creating a transformative museum experience, if creatively and collaboratively designed from a human-centred perspective (see Mason 2022). Such a human-centred perspective is employed in Chronis's framework of narrative construction (2012) to understand lived experiences. This framework consists of three successive stages of *narrative enrichment*, *narrative imagining*, and *narrative closure* to understand how visitors make sense of the exhibition. The framework is anchored in the visitors' point of view, following them as they interpret the exhibition elements according to their own frame of reference which consists of their pre-existing knowledge of the topic, their previous lived experiences, and their own life story.

Similarly, the range of technologies that can be applied to enrich museum experiences seems endless. Based on interviews with museum experience designers, Calvi and Vermeeren (2023) provide an overview of various digital technologies (ranging from apps and simple sensors to robots, Artificial Intelligence and Virtual Reality) and how they may be applied to enrich museum experiences (e.g., for extending the visitor journey, increased engagement, immersion, social experiences, personalisation, etc.). However, their focus is on museum experiences in general, rather than on *transformative* museum experiences. Gaggioli (2016), not specifically focussing on museum experiences, argues that immersive virtual reality holds the highest potential to foster a transformative process. However, as was consistently stated by the museum experience designers interviewed by Calvi and Vermeeren (2023), "technology is not the first element to think of when designing an experience", "technology is not seen as leading, but the museum's values and stories are" (p. 8). Calvi and Vermeeren (2023) also found that nowadays "many design agencies explicitly think about museum visits in terms of journeys or as an experience that is integrated into a bigger (or more holistic) experience in time and place" (p. 11). Extending the visitor journey or seeing it as integrated into a bigger experience in time, is especially important for transformative experiences. Novel technologies provide new opportunities to achieve this, and through that help bridge the gap from experiences in the museum to the transformative steps in people's everyday lives. However, the questions around the optimal length and nature of a transformative visitor journey and how it can be embedded or related to a person's broader transformational journey still deserve further exploration.

In conclusion: Designed museum experiences indeed have the potential to play an important role in people's transformative (learning) experiences in relation to societal challenges. But there are still many design challenges in how to effectively do so, as well as in how technology may support this.

1.4 Who Should We Design Such Experiences for? A Special Focus on Communities

While the transformative experiences mentioned above are addressed to museum audiences *tout court*, a special kind of audience is made up of the communities that are part of the museum ecosystem, which deserve separate attention. As briefly anticipated in the section on the different dynamics between individual and social in the design of transformative experiences, when it comes to communities, the transformative role of museum experiences might be understood and defined in a different way.

With the advent of the New Museology (Morse and Munro 2018), the focus of museum practice has gradually shifted from museum professionals defending their "silos of expertise" onto seeking alliances across disciplines and audiences. As a consequence, the people-centred, much less collection-driven approach to museum practice advocated by the New Museology has put a stronger focus on communities and on their engagement in heritage discourse. It has given them a voice in claiming their own narrative in the otherwise traditional view on heritage and discourse perpetrated by museums as institutions.

It is however with the 2003 UNESCO Convention for the Safeguarding of the Intangible Cultural Heritage, that participatory approaches to cultural heritage have become mainstream in heritage practice. It is its Article 15 in particular that emphasises the need to promote the active engagement of communities "to create, maintain and transmit such heritage, and to involve them actively in management" (Sousa 2018, p. 10). In museums, participation has become a recognised and accepted concept and a practice that is more and more adopted since Nina Simon's seminal book on the participatory museum (2010).

But what does participation have to do with the transformative role of museum experiences? In the academic literature, the attention to community engagement has taken different perspectives: some scholars (see for example Burgers 2021) are interested in lowering the threshold to heritage access and for this reason have been looking into how communities can be involved in its management. Others, like Chmutina et al. (2021) extend community involvement beyond mere management, onto planning and preserving local cultural heritage. Houpert (2019), on the other hand, stresses the importance of engaging the local community even earlier in this process, in determining what heritage is for them and also in identifying which forms this engagement may take. Beyond their intrinsic differences, all these perspectives assume that local communities need to develop a sense of ownership for their heritage. With ownership comes a sense of pride for it, as well as a sense of awareness of the value it represents, leading to a feeling of responsibility for it.

In this sense, the participation of communities in the museum discourse can be considered as transformative to them because it places them right at the centre of museum practice. This new role may become a catalyst for transformation because it contributes to empowering and making them valuable peers for the museum as an institution (Simon 2010). Participatory practices thus represent a way to "connect people, places and collections, and create public value" (McCall and Gray 2014, p. 4). Applying the concept of transformative experiences to participatory museum practices with communities captures nuanced dimensions of change, oftentimes different from the ones typically afforded by museum visits. These changes might not necessarily take place inside the museum spaces, though they may be initiated or punctuated by museum interventions. They also have different temporalities and rhythms of change, often involving long-term collaborations between museums and local communities. These changes and the scales at which they might be experienced vary greatly according to the type of community involved and its needs, the types of collaboration and the heritage or culture-related issues at stake. In other words, they are not prone to generalisation and even what may be considered "best approaches" in engaging communities to make them feel heard and to democratise access to heritage, are local in nature, context-specific and not easily transferable to other contexts. While the UNESCO Convention lists a number of methods to involve communities, some scholars (Burgers 2021; Rodenberg et al. 2023) still contend that "there is much debate, but little research, on current concepts, tools and procedures for democratisation in the access to and definition, appropriation, management and planning of heritage" (Burgers 2021, p. 71). In this introductory chapter, we merely wish to raise awareness of the important transformative potential that community engagement in museums practices has for communities (and oftentimes for museums as well). While the literature offers valuable case studies on how such transformative experiences might unfold, their valences, challenges and their contradictions, there are critical questions being opened up as well. Some questions, with direct concern for this volume, regard the role that technology might play to facilitate this involvement. In a world where digital technologies are pervasive in the lives of museum visitors and increasingly integrated in curatorial and educational practices, how can they be leveraged for creating platforms for communities to come together, negotiate collective views, develop and convey their own discourses and interpretations around heritage? How can museums become "a shared space with communities" (Mason 2022, p. 2)? How can this involvement be sustainable? And ultimately, how can approaches to more elaborate, often long-term community engagement be conflated with or leveraged by the design of transformative experiences *in situ*?

1.5 For What? The Significance and Consequences of (Designing for) Transformative Experiences in Museums

The question of impact is inherent in the design of transformative experiences, yet as argued above, it is also most elusive, as the outcomes are subjective and difficult to articulate. In this section, we would like to open up for debate the very idea of impact and how we might appreciate or assess it, when considering transformative experiences.

In a circular fashion, we would firstly like to bring back into focus the argument on the changing roles of museums in society which opened this introductory chapter. In order to fully appreciate the value of the transformative experiences offered by museums, it is necessary to raise awareness of the different scales at which we might locate change: At micro-scale, we regard the experience itself as a medium for change. At this scale, the impacts are as well anchored in the context and participants that partake in the experience. In close connection to this, at macro-scale, incremental changes have been contributing for years to shifting museums' roles and identities as sociocultural actors. These shifts affect not only museums and their internal structures, but also relationships with other social actors and complex dynamics of cooperation among them. Acknowledging these shifts at macro-scale is important, in our view, for being able to grasp the underpinnings of transformative experiences at the micro-scale. In other words, we need to keep in mind the way museums function in society, how they collaborate with other institutions and how they come to be perceived by citizens, because all of these shape the context within which we can appreciate at face value the impacts of museum experiences on visitors and more broadly their overall societal value (Scott 2009).

To illustrate this, we would like to highlight here one vector of change at the macro-scale, regarding the educational role of museums. While education has traditionally been a core function of the museum, nowadays museums are becoming increasingly important education players as third spaces (Potter and McDougall 2017), where interest-based activities, mediated interactions and porous teacher-student boundaries come together to shape more vibrant, alternative teaching and learning practices. The concept of "experience" is fundamental for the educational role of museums. As Scott (2006, 2009) argued in her well-researched review of museums societal values and impacts, the value of museum education resides in the "unique type of learning experience" (2006, p. 56) it offers, which sets it apart from formal scholarly institutions and underscores its central contribution to out of school education. The growing interest in museum learning reflects broader trends and associated discourses about changing education paradigms, employability, and the future of work. In a world marked by fast change, traditional educational actors are slower to adapt their curricula and learning approaches to meet change and move at equal speed to follow its evolution so that they can train new generations of learners equipped to navigate shifting job market realities. Where schools are slow to move and adapt, the learning experiences that museums offer become valuable, not as replacement, but rather as ways to calm the gap, to fill needs for inspiration, exposure to novelty or to new interpretations. In short, museums can kindle interest in transformative learning (Kitchenham 2008) pathways, or offer spaces for transformative learning episodes that can be followed upon and deepened by learners by accessing other actors, institutions and spaces in the learning ecosystem. For example, a digital crafts workshop in a museum will not prepare a future professional, but might offer a just enough blend of know-how and experience to inspire participants that are interested in this field to assess opportunities against aspirations and gently suggest directions for further training (Sabiescu and Zajzon 2023). This example illustrates how trends shaping learning ecosystems at the macro-scale are brought to bear on the design of micro-scale learning experiences.

In our view, when we seek to appreciate the impacts of situated learning experiences in museums we have to be mindful of how the experience is positioned both at micro and at macro-scale. Acknowledging this complexity, in this volume we endorse an ecosystem approach (Vermeeren et al. 2018a; Sabiescu and Charatzopoulou 2018), seeing museums in networked ecologies of learning spaces, actors and offerings where they perform a unique role, but also where they depend on collaborations with other actors in order to fulfil their educational mission. This perspective is adopted as a means to properly contextualise and calibrate the approaches shaping the design of museum learning experiences, with consideration towards relationships established with broader societal norms, values, practices, spaces and discourses for (out of school) education and learning.

While we focussed above on learning experiences in relation to the educational function of museums, other facets of museum roles and functions can be explored, where the links between micro- and macro-scales appear important for a thorough consideration of impacts. We could, for instance, extend the discussion above on community participation in museum practices, bringing to bear the same dynamic between the micro and the macro-scale. In all these cases, museums can be seen as responsive institutions, stepping in, often as pioneers, to fill the needs of a society pressed by rapid change. In conclusion, an ecosystemic lens enables us to capture and appreciate more thoroughly the scales, mechanisms and trajectories of transformation and change. And an assessment lens that favours more attention to processual, step by step, and multi-scaled change is prone to give us a more comprehensible view of impacts. As suggested as well by Bergevin (2018), this approach would be less concerned with final outcomes and more with on-going processes—appreciating impacts in terms of active engagement of visitors and communities with museums, honouring their perspectives and positionalities.

1.6 The Chapters in This Book

The book is divided in three parts, offering complementary perspectives around transformative museums experiences that reflect the ecosystemic perspective underpinning the thinking and approach to practice that informs this volume: after unpacking the concept of "transformative experience" in relation to museums and museum visitors and associated design approaches in Part I, the chapters in Part II then look at how transformative experiences are emblematic of museums themselves being subjected to change, both within their organisational structures as well as in the way they interpret and act to fulfil their social roles and mandates, and the relationships established with other socio-cultural, economic and political actors and institutions. The final part discusses the role that technologies play in supporting the delivery of transformative experiences, along with their sociocultural and ethical implications.

1.6.1 Part I: Transformative Experiences: Concept and Design Approaches

In Chap. 2, Johan Liedgren, Andrea Gaggioli and Pieter M. A. Desmet sketch an interpretive frame for theorising transformative museum experiences at the junction of the familiar and the unfamiliar, of what is and what could potentially be. This in-between space of liminality is an extension of what museums are already: sites of experience separate from the everyday, by their definition realms where extraordinary experiences (Duerden et al. 2018) are set to be staged. Therefore, the potential for transformative experiences is already embedded in the foundation of museums as liminal spaces. Yet, materialising the transformative potential of such experiences requires an intentional design that, to start with, disengages the visitor from their ordinary, everyday experience flow and patterns of thinking. This space is suspended in between the real and tangible on the one hand, and the imaginative and metaphoric on the other. Liedgren et al. argue that this is an *active* space in the sense that for the transformative experience to emerge, the visitor needs to be immersed enough in order to allow their ordinary flow of thinking and feeling to be disrupted, but still maintain their capacity to make sense of the experience in ways that afford transformation of the self-convictions and beliefs, attitudes and worldviews.

The authors' *Liminal Design Framework* distinguishes three steps for activating this in-between space and engaging the visitors: a Narrative Desire that strikes a balance between being at the same time relevant and unexpected (Step 1), is materialised, instantiated for the visitor as a space of Optimised Abstraction (Step 2). Suspension of Disbelief (Step 3) ensures the continuity of the experience and the ability of the visitor to engage fully and immersively within it. Thus, the visitor is then able to step back at the end and bring its echoes and ramifications back into the ruptured, disrupted flow of the everyday, where the experience will ultimately leave a trace, a seed of transformation. The chapter offers a tapestry of cases in which this three-step model is illustrated by exhibition concepts, museum galleries, or specific hotspots in exhibition trails.

Chapter 3, *Attachments in Museum Experience Design*, by Noémi Zajzon, links conceptually the notion of 'transformative experience' to that of 'attachment', a connection which is hinted at in the subtitle *Displaying relationships and networks of public urban heritage*. The chapter narrative unfolds from an ecosystemic, relational perspective that highlights the role of public attachments in connecting visitors with the subtle messages weaved in the exhibition design, generating engaging experiences that leverage public memories. This connection is explored by examining the design of an historical exhibition that celebrated the figure of a city mayor who left an enduring legacy in Târgu Mureş, a city in Transylvania. The chapter offers a rich theoretical exploration informed by affect theories, symbolic interactionism and science and technology studies, showing how exhibition and experience designers can use public attachments to create engaging, potentially transformative experiences through historical exhibitions, linking fragments of public memory to issues of contemporary relevance.

In *Designing "One Minute" experiences* (Chap. 4) Anders Sundnes Løvlie, Linda Stoltze and Timothy Wray address an interesting research and design question: how to design engaging, stimulating and potentially transformative experiences for visitors, while being aware of their short attention span in engaging with exhibits? The chapter details the design and user testing of *One Minute*, an app that can be used to generate informative content about museum exhibits in a format that is stimulating and interactive. This case opens up valuable points for reflection and discussion around the value of "one minute experiences": as the authors enquire, even though several studies did prove the short attention span of museum visitors while in the galleries, how valuable can a one-minute engagement be? The chapter addresses this question and proposes reflections informed by the literature and the data from the

One Minute study, concluding with an important realisation: that any transformative experience starts with catching and then holding the attention. Thus, short experiences that are engaging, while not transformative in themselves, might set in motion processes of (slow, but real) transformation. One of these may be the creation of a long-term relationship between museums and their visitors, positioning the museum as a friendly, engaging go-to place to enjoy art, learn and reflect.

1.6.2 Part II: The Changing Museum: Structure, Social Role and Relationships

Part II opens with a chapter that looks at the transformative potential of experiences offered by science museums and centres, as well as the major changes undergone by these institutions throughout the past century and since the turn of the century in particular (Chap. 5). Marjoleine G. van der Meij and Christianne J. Blijleven locate the vortex of change around science museums and science centres in the evolution of science communication paradigms, which shifted the communication of science towards more participatory and dialogic models. The chapter offers an outline of the historical evolution of experiences offered by science museums and science centres, showing how along with the integration of more dialogic and participatory approaches, their design started to be more and more considerate of societal issues and actively engaging with them. The chapter offers rich illustrations of recent and contemporary exhibitions that illustrate both the transformation of science museums and centres, as well as their transformative potential when it comes to taking effect on visitors' knowledge, worldviews and attitudes. These are accompanied by reflections on the mindshift needed to fully embrace the dialogic and participatory models that the museums started to be open towards throughout the past decades.

In Chap. 6, *Discovering Volunteers as an Essential Community of Practice in Small Museums in the Netherlands*, Silvia Naldini and Nicholas Clarke highlight the human dimension in the context of change around museums. The chapter reports on a project that involved seven small museums in the Netherlands and tested a method for involving volunteers in ideating and proposing strategies for assessing museum performance and formulating new directions and strategies for museum transformation. The chapter brings a valuable contribution by drawing attention to the context and challenges surrounding small museums, how these are sustained by an often invisible, nonetheless essential, community of volunteers, and how the role of the latter can be leveraged through specific engagement techniques. The workshop-based method outlined by the authors invites volunteers to reflect on the current strategy and activities of the museum and sketch a vision for desired future directions of change, spanning internal museum operations and the relationships established with visitors and surrounding communities.

In Chap. 7, *Third Space Literacies and Museum Learning*, Julian McDougall discusses the transformative dimension of the role that museums have for long filled, that of acting as spaces for non-formal learning. McDougall uses as a central case the newly opened Museum of Homelessness in London, and by comparing it with experiences staged in four other museums, unfolds a poignant argument about the way transformation is embedded in the social and educational function of the museum. Museums, McDougall argues, can reasonably be said to intend a "dynamic pedagogy" where change is embedded, but the extent to which they can deliver on this will depend on the articulation of curational and experience design practices. The Museum of Homelessness makes an excellent case for this argument. After waiting for years to find a physical building, the exhibition narrative has been designed to evoke the experience of homelessness while constantly inviting the visitor to make connections to first space (visitors' own) experiences that are inherently human, personal, and thus engulfing: the need for refuge in difficult times, the need and comfort of finding community, solidarity and eventually the vital necessity to cherish hope and envision (shared and personal) futures. Thus, the museum offers a space for "transformative relations" by leveraging and activating connections to personal histories, something which can be discussed with reflection to the notion of "attachments" discussed earlier in Noémi Zajzon's chapter, only that in here, the focus is on the personal, whereas Zajzon explored the public nature of attachments in relation to history making and historical exhibitions. Ultimately, McDougall's chapter argues that the crux of the transformative potential of museum experiences lies in the intentionality to create a third space of reflexive encounter between what is being exhibited and the visitor's first space, delivered by weaving powerful narratives and themes around the exhibits on display.

The transformative potential of historical exhibitions, addressed by Noémi Zajzon in Part I is explored once again, from a different perspective, by Emilie Sitzia's chapter on *Exhibiting Conflict as a Transformative Strategy* (Chap. 8). Sitzia argues that one direction for transformative exhibitory practices may lie in the possibility to exhibit multiple, even conflicting narratives in the same space. The chapter takes the case of Musée d'Histoire de Marseille (MHM), which has been asked by local citizens to include in its exhibition a narration of the clashes between the citizens and the municipality of Marseille with respect to buildings safety, following a notorious case of building collapse. This case is used by Sitzia, weaved into a rich theoretical discussion that ultimately argues for disruption, conflict as a root node and first step in transformational journeys. Rather than discarding conflict, the chapter invites reflection on how museums can leverage their social and educational role to welcome in their spaces polyvocality, multiplicity of views, even when they conflict, as a way to generate reflexivity and, paradoxically, new pathways to dialogue and understanding.

In Chap. 9, *Ochre Painting Workshops as a Tool for Interactive and Sensory Museum Learning*, Tammy Hodskiss offers a highly original reflection on the engaging and potentially transformative nature of sensorial workshops where visitors are invited to engage hands-on with and learn about ochre rock, painting and art. The ochre workshops are offered by the Origins Centre in South Africa and reflect the museum's approach to learning as an experiential, hands-on, interactive process. Visitors can touch, grind, process, and paint with ochre, as means to learn about its use in cosmetics, medicinal uses, indigenous arts as well as contemporary artistic expressions.

1.6.3 Part III: Supporting Technologies

In Chap. 10, Lora Markova focuses on the documentation and preservation of immersive museum experiences generated via eXtended Reality (XR) technologies such as AR and VR. The chapter starts by exploring the sociocultural value and potentially transformative role of immersive experiences as a rationale for their preservation, drawing on two recent London-based cases of immersive experiences—*Virtual Veronese* (2019, The National Gallery) and *Curious Alice: The VR Experience* (2021, Victoria and Albert Museum). This enquiry is extended into a reflection on how the nature of immersive experiences and the very challenges brought by their preservation call for changes in museum practices and the relationships and collaborations nurtured with other sociocultural and technological organisations. For example, the process of preserving the VR experience offered by *Curious Alice: The VR Experience* would likely have to be sustained by collaborations between the V&A museum's team, including curators, designers and producers, creative technology companies as well as the targeted user communities.

In Chap. 11, *The Phygital Museum Ecosystem*, Alessandra Miano focuses on phygital experiences—museum experiences that leverage and integrate the affordances of digital technology and those of the museum or gallery space to create engaging, potentially engulfing experiences for visitors. Through a review of the literature and a suite of relevant case studies from Dutch museums, Miano defines a taxonomy of phygital museum experiences according to the dynamics between the type of technology used and its integration in the physical space, the use of storytelling and the approach to visitor engagement. The analysis of the cases reveals the transformative potential associated with phygital experiences, stemming from their capacity for immersivity and meaningful interaction. The question of agency appears to be central to this potential. It is by offering visitors the possibility to allow (or stimulate) the installation narrative to unfold, that these experiences are made unique through each episode of interaction, triggering different narrative threads and evoking subjective meanings and understandings.

The two final chapters approach, from different analytical angles, the question of Artificial Intelligence as a mediator of potentially transformative experiences, along with the ethical implications that museums should tackle while considering this potential. In Chap. 12, *Seeing Art Through the Eye of the Algorithm: Artificial Intelligence in the Museum*—Anders Sundnes Løvlie, Louie Søs Meyer, Christian Sivertsen, Peter Kun, Matthias Freiberger and Sebastian Risi weave the chapter narrative around a meaningful question: how does AI affect experiencing art in the museum? The chapter critically analyses different case examples of using AI to support, enhance, enrich, or even distort art experiences, showing how the potential of the technology is taken in very different directions in the world of art and museums: the chapter starts by focussing on the use of AI (in particular computer vision) for analysing digital collections and creating new metadata, thus affording new ways of exploring or linking between collections items; followed by the analysis of generative AI in applications such as computer chatbots, voice assistants, game-play and image generation installations responsive to user input. The analysis then engages with projects that deliberately use AI to show the limitations of the trained algorithms and where it can go wrong, thus inviting reflections and more mature understandings beyond mere enthusiasm for the novelty of the technology. Based on the analysis of these cases, the authors offer an intellectually rich and inquisitive interpretation of the potential and the limitations of AI for shaping the experience of art.

Closing the section on supporting technologies and the book, Kathryn Brown's chapter *Artificial Exchange: Chatbots and the Ethics of Museum Experience Design* is a well documented and profoundly inquisitive essay that reviews and then questions the ascending trend of integrating AI technologies in museums to attract new audiences and uplift the visit experience. One of the arguments advanced in this chapter is that the integration of technologies such as AI in museums and the heritage domain is actually attempting to meet, through new means, ideals that have shaped and moved the New Museology and the participatory wave in museum experience design. Whether the integration and use of AI technologies respond or not to these ideals, is one of the core issues that demand urgent attention. Brown's sharp analysis of the underlying agendas, nuances and outcomes of AI uses in museums suggests that more often than not, these experimental spaces might be at odds with and even demand the reconsideration of established curatorial and educational principles and practices. Ultimately, Brown suggests that museums should question and problematise the types of experiences they seek to create with the help of AI, how these balance the ratio between the human and the technical, and what are the likely implications of integrating these new AI-supported experiences for the evolving sociocultural and educational roles of museums. If, for instance, the integration of AI seeks to attract to museums new audiences that would not otherwise participate in these spaces, what are the implications of these audiences preferring to engage with algorithmic speech rather than human to human conversation?

References

Albert JRI (2018) The informal city in the museum of Barcelona. Mus Int 70(3–4):48–59

Altayli A, Viau-Courville M (2018a) (Special issue editorial) Negotiating multivocal narratives, collective agency and activism in the museum. Mus Int 70(3–4):3–8

Altayli A, Viau-Courville M (2018b) (Special issue) Museums and contested histories. Mus Int 70(3–4):i–ii, 1–145

Baggesen RH (2014) Augmenting the agora: media and civic engagement in museums. MedieKultur J Media Commun Res 30(56):15 pp

Bergevin JL (2018) Narratives of transformation: reframing and naming the impact of activist museum practice on visitors. Thesis, University of Leicester. https://hdl.handle.net/2381/43381

Bull JD (2020) '…Threat and opportunity to be found in the disintegrating world.' (O'Hara 2003, 71)—the potential for transformative museum experiences in the post-COVID era. J Conserv Mus Stud 18(1):3. https://doi.org/10.5334/jcms.203
Burgers GJ (2021) Tourism, leisure and cultural heritage: the challenge of participatory planning and design. In: Tourism and regional science: new roads. Springer Singapore, Singapore, pp 71–85
Calvi L, Hover M (2018) Becoming Vincent: a multifaceted story in a multifaceted ecosystem. In: Museum experience design: crowds, ecosystems and novel technologies, pp 279–300
Calvi L, Vermeeren A (2023) Digitally enriched museum experiences—what technology can do. Mus Manag Curatorsh 39(3):335–356. https://doi.org/10.1080/09647775.2023.2235683
Chisolm MS, Kelly-Hedrick M, Stephens MB, Zahra FS (2020) Transformative learning in the art museum: a methods review. Fam Med 52(10):736–740. https://doi.org/10.22454/FamMed.2020.622085
Chmutina K, Tandon A, Kalkhitashvili M, Tevzadze M, Kobulia I (2021) Connecting heritage, vulnerabilities and capacities through a participatory game. Int J Disaster Risk Reduct 53:102005. https://doi.org/10.1016/j.ijdrr.2020.102005
Chronis A (2012) Tourists as story-builders: narrative construction at a heritage museum. J Travel Tour Mark 29(5):444–459. https://doi.org/10.1080/10548408.2012.691395
Duerden MD, Ward PJ, Freeman PA (2015) Conceptualizing structured experiences: seeking interdisciplinary integration. J Leis Res 47(5):601–620
Duerden MD, Lundberg NR, Ward P, Taniguchi ST, Hill B, Widmer MA, Zabriskie R (2018) From ordinary to extraordinary: a framework of experience types. J Leis Res 49(3–5):196–216. https://doi.org/10.1080/00222216.2018.1528779
Durkheim É (1912/1995) The elementary forms of the religious life (1912, English translation by Joseph Swain: 1915). The Free Press
Gaggioli A (2016) Transformative experience design. In: Human computer confluence: transforming human experience through symbiotic technologies. De Gruyter Open Poland, Warsaw, Poland, pp 97–122
Garner JK, Kaplan A, Pugh K (2016) Museums as contexts for transformative experiences and identity development. J Mus Educ 41(4):341–352. https://doi.org/10.1080/10598650.2016.1199343
Gokcigdem E (ed) (2016) Fostering empathy through museums. Rowman & Littlefield, London
Houpert C (2019) Participatory approaches and social inclusion in cultural heritage. Accessed 02 Feb 2022. Available online: https://eurocities.eu/latest/new-rock-case-studies-inspiring-ideas-for-using-cultural-heritage-to-engage-citizens/
Jefferies K, Lepp A (2012) An investigation of extraordinary experiences. J Park Recreat Adm 30(3):37–51
Kitchenham A (2008) The evolution of John Mezirow's transformative learning theory. J Transform Educ 6(2). https://doi.org/10.1177/1541344608322678
Liedgren J, Desmet PMA, Gaggioli A (2023) Liminal design: a conceptual framework and three step approach for developing technology that delivers transcendence and deeper experiences. Front Psychol 14(2):1043170. https://doi.org/10.3389/fpsyg.2023.1043170
Lynch B (2017) Disturbing the peace: museums, democracy and conflict avoidance. In: Walters D, Laven D, Davis P (eds) Heritage and peacebuilding. Boydell Press, Suffolk, pp 109–126
Mac Devitt A (2016) Editorial of special issue: the role of museums in a changing society. Mus Int 68(3–4). https://doi.org/10.1111/muse.12139
Mason M (2022) The contribution of design thinking to museum digital transformation in post-pandemic times. Multimodal Technol Interact 2022(6):79. https://doi.org/10.3390/mti6090079
McCall V, Gray C (2014) Museums and the 'new museology': theory, practice and organisational change. Mus Manag Curatorsh 29(1):19–35
Message K (2018) The disobedient museum: writing at the edge. Routledge, London and New York
Mezirow J (1978) Perspective transformation. Adult Educ 28:100–110

Morse N, Munro E (2018) Museums' community engagement schemes, austerity and practices of care in two local museum services. Soc Cult Geogr 19(3):357–378

Mouliou M (2018) The museum of our discoveries: empowering young refugees in an urban context. Mus Int 70(3–4):124–133

Murphy O (2018) Coworking spaces, accelerators and incubators: emerging forms of museum practice in an increasingly digital world. Mus Int 70(1–2):62–75. https://doi.org/10.1111/muse.12193

Nohl A-M (2015) Typical phases of transformative learning: a practice-based model. Adult Educ Q 65(1):35–49. https://doi.org/10.1177/0741713614558582

Potter J, McDougall J (2017) Digital media, culture and education: theorising third space literacies. Springer

Rodenberg J, Wagenaar P, Burgers G-J (eds) (2023) Calling on the community understanding participation in the heritage sector, an interactive governance perspective

Rozendaal MC, Vermeeren AP, Issidorides DC (2018) Using mobile technologies to capture the visitor experience. In: Museum experience design: crowds, ecosystems and novel technologies, pp 239–258

Sabiescu A (2018) A critical reflection on three paradigms in museum experience design. In: Museum experience design: crowds, ecosystems and novel technologies, pp 259–276

Sabiescu A, Charatzopoulou K (2018) The museum as ecosystem and museums in learning ecosystems. In: Museum experience design: crowds, ecosystems and novel technologies, pp 325–345

Sabiescu A, Zajzon N (2023) Museums and young people's creative careers. Research report. Connect2Aspire. Available at https://connect2aspire.lboro.ac.uk/wp-content/uploads/2023/07/Connect2Aspire-Museums-report-web.pdf

Samis P, Michaelson M (2016) Creating the visitor-centered museum. Routledge

Scott CA (2006) Museums: impact and value. Cult Trends 15(1):45–75

Scott CA (2009) Exploring the evidence base for museum value. Mus Manag Curatorsh 24(3):195–212

Simon N (2010) The participatory museum. CC-attribution-non-commercial. Accessed 02 Feb 2022. www.participatorymuseum.org

Simon RI (2014) A pedagogy of witnessing: curatorial practice and the pursuit of social justice. SUNY Press, Albany

Soren BJ (2009) Museum experiences that change visitors. Mus Manag Curatorsh 24(3):233–251. https://doi.org/10.1080/09647770903073060

Sousa F (2018) The participation in the safeguarding of the intangible cultural heritage: the role of communities, groups and individuals. Accessed 02 Feb 2022. Available online: memoriamedia.net

Turner V (1969/2008) The ritual process: structure and anti-structure. Aldine Transaction

van der Lans L, Ansems EL, Khan VJ (2018) Paid crowdsourcing as concept and content generator to enhance museum experiences. In: Museum experience design: crowds, ecosystems and novel technologies, pp 137–156

Vermeeren AP, Calvi L, Sabiescu A (2018a) Museum experience design: crowds, ecosystems and novel technologies. Springer International Publishing

Vermeeren AP, Calvi L, Sabiescu A, Trocchianesi R, Stuedahl D, Giaccardi E, Radice S (2018b) Future museum experience design: crowds, ecosystems and novel technologies. Springer International Publishing, pp 1–16

Wheadon N (2022) Museum metamorphosis: cultivating change through cultural citizenship. Rowman & Littlefield Publishers

Wildt A (2018) The city museum as an empathic space. Mus Int 70(3–4):72–83

Wrigglesworth T, Watts LA (2018) The value of user-centric crowdsourcing for cultural heritage: fostering emotional engagement with integrity. In: Museum experience design: crowds, ecosystems and novel technologies, pp 157–179

Link

https://icom.museum/en/resources/standards-guidelines/museum-definition/

Amalia Sabiescu is a senior lecturer in Media and Creative Industries at Loughborough University London. A media and communications scholar with an interdisciplinary research agenda, Dr Sabiescu employs ecological frameworks to study the nexus between social, cultural and digital change. Her research investigates this dynamic in communities, museums and the heritage sector, examining processes of digital transformation and the evolving social and educational roles of museums.

Licia Calvi is a senior lecturer at the Breda University of Applied Sciences, the Netherlands, specialising in the digital transformation of museums, and an adjunct professor in Museum Communication Studies at the University of Bergamo, in Italy. A digital humanist, she investigates how digital technology is used in museums beyond enhancing the visitor experience, to shape (new) museum practices and the role storytelling plays in them.

Arnold Vermeeren is Associate Professor at TU Delft, Faculty of Industrial Design Engineering and Director of the Faculty's MuseumFutures Lab. He was educated as an industrial designer and has been involved in various EU-funded projects on User Experience (UX) as well as a large variety of museum experience-related projects. His current research focuses on designing transformative museum experiences related to societal changes.

Part I
Transformative Experiences: Concept and Design Approaches

Chapter 2
Juxtaposition and the Liminal Exhibit—Inevitable and Surprising, at the Same Time

Johan Liedgren, Andrea Gaggioli, and Pieter M. A. Desmet

I had to take the world of Paterson into a new dimension if I wanted to give it imaginative validity.
William Carlos Williams,
Paterson. New Directions, 1946

Abstract By exploring the potential of liminal design for museums and exhibitions through the intentional juxtaposition of the familiar and the unfamiliar, we offer perspectives to ignite visitors' imagination. The theoretical framework connecting liminality, transformative experiences, and juxtaposition anchors a practical three-step model that showcases how museums can offer liminal experiences with narrative engagement, optimal abstraction, and suspension of disbelief. Concepts are illustrated with examples, including the Seattle Asian Art Museum, Victoria and Albert, Brera, and the Louvre Abu Dhabi. The specific dynamics of interactive technology, immersive exhibits, and multimedia are discussed as additional thresholds and juxtapositions creating liminality that can offer deeper and more meaningful visitor experiences.

J. Liedgren (✉)
Independent Researcher, Seattle, WA, USA
e-mail: johan@liedgren.com

A. Gaggioli
Università Cattolica del Sacro Cuore, Milan, Italy
e-mail: andrea.gaggioli@unicatt.it

P. M. A. Desmet
Delft University of Technology, Delft, The Netherlands
e-mail: P.M.A.Desmet@tudelft.nl

L. Calvi et al. (eds.), *Transformative Museum Experiences*, Springer Series on Cultural Computing, https://doi.org/10.1007/978-3-031-89521-0_2

2.1 Introduction

Aristotle suggested that all good stories need to be both inevitable and surprising—at the same time (Aristotle, Poetics 1452a). The same is arguably true for liminality: it is the unknown, infinite space, and tension suspended in-between two intentionally juxtaposed notions—between what is, and what might be—that tickles and tempts our imagination to fuel deeper liminal experiences. Practitioners of museum design and exhibit curation confront decisions around this very same balance.

Museums are already textbook examples of a liminal space. Liminal spaces are distinctly and deliberately separate from our ordinary reality, akin to cinemas, nightclubs, places of worship, a good book, or a sports arena. All of them are real spaces holding a fictional promise—some offering only a short thrill, others setting up for deep personal transformation. When we enter such a space, we voluntarily leave our ordinary reality behind to participate more fully in another suggested one. Different rules apply. Our attention and attitude are expected to be different. At a museum with objects on display—often long and far removed from their original condition and purpose—practical considerations are removed, and the artifacts are brought in to juxtapose the ordinary and be experienced as abstract examples of a much bigger idea. When participating in such a hypothetical space, we expect, in return, an experience that is freed from ordinary consequences, risks, and restrictions—a safe place to participate in with our imagination for profound and memorable experiences that cannot be held in the transactional nature of ordinary day-to-day life.

2.2 Theoretical Framework

If we want such liminality to come alive during a museum visit, we need to activate the visitor's imagination with disruptions to their established flow of thinking and ordinary use of metaphors (Lima 1995): each part of the museum needs to challenge the expectations a visitor arrives with by suggesting another seemingly contradictory perspective and metaphor. Philosopher Paul Ricoeur distinguishes conventional metaphors, or images that have become clichés, from alive metaphors ("métaphores vives") requiring imaginative work. Only the latter expose the person to some radical newness, which demands the simultaneous experience of both a "logical moment" and a "sensual moment" (Ricoeur 1975).

It is this in-between intentional juxtaposition of different notions—of what is, and what might be—that creates an active liminal space. When the visitor feels safe to explore something unknown, and sees enough promise in the new suggested perspective to warrant sensemaking of the contradictory notions, imagination will play out new possible ways to broker the paradox. This creates a new perspective in making personal sense of it all, and enables a transition back to the ordinary world, still holding some of the liminal insight in place (Stenner 2017; Zittoun and Stenner 2021). Some degree of transformation has taken place.

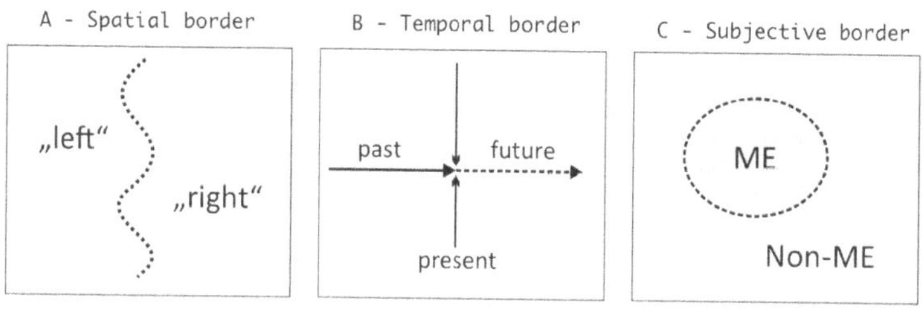

Fig. 2.1 Three semiotic thresholds. Image adapted from De Luca Picione and Valsiner (2017)

If visitors can take in the exhibit without challenging their pre-existing perspective—if no paradox, question, conflict, or juxtaposition between what is and what might be is sensed—no curiosity is required. No imagination is necessary. Consequently, no deeper positive experience is had (Antón et al. 2018). What is left is a simple transaction: a predictable barter between what we came for and what we unsurprisingly got. Our perspective on the world and ourselves is unchanged. Transactionality is antithetical to liminality.

The word liminality stems from Latin's limen, meaning threshold or border. Distinctions are how we make sense of the world: what is me and not me, what is past and what is future, etc. (Fig. 2.1). In routine tasks and transactions, such distinct thresholds need to be clear and fixed to perform the expected efficiently. In a liminal space on the other hand, the threshold itself is a space to be explored. A liminal experience is born by two contrasting notions held in the same context, suggesting a possible synthesis and new meaning. We are presented with an intentional juxtaposition challenging our ordinary thresholds, self and worldview.

The relevant psychological aspect highlighted through these distinctions is that a border is an arbitrary semiotic device which is required for both maintaining stability in our world and—in the liminal space—to be in defiance of status quo, inducing transformation by concurrently posing other possibilities (De Luca Picione and Valsiner 2017). The object world has not changed. But our way of seeing it does, and so does its meaning. Aristotle's suggestion that all good stories need to be both inevitable and surprising, is very much taken to heart.

Intentional juxtapositions propose new semiotic thresholds. The expected object or notion has suddenly been placed inside an unexpected context, challenging our ordinary understanding. Suspended in between these two juxtaposed notions—a very real artifact or painting on one side, and its new proposed context on the other—a liminal space opens up to be explored, suggesting a different perspective and novel meaning. When effective, encountering such juxtaposition can be both tantalizing and destabilizing, triggering curiosity and a desire to explore further.

Tom Hennes captures this idea well as it pertains to museum curation (Hennes 2010, p. 24): "This element of destabilization … is an exciting and important challenge that is essential to creating exhibitions that affect their visitors. While it may at first feel unnerving to museum practitioners to envision their work in this way, it has strong roots in constructivist learning, foreshadowed by Dewey's conception of

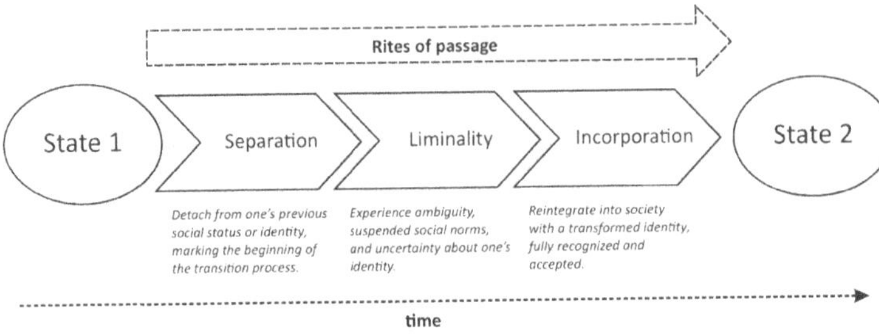

Fig. 2.2 Three distinct phases of separation, liminality and incorporation when moving from one social status to another by Van Gennep (1960). Image adapted from Soderlund and Borg (2018)

experience as beginning with a "perplexing situation" … and progressing through stages of inquiry and reflection."

The same idea aligns with Michel Foucault's notion of heterotopias (Foucault 1986), which he identifies as distinct spaces that disrupt our normal experience of the world. Foucault sets heterotopias apart from utopias, the latter being non-real spaces that propose an idealized society. In contrast, heterotopias are concrete and intrinsic to the societal structure. They are "other" spaces, embodying both presence and absence, representation and challenge, order and disruption. These spaces exist as pockets within the fabric of society, reflecting it, subverting it, and offering a different perspective on what is considered the norm.

Psychologically, a similar relationship to liminality is presented in anthropologist Victor Turner's model of personal transformation (Turner 1974). This transformation requires a temporary suspension of social norms and roles, allowing individuals to experiment with new identities and ways of being. Turner emphasizes the importance of ritual experiences in facilitating personal transformation, building on the seminal work of Van Gennep (1960), who identified three distinct stages that individuals go through to transition from one social status to another (Fig. 2.2).

Once we are through the liminal stage and have incorporated our liminal experience, it becomes, in part, our new reality. Both Van Gennep and Turner stress the importance of ritual and ceremonial practices in facilitating personal transformation during liminality. Turner's process of transformation and temporal limitation is relevant in terms of a museum visit's ability to be memorable and stay relevant after it is over, as well as the implicit need to keep imagination alive throughout the whole visit by continually re-challenging the visitor with the idea of a new proposed perspective. If the juxtaposition has been resolved or is repetitive, our imagination will fade for lack of interest and the rest of the visit will likely turn transactional.

> We shall not cease from
> exploration.
> And the end of all our exploring.
> Will be to arrive where we
> started.

And know the place for the first time.
—T. S. Eliot, Wasteland

2.3 Abstraction, Juxtaposition, and Metaphor

Our view on liminality holds that juxtaposition—meaningful contradiction and paradox—is central to both creating and having meaningful liminal experiences. Three beliefs ground this assumption:

1. That experiences play out over time and are therefore narrative in nature with a beginning, middle, and end (Peirce 1877). A narrative without conflicts, surprises, or relevant unknowns (juxtapositions), simply isn't worth sharing, retelling, or paying attention to.
2. We also suggest that the active imagination stemming from encountered paradoxes are grounded in evolution (Stenner 2017). As life evolved to more complex states, with more mobility and social cooperation, simply reacting to external stimuli and relying on hardcoded biological functions to respond was no longer sufficient for survival. We were forced to predict and make meaning of what is both the bodily us (hunger), and what is outside of us (food), to proactively navigate our environment as well as the intentions and emotions of those around us. Or put another way, to broker the paradox of what is us and simultaneously infer what is not us cannot be fully known (Cangià 2020).
3. Lastly, that a positive disruptive or destabilizing encounter that activates our imagination (as opposed to automatic fight or flight responses) only happens when we, in response, re-imagine an existing notion from a new perspective and thereby are motivated to contemplate the unknown (Zittoun and Cerchia 2013). In this new perspective, far from being opposed to reality, imagination plays a vital role in effecting real-world changes and our adaptation to it.

Humans have in part evolved consciousness to broker these paradoxes: the ability to imagine and play out in our minds scenarios involving the unknown, and then to memorize these hypotheticals as good or bad by inferring emotion to each outcome (Stenner 2017). This is how fictional events can be linked to very real emotions and experiences (Frijda 1986). Consequently, our social well-being also depends on sharing what is unique only to us and thus cannot be fully shared: we combine symbols and abstractions to represent specific unknowns (another paradox) in what then for others will be intentional paradoxes presented to be experienced.

An abstraction by itself is not liminality: the word "snowflake" is simply a direct abstraction pointing to a specific ice crystal. But by suggesting a juxtaposed relationship between two previously unrelated abstractions (relational abstraction) their common structure is rendered more salient (a child is like a snowflake) (Gentner and Hoyos 2017). It is the allegorical use of abstractions that creates a metaphor (What a snowflake!). When a museum juxtaposes a specific collection of artworks with a non-intuitive theme, it works in a related way—and in offering a safe space optimized for contemplating this new and peculiar metaphor in interesting ways, we create a liminal space to experience and explore a novel idea.

The centrality of juxtapositions in creating new and interesting metaphors to support deep and meaningful experiences is further applied in the next section on intentional design.

2.4 Designing for Liminal Spaces

In the practical design of liminal spaces, three distinct aspects are useful to highlight when orchestrating its intentional manifestation, as proposed in our "Liminal Design Framework" (Fig. 2.3; Liedgren et al. 2023). These three facets also map to what activates the imaginative experience for the visitor, from the very beginning—sometimes long before we enter the museum—through to the very end, and potentially long after that; see Fig. 2.4 for real-life examples.

Firstly, **Narrative Desire**: what question or curiosity does the liminal space evoke in order to inspire and motivate visitors to explore something deeply and with curiosity? This question can be considered the new suggested perspective that sets up the juxtaposition to the ordinary or expected that inspires a desire to explore further. The chosen Narrative Desire of course needs to be relevant to the specific exhibit, yet still suggest a new one—otherwise we simply write it off as random. Aristotle's suggestion that all good stories need to be both inevitable and surprising (a paradox!), at the same time, again shows itself as a foundational premise. The depth of our experience will not be greater than the depth of the juxtaposition and the unknown that it holds in its suspension.

For museums, the Narrative Desire can generally be thought of as the theme or the publicly articulated idea of the exhibit. It is this suggested concept that brings a collection of works or samples together as context through a single abstract idea.

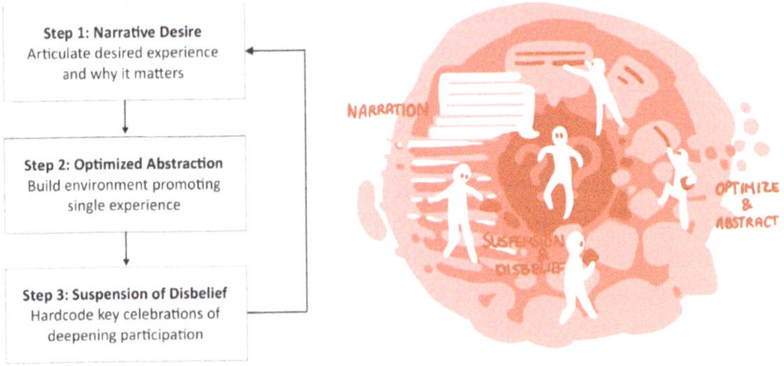

Fig. 2.3 Liminal design framework: a conceptual framework and three-step approach for developing technology that delivers transcendence and deeper experiences. Image adapted from Liedgren et al. (2023), drawing created by Charlotte Peeters Weem

A vivid illustration of **Narrative Desire** can be found in the "Giacometti versus Picasso" exhibition at the Voorlinden museum in 2021. This unique showcase juxtaposed the creations of these two revered artists, who, despite their mutual admiration, never engaged in collaboration or developed a friendship. The exhibition sparks a desire to explore the influence they had on each other's art, with the newly discovered professional intimacy of the distant admirers. Visitors are naturally compelled to delve deeper into the nature of this revealed dialogue, exploring the reciprocal influences that shaped each artist's distinctive style.

A very direct example of **Optimized Abstraction** was *Rothko & Me* at the Stedelijk Museum in 2020. One separate room offered visitors the opportunity to leave the standard shared and sometimes busy museum experience to spend time alone with a single Rothko painting (Grey, Orange on Maroon, No 8, 1960). The 10-minute solitude and undistracted focus - not even cellphones are allowed - nicely juxtaposed the usual crowded and shared experience of the famed artist's work and instead aimed to find a new and private meditative intimacy with the painting. It was an abstraction from the ordinary, neatly optimised to focus our attention on the stated narrative desire.

In the case of **Suspension of Disbelief**, we can look to the Verbeke Foundation. This extraordinary museum includes a diverse array of settings, from lush greenhouses to rugged natural landscapes and weathered industrial structures. Within this eclectic environment, visitors encounter a blend of finalised artworks, deteriorating structures, and ongoing projects, blurring the boundaries between art, context, and artistic practices, each part tying into the overarching theme of transformation. As visitors navigate these dynamic spaces, they stay immersed and interested, and thereby prompted to suspend their disbelief and embrace the ambiguity inherent in the museum's immersive experience.

Fig. 2.4 Examples for the three steps to activate an imaginative experience, **a** Alberto Giacometti, Homme qui marche II (1960), **b** Pablo Picasso, L'Ombre (1953), **c** Mark Rothko, Gray, Orange on Maroon, No. 8 (1960), **d** Peter De Cupere, Earthcar (2007). Photo in **c** by Lotte Stekelenburg, courtesy Depot Boijmans van Beuningen; photo in **d** by G. de Schepper. Other photos sourced from copyright-free online repositories

The novel concept challenges our existing world view and thus the meaning of the artifacts presented and presents the museum collection through the lens of this novel overarching idea to entice visitor's deeper exploration.

Setting goals for the liminal experience should not be seen as a top-down prescriptive ambition to control the visitors' feelings or responses throughout the exhibit. We must always leave narrative room for imagination. Avoid the temptation to simply state what the liminal juxtaposition should mean; doing so robs the experience of its unknown hiding in the juxtaposition, and risks turning the visit limp and transactional. If each step is prescribed, no imagination would be required. In choosing a narrative desire, an intriguing question will always trump the prescriptive answer.

Secondly, **Optimized Abstraction**: At the most rudimentary level, part of the liminal design task is to focus our attention on the Narrative Desire. How do we know we are in a space separate from the ordinary? How do we keep distractions at bay? Museums in part already do this by abstracting exhibited objects, far removed from their original and intended place and use—showcased on pedestals with spot-lighting for easy viewing in a quiet and uncluttered environment.

But the task of Optimized Abstraction gets more complex as we consider its true potential as a language designed to manifest the chosen Narrative Desire. It is the unexpected and the friction of an experience that we remember, not its ease of use.

In what order do we place artifacts? How much space do we give to one piece over another? Which artworks are grouped together, and which are kept apart? What is included, and what is deliberately left out? These decisions shape the balance between the expected and the unexpected, defining the overall experience.

Gilles Deleuze captures this aspect of Optimized Abstraction as the becoming of liminal language: when the language (or abstraction) is "toppled or pushed to a limit" (Deleuze and Guattari 1987), we see past the words and can grasp the essence and idea hiding behind the printed text. This is the experiential difference between a cardiology report and poetry depicting a broken heart. Similarly, the presentational language of museums is established. To create purposeful friction—directing focus on, framing, and placing the objects on display as part of the bigger theme—the expected exhibit language needs to be pushed to create a new temporary language uniquely suited in conveying its bigger idea. Optimized Abstraction is the physical manifestation of both the Narrative Desire, and the third and final aspect of liminal design discussed next: Suspension of Disbelief.

Suspension of Disbelief: How might the liminal space continue to hold the attention of the visitor until the experience is fully concluded? Established perspectives can be found in Erika Fischer-Lichte's work, exploring the transformative potential of theatrical and performative acts. Central to her theory is the concept of "heightened attention," opening up the possibility for catharsis and self-reflection. Fischer-Lichte and Jain (2008) points to the immersive focus and participatory nature in the performance as distinct from day to day, arguing that it offers a unique and intentionally separate space for the audience to confront and transcend societal constraints.

Outside the mechanical task of keeping unrelated and mundane distractions out, the more complex challenge in sustaining the audience's interest and focus on the overarching idea, is a dramatic one: enough disbelief to protect the liminal experience from ordinary constraints. In other words, how do we keep one thematic idea interesting for the entirety of the exhibit? We can consider at least two fundamental aspects:

1. How objects on display differ throughout the exhibit within a single context (Object Switch), providing variety and novel juxtapositions to illustrate a singular thematic exhibit idea.
2. How similar objects are presented in progressively different contexts (Context Switch), each offering a related but novel juxtaposition and suggested meaning to keep the visitor engaged and the thematic questions present.

In both these cases, the juxtaposition itself is "stretched" to make the proposed combination of context and object less obvious as the exhibit progresses. This task is inherently narrative: challenging the visitor's curiosity as the visit progresses, while contextually mining the very same Narrative Desire. This is part of the art of creating liminality, not unrelated to that of gradually raising the stakes to keep a reader captivated during hundreds of book pages during a single story told. The concepts of Object Switch and Context Switch are further explored with real-world examples below.

2.5 The Liminal Exhibit

Can a single piece of art be liminal just by itself? Most definitely. No museum is required for that. We might stumble upon a piece of art in someone's home that moves us to tears. The frame naturally creates a threshold, and the artistic work held inside it provides enough abstraction and juxtaposition to the real world to deliver a version of liminality. Or we might look out over the old city of Rome and experience an overwhelming sense of beauty and history in the moment. And we can fall deeply in love without much help from any institution. Or marvel in awe at our place in the universe while looking out over the billion-year-old rock exposed throughout the Grand Canyon, untouched by any intentional human design or frame. All of these are real liminal experiences, sometimes small and fleeting, and at times profound. But since museums are significant and deliberate enterprises, they are, by definition, defined by their own intentions. And we need to design exhibitions accordingly.

Given this chapter's foundation of intentional juxtapositions, one simplified way to analyze and construct an exhibit is to explore the relationship between the object reality—what we can see on display and its usual presuppositions—and, on the other hand, the articulated intent and reasons for the display proposed as an abstract idea or theme. If there is no interesting distance between the visitor's expectations of the objects on display and the proposed theme, there is no conflict, nor juxtaposition—and no liminality is created.

One very explicit example of a rich and intriguing juxtaposition was Seattle's Asian Art Museum's exhibit of Renegade Edo and Paris: Edo prints juxtaposed alongside vintage posters by Toulouse-Lautrec. The formal exhibit introduction explicitly asked: What do late eighteenth- to nineteenth-century Edo (present-day Tokyo) and late nineteenth-century Paris have in common? With each wall bringing together art from different sides of the world and eras—placed together for viewing side by side—the exhibit invited visitors to experience the formal and thematic parallels between these two collections. It highlighted the shared social impulses behind their burgeoning and more widespread art production. As both featured cities faced profound changes from a rising middle class, how subversive impulses gave rise to vibrant cultures of theater-going, gratuitous pleasure-seeking, and new forms of visual art. Both the art from Edo and Toulouse-Lautrec's debaucherous Moulin Rouge are well-known, but the exhibit asked us to re-see what we already knew—to invite deeper meaning and universality through direct non-obvious comparison and juxtaposition.

If we instead look at the more traditional exhibit structure, it is often sequenced primarily in chronological order. At times, a text description might add quick notes on art history or symbolism for a single work of art—but such exhibits lack the ambition to offer anything thematically challenging or new.

One stand-out exception in elevating a traditional structure is Brera in Milan. Its vast and sprawling collection of priceless art gathered from Napoleon's expansive war territories is mainly offered up for chronological display. But at the very end of the museum, we are offered Hayez's famous The Kiss (https://en.wikipedia.org/wiki/The_Kiss_(Hayez)), a painting portraying two young lovers braving a scandalous unmarried kiss in a show of patriotism—the young man just about to leave for war. One love is sacrificed for another. The painting is brilliantly juxtaposed and surrounded by two thematically similar but very different artistic takes on the same complex patriotism: A Great Sacrifice (https://pinacotecabrera.org/en/collezione-online/opere/il-grande-sacrificio/) paints a more mundane image of a mother sending her son to war—the same composition but here depicted as a motherly embrace. And then hung on the other side: Doleful Premonition (https://pinacotecabrera.org/en/collezione-online/opere/triste-presentimento/) depicting a young woman reading a letter alone in bed, contemplating an image of her beloved patriot (with a small replica of The Kiss placed on the wall behind her!), perhaps longing for his return, or mourning his permanent absence (see Fig. 2.5).

From a liminal point of view, we can imagine a thematic context set and maintained from the very beginning of the Brera visit: to have this tender end cap of Napoleon's conquered treasures conclude with an even more poignant and bittersweet kiss goodbye—speaking not just to one or three paintings, but Brera's entire collection through the lens of both the long lasting beauty of its art treasures (and the hard restoration work required, also on display), then juxtaposed by the horrors of war that brought it together.

What we will discuss next is the core of this exhibit design challenge: how to maintain meaningful surprise—and sustain active liminality—throughout the complete visitor experience.

Fig. 2.5 The Brera in Milan. Left: Girolamo Induno, A Great Sacrifice (1860). Middle: Francesco Hayez, The Kiss (1859). Right: Girolamo Induno, Doleful Premonition (1862). Photo sourced from copyright-free repository

2.6 Suspension of Disbelief

Like Brera, most museums and exhibits are more than a single piece of art, and it is common to offer homogeneous or related collections placed together in distinct sections. A museum visit can be as long as a feature film and share some of its narrative challenges to keep the audience fully engaged for the duration of the visit. No matter how well we handle technical immersion, if the narrative experience doesn't raise the stakes gradually and maintain the promise of meaningful surprise, the visitors' focus and engagement will soon wear thin (Bitgood 2009). All lifeforms stop responding to external stimuli if it is repetitive.

As mentioned above, there are at least two principal ways we can approach this dramatic task of maintaining suspension of disbelief in the context of juxtapositions. If we maintain a singular theme for the whole museum visit, we can change the artifacts that speak to the theme in interesting ways. This would continually challenge and deepen the thematic meaning as exemplified by the objects and escalate the surprise of what the theme can include: this is Object Switch (Fig. 2.7).

Or, another approach: if the museum offers only similar or homogeneous collections, we can instead choose to offer several new juxtaposed perspectives on the same type of artifacts: this is Context Switch (Fig. 2.9). Let's look at examples of both approaches.

2.6.1 *Object Switch*

The maiden exhibit in 2019 at the then just completed 1.3 billion dollar hyper modern structure of the Louvre in Abu Dhabi, presented 55 rooms sequenced into 12 "chapters" holding over 600 widely different pieces of priceless art and artifacts from all

Fig. 2.6 Interior of the Abu Dhabi Louvre Museum, showing reflections of the "Rain of Light" dome. Architect Jean Nouvel. Photo by Nattakit Jeerapatmaitree (Shutterstock)

corners of history and the world (Fig. 2.6). The single overarching theme for all was "Humanity," and stayed persistently consistent throughout the entire museum.

The show opens with "First Villages;" incredible ancient artifacts from every continent, placed side by side to remind us of our shared past and the objects' striking similarities. Next up: "The First Great Powers" and "Great Empires": early trade routes and universal religions that lay the foundation for civilization as we know it, perhaps correctly assumed forgotten in a more Western view of history—and likely a reminder that we are far from Paris. And so the visit moves, from room to room, from one type of artifacts collected from around the world to the next, each collection indirectly juxtaposing a more myopic Western views of both art, history, and museums with its place in the exhibit's larger theme: Humanity—a direct example of Object Switch.

The exhibit's chapter "Challenging Modernism" performs a similar narrative maneuver: first establishing commonality by showing the same artistic trend of modernism from all around the world. Modernism, as a Westerner might remember it, has "just" three walls in one room containing an unprecedented and dizzying collection of major works by Manet, Monet, Caillebotte and Degas, Whistler, Van Gogh, and Cezanne. It's all there: three walls. With a few steps back, you can take it all in at once: potentially a new perspective on its relative size and place in world history. And again, making a point that speaks to the larger theme.

All in all, 600 artifacts, 55 rooms: from stone carvings and pottery from tens of thousands of years ago to early scientific instruments, orientalism in art (here taking on a different meaning), modernism, royal patronage, even including dissident art such as Ai Weiwei's crystal Monument to the Third International. Every single chapter and room challenge us to view the main theme from a new and

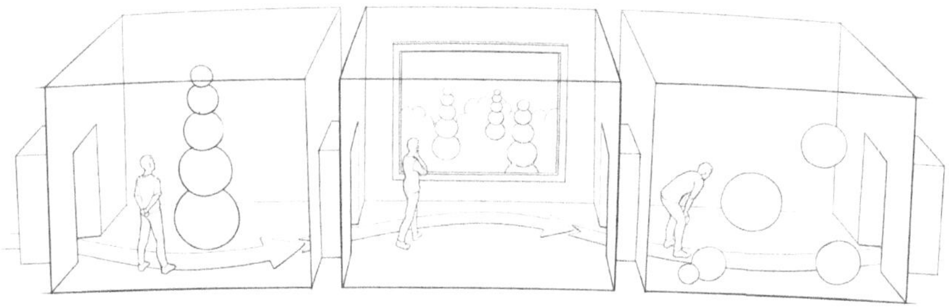

Fig. 2.7 Schematic representation of the "Object Switch" approach to liminal juxtapositioning. Change of the artifacts (from left to middle and right) to deepen the thematic meaning. Drawing by Jort Nijhuis

different angle—always laddering up to showcase the museum's curated version of universality: "Humanity." An ambitious and consistent example of Object Switching.

Furthermore, try to roam the museum, and a polite guard will ensure that you take in the rooms of the exhibit in the precise order that the overarching theme and narrative sequence demand. Although each room and chapter by themselves nicely ladder up to the main theme, the juxtapositions in this ambitious Object Switch are gradually stretched. Whereas the initial room "First Villages" presents straightforward juxtapositions of different artifacts that are both easy to see and grasp as related, the further into the chapters we venture, the juxtapositions reach beyond the obvious and require more imagination to be held in the same thematic context—escalating active participation to ensure sustained conceptual curiosity and suspension of disbelief (Fig. 2.7).

2.6.2 *Context Switch*

Instead of changing the objects on one side of the juxtaposition, Context Switching finds ways to offer new perspectives on objects that remain the same or at least similar. The Sonneveld House in Rotterdam explicitly sets out to do just this while showcasing the modern masterpiece from 1933 meticulously restored—books still on tables and towels in the bathrooms from the family who lived there once (Fig. 2.8). In this sense, the museum has only one "object" on display: the house.

For visitors, however, the house-turned-museum continually strives to create new points of view and discussions for its visitors. The general audio tour will not simply narrate the house's history but will offer several widely different stories of the house. At times the narrated focus is on how the house manifests new versions of the future as seen by the family when the house was built back in 1933. There are also in-depth discussions about modernist architecture, the perspective of a child who used to visit the house regularly and unveiled the mysterious qualities of the laundry elevator and other seemingly uninteresting functional spaces. There is the owner's

Fig. 2.8 Sonneveld house. Architecture by Brinkman en Van der Vlugt. Photos by Johanness Schwartz, courtesy Het Nieuwe Instituut

daughter sharing stories about how they enjoyed hosting parties with their modern pickup record player, and occasionally notes from the house cleaner offering a less than enthusiastic view of what it takes to clean modern design, especially the showers when serving a mistress who had the habit of making her redo the complete bathroom when she missed a single left dried-up water drop. All in all, one central object is continually challenged by suggesting new ways to take it in.

The Sonneveld House further extends this play by introducing contemporary dynamics as well. Mirrored floors installed by the Dutch interior designer Petra Blaisse in 2015 provided new and unexpected perspectives of the residence that one would normally not consider, giving new dimensions that also naturally change with light and climate. Het Nieuwe Instituut (the New Institute) that manages the Sonneveld House "… is developing new ways of exhibiting design, architecture and technology. Inviting artists and designers to install their work in 'house museums' like the Sonneveld is a proven means of encouraging more people to visit. But Ms. Blaisse has gone further by raising questions about the functions of such places and their presumed authenticity" (Rawsthorn 2015). These initiatives are a natural

Fig. 2.9 Schematic representation of the "Context Switch" approach to liminal juxtapositioning. The same artifacts are seen from three different perspectives to deepen the thematic meaning. Drawing by Jort Nijhuis

extension of Context Switching—now not only including one visit, but continually creating new curiosity over time around objects that for good reasons remain the same (Fig. 2.9).

2.7 Whose Exhibit Is It Anyway?

The creative tension between exhibit themes and artifacts, between different art pieces in the same exhibit, or between the history of the museum and the current exhibit—all juxtapose expectations with a challenge to the same by intentionally presenting the two in the same context of an exhibit. Does it matter then in the juxtaposition, which counts as established expectation, and which is deemed the challenge? It does (Obrist and Raza 2014): the curator in charge of theme and art selection will have more agency in suggesting meaning, than any individual static piece of art, no matter how great or famed the artist. No meaningful juxtaposition can be constructed without intention, and it is this intention manifested as exhibition that takes the lead in suggesting meaning.

Whether Dan Brown's bestselling book The DaVinci Code is kitsch or simply an entertaining pageturner can be discussed, but the novel attention it brought to real-world historical sites provides a contemporary example of different contexts competing for ownership of the narrative. When the central location of the book's plot has tourists pile en masse into Paris's heritage site of the San Sulpice church to "study" clues mentioned in the very fictional book as they appear in the very real church, the fictional narrative stands in stark contrast to both the church's historical significance as well as the church's original religious purpose and historical value.

The landmark's heritage is suddenly competing with an American writer's made-up and highly secular narrative. One crafty priest at the church, tired of being asked to point out where the clues were located, taped up simple signs for jetlagged tourists as a make-shift guide to the things mentioned in the "American mystery" book. He also ceased the opportunity to guide his newfound visitors to one last sign written in English and hung over a stack of bibles to cleverly reclaim the narrative with another juxtaposition. The sign read: You've read the book, now read the Book.

2.8 Technology as a Liminal Threshold

Technology and media, such as educational films, computer screens, and interactional stations can play well inside the liminal design framework for museums. They can switch object reality within the liminal space, or suggest a new context for the same object reality. However, what can make multimedia support challenging is the move from say walking around artifacts from ancient Egypt, to moving into a separate dark room where a film about today's Egypt plays. Even if the film's narrative supports the overarching theme directly, the liminal space switch toward another media form will require the visitor to exit the first immersion and invest in a very different one. And once the film is done, and coming back out into the light—the visitor will yet again be required to re-enter the original liminality.

The film about today's Egypt could be placed at either the beginning or the end of the exhibit. We would treat it as a separate liminal space of the exhibit, not nested inside another. Or, when possible, we can try to reduce the liminal thresholds between the film space and the liminal space of objects on display in the main room by making them one and the same. The Royal BC Museum in Victoria Canada for example, in their anthropological section of tools, icons, and totems, offers photographs and film clips of what life was like for the people whose selected artifacts are on display right. There are also real recordings of native languages and singing coming from behind objects in their display cases. The new varied media combination serves as a rich texture and backdrop to each object. It is all part of the same overall exhibit design, and once the visitor has invested in that specific liminality and abstraction to explore, no further switching is required.

A journey through a museum with the often-used audio headset-guide has the same benefit: once this is an integrated part of the user's liminal experience, we don't try to switch the frame of the liminal space, and it might even help provide isolation and solitude to counter the noise and distraction of a public space. It can also be an effective way to support the theme, as it stays with the visitor through the entirety of the exhibit, framing up each part of the exhibit to support the overarching narrative—something that can be challenging to do oneself.

Other museums offer QR codes for the objects to provide more information. This is more challenging and potentially distracting, again, as it asks the visitor to repeatedly move in and out of different media types, and thus immersive contexts.

From a liminal perspective, we need to consider to what extent multimedia additions to an exhibit truly add depth and understanding to the artifacts and art—where additional technology is the only way to access such relevant and surprising perspectives—or, if it simply showcases technology in an attempt to compete for an audience already saturated by entertainment. This question becomes more poignant when analyzing the recent rise in "immersive exhibits" (see below).

2.9 Immersive Exhibits

Hopefully, all exhibits are immersive, although recent and ambitious media projects such as Monet's Lillies, The Klimt Immersive Experience, Refic Anadol's extravagant AI screen at MoMa's ground-floor atrium, MET's Un-framed virtual tour, Louvre's Beyond the Glass (Mona Lisa as virtual person), Live streaming Forbidden City (34 million peak views), or Emanuelle Moreaux' walk through work: Colors, Numbers (Tokyo 2023)—all hint at a growing trend that speaks to liminality in particular ways. With these examples, it is not hard to distinguish between the remotely mediated visits, offering a documentary view in real time of a traditional non-interactive exhibit, and then the art that is created as immersive or interactive but not referring to another artist. Then, there are the immersive exhibits that attempt to bring to life and illustrate well-known artists or works of art, such as that of Klimt and Monet with large screens surrounding the visitor. The question for the latter is to what extent they juxtapose a traditional view of a painting with new suggested meaning to enrich and challenge our understanding, or if they are simply borrowing from masters for spectacle and entertainment to cater to an audience more prone to visually exciting on-demand thrills.

Regardless, the liminal potential of immersive exhibits is real. These spaces can serve as transitional areas, acting as a boundary between reality and imagination. Visitors might be encouraged to interact with the artwork and explore its multiple meanings beyond what the canvas practically can do. They might offer a kaleidoscopic perceptual experience, incorporating signature elements such as color, form, and spatial arrangement to actively engage the visitor's senses and imagination in new ways but still relate to the artworks it plays off of. Such surroundings frequently strive to obscure the distinctions between the observer and the observed, resulting in a distinctive and potentially transforming encounter that complements the original art it derives from.

When we engage with immersive exhibits that reinterpret the works of renowned artists such as Van Gogh or Monet, we enter a space where the original paintings are not physically present. It should be recognized that this immersive experience differs significantly from the original artwork encounter. The immersive exhibit's liminal character and potential lies in deviating from the conventional art experience—inviting visitors to contemplate not just the art itself, but the very act of experiencing art. In essence, it offers a meta-experience, one that revolves around reflecting upon the process of engaging with art and the boundaries of museums.

2.10 Practicalities as Thresholds

In 1988, the Victoria and Albert Museum in London ran ads suggesting it had an "Ace café' with quite a nice museum attached"—and perhaps their pastries are noteworthy. But without assigning the ad more sincerity than went into making it, this does beg the question of how we handle and position all the necessary parts of the museum that are not directly part of the exhibits. A museum is a public place and requires necessities like a coat check, ticket and membership counters, security, bathrooms, and gift shops. How do these practicalities play with the primary liminality and experiences that visitors came for? They are, after all, still thresholds of some kind.

We cannot hide these necessities completely. We can, however, actively exclude them—and in doing so, make them a proactive gesture to highlight what the narrative is, and what it isn't. Practicalities might be tucked away and offered as distinct transactions separate from the "real" museum exhibit. Suppose the threshold between the exhibit and the practicalities that support it are clear, a drink of water or the move from one building to the next, then these can be offered as intentional "palate cleansers" before the next exhibit immersion takes liminal place.

This doesn't mean we must leave the magic and immersive safety of the museum. For example, the Copenhagen National Museum joins several different buildings with expansive, uncluttered, and quiet spaces, all architecturally very different. They become new liminal zones to help us slow down and to help mark experiential thresholds to give each more importance.

Or, we can find ways to integrate the practicalities in the liminal experience. For example, the necessary museum entrance can be treated as a ritual start point: supporting the destabilization and separation from the ordinary reality—stripping the visitor of coat layers and baggage meant for the outside world, to then bring them to the exhibit more exposed and sensitive to what lies ahead. A good example is the coat rack at the museum Boijmans Van Beuningen (Rotterdam), aptly named Merry-Go-Round (Fig. 2.10), serving as a captivating centerpiece at the museum's entrance. Resembling a merry-go-round, it features a vibrant red and white rope pattern, and a unique mechanism made of pulley blocks and weights. Visitors hang their coats on cloth hangers and hoist them up with a rope, securing them with a small key to leave their jackets suspended, floating beneath the ceiling. This fusion of artistic expression and functional utility blurs the conventional boundaries between the two, offering visitors the first step into a liminal space.

Separation from the ordinary and anticipation for what might come next are the key ingredients in building a temporary attitude conducive to deeper engagement and liminality. Consequently, we might not want to have visitors leave on a transactional note by offering whatever will sell at the exit gift shop. More integrated approaches can be found at the Victoria and Albert museum in London, where the fashion galleries have their shop selling catalogs, clothes, and accessories inspired by each landmark exhibition. Or, Cairo's Grand Egyptian Museum—perhaps more to the point by its inaccessible exclusivity—with Nakhla, the standalone boutique of the eponymous jewelry brand, situated at the feet of the iconic statue of Ramesses

Fig. 2.10 Merry-go-round coat rack, Studio Wieki Somers. Photos by Elian Somers, courtesy Studio Wieki Somers

II, offering bold gold necklaces displayed around the necks of a series of obsidian Nefertiti busts, in and of themselves, pricey collector's items.

2.11 Conclusion

As with all narratives and stories—although each part of the experience cannot, and should not, hold the entire narrative—each part needs to serve the overarching theme. The adage that: "Not all parts of the boat should look like a boat" certainly holds true for liminal museum experiences as well. This, of course, is especially relevant when we consider the many interwoven narratives and the multitude of aspects that make up a museum: its mission, individual artworks, curator statements, and exhibits—all engaging in dialogue with each other through juxtaposition.

The organization of these nested thresholds offers a unique opportunity: we are largely incapable of experiencing more than one liminal space concurrently as each liminal space is narrative, finite and requires internal coherence to work (Schütz 1945 p. 554). Liminality is created when intentionally juxtaposing two opposites; nothing more, nothing less. Consequently, the user will confront liminal thresholds one at a time.

With that, we are back to the liminal design framework suggested initially: to consider the museum experience holistically as an Optimized Abstraction supporting the Narrative Desire: the very question that had the visitors arrive curious in the first place. Suspension of Disbelief is held through a carefully orchestrated sequence of juxtapositions and intentional contradictions, renewing and sustaining the visitors' interest as an escalating narrative.

And it is perhaps exactly this focus on liminality as a sequence of intriguing juxtapositions—each holding both the very real and the infinite possibilities of the profound, in a fragile balance of opposites—that makes our rewarding work with museums both inevitable and surprising at the same time.

References

Antón C, Camarero C, Garrido M-J (2018) A journey through the museum: visit factors that prevent or further visitor satiation. Ann Tour Res 73:48–61. https://doi.org/10.1016/j.annals.2018.08.002
Aristotle. Poetics (1452a)
Bitgood S (2009) Museum fatigue: a critical review. Visit Stud J 12(2):93–111
Cangià F (2020) (Im)mobile imagination. On trailing, feeling stuck and imagining work on-the-move. Cult Psychol 26(4):697–712. https://doi.org/10.1177/1354067X19899070
De Luca Picione R, Valsiner J (2017) Psychological functions of semiotic borders in sense-making: liminality of narrative processes. Eur J Psychol 13(3):532–547. https://doi.org/10.5964/ejop.v13i3.1136. PMID: 28904600; PMCID: PMC5590535
Deleuze G, Guattari F (1987) A thousand plateaus: capitalism and schizophrenia. University of Minnesota Press
Fischer-Lichte E, Jain S (2008) The transformative power of performance: a new aesthetics. In: Iris Jane S (trans.). Routledge
Foucault M (1986) Of other spaces. Diacritics 16(1):22–27
Frijda NH (1986) The emotions. Cambridge University Press
Gentner D, Hoyos C (2017) Analogy and abstraction. Top Cogn Sci 9:672–693. https://doi.org/10.1111/tops.12278
Hennes T (2010) Exhibitions: from a perspective of encounter. Curator Mus J 53:21–33. https://doi.org/10.1111/j.2151-6952.2009.00005.x
Liedgren J, Desmet PMA, Gaggioli A (2023) Liminal design: a conceptual framework and three-step approach for developing technology that delivers transcendence and deeper experiences. Front Psychol 14:1043170. https://doi.org/10.3389/fpsyg.2023.1043170
Lima MG (1995) From aesthetics to psychology: notes on Vygotsky's "psychology of art". Anthropol Educ Q 26(4):410–424. http://www.jstor.org/stable/3195754
Obrist HU, Raza A (eds) (2014) Ways of curating. Allen Lane
Peirce CS (1877) The fixation of belief. Popul Sci Mon 12(1):1–15
Rawsthorn A (2015) Showing a Dutch house through the looking glass. The New York Times, 4 Feb 2015. https://www.nytimes.com/2015/02/04/arts/design/showing-a-dutch-house-through-the-looking-glass.html
Ricoeur P (1975) Phenomenology and hermeneutics. Noûs 9(1):85–102
Schütz A (1945) On multiple realities. Philos Phenomenol Res 5(4):533–576
Soderlund J, Borg E (2018) Liminality in management and organization studies: process, position and place. Int J Manag Rev 20(4):880–902
Stenner P (2017) Liminality and experience: a transdisciplinary approach to the psychosocial. Palgrave, London
Turner V (1974) Liminal to liminoid, in play, flow, and ritual: an essay in comparative symbology. Rice Inst Pamphlet Rice Univ Stud 60(3):20–60
Van Gennep A (1960) The rites of passage. In: Vizedom MB, Caffee GL (trans.). University of Chicago Press, Chicago. Original work published 1909, Les rites de passage
Zittoun T, Cerchia F (2013) Imagination as expansion of experience. Integr Psychol Behav Sci 47(3):305–324. https://doi.org/10.1007/s12124-013-9234-2
Zittoun T, Stenner P (2021) Vygotsky's tragedy: Hamlet and the psychology of art. Rev Gen Psychol 25(3):223–238. https://doi.org/10.1177/10892680211013293

Johan Liedgren is a writer, lecturer, filmmaker, and founder of The Liminal Circle, an international think tank and consulting firm focused on exploring Applied Liminality. The work centers on narrative theory and transformational design, aiming to create deeper and more meaningful experiences. This approach intersects technology with liminal spaces, interconnectedness, and narrative models to envision radically new ways for products to engage.

Andrea Gaggioli Ph.D., is Professor of Psychology at the Università Cattolica del Sacro Cuore in Milan, Italy. His work explores the relationship between human experience, digital technologies, and well-being. With a focus on immersive environments such as virtual and augmented reality, his research investigates their potential to enhance emotional health and cognitive function. Gaggioli also serves as the director of the Research Center in Communication Psychology, where he leads studies on how digital media and communication technologies impact psychological processes and human interaction.

Pieter M. A. Desmet Ph.D., is Professor of Design for Experience in the Human-Centered Design Department at Delft University of Technology, The Netherlands. His research focuses on understanding how and why design elicits emotion and contributes to the well-being of individuals and communities. He leads a research group exploring various dimensions of user experience and serves as the director of the Delft Institute of Positive Design, an initiative dedicated to generating knowledge and tools that support designers in creating products and services that foster human flourishing.

Chapter 3
Attachments in Museum Experience Design: Displaying Relationships and Networks of Public Urban Heritage

Noémi Zajzon

Abstract The dynamics of museum experience design processes and practices can be better understood by considering how public attachments shape experiential knowledge practices. Within exhibitions, attachments stipulate participatory forms that bond visitors experience with histories of objects, places and people, creating relationships that museums institutionalise and leverage for public formation. This idea is explored through a historical exhibition reimagining and refurbishing the memorial rooms of György Bernády, reframing his legacy through the social networks he catalysed for the urban transformation, public life, and cultural landscape as a mayor of Târgu Mureș (former Marosvásárhely), an emerging city in early twentieth century Transylvania. Drawing on symbolic interactionism, science and technology studies affect theories, the chapter considers the transformative potential of attachments that museums can harness in their relationships with publics, their role in heritagisation processes and public history, and offers insights for exhibition design research and practice within and beyond cultural institutions.

3.1 Introduction

Although tasked with different knowledge infrastructures, the curatorial projects of museums and exhibition design processes generally share a common concern about how visitor experiences engage and shape publics. With museums redefining themselves through their social agendas and the relationships built with publics (Vermeeren et al. 2018), exhibitions are tasked ever more so to account for the individual and collective experiences, memories and identities they convey and engage (Witcomb 2015) on various narrative scales (Austin 2012). Heritage[1] practices are

[1] Harrison (2012) describes heritage as made in the present and dealing with concerns from and about the past. It manifests in the relationships of contemporary societies have with objects, places, and practices related to the past.

N. Zajzon (✉)
Loughborough University, London, UK
e-mail: N.Zajzon@lboro.ac.uk; zajzonnoemi@gmail.com

L. Calvi et al. (eds.), *Transformative Museum Experiences*, Springer Series on Cultural Computing, https://doi.org/10.1007/978-3-031-89521-0_3

also challenged in terms of their scope, care work, and societal impact (Harrison 2012; Tolia-Kelly et al. 2017). This chapter proposes that attachments can inform these processes reflexively by activating experiential and historical knowledge about public heritage. Discussed through a historical exhibition design project about the urban legacy of a mayor, it demonstrates how narrative objects of a city in transformation mobilise individual and collective values and identity across time and space, informing transformative learning in heritagisation processes.

As sources and resources of internal motivations and external resolution (Gomart and Hennion 1999), attachments have been employed to inform action networks (Latour 1999) and public participation (Marres 2005) by working through their temporal scale and value concerns (Stuedahl et al. 2016) as well as their intertwinement with affect and history (Zajzon 2025). Theories and research on emotions and affects have extended understanding on how thinking and feeling deepen understanding of signification and reflection of individual and social processes (Massumi 1995; Clough and Halley 2007; Holmes 2010; Gregg and Seigworth 2020). Thus, attachments mobilise experiential and historical knowledge that exhibitions can amplify through their multimodal narrative mediums and that museums can harness for reflexive participation in society.

The chapter employs the concept of attachments to reflect on the conceptual translation and implementation of an exhibition commissioned by the Museum Mureș County for the memorial rooms of György Bernády, located in the Palace of Culture, a heritage site in Târgu Mureș in Romania. As reflected in the title, *György Bernády, Relationships and Networks*, the exhibition displays the legacy of this public figure through the social networks he leveraged for the city's urban transformation and cultural landscape. It captures the historical context by working through the cult, canon, heroisation, and identity of Bernády's figure, as recorded and institutionalised, and his vision of a future as a 'town builder' and mayor in the Austro-Hungarian Monarchy. Set up across two rooms, the exhibits present his political trajectory in the Monarchy, membership in the Freemasonry movement, and travel to the United States of America; his commitments and influence as mayor of Târgu Mureș (formerly Marosvásárhely) and sustained connections with architects, artists, and political alliances in Greater Romania, as well as family life.

The narrative works through the character of his figure and public influence, including his political aspirations and urban innovations that shaped the civic public emerging through the Art Nuovo-styled urbanisation of the once-rural city. Most importantly, it tackles Bernády's defining vision for the future of local history, weaving stories about his roles and activities in ways that activate reflection on the contemporary network of practices shaping the city. On the one hand, it unravels his achievements as a mayor and politician, town builder and urban visionary and family figure. On the other hand, it recollects the city in transformation through narrative objects that extend affective bonds through public memory and place identity. Doing so, the exhibition taps into the *public attachments* associated with this urban legacy and cultural heritage animating the personal within the collective past of the city. It activates memories tied to the paving bricks, public buildings, the ornamental details, and decorative programmes that shaped the cultural landscape, as well as recollections of public leisure activities linked to water-related architecture and political experiences associated with public squares.

Interacting with these contents evokes affective responses not only to individual and collective experience of the objecthood inherited through Bernády's legacy but also to the contemporary public heritage practices and the cultural and civic values they uphold. The exhibition concludes with an interactive wall, co-curated by the exhibition curators and designer, that bridges historical perspectives of the thematic exhibits with present-day concerns. The installation encourages visitors to reflect on how *public attachments* resonate with current needs and social issues. By shifting the past into the present, the installation contextualizes public urban heritage within contemporary dynamics, providing an occasion for meaningful dialogue between citizens, domain experts, and municipal decision-makers. Visitors are invited to connect historical transformations of the city with contemporary public affairs, prompting reflection on the role of city governance and civic participation as integral to heritage practices.

Attachments, then, mobilise the experience of participation with objects of public history, in this case, those pertaining to the urban heritage of Târgu Mureș. The chapter reflects on how the thematic exhibits shape the visitor experience, encouraging interaction and participation that extend beyond the exhibition space, activating a sense of ownership and agency towards the city. It examines how attachments can be used in exhibitions to evoke individual and collective experiences, activate agentic capacities, and support transformative learning through engagement with the past. Museum experience design processes can harness such tactics to both consolidate and challenge institutional frames of history through their object-collections and their relationships with publics. Conceptually, attachments can expose tensions in processes of heritagisation and transformation. In practice, they can guide participation in the controversies of institutionalised memory and the public histories of objects, people and places. By engaging with past experiences and trajectories, attachments can shape the methodological implications of exhibition experiences through participatory forms that reflect on the objecthood of museums and the relationships they build within institutional and broader civic contexts.

3.2 Participation, Heritage, Publics in Museum Experience Design

A widely sustained perception about museums is that they collect, preserve, and display for the public good, promising an experience beyond everyday life and a sense of wonder that may be creatively and intellectually rewarding (Gaggioli 2016). According to Gaggioli (2016), this sense of awe is realised through exposure to information that prompts the visitor to reject or be receptive to novelty. With the participatory turn in the cultural and heritage sectors, museum social agendas have been looking to find alignment with citizen humanities and sciences (Pierroux et al. 2020). This implied democratising institutional agendas and practices ranging from content curation, sociotechnical innovations, digitalisation, and media design of the museums' broader mediated communication environment that shape museum interactions with surroundings (Morrison et al. 2010). Transforming museum experiences through participation has shifted the focus from collections to visitor-centred approaches, prioritising long-term dialogue and new relationships while rethinking the role of technology in sustaining these relationships within the broader social context (Vermeeren et al. 2018).

In this context, exhibition design processes are also tasked to create experiences with visitors as users and publics in mind. According to Carpentier (2015), this entails considering the affordance of access, interaction and participation that involve users, publics and audiences as active agents in interpretational and constructional work. Building on these insights, Hetland and Schrøder (2020) distinguish users according to participatory audiences who co-create frames and processes, and citizen publics who actively contribute to the broader societal dialogue. This speaks to the politics of material participation discussed by Marres (2016) also shaping the social organising practices of design (Le Dantec's 2016). Considering museum participation, exhibitions employ various forms of storytelling to weave narratives through the different scales of visitors' experiential engagement with exhibits (Austin 2012, p. 107). Yet despite their multimodal narrative mediums—including visual, textual, and spatial elements—they remain fairly isolated from the post-visitor experiences and the story worlds designed. British sociologist Bennett (2005, p. 6) suggests that museums can use their 'custom-built environments' to shape relationships between people, things and society by 'producing new entities' that extend beyond the institution, influencing various social and civic initiatives. Discussed through the historical exhibition presented here, the chapter suggests that exhibition strategies can leverage the experiential knowledge of public heritage by mobilising attachments across timescales. By reframing the legacy of a political figure through his networks and practices that shaped the urban heritage of Târgu Mureş, the visitor experience extends reflective and agentic capacities to the broader social context.

The exhibits assembling the Bernády legacy—from the museum's collection alongside borrowed, crowdsourced and commissioned source materials—engage visitors' individual and collective experiential knowledge of heritage. According to Harrison (2012), heritage reveals relationships within communities and between people and places, and for communities to display their objects of value is part of their construction of identity, and thereby the value of their heritage. It manifests through a set of attitudes and relationships to the past, and the objects, places and practices selected to exemplify this past. In other words, heritage is 'a past formed in the present and consciously shaped by survivals and memories from history in response to current needs' (Ashworth and Tunbridge 1999, p. 105). This highlights the important role of design in producing heritage (Lees-Maffei and Houze 2021). In this light, exhibition narratives are responsible for how heritage is framed, and for what Harrison (2012, p. 69) calls heritagisation as 'the process by which objects and places are transformed from functional 'things' into objects of display and exhibition'. Furthermore, with heritage as a framework best equipped to bring together and harmonise lifetimes of natural and human histories (Jordheim 2021, p. 185), museum exhibitions are a powerful tool to problematise the objecthood of collections and the structural relations that establish heritage as public good. To consider heritage through Bernády's legacy activates attachments not only to a historical period but also to public practices that preserve values, memories, and personal and group identity. With attachments as an instrumental concept in exhibition design research, the chapter speculates on their transformative role in the relationships that museums establish with their publics.

3.3 Attachments in Museum Exhibition Design

Suspended between the past and the future, loss and becoming, attachments elucidate relationships of identity formation that museums institutionalise to provide continuity to public history. Incorporated into exhibition design processes, attachments can inform participation in museum experience design by sensitising visitors to relationships with objects, places and practices and thereby activating capacities in processes of heritagisation. This complements theoretical views intersecting symbolic interactionism and critical heritage studies looking to overcome binary structures between the tangibility of the material environment and intangible heritage and the affective capacities of artefacts, mediation and social practices (Harrison and Rose 2010).

The sociological perspective, according to which attachments carry sources and resources of experiential knowledge practices (Gomart and Hennion 1999), has enabled greater insight into aspects of time and space, contributing to knowledge infrastructuring within the field of cultural heritage (Stuedahl et al. 2016). It also complements the frame of psychological ownership Baxter and colleagues (2015) mobilise in the context of the user experience of product attachments. According to this view, the motives and routes shape the user experience of object-attachments by developing affordance categories, such as control, intimate knowledge, and self-investment, thereby attending to efficacy and reflectance, self-identity and sense of place. These then inform the principles of the conceptual design by highlighting how product features affect attachments, which corroborates why technology is never the endpoint of the experience but instead shapes motivations and practices, and thereby how we develop capacities to influence the world.

Considering the processes of exhibition development, Gaggioli (2016) suggests that the transformative capacities of experience rely on the epistemic and emotional affordance of content production. He identifies four interrelated aspects of transformative experience design, which are: (1) *transformative medium*, e.g. plays, storytelling, imagery, music, films and paintings; (2) *transformative content*, referring to the content/subject and structure of an experience, which includes epistemic and emotional affordances; (3) *transformative form*, which concerns the style rather than the subject of the experience that is represented; and (4) *transformative purpose* implying a process—rather than an outcome-led thinking and interactive experiences considered through their transformative potentials.

Gaggioli's transformative plan complements the three-level conceptual framework proposed by Mason (2020) to guide visitor experience design in museums. Accordingly, progressing from (1) the experience level, through (2) the structure to (3) the surface level, implies transitioning from units of experience and meta-narrative to interaction spaces and information architecture, and finally to the finer details of physical and digital content, graphics, and layout. Mason highlights the collaborative and iterative process that underpins people-centred problem-framing, which is also foregrounded by Pagotto (2022) in museum experience design practices and interpretation strategies of exhibition development, including interaction, communication, exhibition, educational, and curatorial/artistic design. Pagotto further distinguishes between visitors' interaction modes according to social and individual experience, active and passive engagement, creative expression, additional information, and the continuity/non-continuity of the experience. This parallels Dierking and Falk's (2008) visitor-centred approach to optimise the learning journey by considering the *interactive experience model* that is a shifting interchange between the personal (perception and worldview), social (sharing) and physical (the display culture and built environment) experience. Attachments, this chapter suggests, can inform this interchange by engaging affective values across different time scales and with personal and collective histories. When integrated into exhibitions and their narrative objects, attachments can deepen participation by extending the visitor' learning journey beyond the exhibition space and linking it to wider heritage contexts in the public realm.

Historical exhibitions, like the one discussed here, broaden experience in time through the object network of urban heritage intimate to public history associated with Bernády's legacy. By framing this legacy through the relationships and networks that shaped the city's identity, the exhibition foregrounds the symbolic frameworks and heritage practices that shape urban publics.

3.4 The Exhibition Design Process

The exhibition was conceived with the museum's primary aim to refurbish the memorial rooms in the Palace of Culture and showcase previously unshown archival material of Bernády György's legacy through a more up-to-date exhibition scenography for the local public (Fig. 3.1).

The collaboration started with visual ideation and initial project planning during the funding stage. Over the next year and a half, between the funding application and the design phase, the narrative was developed through ongoing conversations and meetings between the curatorial team and the designer.

These meetings gradually consolidated the exhibition's central concept and explored storytelling approaches by reviewing artefact documentation, refining

Fig. 3.1 Exhibition site, refurbishing work in progress in Room 1. *Source* Author

written texts, selecting exhibition objects, and identifying display constraints, ultimately shaping the visual and spatial development of the overall design. One challenge during the ideation process was the evolving content and uncertainty about which objects would be displayed, which required ongoing changes to simulations and design decisions. Another challenge was adapting the text-heavy narrative to the physical space while making it accessible in three languages,[2] without limiting the exhibits' multimodality or the interpretation of objects.

The process revealed the importance of the methods used to simulate and translate the historical narrative into an exhibition narrative, by thematically grouping and categorising objects and designing a display system that embeds visual and spatial transitions, creating a sense of progression in the visitor journey. Key activities and tools in this process included the digital platforms and online folders for organising, adjusting and finalising content; the drawing tools, including the 3D model that facilitated dialogue between the curatorial team, designer and the production company, the sketchbook documenting conversations, ideas, technical solutions, and photo-documentations of site visits.

Transformative mediums, such as the interactive wall, designed to support the learning journey beyond the exhibition space and museum discourse were also subject to negotiation. Inspired by the historical context and the exhibition's diffuse collection—albeit differently from the historians on the curatorial team—the interactive installation aimed to extend the visitor experience into the realm of civic urban heritage and prompt reflection on ongoing modernisation practices

[2] The exhibition features Romanian as the official language, complemented by Hungarian (the most widely spoken minority language and the former official language in Transylvania during the Kingdom of Hungary and Habsburg Empire) and English to engage an international audience.

in the city. This also ties into the chapter's conceptual argument, namely, that leveraging attachments in exhibition narrative development can enhance reflexive participation transformative for museum experience design.

3.4.1 The Narrative Experience and Storytelling Approach

The exhibition sets off with a timeline positioned to the right at the entrance to Room 1, outlining the key events in Bernády György's life and introducing his early career and gradual evolvement in the political sphere (Fig. 3.2). This chronological departure shifts to a thematic approach, with eleven themes curated by individual historians and art historians serving as distinct chapters in the exhibition. Each chapter explores Bernády's legacy and personality through the lens of relationships and networks, employing a multiperspectival storytelling approach that informs the exhibition's visual and spatial organisation and overall flow.

The first part of the visitor journey focuses on the influence of the Habsburg Empire on Bernády's career, highlighting his trajectory within the Austro-Hungarian Monarchy and his rise as a public figure leading to his role as mayor. Displays on the left showcase scenes and prominent figures (statues) from the public sphere, leading along two stained-glass windows, one featuring the Coat of Arms of Hungary and one of Ferdinand I, emperor of Austria and King of Hungary. Adjacent to this, an outline of Bernády's connections with the Freemasonry movement and his democratic political intentions is presented.

Fig. 3.2 Timeline in Room 1. *Source* Author

Visitors are then guided into a semi-enclosed booth designed to evoke Bernády's study trip to America. This cabin-like space presents episodes from the voyage, illustrating its purpose and activities through images, souvenir objects, guidebooks, travel documents, newspapers, postcards, and an animated film about the trip.

Upon exiting the booth, the visitor journey intersects the period of Bernády's activities as mayor of Târgu Mureş (the front facade and display on the left), his relationships with architects (the wall opposite the booth) and artists (the wall to the right of the booth). Original collection-objects and graphic devices illustrate Bernády's connections, practices and wealth as a mayor, providing a glimpse into his architectural aspirations, with the front of the cabin booth resembling the former Town Hall's facade that used to incorporate the heralds of symbolic personalities (Fig. 3.3). With Bernády as a mayor, visitors are invited to meet the architects, master builders, artists and designers—key networks Bernády leveraged for the town's urban and cultural transformation.

Opposite the booth, the wall display captures the city's transformation during Bernády's era, showcasing completed and unrealised projects, architectural plans, and urban innovations. The display integrates vertically an interactive lightbox showcasing the realised buildings of Târgu Mureş, and continues horizontally with a structure that incorporates a visual slider of the city's transformation from the nineteenth to the twentieth century, along with pull-out drawers containing reproductions of architectural plans (see also Fig. 3.6). Bernády's original work desk, designed by Ede Toroczkai Wigand, is also integrated into this section as a display system. It

Fig. 3.3 View from the main exhibition entrance to Room 1. The cabin booth, which hosts the travel to America also echoes the former Town Hall's facade, once adorned with the heralds of symbolic personalities. *Source* Author

showcases two 3D-printed maquettes of unbuilt masterworks—the National Theatre (1909) and the Maros-Torda County Hall (1909)[3]—alongside an interactive touch-screen providing additional information on architectural competition projects. The desk transitions into the section presenting Bernády's relationships with artists and the role of the Palace of Culture. This area features images, photos, copies of and original artworks, and books from the artists, including four stained glasses originally designed for the former Town Hall, now the residence of the Mureş County Council building.

The exhibition continues with Room 2, split into two compartments featuring four themes. Upon entering the corridor to the left, visitors encounter Bernády as a local politician during Greater Romania, alongside Romanian politicians and locals, and his second term as mayor. Sequences from this period are presented through documents, images, a film, an installation of Bernády's medal collection, and his business cards. Divided by a wall, the second compartment covers the themes of the Family, Myth-building and the Interactive Wall. The Family section integrates Bernády's original bookcase with his library and desk, offering a glimpse into family life, complemented by a film narrating the story of his maid. This transitions into a reflection on Bernády's myth-shaping power, emphasising the importance of demystifying his legacy. The exhibition concludes with an installation that connects the past to the present and visitors to contemporary public life, urban planning and civic welfare. By inviting reflection on topics such as public transport, the built environment, schools, civic participation, residential areas, green spaces, leisure, and tourism, the installation shifts the visitor's perspective to that of a citizen actively shaping society beyond the exhibition space.

3.4.2 Scenographic Strategies and Tactics

Exhibitions are multimodal narratives brought to life through objects and the three-dimensional interpretive power of scenography, in which staging tactics and strategies define the conditions of display and, consequently, the visitor experience. Thus, the development of exhibitions relies on various tools, including plans, sketches and diagrams as well as digital instruments to organise and make sense of the material content, craft storytelling mediums and script the narrative into the space. Exhibitions are also shaped by shifting positionalities within the exhibition team, in this case, negotiating the desired atmosphere and the learning journey with practical constraints, such as limiting the narrative scope and interactive mediums to accommodate multilingual wall texts and larger visitor groups within certain areas.

[3] The 3D-printed models have been reconstructed at the Ybl Miklós Faculty of Architecture and Civil Engineering of Óbuda University based on the original blueprints by Károly Kós and Ede Toroczkai Wigand for the County Hall, and by Marcell Komor and Dezső Jakab for the Theatre, were brought to life by Limes 3D Innohub.

Scripting the exhibition narrative into the space began by dividing it into thematic acts, identifying the levels of narrativity and displays that connect sequences to sustain a sense of progression (Fig. 3.4).

This involved experimenting with the visual and spatial affordances of the mediums and finding alignment between objects and texts to bring the content to life. Engaging with the mediums—images, photographs, documents, original artworks—and inspecting the details and materialities of objects, including the miniature copies of sculptures, souvenir objects, guidebooks, medals, county badges, ornamental details of the furniture, facilitated medium-specific groupings, thematic categorisation, and narrative organising. The specific characteristics of the objects informed the selection of display techniques, ensuring coherence within the display system, for example distinguishing original artefacts from replicas, identifying storytelling approaches to make information tangible, or activating the experiential and interactive dimension of objects. The predominance of two-dimensional mediums led to tactics enhancing the perception of space and depth, such as using archival material as architectural elements within the exhibition space (Fig. 3.5), or extrapolating details and upending proportions.

Refining the details of the visual narrative required ongoing negotiation, including the selection, interpretation, and integration of graphic elements. Playing with scale and depth horizontally and vertically within each compartment helped the composition of the story through the arrangement of objects, as well as finding the touchpoints for interaction shortcuts (Fig. 3.6). By alternating between two-dimensional and three-dimensional elements to present the thematic exhibits, a strategy was developed to optimise material choices (favouring paint over print for large surfaces, and

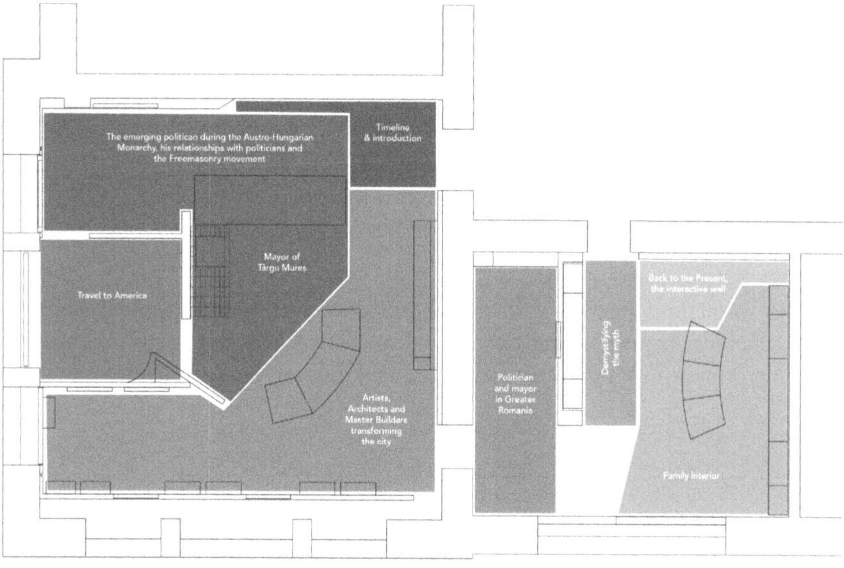

Fig. 3.4 Narrative structure divided into acts. *Source* Author

Fig. 3.5 Exhibition wall render illustrating György Bernády's relationships with the master builders, architects, and the city in transformation. *Source* Author

Fig. 3.6 Display system integrating the interactive map with the lightbox of the realised architectural projects, the interactive visual slider of the city in transformation, and pull-out drawers with the architectural plans of the master builders and architects. *Source* Author

steel over wood for main display structures), enhance the visual atmosphere (through colour schemes, texture, sound, and lighting), and shape the spatial expression (including proportions, perspectives, angles, and light) of the narrative.

3.5 Public Attachments to the City in Transformation

Media entities welcomed the exhibition describing it as showcasing "the Bernády universe" (Nagy Székely 2024) and juxtaposing the social media-free historical context with contemporary digitally networked contexts (Hajnal 2024). Both media framings highlight the exhibition's focus on György Bernády's social networks and practices that shaped the cultural landscape and infrastructure of Târgu Mureș, and the public values attributed to his legacy.

This thematic approach builds on and responds to the varying body of historical research that has significantly increased in Romania after the fall of the communist regime in 1989[4] due to a prominent return towards the past to reclaim lost memories and historical points of reference for the rebirth of the city (Fodor 2015). Historical records reveal how Bernády's memory has been preserved and directed towards future generations to create a role model and to articulate benchmarks for collective identity (György 2014, 2018), and to support the modernisation of public life in a city characterised by a sense of 'catching up' and a quest for 'role models' (Fazakas et al. 2021). His remembrance as the 'town builder' of Târgu Mureș is grounded in his organisational work as a politician, mayor and urban visionary advancing a national industrial development program centred on culture and education and shaped by the Szekler cultural programme that came to define the national architectural modernism of the city[5] (Oniga 2013; Székely 2021). These efforts included innovations in the sewage system, street planning, lighting, and major public buildings; infrastructural transformations around the Mureș River and industrial plants; the modernisation of the city's layout and public life, and architectural developments such as the Art Nouveau style Town Hall, the Chamber of Commerce and Industry, a range of educational, vocational and cultural institutions, including the Palace of Culture that hosted art gallery, music school and public library and marked Târgu Mureș as a 'model city' (Fodor 2021, pp. 126–148). His initiative to establish a committee responsible for the 'beautification' of urban development—promoting visually appealing street designs and architectural plans— became also instrumental in carrying out his urban planning goals.[6]

The exhibition unpacks this legacy through its artistic, technical, political and civic relevance. It focuses on Bernády's relationships and networks through the practices driving his cultural and technical innovations. It showcases Bernády's commitment to culture and education and the connections he cultivated with politicians and cultural

---

[4] The 1989 regime change signals the transition from the communist regime to democratic capitalism.

[5] According to Székely (2021), the national architectural modernism shaping the city in the early twentieth century distinguished Târgu Mureș from its contemporaneous Hungarian cities undergoing modernisation by integrating national iconography, blending peasant-inspired ornamentation with folk ballads and national heroes, and establishing an architecturally focused vocational school disproportionate to the city's scale.

[6] In his chapter, Fodor (2021, pp. 126–148) highlights how Bernády used this platform, comprising of "lay people", i.e., "non-engineers", with a keen interest in "beautifying" urban development, to advance his vision of the 'model city'.

workers of the time, weaving through the symbolic framework and practices that have transformed the city shaping and providing continuity to its urban public during periods of political regimes and transitions. While framing the rebirth of the city through its transformation from a rural to an urban place highlights attachments to the modernisation of public life, remembering its revival through Bernády's legacy has been often linked to collective identity (Fodor 2021, pp. 89–148). It has safeguarded a threatened community life following both the postwar and post-communist regime-change, while ensuring a continuity of the local elite to capture the past through the urban transformation of the city and extend these achievements to the future (György 2014). Communities develop through 'thin' or 'thick attachments' depending on a range of characteristics—of ethnicity, religion, class and politics—and commitments to a common body of symbols that provide group members with shared meanings distinct from relations to others[7] (Crooke 2008, pp. 29–30). These bonds are strengthened by cultural markers embedded in place, history, ethnicity and life experiences, a phenomenon well documented in place attachment studies (Low and Altman 1992; Manzo and Perkins 2006; Manzo and Devine-Wright 2013; Madgin 2021).

By presenting Bernády's legacy through his practices, the exhibition brings heritage-making processes closer to individual and collective experience and participation. These nodes mediate the museum's relationship with its publics and become points of negotiation between curators and exhibition designers over how narrative objects frame the exhibition content and connect with publics . Each thematic compartment includes displays that explore Bernády's social networks across different time periods, activities and contexts. Engaging with these displays elicits experiences that bond visitors with the city. For instance, the wall section on architectural heritage features a multilayered open book that includes an interactive map of the realised buildings in a lightbox and a visual slider of the changing city. When guiding visitors through the exhibition, engagement with these elements elicited stories and affective responses of individual and collective experiences beyond the information displayed. Visitors shared personal reflections—recalling life events in public buildings and squares, recounting observations about the built environment, or telling family stories tied to political developments and regime changes. Some remembered childhood moments linked to the yellow keramit brick, a kerbstone material widely used for paving in public spaces during Bernády's era. These autobiographical stories add depth to local urban identity growing with the city.

The exhibition brings Bernády's legacy closer to visitors, highlighting the social practices behind his impact and making them contemporaneously relevant for public and civic heritage by paralleling enduring relations with current needs and issues. While this could have been more actively addressed during the exhibition development, the reflection in this chapter intends to advance the relevance of attachments

[7] Crooke (2008), writing about how museums can navigate communities, invokes Gerard Delanty's view (2003) of "thin" and "thick" attachments that form communities, but cautions to see these as a means to value or judge them. This speaks to how semiotic communities operate, referenced through the work of Cohen (1985), who suggests that commitments to a common body of symbols provide communities with meanings shared amongst its members and distinct from relations to others outside the group.

in historical exhibitions that engage urban public heritage for museum experience design. It attempts to demonstrate how attachments reserve the power for museums to leverage their objecthood to become cultural and civic actors when developing new directions and relationships with publics.

3.6 Transformative Object Networks and Practices

By focusing on Bernády's network of practices, the exhibition brings urban public modernisation closer to citizens and in relation to contemporary issues. This may be seen as *transformative content* not only for the museum's collection but also for public history. The objects on display articulate public attachments to symbolic representations of the city's history, revealing the intertwinement of urban heritage and identity with modernisation and national imaginaries.

The exhibition incorporates objects from the museum's collection, alongside materials acquired from partner institutions, community contributions and commissioned works as shown in the exhibition layout diagram (Fig. 3.7).

The first compartment features archival materials, including photographs, plaques, diplomas, event invitations, and correspondence, unravelling the relationships that

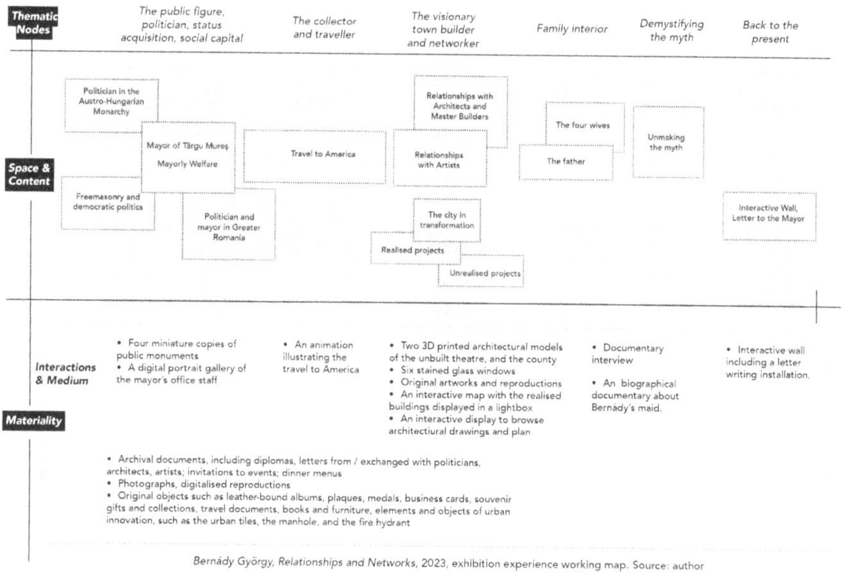

Fig. 3.7 Exhibition layout diagram drafted by the author to identify key touchpoints and interactions along the visitor journey

shaped Bernády's political career, status, and social capital. The display assemblage connecting the sections on the Austro-Hungarian Monarchy and his mayorship presents commemorative statues of heroes from the 1848 revolution alongside the practices of gifting albums for special occasions. The miniature copies of these public monuments illustrate the symbolic politics of the public sphere and the national imagery that shaped collective identity, yet fell victim to iconoclasm following the First World War. The Freemasonry compartment, featuring his diploma and medal alongside an audio testimony from one of the master builders, reveals his political aspirations to use this network effectively for the realisation of his plans.

The exhibition further introduces Bernády's practices as a collector and traveller, showcasing county badges, a collection of medals and souvenirs from his American travel advocating for natural gas.

The compartments detailing his relationships with architects, master builders, artists and designers emphasise his role as a visionary and connector, instrumental in driving urban transformation and intellectual modernisation of Târgu Mureș, commissioning architectural work and decorative programmes from accomplished Hungarian architects, workshops and artists, bringing their expertise to the city and forming lifelong friendships (Fig. 3.8).

Following the regime-change of 1918–1920 from the Monarchy to Greater Romania, the local politician Bernády extended his network with Romanian officials while remaining vocal about the grievances of Transylvanian Hungarians and advocating for political activism (Fig. 3.9, right image).

Throughout the exhibition development, the use of creative technologies for experimentation and interactions within the display system was limited due to budget constraints and the anticipated maintenance work required. Most often, the search for *transformative forms* in the units of visitor experience was found in playing with

Fig. 3.8 View towards the walls depicting Bernády's cultural legacy through his relationships with the architects, master builders and the artists, Room 1. *Source* Author

Fig. 3.9 Photographs illustrating the view into the cabin, travel to America in Room 1 (to the left) and the exhibition compartment on the politician and mayor in Greater Romania, Room 2 (to the right). *Source* Author

the style of the physical interface and finding coherence through the visual and spatial structure and integrated audio-visual mediums.

Original collection-based objects and documents were complemented by interpretation aids such as textual labels (in three languages) and screens for the visitor to delve into and interact with the content displayed. For example, the digital portrait gallery allowed an encounter with the mayor's office staff, whereas the interactive display enabled browsing of the realised and unrealised architectural project plans. Less tangible information required storytelling through *transformative mediums* of audio-visual formatting. For instance, telling the American journey through an animation[8] was an effective way to personify public perceptions of the mayor's motivations and achievements with this travel (Fig. 3.9, left image). The crowd-sourced story about a trouser brace gifted by Bernády to a young boy called Traian Maxim Chirilean, whose grandfather was acting consultant to the mayor, led to tracing Bernády's last living social connection and inspired a documentary interview[9] with him. The video presenting Maxim's story weaves together his childhood memories with broader themes of public life and political transformation that define the figure of the mayor. Another documentary sharing the story of Bernády's maid complements[10] the section on Family life and his relationships with his four wives.

[8] The animation was commissioned from animation director Buzási Gyopár, 2024.

[9] The documentary interview was produced by What's in the Production Box, 2024.

[10] *I was Bernády's maid*. A biographical documentary, by TVR Târgu Mureş, 2009.

Additionally, the commissioned 3D-printed maquettes of the unbuilt Theatre and County Hall more tangible to the public.[11]

These narrative objects extend the museum's collection from the era by addressing gaps in knowledge concerning the less tangible cultural and political dimensions of public life at the time. The four miniature monument replicas evoke the memorial practices emblematic of collective identity, while the animated film on Bernády's American travel reveals how his visions of progress combined the foundational steps of urbanisation and modernisation with imperial modes of gifting and souveniring, contributing to his legacy making. These exhibits, while nurturing intellectual engagement with history and nostalgia for the city's changing identity, convey heritage as an active practice of placemaking and local politics, relevant to museum experience design.

The interactive wall (Fig. 3.10) furthers the exhibition's transformative goal to bridge historical perspectives and prompt reflection on the role of city governance and civic participation as integral to public urban heritage.

Originally intended as a medium to spark dialogue among public and private decision-makers and citizens post-visitor experience, the installation was conceived to host events and debates on pressing issues in local public life and urban development, including housing, transportation, and school system, as well as green spaces and leisure time. Involving visitors in reflecting on how the thematic exhibits relate to present-day issues in the city would have strengthened the exhibition's *transformative content* and further engaged the museum's role within the broader social context (Stuedahl 2018). Due to the required maintenance and organisational demands on museum staff, as well as considerations of public reception, the design was revised into an interactive board that invited visitors—locals, non-locals and children—to leave a message or write a letter to the current mayor on selected themes of contemporary public life.

The concept of public attachments could have been explored more fully with a greater focus on process over outcome and more emphasis on interactive experiences. This exploration would have also benefited from an engaged co-design process, assuming the designer's role as a creative strategist is acknowledged within co-curated initiatives emerging from the collaboration (Austin 2020). From a design research perspective, further exploration is needed to understand how museums can engage public attachments to sustain dialogue and negotiation within the broader context of civic heritage, cultural processes and public politics.

[11] These 3D-printed models were commissioned from and reconstructed by the Ybl Miklós Faculty of Architecture and Civil Engineering of Óbuda University, 2023.

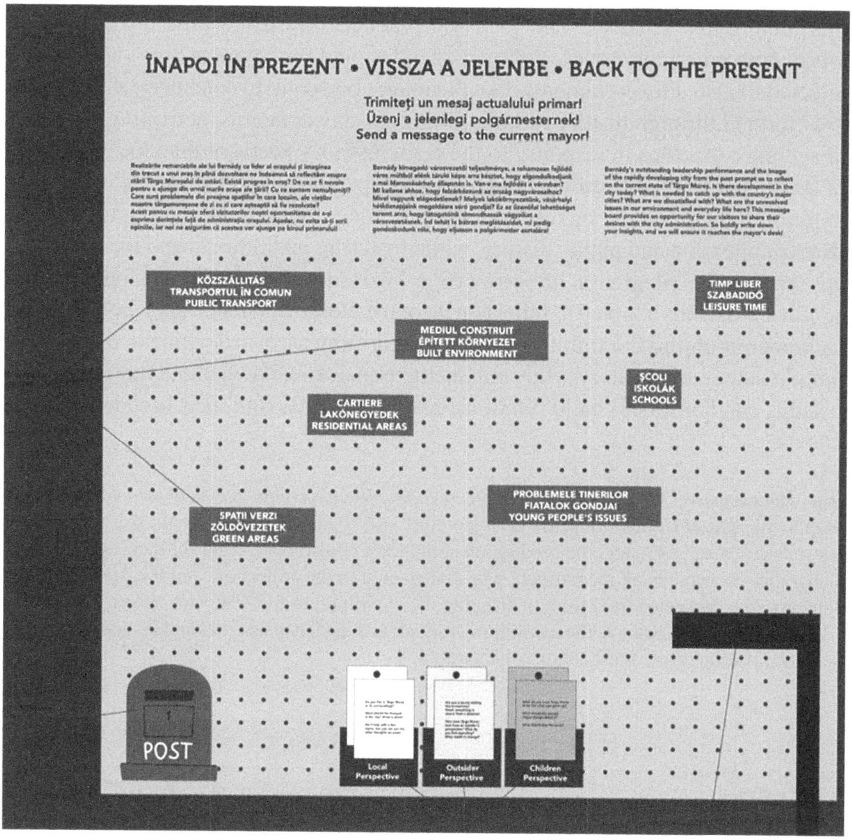

Fig. 3.10 Proposal for the interactive wall, Room 2. *Source* Author

3.7 Conclusion

Historical exhibitions connect the past with the present hoping to provide a comprehensive take on history. The exhibition discussed demonstrates how attachments to urban public heritage can inform this process through narrative objects that mobilise experiential knowledge of the city's history, contributing to museum experience design. By tracing Bernády's practices and social networks, the exhibits unravel the affective and symbolic systems that shaped Târgu Mureş, bringing this legacy closer to visitors. Using a range of mediums—from archival images, documents, original artefacts and replicas to storytelling through animation, 3D-printed architectural models, and both digital and physical interactions—the exhibits draw visitors into the industrial and cultural transformation that branded the city at that time and modelled its identity.

In light of the social networks, the legacy of the politician, mayor, and urban planner lives through the objects of public modernisation and the value system underpinning his practices. The focus on practices illustrates how urban heritage evolves with emerging issues, political agendas, and the relationships cultivated or neglected. It also allows elements, like the interactive wall, to consider public attachments formed through history in light of present-day concerns, activating reflective and agentic capacities in response to the contemporary needs of the city.

Despite the multifaceted challenges posed by an initially diffuse collection, the exhibition transforms the memorial rooms of this public figure, enriching both the museum collection and public history, while fostering institutional and local partnerships through the integration of borrowed, crowdsourced, and commissioned works. The conceptual lens adopted to reflect on it contributes to understanding the capacities attachments mobilise in exhibition design—informing ways to document, display and communicate public history while enhancing transformative visitor experiences that museums can harness to build relationships with publics and their broader heritage contexts.

Acknowledgements The exhibition *György Bernády, Relationships and Networks* was commissioned by the Mureş County Museum between 2021 and 2024. The author would like to thank the museum's curatorial team and the production company's construction team for their expertise and collaboration, as well as all the partners who contributed to the collection, and the translators and volunteers who dedicated their time to bringing the exhibition to life. The views expressed in this work are those of the author as the exhibition designer and design researcher and do not necessarily reflect the position of the museum or collaborators.

References

Ashworth GJ, Tunbridge JE (1999) Old cities, new pasts: heritage planning in selected cities of Central Europe. GeoJournal 49(105–116):105
Austin T (2012) Scales of narrativity. In: Museum making. Routledge, pp 107–118
Austin T (2020) Narrative environments and experience design: space as a medium of communication. Routledge
Baxter WL, Aurisicchio M, Childs PR (2015) A psychological ownership approach to designing object attachment. J Eng Des 26(4–6):140–156
Bennett T (2005) Civic laboratories: museums, cultural objecthood and the governance of the social. Cult Stud 19(5):521–547
Carpentier N (2015) Differentiating between access, interaction and participation. Conjunctions 2(2):7–28
Clough PT, Halley J (2007) The affective turn: theorizing the social. Duke University Press, Durham, NC
Cohen A (1985) The Symbolic Construction of Community. Tavistock, London and New York
Crooke E (2008) Museums and community: ideas, issues and challenges. Routledge
Falk JH, Dierking LD (2008) Enhancing visitor interaction and learning with mobile technologies. In: Digital technologies and the museum experience: handheld guides and other media, pp 19–33
Fazakas L, Ferenczi S, Fodor J, Gál Z (2021) Minta és felzárkózás [Role model and catching up]. Iskola Alapítvány
Fodor J (2015) Bernády a városépítő [Bernády, the town-builder]. Alutus Kiadó, Csíkszereda
Fodor J (2021) The development of Târgu Mureş in the early 20th century, pp 89–123. Mayor György Bernády's role in the urban development of Târgu Mureş, 1902–1912, pp 126–139. In:

Fazakas L, Ferenczi S, Fodor J, Gál Z (eds) Minta és felzárkózás [Role model and catching up]. Iskola Alapítvány
Gaggioli A (2016) Transformative experience design. In: Human computer confluence. Transforming human experience through symbiotic technologies, pp 96–121
Gomart E, Hennion A (1999) A sociology of attachment: music amateurs, drug users. Sociol Rev 47(S1):220–247
Gregg M, Seigworth GJ (eds) (2020) The affect theory reader. Duke University Press
György V (2014) The myth-shaping power of a past vision of the future. Acta Univ Sapientiae Philol 5(2):185–202
György VI (2018) Bernády György és kultusza Marosvásárhelyen. Erdélyi Múzeum-Egyesület
Hajnal C (2024) Bernády did not have Facebook, but he had a network and a system of relationships—the Bernády exhibition reopens in Târgu Mureș. Source: Székelyhon.ro. https://szekelyhon.ro/aktualis/bernadynak-nem-volt-facebookja-de-volt-halozata-es-viszonyrendszere-n-ujranyilt-a-bernady-tarlat-marosvasarhelyen
Harrison R (2012) Heritage: critical approaches. Routledge
Harrison R, Rose D (2010) Intangible heritage. In: Bangstad TR, Pétursdóttir Þ (eds) (2022) Heritage ecologies. Routledge, Taylor & Francis Group, p 238
Hetland P, Schrøder KC (2020) The participatory turn: users, publics, and audiences. In: A history of participation in museums and archives. Routledge, pp 168–185
Holmes M (2010) The emotionalization of reflexivity. Sociol 44(1):139–154
Jordheim H (2021) Mending shattered time: 22 July in Norwegian collective memory. In: Heritage ecologies. Routledge, pp 185–207
Latour B (1999) Factures/fractures: from the concept of network to the concept of attachment. Res Anthropol Aesthet 36(1):20–31
Le Dantec CA (2016) Designing publics. MIT Press
Lees-Maffei G, Houze R (eds) (2021) Design and heritage: the construction of identity and belonging. Routledge
Low SM, Altman I (1992) Place attachment: a conceptual inquiry. In: Place attachment. Springer US, Boston, MA, pp 1–12
Madgin R (2021) Why do historic places matter? Emotional attachments to urban heritage
Manzo L, Devine-Wright P (2013) Place attachment: advances in theory, methods and applications. Routledge
Manzo LC, Perkins DD (2006) Finding common ground: the importance of place attachment to community participation and planning. J Plan Lit 20(4):335–350
Marres NS (2005) No issue, no public: democratic deficits after the displacement of politics. Amsterdam
Marres N (2016) Material participation: technology, the environment and everyday publics. Springer
Mason M (2020) The elements of visitor experience in post-digital museum design. Des Principl Pract 14(1):1–14
Massumi B (1995) The autonomy of affect. Cult Crit 31:83–109
Morrison A, Stuedahl D, Mörtberg C, Wagner I, Liestøl G, Bratteteig T (2010) Analytical perspectives. In: Exploring digital design: multi-disciplinary design practices, pp 55–103
Nagy Székely I (2024) The new Bernády universe has opened. The life of an urban planner in the light of networks. Source: E-Népújság.ro. https://www.e-nepujsag.ro/articles/megnyilt-az-uj-bernady-univerzum
Oniga E (ed) (2013) A marosvásárhelyi Kultúrpalota 1908–1913. Maros Megyei Múzeum, Marosvásárhely
Pagotto MB (2022) Interpretation design in art exhibitions: review of literature and design of a practice cycle. Mus Manag Curatorsh 37(5):471–490
Pierroux P, Bäckström M, Brenna B, Gowlland G, Ween G (2020) Museums as sites of participatory democracy and design. In: A history of participation in museums and archives. Routledge, pp 27–45

Stuedahl D (2018) Participation in design and changing practices of museum development. In: The Routledge handbook of museums, media and communication. Routledge, pp 219–231
Stuedahl D, Runardotter M, Mörtberg CM (2016) Attachments to participatory digital infrastructures in the cultural heritage sector
Székely M (2021) Marosvásárhely 1892–1902: a felkészülés évtizede—Marosvásárhely 1892–1902: the decade of preparation. Ars Hung 47(1):5–28
Tolia-Kelly DP, Waterton E, Watson S (2017) Heritage, affect and emotion. Politics, practices and infrastructures
Vermeeren AP, Calvi L, Sabiescu A, Trocchianesi R, Stuedahl D, Giaccardi E, Radice S (2018) Future museum experience design: crowds, ecosystems and novel technologies. Springer International Publishing, pp 1–16
Witcomb A (2015) Thinking about others through museums and heritage. In: Waterton E, Watson S (eds) The Palgrave handbook of contemporary heritage research. Palgrave Macmillan, London. https://doi.org/10.1057/9781137293565_8
Zajzon N (2025, forthcoming) Redesigning relations: attachments in participatory history making with insights from citizen movements. Design issues, Special Issue on Design and the articulations of pasts.

Noémi Zajzon Ph.D., is a design researcher working at the intersection of visual communication, spatial practices, and participatory design. With a background in visual art histories and narrative environment design, her work spans exhibition-making and research on the politics of participation in design cultures. She has collaborated with museums, NGOs, community and grassroots organisations across the UK and Europe, and been a research associate on various projects at the Free University in Bolzano and at Loughborough University in London.

Chapter 4
Designing "One Minute" Experiences

Anders Sundnes Løvlie, Linda Stoltze, and Timothy Wray

Abstract Several studies have shown that visitors to art museums spend very short time looking at artworks and reading about them. Visitors' attention is fickle. Yet, often the information presented to visitors is written in winding and complicated texts. As information is increasingly offered on small screens such as smartphones, and as museums are striving to reach new and young audience groups, brevity and simplicity are ever more important. This chapter reports on a research-through-design study of a smartphone app called *One Minute* that uses image recognition to identify artworks and offers interpretive text that can be read in a minute. The app was developed by the authors initially as a research experiment, and further developed and deployed at the Brighton Museum and Art Gallery in the UK. The main contribution of the study lies in the design of a format for authoring bite-sized interpretations aiming to awake curiosity. Tests of the app have demonstrated that the format is effective in helping museum curators write simpler and more engaging texts. The app has also been used to engage members of the public to contribute their interpretations of artworks, offering a practical way to invite new voices into the museum.

4.1 Introduction

Museums wish to create transformative experiences for their visitors—experiences that change them in profound ways (Soren 2009). This ambition stands in stark contrast to empirical studies showing that visitors spend very short time looking at art masterpieces and reading about them—typically around 20 seconds, according to two influential studies (Smith and Smith 2001; Smith et al. 2017). How can art museums offer transformative experiences to audiences whose attention is so fickle?

This challenge is further complicated by the fact that looking at art is difficult (Noë 2015). There is a joke that has been repeated so many times it has become a cliché in films, comedy shows and cartoons. It goes something like this: A visitor in a contemporary art gallery looks thoughtfully at a small object on the floor, and makes

A. S. Løvlie (✉) · L. Stoltze · T. Wray
IT University of Copenhagen, Copenhagen, Denmark
e-mail: asun@itu.dk

L. Calvi et al. (eds.), *Transformative Museum Experiences*, Springer Series on Cultural Computing, https://doi.org/10.1007/978-3-031-89521-0_4

intellectual-sounding comments about the aesthetic qualities of the piece. Then a cleaning person passes by and sweeps the object into the trash bin; it wasn't art after all, rather just a piece of trash. The joke exists in numerous variations and has been enacted as a practical joke on unwitting museum visitors—and in fact numerous actual artworks seem to play on the uncertainty underlying it (consider for instance some of Banksy's "museum pranks").[1] The joke might be seen as a satire along the lines of "The Emperor's New Clothes", ridiculing art galleries and art aficionados. But seen from another perspective, the joke speaks to an audience that see themselves as outsiders in the art museum, unable to make sense of the artworks—or even tell the difference between art and a piece of trash. Art museums have often been criticized for implicitly addressing an audience of experts, leaving those without expertise (or confidence/'habitus') lost (Bourdieu et al. 1990; Merriman 1989).

Artwork labels with interpretive text is one way of helping such visitors, offering some helpful background information and suggestions for how to interpret and appreciate the art. Museum professionals are divided about whether or not labels should be offered, where some professionals prefer that the artworks should stand on their own and "speak for themselves", whereas some scholars e.g. in new museology have highlighted interpretive text as a way to help visitors (Vergo 1989; Bennett 1997; Ravelli 2007; Reitstätter et al. 2022).

A common compromise is to avoid text on the museum walls, instead offering interpretation through audio guides or smartphone apps. Such guides are limited by the museum's capacity to produce interesting material about its various exhibitions—and present it in a user-friendly and engaging manner. There is also a design challenge tied to indoor positioning: Since most common positioning techniques such as GPS[2] do not work well indoors (and other techniques such as bluetooth beacons have challenges of their own),[3] it is difficult to detect the visitor's position accurately, meaning that the app cannot automatically detect which artwork the visitor is standing next to. Against these challenges, new AI-powered apps such as *Smartify*™, *Magnus*™, and *Google Lens*™ offer an exciting promise: What if you can point your smartphone camera at any object in the museum, and have the smartphone tell you what you are looking at? This is enabled by computer vision techniques which can match the image of an object against the museum's vast collections database, and return the information found there.

In an early user study looking at the app *Vizgu* used by the National Gallery of Denmark in 2017, we realized that while this idea sounds exciting in theory, in practice it stumbles on an all too familiar obstacle: The information the app was able to return from the museum database often consisted of lengthy academic texts that did not seem engaging for users, and were an ill fit for the mobile screen—in particular when taking into account that users might only be willing to spend a very short time reading about the artwork (see Fig. 4.1).

[1] https://banksyexplained.com/banksy-museum-pranks-2003-2005/.

[2] Global Positioning System.

[3] For more information see for instance Wikipedia's entry on Indoor positioning systems (Wikipedia Contributors 2024).

Fig. 4.1 Artwork information from the National Gallery of Denmark, as seen in the Vizgu app (Rogberg 2018)

The challenges outlined above point to a tricky design problem for museum experience designers: Is it possible to use a smartphone guide app to help museum visitors see the art in a museum, respecting that visitors' are only going to spend a short time in front of the artwork, but still offering an experience that goes beyond providing basic information—inviting curiosity and perhaps inspiring some visitors to look deeper? In the following we present our attempt at creating such an app, called *One Minute*, and some insights and challenges we encountered in this process. One unintended, but promising insight was the potential for such an app to facilitate visitors sharing their own interpretations in a way that could allow museums to navigate the tricky challenge of including external voices, while maintaining editorial control and avoiding the pitfalls of user-generated content.

4.2 Related Work

Many scholars have discussed recommendations for designing interpretive texts (also known as physical museum labels) in a museum context (Bitgood 1991, 2016; Borun and Miller 1980). Designers are encouraged to take a variety of parameters into account when designing interpretive texts. Falk and Dierking (2012) suggest that labels need to offer concrete information, as visitors are found to read labels that will help them to answer their concrete questions about objects. Serrell (2015) emphasizes the need to make connections between object and text in order to encourage reading, for instance by referring directly to details in the object. In addition, designers can position label and object closely together, to enhance the connection (Gammon and Burch 2008).

However, several authors point out that visitors want more than just straightforward information. Bitgood (2000) points out that both visual layout and language style is important in order to catch the visitors' attention, and text should be vivid, pose questions, address the reader directly and use a conversational tone. Bedford (2001) emphasizes the importance of storytelling, as stories encourage personal reflection and public discussion—teaching without preaching. Marengo and Fazekas (2018) suggest that many visitors want to read a description of the characters, time and events that relate to the artwork. Serrell (2015) suggests that labels should be considered as narratives, rather than lists of facts, and good labels should inspire, communicate and help the visitors to get what they are seeking. She also suggests that 140 characters, the length limit of posts to the popular social medium Twitter,[4] can be used as a benchmark for the length of label text.

Turning our attention from physical museum labels to mobile apps, there are various studies that investigate interpretive material in a museum and/or heritage setting, typically using audio (Fagerjord 2015; Lee 2017), audiovisuals (Blythe et al. 2011; vom Lehn and Heath 2003), augmented reality (Bekele et al. 2018), games (Beale 2011; Kidd 2018; Løvlie et al. 2021), and an ever increasing variety of hybrids and other formats (Waern and Løvlie 2022a). Some have also experimented with language styles and narratives, such as the location-aware app Carletto the Spider which was found to support emotional engagement through its "funny" and "lovely" language style, resulting in an informal storytelling experience (Lombardo and Damiano 2012). Similarly, The Horse was designed as an emotional character which was evaluated in the way it managed to appear empathetic towards children (Keil et al. 2013).

While audio guides remain one of the most common formats for interpretive material on mobile apps, the use of headphones limits social interaction between companions (Gammon and Burch 2008; Wessel and Mayr 2007), which is problematic because the social dimension is often an important part of a museum visit (Blud 1990; Eklund 2020; Løvlie et al. 2022). Text-based content allows visitors to browse interpretive material on mobile apps without being prevented from social interaction. However, there is a lack of studies exploring the design of interpretive text in mobile apps.

When providing interpretive material on mobile devices there is a second problem designers must take into account, what is often referred to as the "heads-down phenomenon" (Hsi 2002; Lyons 2009; Petrelli et al. 2013; Walter 1996): The concern that when visitors are invited to use mobile apps, they may end up walking through the museum with their eyes fixed to the mobile screen rather than seeing the precious artefacts exhibited in the museum. Such concerns are widespread among museum professionals, reflecting concerns in society at large about smartphone overuse (Silas et al. 2016; Syvertsen and Enli 2020; Turkle 2011), and have also on some occasions

[4] Later this limit has been increased, and the social media company has been renamed to X.

become topics of controversy in social media and mass media (Waern and Løvlie 2022b).

While we should be cautious not to give in to overly simplistic knee-jerk reactions about the dangers of mobile screens, designers do need to be aware of these concerns as they pervade discourse about technology use in museums. The concerns may be seen through the lens of 'attentional balance' which describes that visitors balance their attention between at least three entities when they visit a cultural heritage site: An information source, companion(s) and the location itself (Woodruff et al. 2001, p. 437). These entities afford different stimuli which allow visitors to have fulfilling, engaging experiences. The information source should help visitors get optimal attentional balance and not hinder it. The concept of attentional balance has been used in research exploring the use of Augmented Reality in museums (Damala et al. 2008; Mason 2016; van der Vaart and Damala 2015).

Much effort has been invested in researching how to use digital technologies to create participatory experiences for visitors (Heath and vom Lehn 2009; Smørdal et al. 2014). Simon (2010) encourages cultural institutions to reconnect with the public by inviting them to engage as active participants instead of passive consumers. She suggests that museums should move from being information providers for visitors to instead support multi directional content experiences. This means the participatory institution will act as a 'platform' that connects different users who are both able to be content creators, consumers, collaborators, distributors and critics. However, this may affect the consistency of the visitor experience as the institution cannot guarantee the quality of the content; instead it provides opportunities for diverse co-produced experiences. When designing for participatory experiences, the key is to find ways amateurs can create and share content that is displayed and communicated attractively. The museum benefits from giving voice to a greater diversity of people who can offer a richer variety of perspectives on the museum's collections.

4.3 One Minute

The design of the *One Minute* app started from the realization that interpretive text in a format such as that shown in Fig. 4.1 did not offer a satisfying experience for (most) museum visitors. As suggested by Falk and Dierking (2012), artwork labels should be written to meet the visitor's immediate informational needs in order to catch their attention. Thus we set out to design for an experience that visitors could have in a short amount of time—hence the name—and that would be immediately engaging while also stimulating the visitor's curiosity to hopefully inspire some visitors to see the art in a new light, possibly leading some to look deeper.

The design process of *One Minute* started as a small student project, and grew through several iterations to a research project involving a larger team of researchers, developers and students. In the initial phases we started by designing a format we thought was highly simplified, and tested and evaluated this design with students at our university, only to learn that we had to simplify further. The design proceeded through several iterations of prototyping, testing, and evaluation, and led to the design of a highly simplified format for interpretive text, which can be seen in Fig. 4.2.

The first screenshot (top left) shows the camera view as the user is pointing the camera at the painting (in this case, *Faun and Nymph* by the Danish painter Edvard Weie at the National Gallery of Denmark). When the camera button at the bottom of the screen is pressed, the app takes a photo and uploads this to a server where an image analysis service (Microsoft Azure) compares the photo to the artwork database. If the app finds a match, the user will see the view in the second screen, confirming that the app has detected the painting. From here the user can swipe with their finger to "flip" through a series of up to 5 virtual cards, each containing 1–3 sentences.

Tests of this design demonstrated that it lived up to the promise in the title: Users were able to read and flip through the cards in less than a minute, and most found the experience simple and engaging. However, the iterative testing and evaluation also taught us something else: While we initially had approached the challenge in the way UX designers usually do—by focusing on designing the interface and the interactions, including the visual and technical parts of the application—there was

Fig. 4.2 Artwork information in the *One Minute* prototype, about the painting Faun and Nymph by Edvard Weie, at the National Gallery of Denmark

something else that mattered more than all of these other elements for the user experience: The text. This may come as no surprise for scholars and professionals in communication, however it required us to shift focus and look for tools outside the UX designer's usual toolbox. (As discussed by Fagerjord (2015), there seems to be a lack of methods for UX evaluation that address the *texts* that form part of a user experience.)

In order to address this challenge we reviewed the academic literature about label writing, which offered some recommendations that we could apply in the prototypes created in the iterative design process described above. This led us to identify a structure for the texts that we found we could apply repeatedly to a variety of artworks, and which resulted in texts that most users found engaging. This structure can be seen in the five text cards in Fig. 4.2, which follow a classic Aristotelian storytelling structure with a beginning (screen 3 in the top row), middle (screen 4 in the top row and 1–2 bottom) and end (screen 3 bottom). The text in the "beginning" screen describes the immediately noticeable elements of the artwork that the user can see in front of them, drawing attention to some interesting aspect or detail. The "middle" section is divided in three screens, the first of which aims to evoke curiosity and provoke reflection, for instance by posing a question or provocative statement to the reader; whereas the next two screens provide explanation and elaboration on the question or statement. The "end" screen rounds off the story.

The use of frequent questions were intended to encourage users to look back at the artwork, partly in order to avoid the "heads-down phenomenon" and help visitors maintain attention towards the artwork, as well as to stimulate reflection and help visitors see the artwork in new ways.

Using this structure helped us create "one minute" experiences that our test users found engaging. However, we wished to test whether these insights could be formalized and applied in a way that was somewhat independent of the writing skills and style of an individual. This led us to design an authoring interface with more detailed guidelines. In order to evaluate this design we set up a two-part test. For the first part we recruited four undergraduate students as well as one professional curator from the National Gallery of Denmark. Each of the test participants were given one image of an artwork as well as the interpretive text about that artwork found in the museum database, and were tasked with rewriting the text according to the guidelines in our authoring interface. They all finished their tasks in a short amount of time. Figures 4.3 and 4.4 show two of the texts written by these test users.

For the second part of the test we recruited five new test participants and showed them the five artworks, the original texts from the museum database as well as the new texts written by the first test participants. Results were clear: All the participants in round 2 found the original texts overwhelming and none of them finished reading the original texts for any of the five artworks. On the other hand, all the five rewritten "one minute" texts were read till the end by all five test users. They found the new texts easier to read, both because of the length and because the language was simpler with fewer difficult words. The simplicity made the reading experience more pleasurable and manageable. Some of the users suggested that the texts could be even shorter. Additionally, elements of the texts referring directly to details in the paintings and

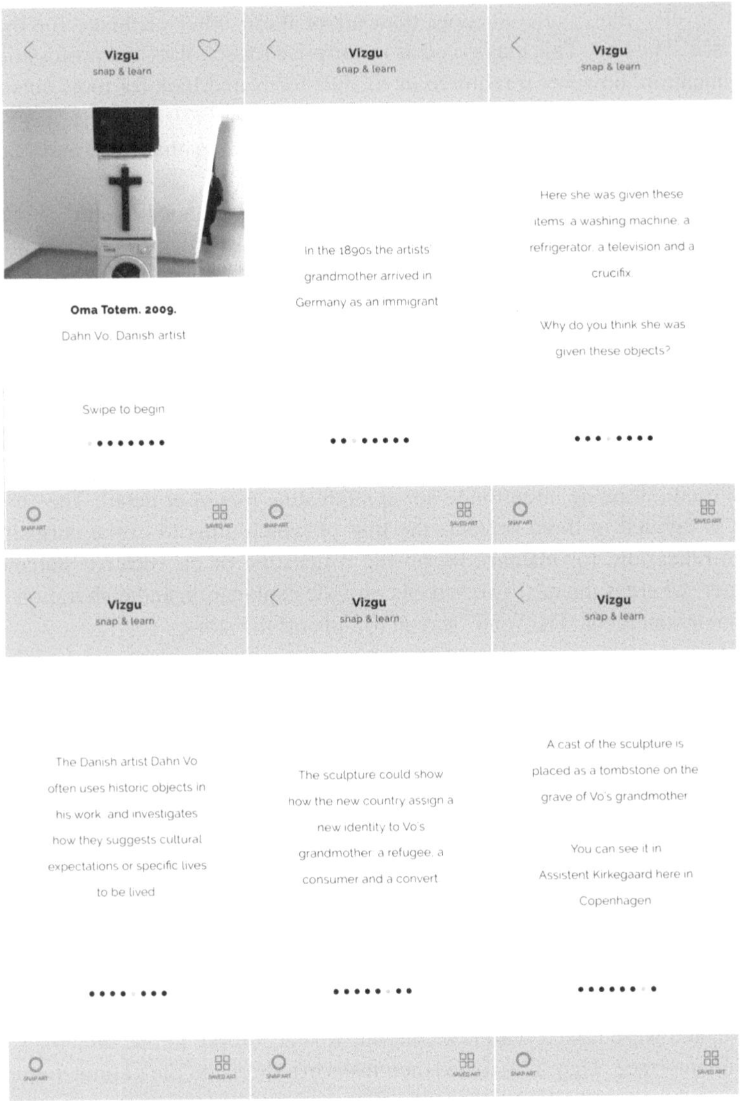

Fig. 4.3 Interpretive text in the *One Minute* format written by a test user who worked as curator at the National Gallery of Denmark, about the artwork *Oma Totem* by Dahn Vo. (The visual interface in these screenshots is an earlier version than the final design seen in Fig. 4.2)

asking questions motivated users to study the artworks more closely while reading the text.

Figure 4.5 shows results from Lix testing (Miltsakaki and Troutt 2008) comparing the original texts (green) with the rewritten "one minute" texts (red). This test provides a quantitative measure of the readability of the texts. Four of the original texts had a

Fig. 4.4 Interpretive text in the *One Minute* format written by a test user who was a student at our university, about the artwork *Fishermen on the Beach on a Peaceful Summer's Night* by Michael Ancher

Lix number above 45, indicating that these texts are difficult to read. In contrast all the rewritten texts had a lower Lix number, four of them below the standard level of 35. The one rewritten text that stands out with a Lix number of 40 was written by the museum curator, indicating (perhaps unsurprisingly) that professional background

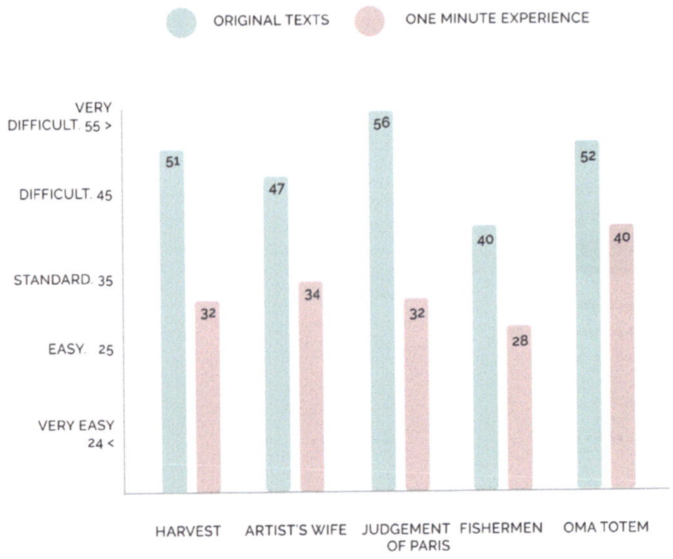

Fig. 4.5 LIX testing of artwork information in the museum database compared to the *One Minute* texts about the same artwork

influences the use of the authoring tool. However, also this text scored significantly lower than the original text (at 52).

4.4 Facilitating Participatory Interpretation

In order to further evaluate and gain insights about the *One Minute* format, we engaged in a collaboration with Brighton Museum and Art Gallery (UK) to use the app to create a visitor experience for their museum. The museum's Digital Manager, Kevin Bacon, suggested that the design offered another interesting opportunity: Could we use this app to invite external voices to offer their interpretation of artworks in the museum? This was envisioned not so much as an exercise in "crowdsourcing content", but rather as a way to include more perspectives on the museum collections on a smaller scale that could be curated to avoid disruptive contributions and other challenges associated with online discourse and social media on a larger scale.

In order to explore this opportunity we built an authoring system implementing the guidelines and interface we had previously designed (Fig. 4.5). We initially had designed the authoring interface to be used on regular computer screens, thinking that the systems would be used by museum professionals working at their desks. However, when considering that the system might be used by external visitors to the museum, we debated whether the authoring system should rather be designed to be used on smartphones in order to enable users to write their text as they were

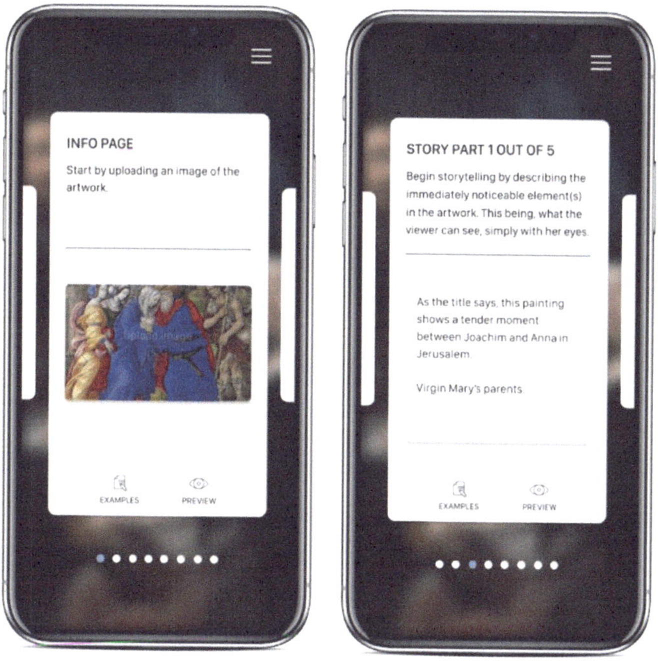

Fig. 4.6 Screenshots from the *One Minute Experience* authoring system

standing in front of the artwork in the museum—in spite of the increased difficulty of typing on a smartphone. Testing internally in the design team made it clear to us that because the *One Minute* texts were so short, it was in fact quite feasible to have users type these texts on their phones—leading us to go for a mobile interface (as we did not have the resources to do both) (Fig. 4.6).

In order to explore how to use the app to facilitate contributions from people other than museum staff, we organised two workshops in the museum on 6 and 7 November 2019. For each workshop 4–5 participants had been recruited from the local community. We started by introducing the participants to the app, after which they were encouraged to walk around the museum, find artworks that interested them and write short stories about them using the authoring interface. The participants wrote in total 24 texts about specific artworks and objects within the museum.[5] These objects were widely distributed throughout both floors of the museum. Figure 4.7 shows a text written by one of the participants.

The following day we organized a test of the *One Minute* visitor experience with the texts written by the workshop participants. We created an exhibition guide (on paper) that listed all the objects that the participants had written about, and encouraged visitors to find the objects, and read their stories. We had a number of smartphones with the app pre-installed to lend for those who couldn't (or wouldn't) use their own

[5] The museum exhibits both art and cultural/historical artefacts.

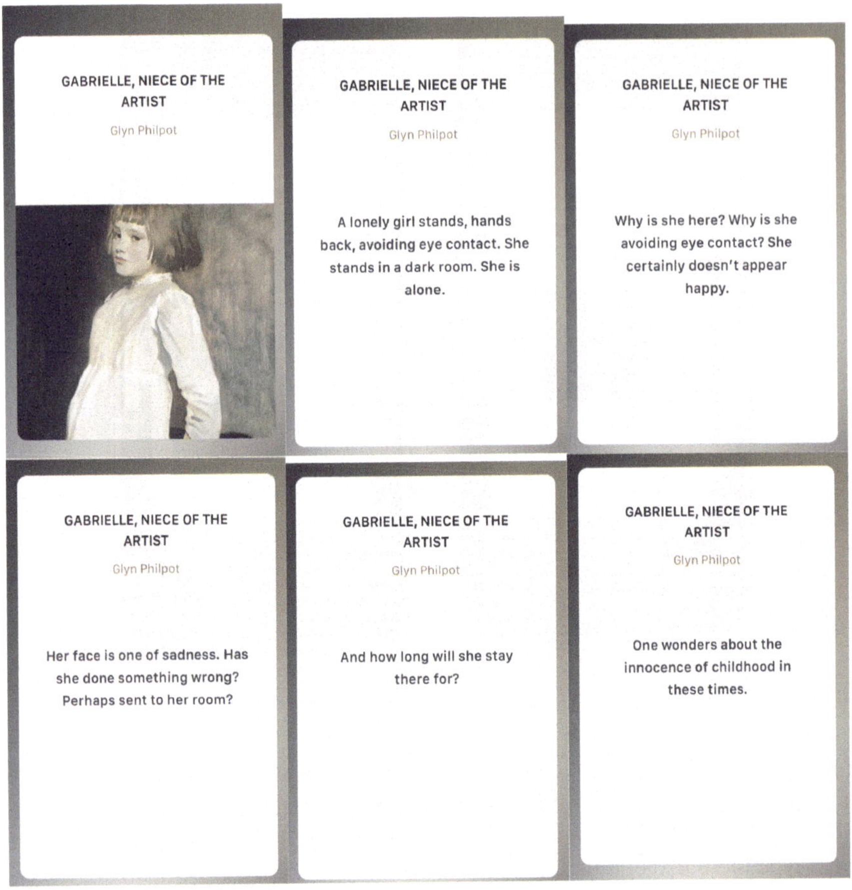

Fig. 4.7 A *One Minute* text written by a workshop participant, about the painting Gabrielle, Niece of the Artist by Glyn Philpot at Brighton Museum and Art Gallery, UK

devices. A total of 40 visitors tried the app. Visitors on average scanned between 5 and 6 artworks, with a median dwell time of 44 s.

14 of the test users were interviewed after trying the app (7 male and 7 female, aged 19–57, 11 local residents and 3 foreign tourists). Most of them were enthusiastic about the experience, indicating that they enjoyed using the app to read about the artwork. We asked all the test participants what they thought about the lengths of the texts: Most felt that they were "just right", although three of the participants felt that some of the texts could have been longer—or have an option to explore more in depth when one's interest had been aroused. And that seemed to happen a lot: When we asked whether there were any of the "One Minute" texts that had made a particular impression on them, all the participants could give examples of texts that had engaged them either by offering them an interesting perspective, sharing

surprising facts, or raising stimulating questions. One participant explained how the app made her reflect on an object that she already knew well:

> Yeah the amber cup which is very easy to walk past, because it's in a dark case… it's just fascinating… 1856 it was found there but it's the only one in the world that's there full together.

In particular the questions asked in the texts were highlighted by many participants, as a stimulating way to invite reflection on the art (although three of the participants also expressed frustration with the questions, in particular when questions were relating to factual matters instead of artwork interpretation). One participant explained how such an interpretive question made him see the painting *Red Scramble* by Frank Stella in a new way:

> I especially remind [sic] the question about… the thing with the squares. Where the question was, like, is this a pyramid or a well? So it made me… I didn't look at it in that way. But with this question I immediately saw that there was more depth in it. So I looked at it in another way.

Several interviewees who knew the museum very well—and even some who were museum employees—said they learned new things about the artworks in the museum, even though they had seen the exhibitions many times before. And some of the participants indicated that using the app made them look longer and deeper, such as this participant reflecting on the painting *Gabrielle, Niece of the Artist* (see Fig. 4.6):

> Well I liked how the app made you question why, you know, why is she so sad? How were children back then, what did they have to go through? Had she done something wrong? Or had she been sent to her room? I don't really think I had ever stood there and thought about that. Why does she look so sad?

It should be noted that participants also had some critical comments. There were some technical challenges and usability problems, as one might expect with an experimental prototype. Furthermore, some participants noted that the *One Minute* format felt more appropriate when applied to artworks in the museum exhibition, than to historical artefacts (as this museum includes exhibitions of historical and archaeological artefacts, as well as art).

Our study ended with the test deployment at Brighton Museum and Art Gallery. However, employees at the museum continued exploring the concept, and tested a new version of the app in 2021. This version had benefited from some further technical development, and could therefore be installed and used by all the visitors on their own phones without any problems. However, there were still issues with the accuracy of the image detection system. The museum's internal report also concluded that it would be necessary to rebuild the app as a web app, in order to overcome the obstacle of users having to download and install the app on their phones. But most importantly visitors responded with enthusiasm to the *One Minute* stories written by museum staff.

4.5 Discussion

What is the value of a One Minute artwork interpretation? The name may seem inviting to visitors, but perhaps also provocative for museum staff with a passion for their exhibits and the ambition to offer deep, transformative experiences. Can a museum app provide a transformative experience in just one minute? Probably not, if what we have in mind is a fundamental personal change, as described by Gaggioli: "A transformative experience can completely alter one's relationship with the self-world: the individual builds up a new worldview, and this new perspective supports lasting change" (Gaggioli 2016, p. 101). The philosopher Paul provides a list of examples of experiences that might cause such fundamental change in a person:

> a horrific physical attack, gaining a new sensory ability, having a traumatic accident, undergoing major surgery, winning an Olympic gold medal, participating in a revolution, having a religious conversion, having a child, experiencing the death of a parent, making a major scientific discovery, or experiencing the death of a child. (Paul 2014, p. 16)

These examples set a high bar for what we should consider 'transformative': Most of us will only experience a few of these events in our lifetime. It is hard to imagine that a museum app might ever facilitate an experience that is even remotely similar in terms of emotional impact and personal change as that of having a child—or losing it. And indeed when museum scholars such as Soren (2009) discuss transformative experiences in museums, the examples they give are of much less intensity—describing moments of emotional reactions, empathy, and awe, rather than personally life-altering events as suggested by Paul and Gaggioli. But these varying uses of the concept seem to raise the question: *How* transformative should we expect a museum experience to be?

Duerden and colleagues define a transformational experience in the following way:

> An experience where the objective elements engage an individual's attention and produce subjective reactions involving strong emotions, the discovery of significant and personally relevant insights, and personal changes in values, beliefs, intentions, or self-perceptions. Most often transformative experiences are characterized by intrinsically motivated, enduring changes in self-perception and behavior. (Duerden et al. 2018, p. 208)

As the authors acknowledge, such personal, enduring changes are relatively rare. For Duerden and colleagues, transformational experiences stand atop a hierarchy of extraordinary experiences that start with "memorable experiences"—experiences which grab one's attention and provoke strong emotions—of which only a subset may be characterized as "meaningful experiences"—if they involve "the discovery of significant and personally relevant insights" (Duerden et al. 2018, pp. 203–206). And only a subset of these already rare meaningful experiences can be characterized as transformational, according to Duerden and colleagues. Even if we might want to believe that a museum exhibition might hold the potential—for some individuals, on some very rare occasions—to facilitate such a profound experience, we would have to acknowledge that this would be a very exceptional incident; most (or very nearly all) visitors would have experiences of less intensity and impact than this.

This leads to two important conclusions: First, facilitating transformative experiences as described by Paul, Gaggioli and Duerden and colleagues is an impossible ideal for museum experience design. Second, focusing exclusively on such a lofty ideal may make us blind to the many positive experiences visitors can have with museum exhibitions—experiences that have somewhat lower intensity and impact, but which nonetheless are good experiences for the visitors: Pleasant, interesting, educational, and perhaps even memorable and meaningful.

In order to avoid being blinded by overly high ideals, we might instead turn the perspective around, and focus on the other end of Duerden and colleagues' hierarchy. If we cannot always hope to design transformative experiences, what can we posit as a more realistic ambition? The baseline in the hierarchy is formed by the first element in the definition cited above: An experience that attracts and holds the individual's attention. An experience that fails to meet this criterion is considered "subconscious". The museum literature is full of evidence that in fact, many visitor experiences fail to meet this criterion: Much of the time, museum exhibits fail to catch the visitor's attention (Bitgood 2009; Eklund 2020; Lykourentzou et al. 2013). This should perhaps not be seen as a disastrous failure: Attention is one of the most scarce resources in contemporary western societies, and there is a myriad of offerings competing for our attention at any moment—even inside the carefully curated environment of the museum—and it would not be realistic to expect any artefact or installation to catch the attention of all (or even most) visitors.

Be that as it may: Sometimes the visitor's attention is indeed caught, such as when a typical visitor spends around 17–21 s looking at a museum's masterpieces (Smith and Smith 2001; Smith et al. 2017). This turns the experience from 'subconscious' to 'conscious', in Duerden and colleagues' terms. In order to come one level deeper, turning the experience from 'ordinary' to 'extraordinary', the experience must also produce "strong subjective reactions" such as strong emotions or "the discovery of significant and personally relevant insights", turning the experience into a 'memorable' or even 'meaningful' one. With this perspective in mind, we might rephrase the question posed in the beginning of this section. Rather than asking whether it is possible to provide a transformative experience in just one minute, we might ask: Can our design attract and hold the visitor's attention for one minute—and produce strong subjective reactions in that time? This is no small ambition, and we should consider it a success even if we achieve this only for some visitors some of the time.

For the One Minute user test, there is indeed some evidence that the app succeeded in meeting these ambitions. First, with a median dwell time of 44 s, it seems that the app indeed managed to attract and hold the users' attention for a significantly longer time than in Smith and colleagues' empirical studies—more than twice as long. The fact that all interviewees could recall elements from the artwork texts that had made a particular impression on them offers further evidence that the app managed both to engage their attention, and to also facilitate an experience that can be characterized as 'memorable' in the straightforward meaning of the word: That it can be recalled. We can see this also in the fact that several interviewees said they learned new things about the artworks in the museum, even though they had seen the exhibitions many times before.

It is not entirely clear whether the experience these visitors had would qualify as 'memorable' in the definition offered by Duerden and colleagues—requiring a strong emotional reaction—or whether it might also include "the discovery of significant and personally relevant insights", making it 'meaningful'. Considering the quotes from test participants presented in the previous section, it seems clear that some participants did indeed see the artworks in new ways and felt that they had insights relating to the museum objects; but whether this meets the bar of "personally relevant" is harder to determine. Certainly, if we disregard Duerden and colleague's definitions and instead consider the everyday meaning of the words, the experience has been both memorable and meaningful for the participants.

There is no evidence in our interviews suggesting that any of the participants experienced "personal changes in values, beliefs, intentions, or self-perceptions", as stated in the definition of a transformative experience. We might perhaps hope that such experience might take place on very rare occasions—that the app might facilitate such a powerful encounter with an artwork or other museum exhibit that it caused a profound change in the visitor. However, instead of fixating on the hypothetical possibility of such life-changing events, it seems more useful to focus on the actual ability of the app to attract and hold the attention of visitors, and—at least for some of them—help them see something new and interesting in the museum objects.

4.6 Conclusion and Future Work

The *One Minute* app sits between two quite different visions for museum experiences: On the one hand, a computer vision paradigm that invites users to "point the camera and we'll tell you what you are looking at", as evidenced by popular museum apps such as Smartify, Vizgu and Magnus. On the other hand, the ambitious ideal set out by literature on transformative experiences in museums, discussed above and elsewhere in this book, in which the goal is not simply to tell visitors what they are looking at but rather to effect deep, personal change.

Held up against these ideals, it is clear that the *One Minute* format goes one step beyond the computer vision paradigm: It does not only offer core facts about objects, it also provides a pedagogical entry point for someone unfamiliar with the artwork, offering some clues about an interpretation and questions for further reflection, while also supporting an attentional balance (Woodruff et al. 2001) between the text and the artwork, and respecting the fact that the visitor may not have more than a short time to invest in this particular artwork before moving on in their visit. On the other hand there is little evidence to suggest that visitors underwent profound, personally transformative experiences while using the app. However, the fact that in our test deployment even museum employees who walked through the museum every day were able to learn something new through using the app, indicates that the compact *One Minute* format was able to provide users with experiences that they found interesting, memorable and meaningful. Perhaps the brevity of the *One Minute* texts was not an obstacle to having a meaningful experience, but rather a stimulating factor?

Should we then take this as a new paradigm—and have all interpretive text be written in bite-size chunks along the lines of the *One Minute* design? That might be disappointing for some audience groups, both those who desire in-depth immersion and study, as well as those who wish that the artwork should be allowed to "speak for itself" free of interpretive text. However, it is possible to offer *One Minute* texts without disrupting the experience of such visitors. The *One Minute* system can be used in a museum without any physical signage at all, as the system only relies on scanning the actual artworks in order to offer information. Thus there should not be any concern that a *One Minute*-style experience would be in the way of longer and deeper engagement with museum exhibits for those who prefer that.

Our workshops at Brighton Museum and Art Gallery demonstrated that the *One Minute* format could be used to invite members of the public to contribute to artwork interpretive text in a manner that was rewarding and engaging both for those writing the texts, and for other visitors to the museum. What we really wished we also could have done, but did not have the time and resources to do within the duration of that project, was to explore how this format could have been used to offer a channel for audience groups with a distinct perspective on the museum exhibitions: What would it be like if we could see the museum exhibits through the eyes of marginalized voices such as refugees, transgender people, or activists? Many museums try to engage such groups through a variety of efforts. One challenge, noted by one of the participants in our project, is that when members of the public are invited to write interpretive text from their own perspective, they sometimes try to mimic the style of museum communication they are familiar with—and end up writing in an overly complicated, intellectual style. The *One Minute* format has demonstrated that it can help users escape such conventions, not just shortening but also simplifying the texts and freeing users to write in a more direct style—thus (hopefully) also allowing them to express their own unique perspectives more directly. Future researchers should explore how to use such a format to engage outside voices in museum interpretation. Perhaps in the future we could use a *One Minute*-style experience to see the museum through other people's eyes—through the eyes of a child, a foreigner, someone from a marginalized minority group—or all of the above? If the experience lasts only one minute and is sufficiently engaging, visitors may have time and patience to listen to multiple stories—thus making room for multiple perspectives. Thus, the brevity of a compact format is not only an obstacle for in-depth experiences—it may also offer an opportunity.

Acknowledgements The *One Minute* project formed part of the GIFT project which received funding from the European Union's Horizon 2020 research and innovation programme under grant agreement No. 727040. We thank Kevin Bacon and his colleagues at the Brighton Museum and Art Gallery for their generous support and thoughtful contributions. Important contributions to the development of the *One Minute* app were made by Mace Ojala, Phillip Raffnsøe, Marek Kisiel and Philip Korsholm.

References

Beale K (2011) Museums at play—games, interaction and learning. MuseumsEtc

Bedford L (2001) Storytelling: the real work of museums. Curator Mus J 44(1):27–34. https://doi.org/10.1111/j.2151-6952.2001.tb00027.x

Bekele MK, Pierdicca R, Frontoni E, Malinverni ES, Gain J (2018) A survey of augmented, virtual, and mixed reality for cultural heritage. J Comput Cult Herit 11(2):7:1–7:36. https://doi.org/10.1145/3145534

Bennett T (1997) Speaking to the eyes: museums, legibility and the social order. In: The politics of display. Routledge

Bitgood S (1991) The ABCs of label design. Visit Stud 3(1):115–129

Bitgood S (2000) The role of attention in designing effective interpretive labels. J Interpret Res 5(2):31–45. https://doi.org/10.1177/109258720000500205

Bitgood S (2009) Museum fatigue: a critical review. Visit Stud 12(2):93–111. https://doi.org/10.1080/10645570903203406

Bitgood S (2016) Intelligent design of interpretive text. Interp News 5:38–44

Blud LM (1990) Social interaction and learning among family groups visiting a museum. Mus Manag Curatorsh 9(1):43–51

Blythe M, McCarthy J, Wright P, Petrelli D (2011) History and experience: storytelling and interaction design. In: Proceedings of HCI 2011—25th BCS conference on human computer interaction, 1 July 2011. https://doi.org/10.14236/ewic/HCI2011.70

Borun M, Miller M (1980) What's in a name? A study of the effectiveness of explanatory labels in a science museum. Franklin Institute Science Museum and Planetarium. https://eric.ed.gov/?id=ED267966

Bourdieu P, Darbel A, Schnapper D (1990) The love of art: European art museums and their public. Stanford University Press

Damala A, Cubaud P, Bationo A, Houlier P, Marchal I (2008) Bridging the gap between the digital and the physical: design and evaluation of a mobile augmented reality guide for the museum visit. In: Proceedings of the 3rd international conference on digital interactive media in entertainment and arts, pp 120–127. https://doi.org/10.1145/1413634.1413660

Duerden MD, Lundberg NR, Ward P, Taniguchi ST, Hill B, Widmer MA, Zabriskie R (2018) From ordinary to extraordinary: a framework of experience types. J Leis Res 49(3–5):196–216. https://doi.org/10.1080/00222216.2018.1528779

Eklund L (2020) A shoe is a shoe is a shoe: interpersonalization and meaning-making in museums—research findings and design implications. Int J Hum-Comput Interact 36(16):1503–1513. https://doi.org/10.1080/10447318.2020.1767982

Fagerjord A (2015) Humanist evaluation methods in locative media design. J Media Innov 2(1):107–122

Falk JH, Dierking LD (2012) The museum experience revisited. Routledge

Gaggioli A (2016) Transformative experience design. In: Gaggioli A, Ferscha A, Riva G, Dunne S, Viaud-Delmon I (eds) Human computer confluence: transforming human experience through symbiotic technologies. De Gruyter Open Poland, pp 97–122. https://doi.org/10.1515/9783110471137-006

Gammon B, Burch A (2008) Designing mobile digital experiences. In: Tallon L (ed) Digital technologies and the museum experience: handheld guides and other media. Rowman Altamira, pp 35–62

Heath C, vom Lehn D (2009) Interactivity and collaboration: new forms of participation in museums, galleries and science centres. In: Parry R (ed) Museums in a digital age. Routledge

Hsi S (2002) The electronic guidebook: a study of user experiences using mobile web content in a museum setting. In: Proceedings. IEEE international workshop on wireless and mobile technologies in education, 2002, pp 48–54. http://ieeexplore.ieee.org/abstract/document/1039220/

Keil J, Pujol L, Roussou M, Engelke T, Schmitt M, Bockholt U, Eleftheratou S (2013) A digital look at physical museum exhibits: designing personalized stories with handheld augmented reality in museums. In: 2013 digital heritage international congress (DigitalHeritage), vol 2, pp 685–688. https://doi.org/10.1109/DigitalHeritage.2013.6744836
Kidd J (2018) "Immersive" heritage encounters. Mus Rev 3(1)
Lee SJ (2017) A review of audio guides in the era of smart tourism. Inf Syst Front 19(4):705–715. https://doi.org/10.1007/s10796-016-9666-6
Lombardo V, Damiano R (2012) Storytelling on mobile devices for cultural heritage. New Rev Hypermed Multimed 18(1–2):11–35. https://doi.org/10.1080/13614568.2012.617846
Løvlie AS, Ryding K, Spence J, Rajkowska P, Waern A, Wray T, Benford S, Preston W, Clare-Thorn E (2021) Playing games with Tito: designing hybrid museum experiences for critical play. J Comput Cult Herit 14(2). https://doi.org/10.1145/3446620
Løvlie AS, Waern A, Eklund L, Spence J, Rajkowska P, Benford S (2022) Hybrid museum experiences. In: Waern A, Løvlie AS (eds) Hybrid museum experiences: theory and design. Amsterdam University Press. https://www.aup.nl/en/book/9789048552849/hybrid-museum-experiences
Lykourentzou I, Claude X, Naudet Y, Tobias E, Antoniou A, Lepouras G, Vassilakis C (2013) Improving museum visitors' quality of experience through intelligent recommendations: a visiting style-based approach. In: Museums as intelligent environments (MasIE2013)—workshop co-located with the 9th international conference on intelligent environments—IE'13, 16 July 2013
Lyons L (2009) Designing opportunistic user interfaces to support a collaborative museum exhibit. In: Proceedings of the 9th international conference on computer supported collaborative learning, vol 1, pp 375–384. https://dl.acm.org/doi/10.5555/1600053.1600110
Marengo L, Fazekas G (2018) I wonder... Inquiry techniques as a method to gain insights into people's encounters with visual art. In: MW18: museums and the web 2018, Vancouver, Canada. https://mw18.mwconf.org/paper/i-wonder-inquiry-techniques-as-a-method-to-gain-insights-into-peoples-encounters-with-visual-art/index.html
Mason M (2016) The MIT museum glassware prototype: visitor experience exploration for designing smart glasses. J Comput Cult Herit 9(3):1–28. https://doi.org/10.1145/2872278
Merriman N (1989) Museum visiting as a cultural phenomenon. In: Vergo P (ed) The new museology. Reaktion Books. https://reaktionbooks.co.uk/work/the-new-museology
Miltsakaki E, Troutt A (2008) Real time web text classification and analysis of reading difficulty. In: Tetreault J, Burstein J, De Felice R (eds) Proceedings of the third workshop on innovative use of NLP for building educational applications. Association for Computational Linguistics, pp 89–97. https://aclanthology.org/W08-0911
Noë A (2015) Strange tools: art and human nature. Macmillan
Paul LA (2014) Transformative experience, 1st edn. University Press. https://doi.org/10.1093/acprof:oso/9780198717959.001.0001
Petrelli D, Ciolfi L, van Dijk D, Hornecker E, Not E, Schmidt A (2013) Integrating material and digital: a new way for cultural heritage. Interactions 20(4):58–63. https://doi.org/10.1145/2486227.2486239
Ravelli L (2007) Museum texts: communication frameworks. Routledge
Reitstätter L, Galter K, Bakondi F (2022) Looking to read: how visitors use exhibit labels in the art museum. Visit Stud 25(2):127–150. https://doi.org/10.1080/10645578.2021.2018251
Rogberg L (2018) Engaging young adults to read about artworks. Rethinking interpretive text through user-centered design. B.Sc. thesis, IT University of Copenhagen. https://gifting.digital/wp-content/uploads/2019/09/ny-LindaRogberg-1994575-Spring-2018-BachelorThesis-5.pdf
Serrell B (2015) Exhibit labels: an interpretive approach, 2nd edn. Rowman & Littlefield
Silas E, Løvlie AS, Ling R (2016) The smartphone's role in the contemporary backpacking experience. Network Knowl J MeCCSA Postgrad Netw 9(6):40–53
Simon N (2010) The participatory museum. Museum 2.0. http://www.participatorymuseum.org/
Smith JK, Smith LF (2001) Spending time on art. Empir Stud Arts 19:229–236

Smith LF, Smith JK, Tinio PPL (2017) Time spent viewing art and reading labels. Psychol Aesthet Creat Arts 11(1):77–85
Smørdal O, Stuedahl D, Sem I (2014) Experimental zones: two cases of exploring frames of participation in a dialogic museum. Digit Creat 25(3):224–232. https://doi.org/10.1080/14626268.2014.904366
Soren BJ (2009) Museum experiences that change visitors. Mus Manag Curatorsh 24(3):233–251. https://doi.org/10.1080/09647770903073060
Syvertsen T, Enli G (2020) Digital detox: media resistance and the promise of authenticity. Convergence 26(5–6):1269–1283. https://doi.org/10.1177/1354856519847325
Turkle S (2011) Alone together: why we expect more from technology and less from each other. Basic Books. https://www.basicbooks.com/titles/sherry-turkle/alone-together/9780465093656/
van der Vaart M, Damala A (2015) Through the Loupe: visitor engagement with a primarily text-based handheld AR application. In: 2015 digital heritage, vol 2, pp 565–572. https://doi.org/10.1109/DigitalHeritage.2015.7419574
Vergo P (1989) The reticent object. In: Vergo P (ed) The new museology. Reaktion Books
vom Lehn D, Heath C (2003) Displacing the object: mobile technologies and interpretive resources. In: International cultural heritage informatics meeting: proceedings from ICHIM03. http://www.archimuse.com/publishing/ichim03/088C.pdf
Waern A, Løvlie AS (eds) (2022a) Hybrid museum experiences. Amsterdam University Press. https://www.aup.nl/en/book/9789048552849/hybrid-museum-experiences
Waern A, Løvlie AS (2022b) Remediating, reframing and restaging the museum. In: Waern A, Løvlie AS (eds) Hybrid museum experiences: theory and design. Amsterdam University Press, pp 197–211
Walter T (1996) From museum to morgue? Electronic guides in Roman Bath. Tour Manage 17(4):241–245. https://doi.org/10.1016/0261-5177(96)00015-5
Wessel D, Mayr E (2007) Potentials and challenges of mobile media in museums. Int J Interact Mob Technol (iJIM) 1(1). http://journals.sfu.ca/onlinejour/index.php/i-jim/article/view/165
Wikipedia Contributors (2024) Indoor positioning system. In: Wikipedia, the free encyclopedia. Wikimedia Foundation. https://en.wikipedia.org/w/index.php?title=Indoor_positioning_system&oldid=1240842951
Woodruff A, Aoki P, Hurst A, Szymanski M (2001) Electronic guidebooks and visitor attention. In: Bearman D, Garzotto F (eds) International cultural heritage informatics meeting: proceedings from ICHIM01. Archives & museum informatics. http://www.archimuse.com/publishing/ichim01_vol1/woodruff.pdf

Anders Sundnes Løvlie is Associate Professor at the IT University of Copenhagen and head of the research group for Media, Art and Design. His research interests include humanistic HCI, experience design, artificial intelligence, and museums. He was coordinator for the EU-funded research project GIFT, in which the research reported in this book chapter was carried out.

Linda Stoltze is Senior UX Designer with a background from the IT University of Copenhagen, where she explored learning experiences in multiple theses. She has worked across a range of industries, most recently in FinTech, designing solutions that balance user needs and business goals. She's further interested in exploring artificial intelligence in her work as a designer.

Timothy Wray is a postdoctoral researcher whose work explores how technology could be used to support meaningful visitor engagement with museums. His prior research examined how computational methods can be used to support engagement, discovery, and serendipity within online museum collections. He is also a UX/UI designer and web developer who has worked extensively within museums, non-profit organizations, and has also extensive development experience within the commercial sector. He has designed and taught web development and interaction design courses at the IT University of Copenhagen. He is also a visual artist and musician who creates performances that combine his own piano compositions with real-time, generative visuals.

Part II
The Changing Museum: Structure, Social Role and Relationships

Chapter 5
Transformative Experience Design in Science and Technology Centres and Museums; Assumption Shifts, Co-curation, Polyvocality, and Controversies

Marjoleine G. van der Meij and Christianne K. J. Blijleven

Abstract Science centres and science museums (SCMs) are increasingly experimenting with new roles at the science-society nexus, especially in light of complex societal challenges and system transformations urgently needed to address these challenges. From being merely focused on edutainment, and conservation of technoscientific objects in the case of science museums, SCMs increasingly design experiences that aim for societal transformation as well. In the last century, first steps towards this experimentation have been taken by pioneering researchers and practitioners in the science communication and museology field. In this chapter, we highlight the foundations that were built over time in designing contemporary transformative experiences in SCMs, and illustrate commonly used design features. The chapter glances over several contemporary exhibitions in Europe. aimed at societal transformation, which are framed in recent science communication and science museology literature. Drawing from our experiences in collaborating with SCM professionals, we end our chapter by highlighting complexities for organisations and professionals in designing such transformative experiences. To mitigate these challenges, we propose a tentative framework for transformative experience design—as opposed to merely edutainment focused experience design—for SCM professionals.

We would like to emphasise that contemporary SCM experiences are not 'better' or 'more transformative' by definition, or fully new. The contemporary transformative exhibitions that we describe in this chapter, have predecessors in the beginning of the nineteenth century, and alternatively, the 'traditional' experience designs that we describe in this chapter can still be very impactful today.

M. G. van der Meij (✉) · C. K. J. Blijleven
VU University Amsterdam, Amsterdam, The Netherlands
e-mail: m.g.vander.meij@vu.nl

C. K. J. Blijleven
e-mail: k.j.blijleven@vu.nl

L. Calvi et al. (eds.), *Transformative Museum Experiences*, Springer Series on Cultural Computing, https://doi.org/10.1007/978-3-031-89521-0_5

5.1 Introduction

Science centres and museums (SCMs) are buildings—or other types of spaces—that offer interactive experiences on science- and/or technology-related objects and developments. Where SCMs often cover a range of sciences or technologies, varying from natural sciences to social sciences, arts and humanities, some SCMs primarily focus on one field (e.g. biology in zoos). Furthermore, some SCMs are directly affiliated with universities or research institutes, others are independent organisations with or without in-house researchers. SCMs are usually sponsored by governments and industry, but income can also be solely generated from ticket sales. Some SCMs have in-house exhibition and content developers and builders, others assign design consultancies to do so.

By offering museum experiences that facilitate interaction between visitors and science and/or technology, SCMs are often considered as the most 'material' form of science communication. With their relatively high number of visitors, in the Netherlands (17 million residents) over 5 million visitors on a yearly basis (VSC 2024), SCMs are seen as impactful connectors between science and society. In that sense, one could say, SCMs have a highly transformative potential, making it worthwhile to study their contemporary experience designs, and how these have evolved over time.

In Europe, most science centres and museums are connected through their membership of ECSITE,[1] the European Network of Science Centres and Museums; elsewhere in the world similar umbrella organisations exist. These network organisations facilitate a high level of knowledge exchange among SCM professionals. Moreover, it is common practice that a design company or one SCM develops an exhibition and offers it for sale or rent to other science centres and museums. Furthermore, science centres tend to purchase and display ready-made exhibits about science phenomena (e.g. the Exploratorium cookbook of Bruman and The Exploratorium Staff 1991), of which the Bernoulli blower is a well-known example (see Fig. 5.1). As a result of this connectivity and standardisation, certain typologies can be identified in the experience designs of many SCMs.

Since SCMs are focused on science and technology communication, their practices are closely intertwined with developments in the wider science communication research and practitioner field (Schiele 2018). For example, as we will see later in this chapter, where the science communication field has shifted from 'deficit thinking'—characterised by a focus on dissemination of scientific knowledge—to 'dialogue and participation', many SCMs have expanded their predominant *edutainer* role with the role of a science-society interaction *facilitator*, such as public or stakeholder

[1] See https://www.ecsite.eu; similar to Network of European Museum Organisations (NEMO), ECSITE organises conferences and other forms of exchange between SCM professionals, and, amongst others, advocates for inclusive national and international policy development processes on science, science communication, science education and technological innovation. Where NEMO liaises to the cultural sector, ECSITE liaises organisations in the science, technology, and innovation sector.

Fig. 5.1 The Bernoulli blower, a typical exhibit that can be found in many science centres, in different manifestations (here a sketch, by Marjoleine van der Meij). The blower lifts a ball. Visitors can throw the ball in the air stream to see how it lifts and balances itself in the middle (the Bernoulli principle), and they can turn the blower sidewards to find out that the ball eventually falls down (gravity). Usually, the explanation about these phenomena is given in a text label, but central to the experience is the physically interactive, entertaining, engagement (cf. Allen 2004)

engagement, deliberation and participation in science and technology governance (see, e.g., in Bell 2008; Fraaije et al. 2023). Before investigating design ingredients of contemporary transformative experiences in SCMs, therefore, we first want to highlight this major paradigm shift in recent science communication understandings and practices.

5.2 Paradigm Shift in Science Communication

The science communication field covers the investigation and shaping of communication processes and products among professionals engaged in scientific research or innovation, or between the science or tech world and societal actors, wherein the communicated content has a link with science and technology. In the last century, the field has experienced a paradigm shift from so-called 'deficit thinking' to 'dialogue and participation' (van Dam et al. 2020; see Fig. 5.2).

It could be argued that until late in the twentieth century, science communication predominantly focused on bringing scientific knowledge to 'lay people', meaning people outside the scientific world (cf. Achiam and Sølberg 2017; Pedretti and

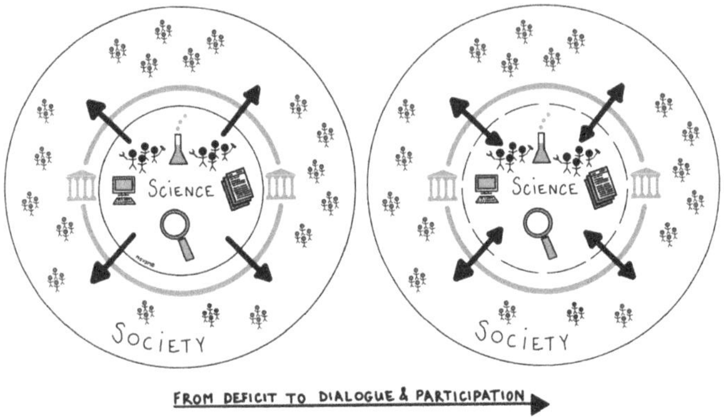

Fig. 5.2 Schematic representation of the paradigm shift in science communication, moving from 'deficit thinking' to dialogue and participation. The former focused on one-way communication *from* science *to* society, via mediators (the grey circle) such as SCMs. The latter comprises two-way communication *between* science and society or *between* mediators (such as SCMs) and society, wherein mediators play a facilitative role

Lannini 2020). The communication thus was a one-way flow *from* science *to* society, via 'intermediaries' such as journalists or other professional communicators, or via scientists who stepped into the media spotlight themselves. The goal of the communication was often threefold: education, entertainment, and nurturing positive attitudes towards science to maintain the support for public funding for scientific research. The following assumptions were dominant in this type of communication (derived from Gibbons 1999; van Dam et al. 2020; Irwin 2021), and in many science communication practices still are:

- The process of scientific knowledge production provides us with solid answers to all societal questions.
- Scientific knowledge production results in certain outcomes, like new knowledge and technological innovations, and these will inherently bring progress to society.
- Lay people have a 'deficit' in their knowledge, which needs to be 'filled' through communication about scientific knowledge.
- Lay people passively receive and perceive the communicated knowledge in literally the same way as intended by science communicators.
- If lay people have more science-related knowledge, they would inherently develop a (more) positive attitude towards science, and accept and trust scientific research outcomes and implementations thereof, such as technological innovations.

As one can see, reading this now, years later, there was little reciprocity in this approach to science communication. This so-called deficit thinking represents a certain ignorance of social and psychological processes that are generally involved in communication, and little nuance in ideas about the multifaceted science-society nexus.

A complex set of events and developments in the late twentieth century impacted the roles and perceptions of science and technology in society, and, in parallel, science communication. These include gradual developments such as globalisation and major changes in the media landscape (from traditional to new media) (van Dam et al. 2020). Some singular, disruptive events or major new science applications had an impact as well: think of the Chernobyl disaster, despite scientists' earlier claims on the safety of nuclear plants; the silent implementation of Genetically Modified Organisms (GMO) in food and the protests this incited[2]; or the poorly executed risk communication around Mad Cow Disease (Irwin 2021). These developments made commonly held assumptions in science and science communication tilt towards the following (derived from Gibbons 1999; van Dam et al. 2020; Irwin 2021):

- Scientific knowledge production alone is not enough to answer societal questions or tackle societal challenges.
- Scientific research and technological innovations can also have (potentially) harmful impacts on society.
- Lay people are actively seeking and processing a lot of information about science and technology themselves (e.g. through media).
- Once you communicate about science, people's reception process is an active co-production process of the communicator's communicated content and the receiver's earlier knowledge, experiences and worldviews; and receivers can actually talk back or talk about it (e.g. via media, or mouth-to-mouth).
- The more knowledgeable (lay) people become, the more nuanced their attitudes to science can become, as well as their acceptance and trust regarding scientific research outcomes and implementations (e.g. technological innovations) in society.

A first response of the science communication field was to become more of a watchdog, moving away from the earlier applied 'cheerleading of science' towards critical observation (van Dam et al. 2020). But various new visions also emerged among scholars and practitioners in the science communication field on knowledge production, inspired by science and technology studies, ethics and philosophy, such as 'socially robust science', 'mode-2 knowledge production', and 'responsible research and innovation' (e.g. Gibbons 1999; Nowotny et al. 2001, 2003; Owen et al. 2012). Generally speaking, these new visions promoted the idea that knowledge production should happen through interaction with societal actors, and through collaboration between scientific disciplines, to align knowledge production with societal interests and to assure that the outcomes of knowledge production would provide urgently needed answers or solutions to contemporary, often highly complex, societal challenges. Terms like knowledge co-production and transdisciplinarity gained traction.

In parallel, ideas about science communication shifted from 'deficit thinking' to 'dialogue and participation', which is a shift to be aware of when we discuss

[2] An interesting example of how exhibitions on GMOs have approached knowledge infrastructures beyond 'deficit thinking' can be found in Kraeftner et al. (2007).

pioneering ideas in science museology later in this chapter (see Fig. 5.2). Science communicators increasingly realised the importance of science communication centring around building relationships between science and society through dialogue and participation processes (Bucchi and Trench 2008; Irwin 2021). Participation involved, amongst others, knowledge co-production between science and non-science actors to address complex societal challenges, with science communicators taking the role of facilitators (ibid.). Dialogue meant that, in addition to 'traditional' unidirectional communication processes, science communicators started to experiment with 'multi-directionality' (communication '*between*' actors), such as facilitation of public or stakeholder deliberation on science and technology (ibid.). Examples of these are national dialogues about emerging technologies and potentially controversial scientific research (nano, synthetic biology, artificial intelligence), aimed at promoting mutual understanding between different actors, or, even, the shaping of science and technology research agendas (governance) (see, e.g. in Gazsó et al. 2012; Stemerding and Rerimassie 2013).

5.3 Science Museums, How They Started

This context of historical developments in the science communication field, and its recent major paradigm shift, is important to have in mind when approaching contemporary transformative exhibition design in SCMs. First, this context illuminates historical and contemporary views in science museology, as a similar shift from deficit thinking to dialogue and participation can be seen in SCMs (Hudson 1987; Bradburne 2000; Schiele 2018). Second, this context explains the shift in role-perceptions of SCMs at the science-society nexus (Achiam and Sølberg 2017), as well as shifts in designing experiences through exhibitions and other content (demonstrations, shows, events, and programmes). The following sections aim to sketch historical developments in SCMs in this light.

Arguably the first type of science museum—we purposefully say museum here—originated during the Enlightenment, during which an (elite) scientific community aimed at applying the scientific method to systematically approach science (e.g. phenomena) and nature (e.g. taxonomy) (Hudson 1987). During this era, private collections consisted of objects linked to art, science and technology, often displayed in so-called 'curiosity cabinets' (ibid.). While many of these collections were primarily accessible to a privileged audience, that is, acquaintances and friends of (wealthy) collectors, many collections were later released to the general audience (ibid.). The collections varied from scale models of the universe and large telescopes, to wooden cabinets and display cases with minerals or 'creatures' in formaldehyde—of which a typical one was, for example, the 'conjoined twins'. The objects were often accompanied by text labels, with the (anonymous) curator's explanation of what it is, the date and place of origin, and the maker's name if applicable (Bradburne 2000). For the 'new' general audience, these collections were observed and experienced with a certain awe, not only because of their content, but also as they

Fig. 5.3 Various exhibit typologies: **a** oval room with minerals and instruments, in Teylers Museum. Photography: Mike Bink. **b** Typical physically interactive exhibit, allowing kids to experience the water cycle, in NEMO science museum. Photography: Elekes Andor, via Wikimedia Commons. **c** Typical chemistry laboratory for hands-on learning about the scientific research method. Photography: Elekes Andor, via Wikimedia Commons. **d** Fin whale Leo from GUM and Plantentuin (UGent), controversially placed in the Sint-Baafs Cathedral. Photography: Myriam Devriendt. **e** Board game on smart city technologies, developed and implemented in the dialogue and participation process of NEMO Kennislink, partner of NEMO science museum. Photography: Springstof Media for VU University Amsterdam. **f** Typical example of collecting visitor ideas, here around the complex societal question 'what would you do if… the country would be flooded?' (Watersnoodmuseum, Netherlands; not further described in this chapter). Photography: Marjoleine van der Meij

rarely came across such objects in daily life. (ibid.; Hudson 1987). This design type can be observed in Teylers Museum[3] (Haarlem, Netherlands), founded in 1784 and still open to the general public today. Its original oval-shaped central hall contains wooden glass display cases showing minerals, stones, and instruments that were used to study and illustrate natural phenomena, such as stargazers, world globes, and microscopes (see Fig. 5.3a).

Industrialisation triggered the rise of a new type of museum, or made existing 'early science museums' expand their collections (Hudson 1987). In this era, many

[3] See: https://teylersmuseum.nl/en.

processes previously performed by human hands and labour, or animal power, were mechanised. This was also the period wherein the mechanics' institutes were founded to promote research and industrialisation (Kelly 1952). One of their promotional activities were international industrial exhibitions: the World's Fair. Apart from diplomatic relationships and commercial aims, these World's Fairs aimed at displaying the newest inventions and (working) machines in pavilions of various nations. The demonstrations of working machines, or 'schnittmodells' (Maas 2013) thereof, were merely aimed at explaining their functioning, in the assumption that this would make visitors realise the progress that industrialisation brought and potentially inspire specialist audiences to improve their own work. Several world fairs laid out the foundations of national science museums, whose display of objects sometimes hardly differed from trade shows (Hudson 1987; Morris 2010), such as, for example, the Science Museum in London, Vienna's Technische Museum, Smithsonian in Washington, and the Museum of Science and Industry in Chicago. In addition to glass display cases, these science museums display large collections of machinery, often categorised in thematic halls or rooms; at regular intervals, so-called 'demonstrators' run shows, for example, on how an electricity generator works. The objects and demonstrations are accompanied by visual and textual explanations of the machine's working mechanism, the inventor, and other factual information.

Up to this point, the experience design of science museums was rooted in assumptions very similar to those for 'deficit thinking' in science communication, as described above. The science museum—like science—positioned itself as an authority, communicating to visitors ('lay people') about science and technology to improve understanding and promote science and technology (Hudson 1987; Bradburne 2000). In that sense, experiences merely aimed to 'transform' the science and technology attitudes of the (passive) visitors.

5.4 Science Centres, the Era of Physical Interactivity

Already in the first half of the twentieth century, museum professionals realised that exhibiting objects and demonstrating working machines alone was not enough to engage and educate visitors or to show them the impacts of science and technology on society. This realisation resulted in the rise of a new type of science museum, which was, as some say, the starting point of the word 'science centre' (Hudson 1987). The idea behind science centres was that if visitors have a physically interactive experience, the experience is memorable and they then eventually develop a positive association with science and technology (Bradburne 2000; Allen 2004). Such an experience would also result in an interest in science and technology in the future, which would manifest itself in acceptance of its outcomes or science and technology job interests. Famous science centre pioneers were Palais de la Découverte in Paris, the Exploratorium in San Francisco, and the Ontario Science Centre in Toronto, most of which still exist in the same form.

Typical science centres offer physically interactive visitor experiences; the exhibits relate to science and technology and are tailor-made for specific target groups (see, for example, Figs. 5.1 and 5.3b). The science centre is typically a large space, packed with objects, lights, and audio(-visuals). The exhibits have catchy shapes, a high variety of colours, bulky texts, and steps, turning wheels or buttons that can be pushed, or other objects that visitors can move around to operate exhibits and physically engage in the experience. The explanation or educational elements that link to science or technology at stake are secondary, often packaged in a small 'instruction and explanation' text label (Bradburne 2000). So-called 'explainers' are present to support visitors in their learning experience. Due to this physical interactivity, omnipresent in science centres, they generally appeal more to children than science museums did hitherto.

A few features can be seen in the experience designs of science centres that differ from science museum exhibits (Allen 2004). First, the exhibits are not only designed for a high degree of physical interactivity between visitors and objects, but also for interactivity among members of a family or visitor-group, or (even) between visitors that are unfamiliar to one another (see Fig. 5.3b). In designing the exhibits, therefore, much attention is paid to different learning styles (visual, textual, spatial, musical, etc.) through a multi-layered experience, for example by inviting multiple visitors to take on different roles in the interaction, and offering optional explanatory information for those who want to know more about the topic at stake in other ways (ibid.). Furthermore, science centres typically also provide experiences through which visitors interactively get introduced into knowledge production methods. Many science centres host tinkering studios, inviting visitors to learn about programming, hydrology, aerospace, or gravity principles through trial and error, and (chemistry) labs wherein visitors can do small step-wise experiments and thereby learn to formulate a research question, observe systematically, and derive conclusions (see Fig. 5.3c).

A typical complexity in designing science centre experiences is cognitive overload (Allen 2004). Although physical interactivity is key in the science centre to ensure memorable experiences, visitors can get lost. To prevent this, designers need to pay much attention to 'immediate apprehendability': exhibits must be just challenging enough, enabling visitors to learn something new, yet also approachable enough to prevent them from being distracted too soon or refraining to engage at all (ibid.). Furthermore, it can be hard to grasp what knowledge is communicated through the interactive exhibits, if the 'fun' dominates. Grouping exhibits thematically can help mitigate this. Such 'conceptual coherence' (ibid.) can be realised through design features such as look and feel, routing, and texts.

In science centres, the perception of 'visitors' has shifted to them being 'users' (Bradburne 2000). In that, an important shift in thinking occurred with the rise of science centres, that is, visitors—thus users—can also be active co-constructors of the experience and hence co-developers of what they take away from engaging with an exhibit (ibid.). This also means that the experience designer should less strictly pre-define the exact 'learning about science or technology' that takes place. Science centres therefore became museal spaces where the experience developers moved away from at least two commonly held assumptions in 'deficit thinking', as sketched in our introduction about the paradigm shift in science communication: the visitor was no longer seen as a passive, literal receiver of scientific knowledge; and the science centre saw itself less as an authority, and instead more as a facilitator of free choice learning (cf. Dierking and Falk 1998).

Nevertheless, it could be argued that the transformative potential of experience designs in SCMs remained largely unidirectional. In line with 'deficit thinking' in science communication, science museums as well as science centres merely focused on transforming the visitor's knowledge levels or attitudes, albeit in different ways. The mere take home message of SCMs was, and in many SCMs still is, one of a 'science and technology cheerleader': '*this is scientific knowledge you should be aware of*', and '*see how cool it is*'. Where in traditional science museums this was realised through a more passive experience, with object displays or machine demonstrations, science centres wrapped this in a more dynamic user experience.

5.5 Towards Contemporary Transformative Experiences in SCMs

The transformative capacity of SCMs expanded through new types of experiences later in the twentieth century. For many SCM curators, rapid technological innovations in many sectors, the unprecedented scale of global conflicts, but also environmental and health issues around the world, combined with the increased mechanisation of goods and services, and networks of global communication, resulted in the realisation that science and technology, and its associated objects, could and should not be displayed in isolation from their societal contexts (Hudson 1987; Macdonald 2002; Pedretti and Lannini 2020). The idea behind new display techniques was that a plurality of stories can be told about science and technology in relation to society; both critical and positive. It aligned well with the watchdog role that the science communication field was adopting more and more at that time (van Dam et al. 2020). It also aligned with the first experiments in science-society dialogue and participation, which was the science communication's field response strategy to the increasing awareness of social controversies around science and technology (Irwin 2021).

SCM experiences about science's and technology's social controversies became more prominently documented through scientific investigations since the '00s. Let us glance over various examples to illustrate the paradigm shift that this way of exhibiting entails.

Skydsgaard et al. (2016) describe a research into visitor experiences of 'Dear difficult body', an exhibition about the human body in the Steno Museum, Aarhus, Denmark.[4] Although much can be scientifically explained about the human body,

[4] This exhibition still exists: https://sciencemuseerne.dk/en/steno-museum/exhibitions/dear-difficult-body.

the Steno exhibit developers installed interactive exhibits that focus on experiential knowledge. The exhibition displays various narratives of youngsters, mirroring the age of its target audience, in which they share their positive and negative perceptions of their own body, including narratives of—for some visitors—controversial topics like anorexia, obesity, and body ideals in play dolls. Visitors are also invited to express their own thoughts, through choice films, quizzes, or paper sticky notes and drawings. The developers collected and analysed about 2000 visitor notes and, based on that analyses, they launched an online interactive platform 'Straight from the heart', in which 'bodily stories' are shared to help youngsters further navigating body image challenges through peer knowledge.[5] This exhibition, with its make-do experience design, which may seem somewhat messy to some visitors, encourages its target group to think for themselves about their body, express themselves, and build upon the input of previous exhibit users.

Horst and Michael (2011), alternatively, created an exhibition in a shopping mall in Copenhagen on biotechnology. While refraining from explaining the technology in too much detail, the various exhibits concerned narratives and artist impressions of biotechnology to make shoppers think about biotechnology, its role in society, its governance, and potential controversies (ibid.). It posed ethical questions to visitors, e.g. the need for biotechnology regulations. Moreover, users could freely explore different forms of input (visuals, texts, artist impressions) and express their own ideas through quizzes and fill-in exercises (Horst 2011).

These newer types of 'science in context' experiences, which tend to address public controversies around science and technology, focus more on daily life in the design of visuals and exhibits, and often contain written or audio(-visual) narratives or arts-based objects that represent different perspectives, especially of those outside the science or tech world. In that, there is openness for diversity, and different forms of knowledge production that can complement one another, and a move away from strict 'facts' about, or produced by, science or technological innovators.

A fundamentally new, and thus for some SCMs exciting, element in this exhibition typology, is the stepping away from the idea that science needs to come with ready-made answers or solutions to societal challenges—and thus that SCMs should communicate state-of-the-art scientific knowledge. Doom (2020) makes a similar plea and reinforces it. Using the Ghent University Museum (GUM) as a case, Doom advocates for open-ended and art-science crossing SCM experiences, triggering doubt, frustration or irritation about science and technology. For example, when curating the UGent university heritage, tasked with bringing heritage in dialogue with the city, Doom's team hung a fin whale skeleton into a cathedral (see Fig. 5.3d), while the washing ashore of fin whales is seen as a predictor of the devil's arrival in religious circles. Visitor reactions ranged from amazement to accusations of blasphemy (ibid.).

When designing science museum experiences in which there is space for diverse perspectives and doubt, SCM professionals are exposed to various challenges. First, SCMs generally fear to be blamed for 'being too critical on science', since external

[5] See: http://kaerekrop.dk.

stakeholders traditionally expect the SCM to cheerlead science and technology (Delicado 2009). Such an unexpected critical stance in experience designs, could then result in sponsoring and visitor stops (ibid.). Moreover, staging controversies in science museums may be slightly complex for young children, since it is more 'minds-on' than 'hands-on' (ibid.). Hence it requires—or results in—a partial target group shift towards adolescents and adults (ibid.). A solution to this can be diversification of exhibits in the SCM, by hosting different experience typologies spread over the building, but this can challenge conceptual coherence. On top of that, a certain courage is required among SCM professionals to be vulnerable in exhibitions, for example by communicating that 'science does not have the answer either' (Doom 2020).

In conversations that we are currently having with science museum professionals,[6] we see a growing courage to address these challenges. Some SCMs report to us that they are critically reconsidering their sponsor deals with the tech and science sector, and decide, for example, that fossil fuel industry, aeroplane brands, or banks investing in weapons may not fit on their sponsor list anymore. Also, some SCMs reported to us that a shift from children to adults is desirable, at least for a number of their exhibitions, to target families and groups of tourists.

The open-ended, polyvocal and arts embracing experience designs tend to have transformative capacity of a new order. The experiences humbly encourage visitors to welcome various ways of thinking about science and technology, and their roles in society. On top of that, the experiences can transform the makers in turn. The input of visitors can transform the experience designers as well, e.g. by confronting them with their own biases (Horst and Michael 2011).

Some scholars and practitioners, however, plead for even more participation of visitors in SCMs, including the institutional governance of the SCM itself (Bandelli and Konijn 2015). Moreover, the realisation of direct interaction between science and society, what one could call 'transformative reciprocity', transforming both societal as well as tech or scientific actors, seems to emerge in SCM experience design.

5.6 Where We Are Now

In the last two decades, some SCMs have experimented with taking new roles that twin the dialogue and participation paradigm in science communication, specifically to reshape their roles as intermediaries and brokers in complex societal challenges (Achiam and Sølberg 2017; Bandelli and Konijn 2015; Pedretti and Lannini 2020). By doing so, they also begin to contribute to societal transformation in response to

[6] In our project Science Museums of the Future, we investigate how science centres and museums are experimenting with newer roles in society (moving away from edutainment), for which we engage in close interactions with many SCM professionals from 2023 until 2027: https://vu.nl/en/about-vu/research-institutes/athena-institute/more-about/science-museums-of-the-future.

Fig. 5.4 The Smoker, an automatic machine that produces smoke and waltz music, made by Jean Marie Phalibois or Douillon (± 1880); one of the collection items steeped in colonialism and slavery that Museum Speelklok had identified in context of the SWING programme[7] (left). Portrait of Witte de With, naval officer employed by the VOC, WIC and navy, and husband of Hillegont van Goch, created by Jan Daemen Cool and Hendrick Martensz. Sorgh (1654); one of the collection items about which Maritime Museum Rotterdam collected visitor feedback in the light of its connections to colonialism and slavery[8] (right)

complex societal challenges such as growing inequalities and climate change. We finish this chapter by highlighting a few contemporary, pioneering examples.

In 2021, Museum Speelklok in Utrecht, Netherlands, for example, invited guest curator Garjan Sterk to uncover stories of colonialism and slavery connected to the SCM's collection of automatic music instruments (see, for example, Fig. 5.4). These stories were shared with staff, visitors, and experts through guest lectures and musical performances (van Dijk 2022). Among the SCM's staff and curatorial researchers, the programme sparked an interdisciplinary search for how to display the uncovered stories. It meant renewal in the ways through which the collection was interpreted and presented for many years. Where the museum's focus lies on the cheerfulness of the music machines, it currently embeds critical stories in its informative materials as well, for example on how some objects display people of colour in a racist way (Vliet and McGinn, n.d.).

[7] Amongst others, the analysis of this collection item was: the Smoker has a suit, curly hair, full red lips, and earrings. Such a standardised and exaggerated representation brutally ignored individual and cultural characteristics of people of colour (van Dijk 2022).

[8] The following text was provided to visitors to reflect on this painting: 'Witte de With proudly portrays himself here, as a successful man, by one of Rotterdam's best portraitists, Jan Daemen Cool. What the painting does not show is that Witte de With was a violent man, who had a part in

In COVID times, the Maritime Museum in Rotterdam, Netherlands, organised a similar guest curatorship and co-creation process, albeit publicly, in its entrance hall and online due to the restrictions imposed by the pandemic. Visitors were invited to think about how the museum should display its collection of colonial objects and paintings of the Dutch fleet and maritime leaders (see Fig. 5.4). The various outcomes of the dialogue process were presented (online) accordingly, accompanied by the staff's own learning curve.[9] Amongst others, as they describe, the dialogue made SCM staff realise that they want to continue co-creating their museum conservation practices and museum experiences with special attention for diversity and inclusion. This ambition is reflected in the recently opened co-curated exhibition 'Anchored?! Ten stories of migration across the sea'.[10]

An example of facilitation for societal transformation is the dialogue process between smart technology developers and citizens in NEMO Science Museum (Amsterdam, Netherlands). Through collaborative research between SCM staff and science communication and design scholars, various dialogue tools were developed and implemented: a board game, reflexive conversations, a video art installation, and theatrical performances (van der Meij et al. 2023; Fraaije et al. 2023; see Fig. 5.3e). The dialogue experiment resulted in more rigorous citizen participation in a specific area of Amsterdam to inclusively design a smart surveillance system. These dialogues about smart cities were one of the many impulses that contributed in the run-up to the foundation of NEMO, The Studio[11] and its exhibition about data, 'Bits of you'. This spin-off space of NEMO Science Museum targets slightly older visitors and hosts interactive experiences and events about controversial topics such as energy (over-) consumption and the aging population.

Drawing from these examples, the design of these dialogue and participation experiences in SCMs require a mind shift: apart from refraining from the tendency to be an authority who provides solid answers or solutions to complex societal challenges, and more openness to critical voices than solely cheerleading science and technology, it requires:

- A facilitative role, including reflection on institutional learning curves and positionality, values and assumptions.
- Postponing of judgements, openness to different forms of knowledge.
- In addition to the material experiences: organising events and longer-term processes.

---

the murder of the inhabitants of Ambon and the destruction of their clove trees in 1625' (derived from https://maritiemmuseum.nl/dialoog).

[9] See for more information (in Dutch): https://maritiemmuseum.nl/dialoog.

[10] See: https://maritiemmuseum.nl/en/exhibitions/verankerd.

[11] See: https://www.nemosciencemuseum.nl/en/studio/.

Based on conversations that we held with SCM staff in the last few years,[12] we reckon that dialogue and participation, and the mind shift needed for doing this, can be difficult especially for established curators and in-house researchers, and visitors with more conventional expectations. They often desire that science museums maintain an authoritarian role through disseminating scientifically generated knowledge. This is an understandable desire especially considering current flows of disinformation and misinformation circulating in society. However, debunking, while pretending that there is a wide consensus about the 'scientific facts', can actually fuel skepticism (Harambam 2021, 2023). In times of high polarisation it becomes more important to engage in conversations, take people seriously by listening to the concerns underlying their opinions, communicate richly, and emphasise complexity and uncertainty (ibid.).

Furthermore, when implementing experiences for dialogue and participation, finances and flexibility can also become an issue, as most exhibitions are only affordable when displayed in the museum for a few years, while developments in society and controversies around science and technology can change very rapidly. Also, adopting the dialogue and participation paradigm brings along a responsibility for SCMs to ensure a good follow up. Once visitors have exchanged their thoughts during dialogue and participation processes, they expect that this input is used, e.g. in science or technology governance (Bell 2008). Ensuring a good follow up then requires that the SCM is robustly embedded in the systems that are aimed to be transformed, such as science or technology governance and funding structures.

5.7 Concluding Remarks

What are the 'new aesthetics' of contemporary transformative experiences in SCMs? Without being disrespectful to the beautiful experiments, their aesthetics might be experienced as somewhat disorderly, outspoken, or, in opposite, humble: a mix of handwritten notes, (in)formally curated texts, everyday objects, science-related objects, artistic objects, and (audio-visual) narratives, e.g. about lived experiences, presented via headphones or speakers (see a visual summary in Fig. 5.5).

---

[12] While some of these observations have been made during earlier project work (e.g. the NEMO smart city case), most of our current fieldwork is part of the Science Museums of the Future project, in which we also foster a learning community around new roles for SCMs, e.g. through reflexive workshops with SCM professionals.

Fig. 5.5 An artist's impression based on observing various contemporary transformative experiences of SCMs; make-do activities, artistic objects to stimulate further (critical) thinking, and perspectives of visitors collected through sticky notes or video-recording (drawing: M. G. van der Meij)

But foremost, the transformative key ingredients in the designed experiences are not to be seen in the materials. They are to be experienced through interactions with exhibits, events, and involved professionals who develop and execute them. The professionals involved in the development of experiences can be educators, curators, content designers, or (internal) researchers, while hosts, facilitators, or explainers are usually involved in performing or running the experiences. To design contemporary transformative experiences, institutions and professionals need to adopt new curatorial approaches. Based on our described paradigm shifts in science communication and science museology, and the various examples, we conclude this chapter by offering a tentative framework for (assumptions in) designing transformative experiences in SCMs (see Table 5.1). In the framework, we contrast predominantly held assumptions in SCM experience design, rooted in deficit thinking, with assumptions that support contemporary SCM experience design. May this be a starting point for the further futuring of transformative SCM experience design.

Table 5.1 Tentative framework for (assumptions in) designing contemporary transformative experiences

	Topic/level	Predominant experience design assumptions (rooted in deficit thinking)	Transformative experience design assumptions (rooted in dialogue and participation)
Science and society	Science is…	The process of arriving at an objective truth, most importantly through natural sciences and mathematics	A dynamic, ever evolving, human process of systematic knowledge production, in which all science fields are relevant
	The relationship between science and society is…	Hierarchical, wherein science has power or authority over society; society needs science	Horizontal, science and society 'need' one another just as much; power balance
Science communication, science centres and science museums	The role of the science centre or museum is…	That of an authority: educating visitors about scientific facts	Facilitative: engaging visitors in meaning making about science and technology, or in new (transdisciplinary) knowledge production
	The direction of science communication is…	*From* science, via mediators such as SCMs etc., *to* visitors	Among visitors; or *between* visitors and the SCM, science-related actors or other 'experts'
Knowledge	Knowledge production is…	A continuous neutral process wherein scientific experts develop and gain new insights	A continuous value-laden process wherein various types of experts[a] around a specific topic (challenge, wicked problem) co-create new meaning and knowledge
	The knowledge to communicate is…	Certain and factual	Unfinished, pluralist, inclusive of nuances in terms of uncertainties and differences in perspectives, plus underlying aspects such as values and assumptions

(continued)

Table 5.1 (continued)

	Topic/level	Predominant experience design assumptions (rooted in deficit thinking)	Transformative experience design assumptions (rooted in dialogue and participation)
	The learning outcome/ take home message of the exhibition is…	'This scientific knowledge is what you should know/be aware of'	'These are various ways of looking at [topic X], please continue questioning and thinking about it; there is no definitive answer (yet)'
Visitor interactions	The visitor is…	A passive and literal receiver of knowledge; audience	An active co-constructor of meaning and knowledge; user
	The visitor-exhibit interaction is…	Static or dynamic, eyes-on, minds-on, hands-on; predefined	Minds-on, hearts-on, plurifold and open-ended
	The experience designer is…	An anonymous authority, cheerleader of science, scientific knowledge and technology	A visible facilitator, open to different perspectives, explicit about own positionality
	The transformation that takes place is…	At the visitor-side, namely in its knowledge levels or attitudes	At the side of the visitor as well as the SCM staff and (potentially) other actors

[a] Including people with experiential expertise, being experiences gained in daily life concerning the topic at stake; formerly seen as (subordinate) 'lay knowledge'

References

Achiam M, Sølberg J (2017) Nine meta-functions for science museums and science centres. Mus Manag Curatorsh 32(2):123–143

Allen S (2004) Designs for learning: studying science museum exhibits that do more than entertain. Sci Educ 88(S1):S17–S33

Bandelli A, Konijn EA (2015) Public participation and scientific citizenship in the science museum in London: visitors' perceptions of the museum as a broker. Visit Stud 18(2):131–149

Bell L (2008) Engaging the public in technology policy; a new role to science museums. Sci Commun 29(3):285–406

Bradburne JM (2000) Interaction in the museum: observing, supporting, learning. Dissertation, Libri Books on Demand

Bruman R, The Exploratorium Staff (1991) Exploratorium cookbook I: a construction manual for Exploratorium exhibits. The Exploratorium, University of Michigan. ISBN 0943451280

Bucchi M, Trench B (eds) (2008) Handbook of public communication of science and technology. Routledge, Oxon

Delicado A (2009) Scientific controversies in museums: notes from a semi-peripheral country. Public Underst Sci 18(6):759–767

Dierking LD, Falk JH (1998) Understanding free-choice learning: a review of the research and its application to museum web sites. In: Museums and the web, vol 98, Apr 1998

Doom M (2020) Museum of doubt. Academia Press

Douma J (1994) A discourse, prototyping for the 21st century

Fraaije A, van der Meij MG, Vermeeren A, Kupper F, Broerse JEW (2023) Creating room for citizen perspectives in 'smart city' Amsterdam through interactive theatre. Res All 7(1)

Gazsó A, Hauser C, Kaiser M (2012) Regulating nanotechnologies by dialogue. Eur J Risk Regul 3(1):103–108

Gibbons M (1999) Science's new social contract with society. Nature 402(Suppl 6761):C81–C84

Harambam J (2021) Against modernist illusions: why we need more democratic and constructivist alternatives to debunking conspiracy theories. J Cult Res 25(1):104–122

Harambam J (2023) Distrusting consensus: how a uniform corona pandemic narrative fostered suspicion and conspiracy theories. J Digit Soc Res 5(3):109–139

Horst M (2011) Taking our own medicine: on an experiment in science communication. Sci Eng Ethics 17:801–815

Horst M, Michael M (2011) On the shoulders of idiots: re-thinking science communication as 'event'. Sci Cult 20(3):283–306

Hudson K (1987) Museums of influence. Cambridge University Press, Bath, Avon

Irwin A (2021) Risk, science and public communication: third-order thinking about scientific culture. In: Routledge handbook of public communication of science and technology. Routledge, pp 147–162

Kelly T (1952) The origin of mechanics' institutes. Br J Educ Stud 1(1):17–27

Kraeftner B, Kroell J, Warner I (2007) Walking on a storyboard, performing shared incompetence: exhibiting "science" in the public realm. In: Exhibition experiments, pp 109–131

Maas A (2013) How to put a black box in a showcase: history of science museums and recent heritage. Stud Hist Philos Sci Part A 44(4):660–668

Macdonald S (2002) Behind the scenes at the science museum. Routledge

Morris P (ed) (2010) Science for the nation: perspectives on the history of the science museum. Springer

Nowotny H, Scott P, Gibbons M (2001) Re-thinking science—knowledge and the public in an age of uncertainty. Polity Press, Cambridge

Nowotny H, Scott P, Gibbons M (2003) Introduction: 'mode 2' revisited: the new production of knowledge. Minerva 41(3):179–194

Owen R, Macnaghten P, Stilgoe J (2012) Responsible research and innovation: from science in society to science for society, with society. Sci Public Policy 39(6):751–760

Pedretti E, Lannini AMN (2020) Towards fourth-generation science museums: changing goals, changing roles. Can J Sci Math Technol Educ 20:700–714

Schiele B (2018) Cultures of scientific culture. Cult Sci 1(1):15–23

Skydsgaard MA, Møller Andersen H, King H (2016) Designing museum exhibits that facilitate visitor reflection and discussion. Mus Manag Curatorsh 31(1):48–68

Stemerding D, Rerimassie V (2013) Discourses on synthetic biology in Europe. Rathenau Instituut, The Hague

van Dam F, de Bakker L, Dijkstra AM, Jensen EA (eds) (2020) Science communication: an introduction, vol 1. World Scientific

van der Meij MG, Fraaije A, Broerse JEW, Kupper F (2023) Guiding visions of corporate smart city innovators: identifying opportunities for participatory futuring. Futures 154:1–12. Article 103269

van Dijk M (2022) SWING, the power of black music, a polyvocal perspective on the collection. Accessed 15 Sept 2024. https://www.museumspeelklok.nl/app/uploads/2024/06/SWING-Programmaboekje-Concertreeks.pdf

Vliet D, McGinn C (n.d.) Broken heritage machines: affect and proximity to power in the decolonization of racialised European musical automata collections

VSC (2022) Annual report of Dutch association for science centres and museums. Accessed 17 Apr 2024. https://www.vsc-netwerk.nl/files/231013-vsc-jaarverslag-2022.pdf

Marjoleine G. van der Meij Ph.D., is Assistant Professor Design for Participatory Transformation in Athena Institute, VU University Amsterdam. In her work she shapes and studies participatory system transformation trajectories, amongst which in the context of science centres and museums. In line with her educational background in engineering and social sciences, she combines design (methodologies) with science communication. Her teaching covers many aspects of science communication, amongst which the designing of transformative science centre and museum experiences through facilitating collaborations between students and practitioners.

Christianne K. J. Blijleven is a Ph.D. student at the Athena Institute, VU University Amsterdam, where she investigates the contemporary roles that science centres and museums take on in the light of complex societal challenges. She has a background in cultural leadership studies. During her Master programme, she spent some time as a researcher behind the scenes at the Science Museum in London, and developed an expertise in experimental display practices, particularly in the context of historical media objects and histories of use.

Chapter 6
Discovering Volunteers as an Essential Community of Practice in Small Museums in the Netherlands

Silvia Naldini and Nicholas J. Clarke

Abstract Museum volunteers form a community of practice that potentially connects a museum to our ever-more diverse society, which includes newcomers and immigrants with diverse ethnic and cultural backgrounds, who are often marginalised. This community of practice holds the means to inform proactive transformations of small museums to become cultural hubs for social contacts. This aligns with the Council of Europe's Faro Convention which democratises the ownership, use and interpretation of cultural heritage. The Small Museums Change research project, which is reported in this chapter, developed a method to assist small museums to define transformation directions by facilitating volunteers to express their assessment of the museum, and express wishes and ambitions as guideline towards an integral transformation. The method proved successful in defining the core qualities and values and in identifying key ambitions for future planning for the seven small museums in the Netherlands that participated in the project. This chapter describes the method developed, highlights its outcomes and successes, and reflects on its value identifying hitherto undiscovered potentials. The method also proved to be valuable as tool to support volunteers as invaluable community to safeguard and further develop museum experiences for community engagement.

S. Naldini (✉)
Heritage and Architecture, Faculty of Architecture and the Built Environment, Delft University of Technology, Delft,
The Netherlands
e-mail: s.naldini@tudelft.nl

N. J. Clarke
Department of Architecture, University of Pretoria, Pretoria, South Africa
e-mail: njc.arch@gmail.com

L. Calvi et al. (eds.), *Transformative Museum Experiences*, Springer Series on Cultural Computing, https://doi.org/10.1007/978-3-031-89521-0_6

6.1 Introduction

Museums are reassessing their relationship to society, both globally and in the Netherlands. They are transitioning from being repositories of artefacts into social hubs that seek to be relevant to local and international contemporary discussions. At the same time our understanding of the museum has evolved from being only a building containing objects to a place where action and interaction with the public occur. The museum is no more only a repository for items of value. The museum is now a value-creator. In this architecture is not the focus of what a museum is (the *purpose*), it is merely a facilitating agent (one of the *means*).

Volunteers have a key role to play in this transition in those countries where volunteerism forms an integral part of the museum landscape. So prevalent is volunteerism in the Dutch museum landscape that the national Dutch Museum Association scan fully justify the statement that: "Almost all Dutch museums work with volunteers" (Museumvereniging, n.d.).

Dutch museums face growing pressure to professionalise, to improve the curating and digitalisation of collections and upgrade their facilities and operations to reduce their ecological footprints, while also adapting to, and leading the charge on reassessing dominant social narratives and norms.

In essence all museums need to continuously transform in order to meet the expectations of their public, both their loyal visitors and the communities attached to the museum and in order to reach new public audiences. Museums need to be sensitive to and reinterpret social needs and innovate if they wish to continue to attract visitors. In the Dutch context, museum volunteers have a key role to play in this transition and in many instances are instrumental in the implementation of change. They are the presenters of cultural heritage, they often present the narratives related to the museum's collection to visitors, and are essential to back-of-house operations.

The criteria used for the *Small Museums Change* study were derived from the outcomes of the *Metamorphosis* research project on the transformation of large/iconic museums in the Netherlands resultant from that country's Delta Plan for Culture. That project highlighted that a broad participation and support of stakeholders is key for a durable transformation. This conclusion points to the principles embodied in volunteering: participation and (mutual) support. The most important point of departure of this exercise was that the volunteers form a community working in the museum but are at the same time also strongly linked to the area and its population where the museum is located.

This chapter presents the background, method and outcomes of the *Small Museums Change* research project, which aimed to show that volunteers form not only an essential source of knowledge about their museum and its context in society, but also a community of practice essential to achieve sustainable and durable small museums. It describes how the roles and ambitions of museums are evolving, in part due to external pressure, but also to a changing awareness of their social role amongst museum institutions. It then discusses museum volunteers as an essential community of practice and presents the method of engagement that was developed to engage these volunteer communities associated with small museums in the Netherlands. Finally, following the presentation of a case study, it outlines the hitherto untapped potential of small museum volunteer communities as change agents.

6.2 Small Museums Change

Approximately 50% of museums in the Netherlands are categorised by the Dutch Museums Association as 'small': museums with an annual turnover of less than €400,000 (in comparison to 'large museums' with a turnover of at least 8 times larger) (Museumvereniging and Stichting Museana 2022). For the purposes of the research, museums were deemed to be 'small', when they are staffed mainly by volunteers and with a formally employed staffing component of a maximum of 2fte (full time equivalent).

Due to their reliance on volunteers, small museums often have a very close relationship to their communities, as the volunteers often live in proximity to the museum, or form part of a community with a specific scientific or historic interest. The role of small museums and their community of volunteers in the Netherlands has received attention from the Cultural Heritage Agency of the Netherlands (RCE) through research carried out in the context of the process towards the ratification and implementation of the Council of Europe Framework Convention on the Value of Cultural Heritage for Society (Faro Convention) (Council of Europe 2005) by the Netherlands (Cultural Heritage Agency of the Netherlands, n.d.).[1] Research undertaken independently but in parallel at the Delft University of Technology showed that museums are developing towards becoming cultural hubs for social contacts (Roos et al. 2019).

These points of departure led to a research project titled *Small Museums Change*, which aimed at exploring and supporting the transformation of small museums and their social contexts specifically, with a focus on museum volunteers. The project focussed on direct engagement with museum management and the volunteer communities in the form of structured engagements, to deliver direct advice to museums, but also to reflect on the acknowledged and untapped value of the volunteer for the small museum in its continuous transformation.

6.3 A Landscape in Transformation

The main characteristic of 'modern' museums is that they are open to the general public. Museums have over time transitioned from private collections accessible to selected guests for contemplation and study, into institutions formally accessible

[1] The Netherlands ratified the Faro Convention in January 2024.

to everyone. An early example of such a publicly accessible private collection in the Netherlands is the Teylers Museum in Haarlem, which already in 1784 opened its doors to the general public (Teylers Museum, n.d.). Even though museums in the nineteenth century were open to the public at large, the visitors they attracted still were—in line with their didactic aims—mainly scholars, and people who could appreciate art. These visitors represented a very small portion of society.

Over the course of time, museums have radically changed their relationship to society. Presently, they don't only have the task of preserving and displaying their collections, but have also acquired an important societal role. In the International Council of Museums (ICOM) definition of what constitutes a museum, adopted in 2022 (ICOM 2022), their fundamental status as being 'open to the public' is addressed first. This is followed by other relevant conditions: a museum should be 'accessible and inclusive' and 'foster diversity and sustainability'. Museums encourage the 'participation of communities', offering 'experiences' which are meant among other things for 'knowledge sharing'. The ICOM definition provides not only a description of museums with their task and mission, but also, implicitly, an encouragement to engage in actions and changes meant to meet the essential characteristics addressed.[2]

'Open to the public' is a precondition for achieving accessibility and inclusiveness. Moreover, the attachment of communities, also of various origin, including for example immigrants, not only reflects a very democratic approach, in line with the Faro Convention, but is essential for the continued existence of the museum and the creation of new narratives. Community engagement has become an even greater imperative for small museums than before, for their financial health and sustainability. The volunteer plays a key role, not only in providing resources for the operation of the museum, but also acting as a link into their associated social networks and therefore providing an important conduit in museums' efforts to foster social inclusion.

The current continuous transformation of the Dutch museum landscape can be traced back to a national subsidy programme, the so-called *Deltaplan voor het Cultuurbehoud* (Delta Plan for Culture Preservation), which was implemented from 1990 to 1994 with the aim to safeguard collections in Dutch Museums. The programme was extended to 1998 with as aim to reduce the backlog in the conservation and management of Dutch museums, libraries and archives, specifically the (climatic) conditions in which collections were curated and displayed (Ministerie van Welzijn, Volksgezondheid en Cultuur 1990).

A review of the legacy of the Delta Plan was undertaken at the Section for Heritage and Architecture at the Faculty of Architecture of the Delft University of Technology during 2017–2019, published under the title *Metamorphosis: the transformation of the Dutch Museum* (Roos et al. 2019).

[2] "A museum is a not-for-profit, permanent institution in the service of society that researches, collects, conserves, interprets and exhibits tangible and intangible heritage. Open to the public, accessible and inclusive, museums foster diversity and sustainability. They operate and communicate ethically, professionally and with the participation of communities, offering varied experiences for education, enjoyment, reflection and knowledge sharing."

Metamorphosis confirmed that the Delta Plan resulted in a professionalisation in the Netherlands in museum management, the definition of the key objectives of individual museums and stimulated growth towards a greater financial independence. The benefits, however, were most evident amongst large (national) museum institutions with an established national reputation, large operating budgets and professionalised management and operations staff. The implementation of the Delta Plan provided a vehicle for the realisation of great political, architectural and museological ambitions, all expressed through grand architectural interventions.

Consequently, as *Metamorphosis* illustrates, the transformation of a museum was and still is often approached as an architectural problem. By placing the architectural programme at the core of a museum, the projects delivered by the Delta Plan were often inflexible "outwardly impressive and interesting (autonomous) buildings", that "... often fail to fully accommodate the daily operation of the museum including changing exhibitions, visitor flows and preservation of the collection". In instances they even became unworkable in the longer term, because they were devised to achieve individual architectural and political ambitions: they were not the result of a design project that was founded on an understanding of a shared vision on the museum and its mission (Roos et al. 2019, pp. 57–58). The Delta Plan resulted in projects at an architectural and collections level. Following its retrospective analysis of the successes or not of this programme, the *Metamorphosis* project, highlighted that dialogue, which should include all stakeholders, is key to the success of the transformation of a museum. Integrality and the involvement of people is essential to achieve durable and sustainable success.

In the light of the scale of contribution of volunteers to Dutch museums and internationally, it is evident that involving volunteers as a key stakeholder group is essential for small museums' continued existence and continued transformation. Yet the tacit knowledge of the volunteer has to date remained largely untapped, their impact unacknowledged and consequently their continued contribution has become tenuous.

6.4 Small Museums in Transformation

Small museums in the Netherlands face an uncertain future due to reduced subsidies, increased energy costs and building performance requirements, changing social views of the (residue of) the past and other demands (Fig. 6.1). Attracting visitors is key for the short-term survival of small museums as income from entry fees contributes to independence from sponsors and governmental/municipal policies (Roos et al. 2019, p. 13). The precarious nature of the financial dependency and limited resources of museums became critical during and after the COVID-19 pandemic. While the total costs for museums in the Netherlands rose by 14% over the period 2021–22, subsidies only increased by 1% (Museumvereniging and Stichting Museana 2022). Especially small museums suffered from increased costs

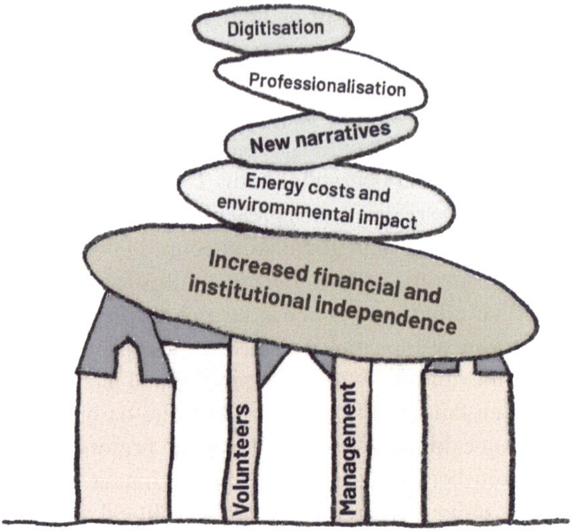

Fig. 6.1 Small museums under pressure face an uncertain future (Naldini and Clarke 2023)

and reduced incomes. A Dutch example is Museum De Voorde, in Zoetermeer, which was forced to close in 2022 due to a lack of municipal funding.

Deploying volunteers can provide a quick and efficient answer to financial strain. The *Metamorphosis* project collected the staffing figures of 15 Dutch museums that had undergone architectural transformations as result of the Delta Plan. This data showed a general increase in the number and contribution of volunteers to the core tasks of museums. One director interviewed as part of the *Metamorphosis* project recalled that in response to severe economic challenges in 2012, the museum changed course, through a reorganisation with a new reliance on a large number of volunteers and a very reduced staff component (Roos et al. 2019, p. 127). A year later the museum could report that it was financially independent.

Museums age. This often becomes visible in out-dated and deteriorated collection displays (for instance due to unreadable cards, poor lighting, …) and a deficit of means with which to provide their public active and enriching experiences. As often stated, technology can help engaging a broad audience (Rozendaal et al. 2018), which is surely of fundamental importance for museums in general, and yet very difficult to achieve in small museums, as in most cases they suffer financial distress. Small museums, with small buffers and reliant on volunteers, have relatively limited resources with which to effect change.

Yet, it would be a mistake to think that an increase in size and status could provide a useful response to these challenges. Small museums do not necessarily need to become larger to remain or become successful. Their nature and uniqueness lie in their size. They can be lean and mean, unhampered by institutional culture and long-term administrative encumberments and commitments to the body politic. Scale can be sought in networking and connecting on different levels with other museums and institutions to foster resilience. Such activities do not alter the nature of the individual museum, but rather define it better and can result in knowledge dissemination and exchange beyond the boundaries of the place where the museum lies and of its country. Networking can enhance the cultural value of a museum and should be encouraged. For small museums with limited means, volunteers form an untapped resource—they provide an entry into networks with links to highly diverse social, religious, business and other communities.

6.5 The Unseen Community: Volunteerism in Dutch Small Museums

The contribution of volunteers to the museum landscape in the Netherlands cannot be overstated, and this is especially true for small museums. Put simply, small museums rely on volunteerism and without volunteers there will be no small museums.

According to research undertaken by the Dutch Museum Association, 66% of the total employment at Dutch museums in 2020 was provided by unpaid volunteers or interns. The main reason Dutch museums are so reliant is financial. The same research highlighted that approximately 1 in 5 small museums are managed entirely by volunteers (Museumvereniging, n.d.). These small Dutch museums today face unprecedented pressure to transform and become more (financially) independent, while diversifying and rescripting narratives to align with societal developments.

Museum volunteer communities are often thought to consist of retired people—but this is not the case. While it is true that many volunteers are retired, the community also includes (young) people undertaking internships and individuals with special/thematic interests or with a strong historical association with a museum or community. The volunteer community is in fact a varied community, representing all of society: from former manual labourers to highly educated knowledge workers. Not all museum volunteers have a background in museology, in fact, a museum background amongst volunteers would be an exception.

Visitors are fundamental to guarantee the existence of the museum. Visitor engagement aims at offering visitors a personal experience of the museum, thereby stimulating repeat visits. Engagement is nowadays entrusted to the museum actors (the volunteers), being the custodians and tellers of the museum narratives, and implies the creation of the means for interaction with the museum's collection, which is the tangible context for the stories.

Placing volunteers central to museum presentation and management brings its own set of challenges. As the contribution of volunteers is just that, *voluntary*, issues of accuracy, responsibility and capacity arise. Well intended actions can lead to detrimental consequences with limited recourse available for correcting mistakes.

The noble act of volunteerism therefore brings with it many challenges. Providing training for volunteers can lead to significant outcomes but may require certainty that individuals are committed to roles or institutions. This may require contractual commitments, which if not carefully considered, may be counterproductive as entering into a contract could be seen by individual volunteers as a means to reduce their freedom to choose when they want to commit to tasks. Contractual agreements could in turn have legal repercussions, not least in terms of labour law. These, and others, are all aspects that small museums are poorly equipped or resourced to deal with. A key consideration for the continued contribution of volunteers in the small museum sector is to find ways to give volunteers a role that provides them with choice and agency to contribute in meaningful ways to the conservation and preservation of a museum's narrative and collection, while also engendering a sense of belonging.

Small museums need to change to keep up with changing social circumstances and to become financially resilient, but engendering change requires key ingredients. The Dannemiller–Gleicher Formula for Change ($C = D \cdot V \cdot F > R$) posits that transformative change (C) takes place when the product of the dissatisfaction with the status quo (D), a vision of what is possible (V), and (importantly) first concrete steps (F), exceed the resistance to change (R) (Clarke 2021).

The transformation of a small museum should be guided by a vision shared by the management team running it (often largely or entirely volunteer), with continuous support of the other volunteers. As volunteers form a community of practice essential for keeping their museum alive, they are best positioned to reflect on the limits and especially the potentialities of their museum, and with guidance to develop a vision to feed the design of future transformations. Their dissatisfaction with the status quo (D) is often the greatest. At the same time, addressing the causes of dissatisfaction through the implementation of first steps (F) will often require their personal time and energy.

The transformation of a museum in which volunteers have a meaningful role demands that each volunteer needs to be aware of their own role within the museum in its present state and the tasks and responsibilities which the envisioned change would mean for them as community and individually. Finally, in view of a transformation, it is important that they reflect on their own will to change, their attitude towards growing in knowledge (e.g., following topical courses, changing roles), and be willing to adapt to meet the needs related to their future tasks.

6.6 *Small Museums Change*: Discovering the Vision of the Small Museum and the Ambitions of the Volunteers

The conclusions presented by the *Metamorphosis* research project highlight that successful museum transformations rely on the engagement of different actors, the analysis of different needs and an ability to remain adaptable, among others (Roos et al. 2019). *Metamorphosis* also concluded that volunteers are not often seen as knowledge resource or given agency in strategic thinking about the continuous transformation of the museum to which they dedicate their time and energy. This omission is problematic as the volunteers play a critical role in the managing of Dutch museums, and they form a community of practice with a vast experience of museum management and operation. They are also in effect the users of the facilities and the guardians of its collection and narrative,

Following on from *Metamorphosis*, the *Small Museums Change* project, spearheaded by the authors, sought to further explore the role of volunteers, understand their critical contributions and understand if and how giving volunteers a greater voice could lead to more durable museum transformations. The growing social role of museums in general, and evidenced by the conclusions of *Metamorphosis*, was a fundamental point of departure for the *Small Museums Change* project, which, aligned with the ambit of the Faro Convention, aimed to uncover the potential of small museums to become cultural hubs for social contacts.

Seven small museums—each faced with an imminent transformation, located in a different socio-economic and geographic context, and each with a unique collection or narrative—were identified to partner in the research project.[3] Pertinent basic information was collected on the partner museums, including their buildings, the spatial organisation of their offering, their collections, curation and policies, annual visitor numbers, number of employees and volunteers and how the management system is structured and operates.

The main focus of the research was to establish how engagement of volunteers through stakeholder engagement workshops and feedback sessions could benefit small museums in transformation. To this aim, individual half-day workshops were held with the volunteers of each participating museum. The aim of the workshops was to define a commonly held vision of the volunteers for the future of their museum. This focus stimulated interest and, as a result, debate amongst the volunteers.

The workshops were meant to give the volunteers a voice. Employed staff and high-level management (even when these were volunteers) were excluded from the discussion to provide a level playing field in the discussion. The workshops and the feedback provided were also meant to assist the volunteer corps to reflect on their current and possible future roles and to increase their sense of belonging, through making the value of their personal contribution explicit.

An important ambition was to assist the volunteers to come to see the museum as a complex organism, including material and immaterial components, connected through networks, which all need to be addressed in the process of change. The definition of museums as ecosystems (Vermeeren et al. 2018) helps in understanding the dilemmas of a multifaceted reality and the need for a shared vision. Therefore, a co-creative approach was deemed necessary, involving actors working in the museum, but also stakeholders from the outside. The aim of the workshops was to help the volunteers analyse the present state of the museum and discuss and clearly express their wishes and ambitions.

A strategic aim was for the outcomes of the workshops to be useful as information to underpin a design process or a change in the building or to create new narratives

[3] Museum Thorn, Thorn, Limburg; Dutch Museum of Lithography, Valkenswaard, Brabant; Museum Paul Tetar van Elven, Delft, South Holland; Dutch Museum of Working-class Districts, Utrecht, Utrecht; House van Meerten, Delft, South Holland; Luther Museum, Amsterdam, North Holland; Streekmuseum Vredegoed, Tienhoven, Utrecht.

related to the collection, all of which should be directed by their commonly held vision for 'their' small museum.

6.7 Methods of Engagement

A bespoke engagement method was developed for *Small Museums Change*, based on experiences from preceding research projects. The basic information collected on each museum followed the model developed for *Metamorphosis*.

The analysis of the spatial structure of the museum and its relationship to visitor experience was founded on Dorus Hoebink's theory of the museum as social performance (Hoebink 2016), which compares a museum with the stage of a theatrical performance. In particular, Hoebink's approach to the assessment of the museum spaces as dynamic/static was referred to for the analysis of the small museums, where warming up/cooling down areas were identified as well. This part formed a preliminary study of the museums in terms of space/routing and display of the collection (Fig. 6.2). Analysing the spatial logic of a museum building shows where the experience offered to the public has changed, because the transformation of a museum as institution is often aligned with its architectural transformation.

Hoebink additionally developed a visual representation of the character of the museum as social performance in the form of a heptagram, with seven elements (Fig. 6.3). This visualisation makes it possible to not only express in simple terms the current character of a museum as social performance, but also to map an ambition for the future for the same. The heptagram helps to map the focus of a museum shows what to focus of a museum is, and can be used to illustrate a change in focus.

Hoebink's heptagram was slightly altered for the purpose of *Small Museums Change* to better reflect the situation of the small museums and serve the aim of involving the volunteers in the definition of its narratives and their conveyance to the public (Fig. 6.4). The use of this tool made it possible to, subsequent to each workshop, present the current and wished-for character of each museum to be clearly visualised in a way that enables comparisons between different museums.

The process and tools developed for the volunteer workshops is based on the 'Kansenkaarten Kerken' (transl. opportunity cards for churches), which presents opportunities for reuse of vacant churches in the Netherlands based on the involvement of stakeholders and ordinary people connected with the church in different ways (Remøy and Clarke 2021) (Fig. 6.4). The museum is conceptualised as consisting of two inter-linked domains: the building and facilities (the *means*) and the collection and society (the *purpose*). These domains are each divided into six layers (Fig. 6.5), resulting in 12 layers in total.

The research method has at is core one-day workshops that are held at each participating small museum (Fig. 6.6). During these workshops, volunteers are asked to reflect and deliberate on the 12 layers connected with the museum, its collection, society, the building and its facilities. A key aim to the method developed is that the engagement method is low-key and low-tech and the outcomes can be validated.

Fig. 6.2 An example of analysis of museum in terms of dynamic/static spaces; in this instance the Dutch Museum of Lithography (Naldini and Clarke 2023)

Fig. 6.3 A visual representation of the character of the museum as social performance in the form of a heptagram as developed by Hoebink, with seven elements (Roos et al. 2019)

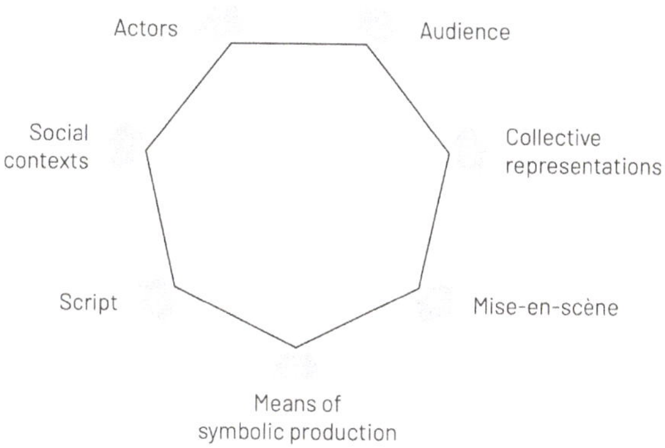

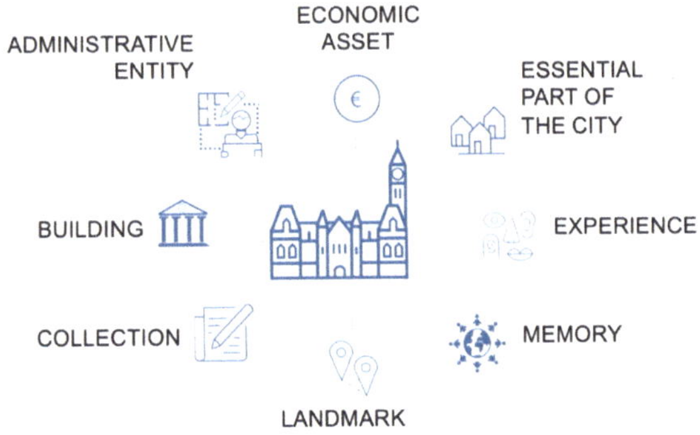

Fig. 6.4 A schematic representation of a church building in its context (Remøy and Clarke 2021)

	Layer	Bearers	Opportunities	Wishes
COLLECTION AND SOCIETY	Narrative (Story)			
	Collection			
	Science and Research			
	Responsibility			
	Society			
	Connectivity			
BUILDING AND FACILITIES	Location			
	Building			
	Exposition/ presentation			
	Facilities			
	Accessibility			
	Visibility			

Fig. 6.5 Conceptualised framework diagramme of the domains and layers defined for the museum, used for the volunteer workshops. *Source* Authors from Naldini and Clarke (2023)

The risk that the discussion during workshops would be merely theoretical, even though based on facts concerning the museum (visitor amount, use of spaces, facilities, etc.) and on the personal experience of the volunteers, was mitigated by the method's strong link to practice. This basic analysis structure forms the backbone of the workshops. The method includes dividing the volunteers into an equal number of groups of maximum five people. Each group is given the opportunity to identify the 'bearers' and opportunities related to an individual layer and note their wishes on A1 sheets using Post-it notes. The sheets are subsequently rotated between the groups to allow for peer review and addition of views by all participants. Reviewing groups can add a 'plus' (+) or a 'minus' (−) sign to indicate their agreement or add additional insights. A plenary presentation of the results signals the end of the individual workshops.

Following each workshop, the data gathered is consolidated by the researchers. A feedback session presents the consolidated outcomes of the workshops to all volunteer groups and museum management teams, to validate the conclusions, following which final reports are submitted to each museum.

Fig. 6.6 Volunteers in discussion during a workshop on 22 October 2022. *Source* Clarke

6.8 Pilot Case Study: Museum Thorn

The research component on Museum Thorn, located in the white city of Thorn, was used as an experiment to validate the designed method. Museum Thorn was, at that time, located in a part of the monumental former courthouse (or 'Dinghuis' in Dutch). The museum management were in discussion to rent some extra floor space, to be able to extend the display areas of the museum in the monumental building.[4]

A first preparatory meeting of the research team, supported by architect Job Roos (Braaksma and Roos Architects), was held with the management of Museum Thorn to establish modes of engagement and outline the expectations and limitations of all parties. To better understand the aim of the envisaged change of the museum,

[4] The Dinghuis is owned by the Bernoster–Kemmers Foundation and both the museum management and the Foundation expressed their interest in a pro-active research project to further define a possible extension intervention.

the discussion was focussed on the 'bearers' of the museum: its central location and proximity to the historical Abbey, its location in the historical Dinghuis, a large-scale model of the village dating to the 1980s called the 'panorama of Thorn' and its public amenities (Naldini and Clarke 2023, p. 46). This resulted in two narrative lines emerging as being the most important form of 'heritage' of the museum: the connecting role of the musical traditions of the village and the role of genteel women from the Middle-Ages. The latter narrative has a wider European reach. The mission of the museum was expressed as to tell these stories to the visitors and preserve this immaterial heritage for future generations. The museum's collection consist of artefacts from the village and aim to tell story of the village, but the discussions uncovered that the collection was far less important to the narrative of the museum than the village itself. The meeting concluded that an effective change could only be expected through strong and interactive storytelling focussing on the village and not on the artefacts. This required a script that engages visitors and leads them through the whole village, of Thorn, which should become the 'museum outside the museum'.

The subsequent workshop with the volunteers, including the management team (formed by volunteers) confirmed this approach. The outcomes include that the presentation of the narratives should not be entrusted to the material kept in the building, but on an interactive experience of significant parts of the village Thorn. This shift in focus is clearly illustrated in the outcomes of the workshop as illustrated in the heptagram (Fig. 6.7) which illustrates how the museum volunteers wished to move towards no longer using the collection for supporting the narratives but work at a script for a routing involving the whole village.

However, the engagements were followed by strict restrictions during the time of the COVID-19 pandemic. The financial difficulties and the restrictions during the time of the pandemic made it very difficult for the museum management to keep paying the rent for the museum building, let alone extend their facilities. Together with the outcomes of the discussions, this situation brought the museum change its strategic vision: the decision was taken to strengthen the narrative and the script

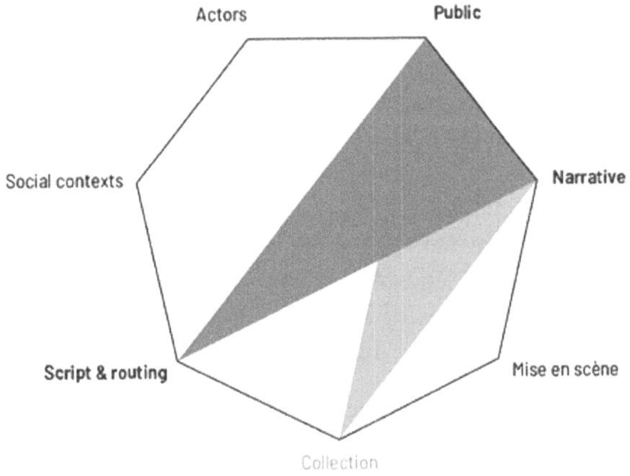

Fig. 6.7 Outcomes of the meeting and the workshop at Museum Thorn. *Source* Authors

Fig. 6.8 The village of Thorn, with the Abbey at it centre, photographed in 2022 *Source* Naldini

to engage the public, not by developing a larger inhouse display area, but rather to diffuse the museum by using the whole village as exhibition under the motto 'Binnenste Buiten' (trans. inside-out) (Fig. 6.8). By activating the social networks of its volunteers, it now hoped to develop new narratives, also because contributions could be sought by newcomers to the region who approach cultural heritage from a different cultural perspective. This went along with a general decision to strengthen the network of the museum, based on its core narratives, through the identification of stakeholders inside and outside the village, and thereby to embed the museum in a larger network. These initiatives, it was considered, could lead to an improved financial stability, as the museum as institution would have no overheads to be able to utilise the village as part of an extended museum offering, while being able to draw more visitors.

The outcomes of the workshop reported in graphic form (Fig. 6.9) show the present situation of the museum (light grey) and the intended course for its future (dark grey). The building, on which all attention had originally been focussed, but also the collection and its display, have become less important than the narrative and social networks. The location of the museum is now seen as being very important, as in the new approach the whole village of Thorn has been conceptualised as both the diffused museum and the setting for its storytelling. Accessibility, but especially visibility are now important factors to be considered in planning changes. The museum's new mission includes a societal goal, which consequently calls for a research network that extend beyond the Village of Thorn to a European level, as one of the museum's new core narratives, that of the genteel women, has a European character.

The meeting and the volunteer workshop at Museum Thorn delivered interesting results for the development of the museum and radically changed the original developmental plan, which included disconnected ideas for transformation such as extending the museum or improved collaboration with the Thorn Abbey, into an *integral transformation plan*. An integral transformation plan is meant to reach the main goals addressed by the community of the volunteers considering different aspects of

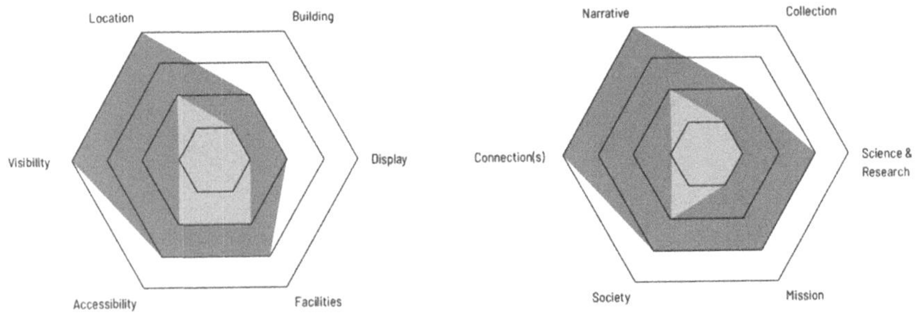

Fig. 6.9 Outcomes of the workshop with volunteers of Museum Thorn presenting the current nature of the museum (light grey) and a wished-for future course (dark grey). Making the most of the location (the whole village) and increasing the visibility of the museum are the first aims. *Source* Authors

the museum mission—from the narratives, to the visibility and accessibility, to the museum building. The engagement also again highlighted how crucial narratives are for preserving the heritage, and the connection with communities and stakeholders. Ensuring such links are established and maintained is considered to be means for social interaction and financial resilience.

6.9 General Case Study Conclusions

The internal evaluation of the Museum Thorn trial case study showed that the method developed provided very useful and delivered significant new insights. This validation led to the choice to use the method in engagements with six additional small museums. All workshops were volunteer-focussed and, following analysis and consolidation by the researchers, the results were reported to the volunteers and discussed. In all workshops, the volunteers successfully expressed their wishes and ambitions, based on which the researchers could distil a vision for the future of the museum. Most importantly, volunteers were encouraged to express their attitude towards society and engagement of the public.

The volunteers indeed proved to represent a very important link between the museum and its immediate geographical and socio-cultural environment. Most volunteer groups wanted to strengthen their small museum's social contacts, indicating a both a wish and a latent potential with regard to the interaction of the museum with society. Various initiatives emerged from the workshops, which confirmed the assumption that museums can become cultural heritage hubs for social contacts. Some already existed, others were novel.

As case in point, the volunteers of the Dutch Museum of Working-class Districts (Volksbuurt Museum) in Utrecht—which is devoted to the history and heritage of its own quarter—invite its less mobile and other marginalised local community groups (which are seen as the museum's 'neighbours') to coffee in the museum once a week

Fig. 6.10 The Dutch Museum of Working Class Neighbourhoods has in interactive display that invites visitors to experience the smell of the city quarter at the turn of the previous century (Naldini 2023)

(Fig. 6.10). This is intended to enhance socialisation and plans exist to extend this initiative and invite resident youth to similar meetings.

The above leads to the conclusions that, thanks to their volunteers, small museums can go beyond merely presenting a narrative, and generate a greater social contribution by addressing issues at play in their immediate geographic vicinity (Fig. 6.11). This indicates that small museums have a role to play in furthering democracy and integration. This is also in line with the foundational principles expressed in the Faro Convention. Engendering social contacts is extremely important in the current context of large migration flows and intolerance.

The bottom-up character of volunteer initiatives resonates with other outcomes of the workshops: volunteers want agency in decisions about the future of their museums and are prepared to modify their own functioning to this aim. Unsurprisingly, they express a belief in the mission defined for their museum. They also know that a successful transformation requires the integration of the expertise from different fields of specialisation, from architects to conservators, engineers to educators. This integral character of the transformation needs to direct future actions, including the maintenance of the building and facilities, the acquisition and de-acquisition of the collection, and changes in the complex fields of accessibility and visibility. They are not averse to new technologies or to projects being entrusted to specialists and university students, even if such actors do not directly belong to the volunteer group of the museum.

The engagement method applied in the project led to outcomes that can be understood and used by the volunteers and management of the museum alike. This validated the approach and method. The most important measure of validation, however, was represented by the positive reactions of the participants, who, in many instances, asserted that the project provided for the very first time a forum in which they could contribute their perspectives to the future of their museum. Only in the case of the Dutch Museum of Working Class Neighbourhoods had the volunteers been asked

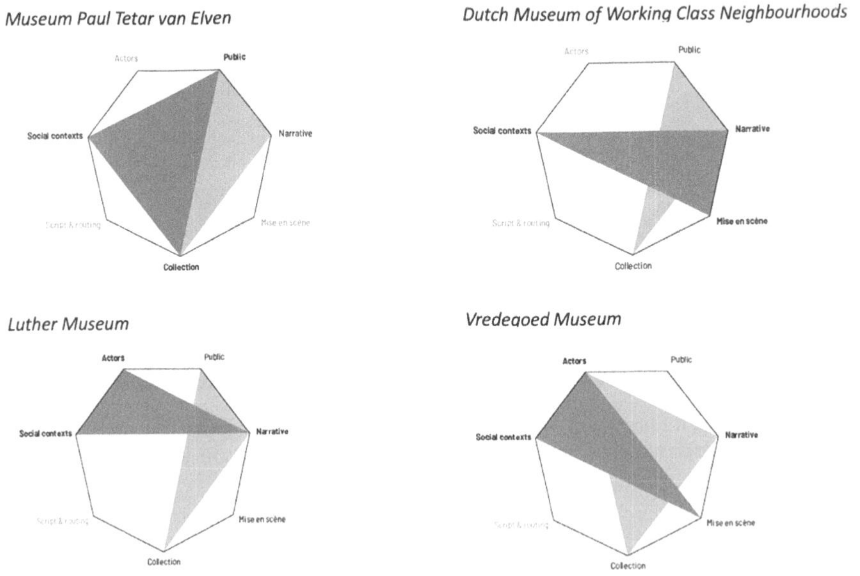

Fig. 6.11 Outcomes of the workshop with volunteers of 4 museums. Enhancing social contacts is deemed crucial for the future of the museum. *Source* Authors

before, by the director, to participate in a workshop. As already noted, three of the seven museums already applied some of the outcomes of the project to substantiate and redirect their policies, even before the conclusion of the research project. The outcomes were elaborated and graphically represented in English, aiming at providing students and interested volunteers abroad with a research instrument. The results were peer-reviewed before publication as open-source book titled *Small Museums Change: Volunteers for Social Engagement* (Naldini and Clarke 2023). The outcomes as presented by the volunteers were reported in Dutch in the appendix of the book, to allow all participants to understand thoroughly and use them.

6.10 Conclusions: Democratising the Volunteer as Change Agent

A transformation of especially small museums cannot be entrusted to the director or specialists such as architects alone, even when it concerns the building. Some of the key actors and community with the tacit knowledge of the museum are the volunteers. The method developed for the *Small Museums Change* project provides one way for architects and other specialists to tap into the lived experiences of the volunteers.

When looking from the museum outwards, volunteers are a ready conduit with which to connect to society, including to marginalised communities. In this sense, the volunteers are the link between the museum and different people with different expectations and needs.

During the workshops, it soon became evident that, as anticipated, some participants had never been asked about their vision on the museum before, even though small museums depend on volunteers for daily operations and the implementation of any change. The discussions in and between the groups were fruitful, leading to new insights into the wishes and needs of the volunteers, and opportunities for future change in the management, but especially the narrative of each museum, which was appreciated and positively valued. The usefulness of the project is evidenced by the fact that the museum directors of three of the seven museums indicated to the researchers that the interim outcomes of the workshop were being used to reshape their development policies—while the research was still ongoing.

The project has discovered that volunteers cherish the ambition of their museum to become more inclusive, dynamic and pluralist. These perspectives align strongly with the principles embodied in the Faro Convention. Bolstering social networks can also support the financial independence of small museums.

The active involvement of the volunteers implies the identification and definition of roles, tasks and responsibilities. Volunteers can apply their knowledge and skills to fulfil museum tasks and further develop them for an effective understanding and consequent use of available knowledge resources. For specific, new functions, emerging from the vision for the future of the museum, also calls for volunteers can be consequently better facilitated. Volunteers across the board expressed the wish to improve their knowledge and skillsets to be able to better contribute to their museums. Positive facilitation of volunteers however may require a clearer definition of their tasks and responsibilities. Exploring the legal ramifications of contractual agreements might be beyond the abilities and resources of many small museums, as are for instance some of the specialist knowledge required to effectively curate their collections. They need institutional support.

Because of the role that small museums and volunteers play in enhancing social contacts, they should receive better recognition—also in terms of funding to support their durable change and financial independence.

Small Museums Change has conclusively shown that small museums are anchors for many Dutch communities. However, small museums in the Netherlands, and elsewhere, find themselves in a landscape of change and must consequently continuously transform to be able to survive. Smallness is an essential characteristic of these institutions, and transformations should aim to preserve it. Smallness does not equal weakness. Small museums often and continuously achieve the impossible: they transform with limited resources and adjust to changing conditions, including rising costs and changing social perspectives. This is only possible due to the dedication of the museum's community.

But the resilience and flexibility of small museums in the face of change depends to a great extent on the engagement of the volunteers and their skillsets. This is why engaging the volunteer communities of small museums is essential to their durable transformation. These communities of practice are an important, if not most important resource a small museum has at its disposal. Giving them a voice at a most basic level provides valuable insights into the operational challenges of museums. At a more fundamental level, engaging the resident volunteer community in the management of small museums taking their wishes into account in strategic planning and decision making, strengthens a sense of belonging, engenders commitment, and can greatly facilitate the diversification of museum narratives, thereby improving access to and democratising cultural heritage.

Acknowledgements The authors wish to acknowledge the contributions of and thank all the dedicated volunteers of the seven museums, as well as their management teams, for participating in the workshops. The *Small Museums Change* project was made possible by a generous grant by the Rondeltappe Bernoster Kemmers Foundation. A special word of thanks to Rosa de Wolf who assisted us at the beginning of the research and Julie Vrindts who worked during the compilation of the results of *Small Museums Change*. We also acknowledge the contributions of Prudence King, Bart Ankersmit and Marzia Loddo for their continuous support throughout the project.

We also want to thank Job Roos (Braaksma and Roos architects), Wessel de Jonge Architects (WDJA) and Michaela Hansen (RCE, Faro project) for the discussion on the outcomes of the research.

References

Clarke NJ (2021) How heritage learns: Dutch public housing heritage evolution in ecosystemic perspective. A+BE Architecture and the Built Environment, TU Delft BK, Delft

Council of Europe (2005) Faro Convention of the Council of Europe, participation in cultural heritage. Accessed 12 July 2024. https://rm.coe.int/1680083746

Cultural Heritage Agency of the Netherlands (n.d.) Faro—participation in cultural heritage. Accessed 11 Dec 2024. https://english.cultureelerfgoed.nl/topics/faro---participation-in-cultural-heritage

Hoebink D (2016) Erfgoed als Schouwspel, Over musea als opvoeringen van gemeenschapsculturen. Erasmus Universiteit, Rotterdam. https://repub.eur.nl/pub/79796

ICOM (International Council on Museums) (2022) Museum definition. Accessed 24 May 2024. https://icom.museum/en/resources/standards-guidelines/museum-definition/

Ministerie van Welzijn, Volksgezondheid en Cultuur (1990) Deltaplan voor het cultuurbehoud. Onderdeel: plan van aanpak achterstanden musea, archieven, monumentenzorg, archeologie. Ministerie van Welzijn, Volksgezondheid en Cultuur, Den Haag

Museumvereniging (n.d.) Musea en vrijwilligers. Accessed 15 June 2024. https://museumvereniging.nl/kennisbank/musea-en-vrijwilligers/

Museumvereniging and Stichting Museana (2022) Trends in de museum sector. Museumscijfers 2022. Accessed 16 Apr 2024. https://museumvereniging.nl/wp-content/uploads/2023/10/2022_Museumcijfers.pdf

Naldini S, Clarke N (2023) Small museums change: volunteers for social engagement. BK Books, Delft. https://books.bk.tudelft.nl/press/catalog/book/805

Remøy H, Clarke N (2021) Kerkenvisie of visioen: De maatschappelijke waarde en duurzaamheid van kerken gewaarborgd in een kerkenvisie voor de Oost-Achterhoek. In: Zijlstra H, Nijhuis S, Quist W et al (eds) Karakteristiek Duurzaam Erfgoed in Gelderland: KaDEr-stellingen Ervaringen en stellingnames na een vierjarige samenwerking tussen de Provincie Gelderland en de TU Delft faculteit Bouwkunde 2017–2021. TU Delft Open, Delft. https://books.bk.tudelft.nl/press/catalog/book/797

Roos J, Hoebink D, Kok A (2019) Metamorphosis: the transformation of Dutch museums. BK Books, Delft. https://books.bk.tudelft.nl/press/catalog/book/697

Rozendaal MC, Vermeeren APOS, Issidorides DC (2018) Using mobile technologies to capture the visitor experience. In: Vermeeren A, Calvi L, Sabiescu A (eds) Museum experience design crowds, ecosystems and novel technologies. Springer, Germany

Teylers Museum (n.d.) Hoe is Teylers Museum ontstaan? Ontdek. Accessed 12 May 2024. https://www.teylersmuseum.nl/nl

Vermeeren APOS, Calvi L, Sabiescu A, Trocchianesi R, Stuedahl D, Giaccardi E, Radice S (2018) Future museum experience design: crowds, ecosystems and novel technologies. In: Vermeeren A, Calvi L Sabiescu A (eds) Museum experience design: crowds, ecosystems and novel technologies. Springer, Germany

Silvia Naldini is Lecturer and Researcher in Building Conservation at the Faculty of Architecture, Delft University of Technology. She has a recognised international position in the field of investigation and diagnosis of damage processes in heritage buildings, value assessment and methods of conservation.

She has done research on the integral transformation of Dutch museums after the 1990s and on proactive transformation of Regional/small Museums run by volunteers, aiming at preserving Culture Heritage and stimulating social cohesion.

Nicholas J. Clarke is an architect and director of Heritage Futures, a built heritage consultancy based in The Netherlands. He obtained his professional degree from the University of Pretoria (South Africa), continued his studies at Cambridge University and defended his Ph.D. at the Delft University of Technology. His architectural practice includes restoration, reuse, impact assessment with a focus on the interface of heritage and sustainable development. Nicholas is a Research Associate of the Department of Architecture at the University of Pretoria, South Africa.

Chapter 7
Third Space Literacies and Museum Learning

Julian McDougall

Abstract Scholarly interest is growing in the non-formal pedagogic experiences which museums can enable. This includes attention to how museums can be situated in the networked ecology of learning spaces as well as the various new literacy repertoires which museum visitors practice to engage with these experiences. This can resonate with scholarly attention to curation as a new literacy practice, intersecting with the long-standing practice of museum curation as storytelling and a form of narratological secondary-encoding of that which is curated, whereby museums are understood to be third spaces. This chapter offers a theoretical overview of third space literacies and an application of this conceptual framing to curational practices in physical museum spaces, before applying these ideas to a case study on the Museum of Homelessness, in comparison with four other museums. In this analysis, the paradoxical tensions inherent to space and intentionality are further explored with an interest in how we experience such tensions in transformative ways.

7.1 Space

Museums are often described as 'third spaces' for non-formal learning (Bhabha 1994; Gutierrez 2008). This has usually been a way to theorise the physical space of a museum as a nuanced, complex mapping of what can be learned when we visit. Museums are understood in this way to exist in between our first space personal histories and lived experiences and the second spaces we inhabit in our official, institutionalised educational encounters.

Curation is understood as a new literacy practice in the everyday first space (Potter and McDougall 2017), intersecting with the long-standing practice of museum curation as storytelling and a form of narratological 'secondary-encoding' of that which is curated (McDougall 2019; McDougall and O'Connor 2015), situating museums as third spaces.

J. McDougall (✉)
Bournemouth University, Bournemouth, UK
e-mail: jmcdougall@bournemouth.ac.uk

L. Calvi et al. (eds.), *Transformative Museum Experiences*, Springer Series on Cultural Computing, https://doi.org/10.1007/978-3-031-89521-0_7

This concept of the 'third space' is long-established and applied frequently to educational contexts, especially non-formal and informal learning spaces, including museums. Third space was developed and applied to a sociocultural perspective of 'rich' settings for the development of literacy practices by Gutierrez (2008), following Bhabha (1994):

> This third space involves a simultaneous coming and going in a borderland zone between different modes of action. A prerequisite for this is that we must believe that we can inhabit these different sites, making each a space of relative comfort. To do so will require inventing creative ways to cross perceived and real "borders." The third space is thus a place of invention and transformational encounters, a dynamic in-between space that is imbued with the traces, relays, ambivalences, ambiguities and contradictions, with the feelings and practices of both sites, to fashion something different, unexpected. (Bhabha 1994, p. 406)

How, then, can we apply these ideas about invention and encounter, and think about this third space, to better understand how these elements converge in '*design approaches and supporting technologies for crafting transformative experiences*' (Calvi et al. 2024) in museums?

> One of the journeys we make in a museum is from material culture to non-material culture and a deeper understanding of ourselves, others and the world in which we live. (Talboys 2011, p. 101)

> Museums usually hold great treasures like paintings in golden frames, marble statues, or grand old books. Our treasures might look ordinary in comparison—they include bin bags, tobacco, and a comb. But each is a fragment of a life lived. The stories they tell challenge stereotypes about what it means to be homeless and reveal a history that's too often hidden. (Museum of Homelessness Co-Founders, Youde 2017)

Third space is primarily metaphorical, conveying and enabling different ideas about learning. But it can also be physical, virtual or hybrid. What characterises third space is a domain in between the first space of home, family, community and everyday life and the second spaces of formal education, work or institutions (or research). In this *in between* space, meanings and learning are exchanged, and new knowledge is generated in this exchange. People take these things back to their first spaces. But also—and crucially, the second space is also in some way changed. So, this third space is a 'semi-permeable membrane' (Potter 2012) in which things flow in two ways. This is crucial because it means that if an activity is set up which is extra to, or alternative to, a conventional learning space, but the knowledge generated remains hierarchical, so that the participants or audience are rendered as the beneficiaries of the facilitators' transmission, then it should not qualify as a 'third space', as the second space is unchanged. In previous work (Potter and McDougall 2017), we accounted for this distinction, by posing two criteria questions for learning in third spaces:

> *What happens to people doing education in a third space?*
> *How do engagements in the third space influence practices back in the second space?*

Therefore, according to this threshold qualification, we can say, perhaps reluctantly, that teachers bringing students to a museum for a curricular activity do not 'count' as a third space experience if nothing changes in the return to school and likewise nothing is brought into the learning dynamic from home, or returns there with a shift in the nature of knowledge, no more reciprocal epistemology. In this sense, the equation with transformative museum experiences is clear—the transformation is not bound by/to the time and space of the museum visit, but in this flows through the membrane from and back to the first and second spaces.

When a third space is a physical location, common examples are such things as a club, community setting, after-school activity—or a museum. When the space is metaphorical, then it can take place in a second space location (such as a classroom), but the learning is negotiated through more agentive activity which is reflexive for both learners and educators, even in a formal setting. An example might be a school library, a physical second space location but metaphorically 'in between' subject learning and non-formal learning (see McDavitt and McDougall 2023). When the third space is virtual, or hybrid, things get complicated. A digital/virtual space might appear to be configured socio-materially as a third space, by definition, when students are engaging with second space education—school—from the first space. However, when we assess the qualities of a digital third space, we are looking for the same shift in knowledge negotiation as set out above. This means that online learning, or a virtual museum, is still only a third space if we can identify these same flows of knowledge between first and second spaces. For example, during the pandemic-enforced 'online pivot', learning design decisions were made in real time, often in collaboration with students, as the second space became, by necessity, a third space. This led to a set of optimistic principles for how we might take these transformative experiences in learning and teaching back, after the COVID-19 pandemic, to pedagogy and learning—understanding teaching spaces as a multiplicity of places, often making sessions open beyond the enrolled class, flipping time, so the default was asynchronous, with 'real time' as supplement, embracing dynamic practices whereby the direction of flow was not about static content being delivered but about open, agentive and productive spaces for both learners and educators. This resulted, often, in a more reflexive 'pedagogy of the inexpert', a more porous expertise, understanding that we 'own' the curriculum but not the social practices of teaching and learning if that was ever the case. But when restrictions were lifted and we returned to either campus or online or blended, something of a 'normal new' took hold and this means that we can only look back at the online learning moment during the pandemic as 'third space' if it led to ongoing transformative experiences after the enforcement.

Much of the literature on museums as third spaces (or 'third places'—a term we can take here as interchangeable, whilst acknowledging there are nuances of difference) is focussed on the potential of exhibition design for transcultural identity work, in particular where indigenous and colonial epistemologies are at play. Understood in this way, a museum can enable new dialogic and intercultural engagement with and between publics and a learning environment for working with historical cultural tensions, in the pursuit of more empathetic cultural relations between visitors in the everyday first spaces of their lives in the present. Curators, it is argued, can facilitate such third spaces if they actively engage with the first space socio-cultural lived experiences of their visitors, so that empathy flows both ways, rather than imposing a 'preferred response' through the curation of the cultural textuality being displayed, so that when we go to a museum we can experience '*interaction with museum resources and with each other, to create, exchange and share information and meaning in real or virtual time and space*' (Silverman 2009, p. 15).

When we put the concept of third space together with ideas about dynamic literacy practices, we also come to identify curation as a literacy practice for everyone as well as a specialist practice for museums. Curation is the process of looking after and conserving artefacts, cultural texts and practices for present and future generations. This requires specialist knowledge and museum exhibitions are where the tacit and specific knowledge of the curator became public and open to interpretation. Curation is about storying, engagement, and informing and is personal, cultural and political, a meta-level intertextual activity of collecting, cataloguing, arranging and assembling for exhibition. But clearly, we do this in our everyday textual lives, more visible now in social media, so the practice is not restricted to professional museum practitioners. This is more overt in terms of digital curation of life in social media:

> If there is an overarching new cultural and literacy practice in the production and sharing of new media of all kinds, it is this metaphorical, meta-combination of literacies into what I've called a new "curatorship of the self," an expression of the anchored aspects of our identity and our transient affiliations and choices. These are exhibitions assembled, presented, dismantled, and reassembled for different audiences: family, friends, coworkers, employers, fellow campaigners, and so on. In each of these cases, some kind of textual design is employed, either in the components of the individual text, a video clip of some sort, or in their assembly from a range of different material and modes of production into a new whole. In these cases, the decisions and intentions of the designers of these texts are important intertextually; that is, these texts of all kinds, markers, and modes of expression that work together to make meaning on the screen in representing the self. (Potter 2012, pp. 2–3)

The reason why 'digital curation' is so immediately recognisable as a practice is because it describes the reflexive impulse we now have to narrate our experiences, an everyday process of telling, and negotiation, the narrative of self. When we use social media, the viral exchanges of these curational practices create a kind of live, ongoing montage of all of our selves, as we link and respond. However, we can also think of analogue age curational practices, what we have called 'Doing Text', from making mix-tapes to writing fanzines to placing books on coffee tables and curating art on our own walls.

Therefore, there are two important implications of how digital media life has brought curation to prominence as a literacy practice for our interests here:

1. Digital curation in the first space brings to the foreground the ways in which curation has always been a literacy practice. The digital makes this more visible, and is thus helpful for our understanding of the 'always-already' of curation.
2. This 'surfacing' of curation in the first space offers new ways to think about the dynamic relationship between museum curation, everyday curation and transformative experiences in museums, and for thinking in new ways about how these curational practices intersect in third spaces.

7.2 Museums as Third Spaces

Museums are not inherently third spaces. Rather, exhibitions can be, if visitors can experience them as such, and learn in attendant ways, in terms of the knowledge exchange practices discussed above. Museums can become third spaces when visitors may actively engage in exploration of complex multitudes of identities, across cultural and psychological boundaries, and engage in dialogues (Du and Cui 2021, p. 79).

Museums are always-already negotiated spaces, but this comes to the foreground in third space when an exhibition can bear witness to habitus.

Habitus (Bourdieu 1984) consists of our thoughts, beliefs and interests and is created through family, class, culture, social settings and education. Habitus has the potential to influence actions and to construct social worlds, as well as being continually influenced by the external circumstances in which we live. Habitus is fluid (changing for example with age, travel, education, aesthetic experience, parenthood) and no two individual's habitus will be the same.

The significance of habitus in experiencing museums might be simply the various ways of being at play in the space, those of the visitors, of the 'objects', of the display, artists, perhaps. Or it might be more significant as 'habitus clash' when competing value regimes and/or epistemologies come into contact with one another. Our interest here is on the configuration of meanings in spaces and how hierarchies are disrupted. When we think about this with regard to after-school clubs or community learning spaces, then these have different 'signature pedagogies' to what happens in classrooms during the school day, because they operate in these third spaces with obligations for the values and cultures of the participants to be known. Third spaces are thus contested, negotiated and political. In the museum, they require, therefore, a similar kind of design thinking, a 'signature curation', which is itself a shift in pedagogy also.

The common thread running through the diverse range of work about third space museum design is the meeting point between the museum entity (which, again, can be virtual, or a physical space in a building), objects and artefacts and things which are intangible, which are 'exhibited' in thoughts and ideas. This is the distinction between dynamic and static. Just as the education system tends to try to 'halt' the dynamic flow of literacies in order to assess it as a form of 'schooled' knowledge, as opposed to a living, situated set of negotiations with language and culture, so can a museum unintentionally 'freeze' intangible things such as culture, identity and heritage through the anchorage of objects and 'works'. When we are thinking about art exhibitions, then third space clearly foregrounds the tension between the desire for visitors' first space knowledge repertoires to be valued and the valuing the creative labour of the artist:

> Museums must embrace Bhabha's calling for a fluid identity and begin to understand that binary boundaries are dissolving and we must adapt to a constantly shifting and changing milieu of ideas, events, appearances, and meanings. Museums must adopt new mentalities; namely, a mindset that keeps the consciousness of and theorizing of culture and hybrid identity radically open. This is not an argument that rejects the location and origin of the

artwork and the artist as important – clearly, these are vital to fully understanding the piece and its symbols of representation. Rather, I hope this acts as a call to consciousness for museums to not simply rely on notions of geography and origin as criteria for exhibitions. (DiGiovanna 2015, pp. 72–73)

7.3 Curation and Learning

The received understanding of curation is that this is about conserving artefacts, cultural texts and practices for present and future generations, using specific sets of skills and knowledge gained over time. Curation demands specific expertise and the pedagogical ability to share this knowledge for now and the future. Museum spaces are where this curational practice is made public and open to interpretation.

Curation is also concerned with weaving narratives between these artefacts, texts and practices. In a gallery context, it might also mean assembling a series of artworks in a particular sequence and context in order to tell a *new* story about an artistic movement or about a single artist's life and development. Curators at the Tate Modern Gallery in London told a new story about Paul Klee by, for the first time, hanging his paintings according to the numbering he himself gave them. In this way, curation, even in its most traditional form, implies a level of storying, working with evolving knowledge and shifting perspectives, of uncovering and revealing things previously not well understood or even deliberately covered up. Sometimes this can be politically or socially motivated as in Rozsika Parker and Griselda Pollock's 'Old Mistresses' which inspired the feminist reclaiming of women's art from more patriarchal accounts of art history. Exhibitions followed in later years in which the curators uncovered and retold stories of women artists whose work represented a much-needed feminist retelling of the story of art history. Other examples include the curated claims and counter-claims made on behalf of the various interests represented in the slavery museum in Liverpool or, in another case, the indigenous people's gallery in the Melbourne Museum, which houses a collection of cultural artefacts from indigenous tribes, a retelling in the twenty-first century of one version of the story of part of Australia, a culturally problematic and sensitive practice relating to the cultural identity of that nation.

When the English artist Grayson Perry was commissioned to curate his own art alongside the British Museum's collection, he was curating his own identity as an artist intertextually with the established archive in a curational gesture that we can think about here as representative of third space:

> The British Museum holds eight million objects from every corner of the globe. Why not, I thought, make the works I am inspired to create and find objects in this vast collection that respond to them? Somewhere in its endless storerooms there must be objects that echo my concerns and styles. (Perry 2011, p. 11)

In this most strikingly 'establishment' environment, Perry's approach resonates with the 'postmodern' meaning-making we engage in with digital social media. We post images of ourselves in space with our affiliations, bring ourselves into being in the world by curating ourselves into it; so that these 'concerns and styles' are mirrored amongst peers, liked and shared, a tapestry of curation.

But even when curation seems to be a second space practice, it is never so straightforward. Consider an exhibition in Birmingham, England about 'Children's Lives'. On entering the gallery, the visitor is asked 'What is a Child?'. This frames a set of images and artefacts which are curated in a non-linear modality, but with a thematic sequencing which encourages a particular journey through the space—a preferred curational narrative. This narrative locates the child in a proximal relation to a context—'At Home'; 'Outside'; 'In Care'; 'On the Move'; 'Imagined' and then, finally, arriving at the present day, a simulation of a teenager's bedroom 'It's all about us'.

Each element is both informed by and forms a 'figured world' (Gee 2015) according to which the images, artefacts, thematic framing and 'anchoring' text on the gallery walls articulate assumptions about childhood. Such figured worlds are perhaps never more entrenched than with regard to how we 'read' childhood. These meanings '*need not be fully in any parent or child's head, consciously or unconsciously, because they are available in the culture in which these parents live – through the media, through written materials and through interaction with others in the society*' (Gee 2015, p. 86).

The *Children's Lives* exhibition declared the (worthy) objective to '*hear children's voices and to see them as independent social actors*', but the conventions of the gallery space, the textual form of the exhibition, could not evade, nor avoid reconstructing, the figured discursive worlds which frame the child as the object of adult frames of reference. The exhibition both acknowledged and, reflexively, sought to resist this:

> Children were observed, recorded, described and measured and the data generated produced the ideal of a 'normal child' against whom all other children were assessed so as to identify and regulate those who did not conform. (Birmingham Museum and Art Gallery 2012)

However, this recognition by the exhibition of the paradoxes of representation and regulation of childhood was in tension, paradoxically, with the second space, curation and discursive dynamics of itself, being complicit in reproducing that which it set out to deconstruct. The conventions of discursive framing that an exhibition will always-already reproduce were at odds with curators' intentionality—to bear witness to the paradox of childhood in representation (see McDougall and O'Connor 2015).

We can conclude from this that professional museum curation can be thought about as a formal, professional 'system world' manifestation of everyday curation. If so, this is still never simply about linear narrative, as the nature of the museum space will always complicate the textual experience of what is 'being curated' in the operation of 'secondary-encoding'. *Children's Lives* presents the paradox whereby the exhibition reinforces the constructed nature of childhood at the same time as attempting to challenge it, and in this paradox was an opportunity for the exhibition to be transformative—radical and transgressive in a sense of indeterminate reflexivity. Whilst the curation largely constructed a figured world in which historical images were anchored by text reinforcing the 'factual' status of photographs and artefacts, the emotional interplay between image and reception carried a tension. At the same time, the one space in which images are presented as aesthetic and representational—the presentation of a 'typical' teenager space with an absence of framing text or commentary—generates a further paradox in the requirement for visitors to 'shift' reception mode in this way. This space, coming at the end of the chronological narrative, offers a way of seeing the representational status of everything a visitor will engage with before. In this way, the exhibition finally fulfils the objective to address the paradox '*What is a Child?*', but through the tensions and ambivalences created by its own discursive and spatial frame of reference. This is all not to deny the exhibition any third space affordances, or the visitor any space to engage with a transformative negotiation of culture. Indeed, in another room, visitors are asked to share their memories of childhood. Whilst many chose to reminisce about climbing apple trees and favourite story books, others felt compelled to share distressing aspects of their childhoods such as 'being abused' or 'being shot in the leg at the age of seven', perhaps through a genuine desire to be heard, or a more intangible urge to disturb the fantasy held dear by many, of childhood as a happy time for all. Here more than anywhere in the exhibition, the construction of, and resistance to, figured worlds is laid bare, hereby opposing any possibility for the exhibition to be presenting 'typical' experiences and stating instead that the majority of childhood experiences would exist outside of these polarised social practices. Again, what this interaction does is to unmask the representational nature of *Children's Lives*, as the most forthright opponent of its discourse uses the term: '*I don't see anything of my childhood represented here*'.

In the *Comrades and Curators* project (McDougall 2019), funded by the Bill Douglas Museum and Archive in Exeter, three museums were connected around *Comrades*, a Bill Douglas film about the historical/political narrative of the Tolpuddle Martyrs, to understand contrasting ways of curating this social history in the museums in Exeter, Tolpuddle and Dorchester. The three curators were interviewed about their formal curation practices at their museums and how they understood the social practice of curating history and they came together at the Exeter museum to take part in an exercise, mapping one another's identities as curators. All of the curators readily expressed their personal investment in their museums, described in each case as a project, and with a clear sense that personal perspectives on the issues being curated were inseparable from the work. This was a nuanced, complex mapping of spaces, between first space personal histories and the narrative/political curation of social history in the second space of the museum. Here, the three curators offer specific examples of curational approaches:

> I try to create a very basic over-arching narrative, that this is the people's history of cinema, as opposed to technology or machines, this is about how people have interacted with films. It's also about how different ways of seeing culminating in the invention of cinema, and these ways of seeing are important in their own sense and how the sensation and wonder they each create are tied in with different aspects of social history, democratisation, urbanization, those kinds of things.
>
> There's a small number of people who are actually cross with what they see as the politicization of this piece of history. They want it to be much safer history, disarmed history.

> What I care about is that you come away with something. We're talking about lots of different areas of history, but the one thing I do hope comes across is the idea of how the law affects our society today and we can affect it today as well, so looking for history to get that across, that you have a voice and you have agency.

The curators agreed on shared themes—curation as storytelling, access to culture—often framed in relation to social class—and the awareness of beauty in the everyday, curating social history as hopeful and optimistic, but also dialogic—'*making things available to people to enable them to make their own reflections on them*', again evoking the social practice of the reflexive, dynamic literacy practice which resonates with both Grayson Perry in the British Museum and all of us in social media. Two findings emerged as most prominent—(1) that pedagogic literacy practices of museum curation are bound up in the personal histories and transition points of practitioners and (2) that the curation of social history cannot be separated from experiences of struggle, loss and adversity and as such curation can never be separated from the personal and is never 'neutral'.

Despite the deeply reflexive articulations by the curators participating in the project, the three museums discussed in the *Comrades and Curators* project offered limited potential for transformation, despite the radical history being curated in different ways, due to the 'heavy second spaces' they each move their visitors through.

7.4 Flipped Roles, Shifting Structures: The Museum of Homelessness

The Museum of Homelessness (MoH) was founded in 2015 and exhibits artefacts and curates the narration of related stories in an equal relation. The museum is now in a physical location, in Finsbury Park, London (see Fig. 7.1), but was previously nomadic and sometimes virtual or blended. MoH is a community-led organisation combining the practices of a working 'social justice museum' with activism. The latter is manifested in curation, rather than the object of it, as with the Tolpuddle museum, for example:

> We've really tried to be careful about how we think of it, because curators hold so much power. (Jessica Turtle, Museum of Homelessness, in Greig 2020)

The objectives of the museum are to curate a national collection for homelessness (in this sense the 'of' in the name may be out of step) and for the museum to generate and be a form itself of activism in support of the homeless community. The museum's curation of 'object stories'—live performances of narratives from people with direct lived experience of homelessness—has its origin in a collaboration with the 'objects' of the exhibition, the artefacts and people with experience of homeless thus in this dynamic subject–object third space relation.

Nomadic for its first decade, MoH curated 'pop up' exhibitions, beginning at Beaconsfield Gallery Vauxhall in 2016. This was the outcome of the organisation training people who had experienced homelessness in storytelling, theming,

Fig. 7.1 MoH sign. Physical space, place of refuge

object curation, design and labelling. Expansion followed with a weekend at Tate Modern, for State of the Nation consisting of speakers, workshops, performances and installations, again all planned and realised by people with experience of homelessness.

The museum's growing archive of objects is symbolic of the key themes curated—finding refuge, sharing resources, questioning everything, building community and rewriting the future. Some examples are a naloxone kit, the emergency antidote for a drug overdose, a trolley used to distribute emergency supplies during the pandemic, a stick carved over time for stability and protection, a paper swan made by a detainee in Yarl's Wood Immigration Removal Centre, a bed donated by a winter homelessness shelter worker, a fabric banner an activist involved in the Focus E15 campaign in east London had used to show solidarity with rough sleepers in Stratford and a steel pot used on soup runs. A black bin bag is given curational prominence, received with emotional familiarity by visitors with the shared lived experience. Disposable for the majority, environmentally infamous, the bin bag has a special status among this community for its insulation and water-resistant properties, for keeping a person warm and their possessions dry. These objects are stored in boxes on shelves in the museum's main space now it has its permanent home. This is an archive of items donated as pivotal symbols in the experience of homelessness or given by community members to one another, connoting support, critical moments in resilience and trust.

MoH describes its approach to curation, crucially, as 'centering' (and paying) people with lived experience, in order to situate people experiencing homelessness as curators *and* custodians, as opposed to themselves being artefacts to be understood. In this, we can see the shift from curating artefacts to the more dynamic 'artefactual literacy' which we associate with the third space. But going further, the museum's activism is not only about lobbying for direct action to intervene in homelessness and uplifting the voices of those with experience, but also to deconstruct and oppose the practices of cultural institutions:

> We can't expect museums whose histories are steeped in elitism and oppression to be the voice of a new culture being ushered in. We need to mount alternatives, and starve the legacy institutions of their revenue. This is why these smaller museums are so interesting. If there isn't a museum that represents your community, then make one. (Turtle 2020)

The museum has no separate existence in isolation from its life as a community space, so that the people it exists to support gain a direct, physical and relational benefit from it. The museum thus curates homelessness as both a validated experience and a crisis to be resolved, but the crisis is for us all—'the apocalypse'. This is designed as a transformative experience through the ways in which visitors' habitus comes into contact with these lived experiences as both artefacts and 'resources of hope'—engaging with, and learning about, homelessness as a hitherto un-curated heritage (Youde 2017). The transformative experience is thus embodied and personalised through the encounter with the museum's 'artefactual curators'. This is the third space.

The community, in both narrating and curating their homelessness, make connections between their lived experiences and historical and policy events as these structural relations are deconstructed in the act of textualising. Counter-representation works here alongside a kind of radical pedagogy of validation, and we can see in these practices the kinds of rich exchanges described, and advocated for, in the work of Bhaba and Guitterez. During the nomadic phase as a 'street museum', this offered both a way to exhibit and provide food and resources, this being an extension of the modus operandi 'praxis' of the museum.

It is important to stress the ethical work done here, as the core objective of the museum is to avoid any possibility of exploitation or 'poverty tourism'. For this reason, actors narrate participants' experiences and the meanings they make with artefacts, working from recordings, thus removing the need to share traumatic memories in public. In all of these ways, the museum's '*engagement with the subsistence struggles of unhoused communities has led to an ethos of flexibility and responsiveness to its community's needs, reflective of a larger, growing movement to reconfigure museums as spaces for civic engagement and community service*' (O'Brassill-Kulfan 2023).

7.5 Transformative Relations

As this chapter was written, the museum was conducting its opening programme in its new physical location: *How to Survive the Apocalypse: Wisdoms from our Community*. As visitors pass through the spaces, and thus the narrative, we are given a ribbon (see Fig. 7.2) for each themed space or performance—refuge, resources, questioning, community and solidarity, hope for the future.

Fig. 7.2 Ribbons. The museum of homelessness: resources of hope

We begin in the community garden, outside the museum's location in the old ranger's house in the park (see Fig. 7.3)—itself the subject of a community history. Going indoors, we see a screening from a pirate radio associate, then move into the main space where we encounter the archive, stored in boxes, reached by ladders and extracted for the storytelling (see Fig. 7.4).

Fig. 7.3 Assembly point sign. Curation—surviving the apocalypse

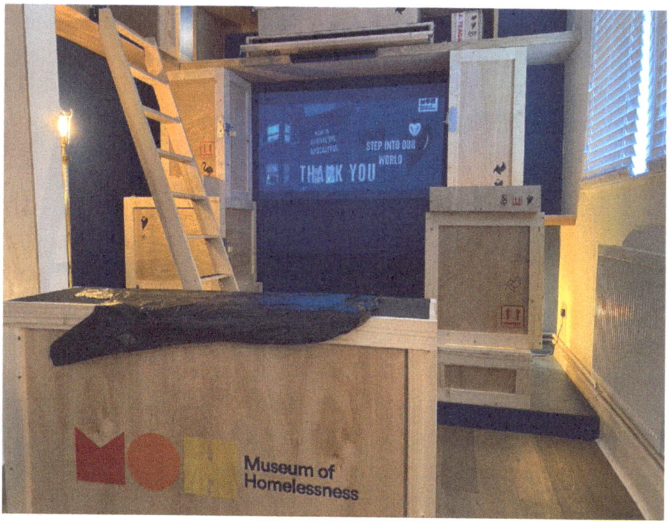

Fig. 7.4 Main space image. With the archive

In each space, community members present stories, with objects. These objects are both directly significant to the donator's experience of homelessness and symbolic in their representation of the survival 'tips' we are given. If a visitor's expectation is for a more conventionally curational and second space pedagogical encounter with the subject of the 'of' in the museum's name, the experience of learning about resources, resilience, connection and solidarity *from*, or *with*, but not 'of', decentre this framing. The experience is in a reciprocal relation with visitors' (future) first spaces.

In this museum, visitors are immersed in the third space immediately, as the storying of each curated object is followed by the expectation of a verbal response, not only to the wisdom imparted but also to share lived experience. As we move through each space … we soon come to understand that we are learning, not 'about' homelessness, but about the skills and values we will ourselves need to survive an apocalypse. In this way, the museum curates through:

> … an approach that looks to smash the traditional model of glass cases and guarded access, we instead present our objects through a tour that includes performance, poetry, object handling, chats, and much more… visitors should expect to have a better chance of surviving the apocalypse after a glimpse into our world. We can offer no guarantees, but in the words of one of the guides to our show: 'Our solidarity is our most potent weapon'. (Museum of Homelessness 2024)

Visitors with experience of homelessness can, if they wish, share their own stories, talk about objects which equate, provide other survival strategies. Those from relative privilege can reflect on what they are learning, or ask questions for deeper understanding. In a sense, this can be the same as a more conventional pedagogic encounter, such as asking the guide in the Shire Hall about the Tolpuddle story, or for more explanation of magic lanterns in the Bill Douglas archive. Except it isn't, because the invitation is not to ask, but respond, reflect, interpret in the moment. To bring, take away, in a transformative relation. Every visitor's response shifts the curation, to be unique, deeply situated in the dialogue. Every visitor will experience a shift in their own encounter with the 'of', this could not be avoided. The third space membrane, in action.

The Museum of Homelessness transforms. In one sense, it has the exact same intention as *Children's Lives*. It seeks to ask 'what is the experience of homelessness?' It wants visitors to engage in the same way, with an archive of the 'topic'. The fact that we were or are all children, whilst some of us are fortunate enough to never be homeless, but many of the visitors to the latter experience have been or are, is of course a huge distinction. However, at the same time, the intention to present the question, to engage the visitor in a reflexive encounter between the gallery and their first spaces—of childhood and of living conditions, is different to an intention to present a static display of the thing in question.

It is reasonable to suggest that all museums *intend* a dynamic pedagogy, a third space. Through the textual articulation methods used in the *Comrades* project, the curators all conveyed this hope. However, the potential to achieve this kind of transformation resides in the curational practices, the extent of the claim for a story, or a theme, or an experience, shared or other or both, to be 'known'—*through* a gaze, the question—'what is?'—reinforced, albeit unanswered, or more or less challenged.

The Museum of Homelessness seems different. It seems to want us to learn *from* the 'of', immersion in the space, this third space, not to learn *about* homelessness but *from* those who have been or are, or are sometimes homeless—categories deliberately ambiguous, for what we need ourselves, for our first space survival. The transformative experience is generated by this museum being at once *about* a community from which and whom we have much to learn, or of which we may be part, before, now or in the future and also in how this museum is *of* and *for* and *is*.

References

Bhabha H (1994) The location of culture. Routledge, London

Birmingham Museum and Art Gallery (2012) Children's Lives Exhibition Guide

Bourdieu P (1984) Distinction: a social critique of the judgement of taste. Routledge, London

Calvi L, Vermeeren L, Sabiescu A (2024) Transforming the museum experience. Springer, Switzerland

DiGiovanna R (2015) Neither here nor there: borrowed bodies, third space, and the museum. Pursuit J Undergrad Res Univ Tennessee 6(1). Article 9

Du J, Cui M (2021) Intercultural dialogues in third spaces: a study of learning experiences of museum visitors. J Transcult Commun. https://doi.org/10.1515/jtc-2021-2007

Gee JP (2015) The new literacy studies. In: Rowsell J, Pahl K (eds) The Routledge handbook of literacy studies. Routledge, London

Greig J (2020) Inside the museum examining Britain's homelessness crisis. Vice, 8.10.20. https://www.vice.com/en/article/m7jyex/museum-of-homelessness-london-uk

Gutierrez K (2008) Developing a sociocultural literacy in the third space. Read Res Q 43:148–164

McDavitt S, McDougall J (2023) Media literacy in the third space school library. J Media Lit Spec Issue
McDougall J (2019) Comrades and curators. J Vis Lit 38(4):245–261
McDougall J, O'Connor J (2015) 'Orphans and rich people': a critical analysis of the 'children's lives' exhibition in Birmingham, UK' in children and society 29:321–330. https://doi.org/10.1111/chso.12025
Museum of Homelessness. London. Accessed 21.6.24. https://museumofhomelessness.org/
O'Brassill-Kulfan K (2023) Interpreting and commemorating homelessness and poverty. Public Hist. https://online.ucpress.edu/tph/article/45/1/25/195210/People-First-Interpreting-and-Commemorating
Perry G (2011) The tomb of the unknown craftsman. The British Museum Press, London
Potter J (2012) Digital media and learner identity: the new curatorship. Palgrave MacMillan, New York
Potter J, McDougall J (2017) Digital media, education and culture: theorising third space literacy. Palgrave MacMillan, London
Silverman LH (2009) The social work of museums. Routledge, Oxon
Talboys GK (2011) Museum educator's handbook. Routledge, Farnham
Youde K (2017) Homelessness: a history. Inside Housing, 02.08.17. https://www.insidehousing.co.uk/insight/insight

Julian McDougall (he/his) is Professor in Media and Education at Bournemouth University and a writer/researcher in media literacy and media education. He is co-editor of the *Journal of Media Literacy Education* and *Routledge Research in Media Literacy and Education*, Chair of the Media and Information Literacy Alliance, media literacy consultant with Ofcom and advisor to the UK Government All Party Parliamentary Group on Political and Media Literacy. His latest book has been published by Palgrave in 2025—*Media Literacy for the Communication Ecosystem: A Theory of Change for a Healthier Future.*

Chapter 8
Exhibiting Conflict as a Transformative Strategy: Writing Contemporary History with the Local Community

Emilie Sitzia

Abstract In 2018, in the popular neighbourhood of Noailles in Marseille, buildings collapsed in the rue d'Aubagne. Tragically, eight people died. In the month that followed, around 4500 people were evacuated from buildings deemed by the municipality as too dangerous to live in. Chains and locks were installed overnight, locking the inhabitants, often from low-income communities out of their homes. These locks, which were meant to keep inhabitants safe, became the symbol of the municipality's lack of care for infrastructure, the trauma of inhabitants and the social divide of Marseille. Civil society asked the Musée d'histoire de la ville de Marseille to integrate this history into the institution, to memorialise these events. Since then, the association "Noailles Debout" has been working with the Musée d'histoire de la ville de Marseille and with the wider public to create a polyvocal exhibition where objects such as the chain and lock are presented as a *chose commune* (a shared object) and are surrounded by multiple voices to capture various facets of this crisis. The museum thereby becomes a space where conflict is exhibited, where points of view clash and are put into dialogue. It becomes a space where transformative learning can take place. In this chapter, I propose to explore the working process, the collection process, and the tools used to display multiple narratives in the museum space. I will pay particular attention to the transformative impact of such a practice on the institution itself, on the participants and on audiences.

8.1 Introduction

In 2018, in the popular neighbourhood of Noailles in Marseille, buildings collapsed in the rue d'Aubagne. Tragically, eight people died. In the month that followed, around 4500 people were evacuated from buildings the municipality deemed too

E. Sitzia
University of Amsterdam, Amsterdam, The Netherlands

E. Sitzia (✉)
Maastricht University, Maastricht, The Netherlands
e-mail: emilie.sitzia@maastrichtuniversity.nl

L. Calvi et al. (eds.), *Transformative Museum Experiences*, Springer Series on Cultural Computing, https://doi.org/10.1007/978-3-031-89521-0_8

dangerous to live in. Chains and locks were installed overnight, locking the inhabitants, often from low-income communities, out of their homes. Inhabitants were often given no more than 10 min to pack what they could before being barred, often permanently, from their homes. These locks and chains were meant to keep inhabitants safe; however, they also became the symbol of the municipality's lack of care for infrastructure, of the conflict between the municipality and the inhabitants, of the trauma of inhabitants and of the social divide of Marseille.

Following these events, civil society asked the Musée d'histoire de la ville de Marseille (MHM) to integrate this trauma into the history of the city told in that institution; that is, to memorialise this conflict between the local population and the municipality. They wanted to make sure this event would not be forgotten as many building collapses had already happened in the past in working-class areas in Marseille. Since then, the association "Noailles Debout" has been working with the MHM and the wider public to create an evolutive polyvocal exhibition where objects such as the chain and lock are presented as a *chose commune* (Fig. 8.1) and are surrounded by multiple voices to capture various facets of this crisis. In this way, the museum becomes a space where conflict is exhibited, where points of view clash and are put into dialogue. It thus becomes a space where transformative learning can take place.

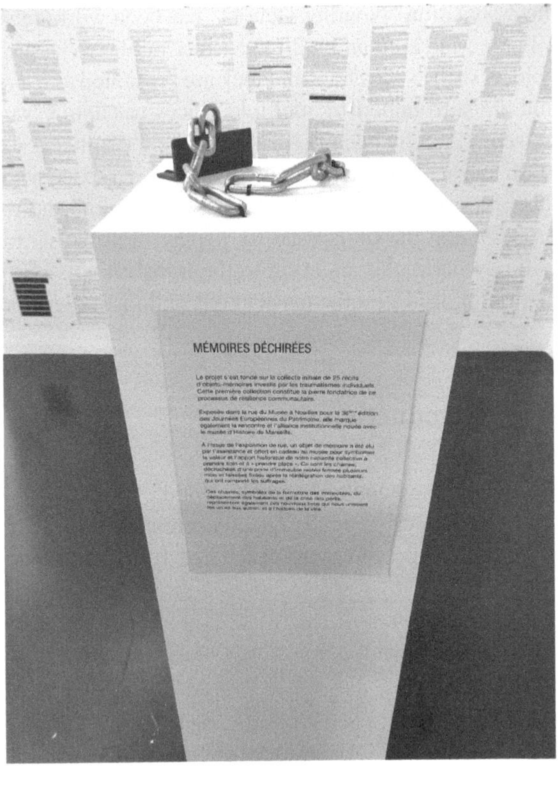

Fig. 8.1 Torn memories, exhibition of chains at the Musée de la ville de Marseille. Photo Emilie Sitzia

The foregoing example at the MHM fits within a wider theorisation of museums that dates back to the early 2000s. More specifically, museums have recently been acknowledged as a cultural battlefield (Borg and Mayo 2010, p. 37; Black 2005) and places of agonism (Mouffe 2016). The transformative potential of museums as sites of sharing, writing and rewriting history has been recognised (Lynch 2011; Janes and Sandell 2019), and they have been hailed as potential agents of change (Sandell 2003; Coffee 2008; Sandell and Nightingale 2012; Golding and Modest 2013). Despite this theoretical recognition, however, in practice, cultural institutions often shy away from conflict or the representation of conflictual history, instead looking for consensus narratives. Situated between the theorisation of the museum as an agent of change and the real-world tendency to seek consensus narratives, the MHM's exhibition described here provides a useful case study to test theories of transformative learning and the place conflict can have within this process.

This study is timely, too, as it comes at a moment when society is increasingly polarised and histories have difficulties coexisting in exhibition spaces. In this light, it seems important to reiterate Schulman's (2017) point that "conflict is not abuse." Often, to start repair and redress processes, such conflicts need to be exhibited and acknowledged. Instead of being seen as destructive or dangerous, conflict (at least in some form) should be seen as an integral part of transformative learning experiences. Whether we are thinking of the acquisition of women's voting rights, the end of Apartheid, the HIV crisis, the legalisation of same-sex marriage, for example, we see that conflict is part of deep individual and societal changes.

When investigating transformative learning experiences, Duerden and Rossman's interdisciplinary study on *Designing Experiences* (2019) provides helpful categorisation insights. Writing about experience participants, the authors distinguish between memorable experiences triggered by emotion (p. 36) and meaningful experiences that provide insights about ourselves and the world that are triggered by a sense of discovery. They note that "meaningful experiences are often the result of co-creation in which participants play an active engaged role in the experience" (Duerden and Rossman 2019, p. 37). Meaningful experiences allows for a shared social experience as well as leaves room for personal reflection.

According to Duerden and Rossman, the trigger for short- or long-term change can also create a transformational experience, which goes further than the meaningful experiences just described, as it offers perspective, attitude or behavioural change. It is not clear from their research if emotion, discovery, and change are a consequence of the experiences or if they are a necessary ingredient to trigger the experiences, or if they are both. They also highlight that there is a need for the repetition of one or two micro-experiences for transformation to take place (p. 39). In any case, it seems that conflict should be able to serve as a trigger for such transformational experiences as it often involves an emotional charge, a discovery/surprise and potentially leads to a shift in behaviour at an individual or societal level. In Schulman's book (2017), talking about conflicts during the HIV crisis, she highlights that through conflict "attitude, treatment, laws, have been transformed in significant ways" (p. 23). Indeed, conflict when looked at through a transformative lens is part of an individual and social growth process. Such conflicts can be seen as transformative triggers or what Jarvis calls "disjunctures."

Indeed, literature on learning in general and on transformative learning in particular sheds some more light on the transformative process. Peter Jarvis writes that "all human learning begins with disjuncture—with either an overt question or with a sense of unknowing" (Jarvis 2009, p. 22). For him, social interaction and this disjunction moment are essential to processes of learning (see Fig. 8.2). According to Jarvis, a person takes the life-world for granted until that individual is confronted with a disjuncture. This disjuncture then needs to be given meaning and a resolution to be practised. This allows the individual to readjust their perception of the world and carry on taking the life-world for granted, having integrated new knowledge. Conflict is a form of disjunction where the life-world of two individuals, or of individuals and institutions clash. As such (and if a resolution is practised), it can potentially trigger learning processes.

Building on Mezirow (2006, 2009), Illeris proposes a definition of transformative learning that is somewhat broader and links transformative learning and matters of identity more firmly. He identifies the target area of transformative learning (that which is transformed) as covering "the cognitive, the emotional, and the social dimensions" (Illeris 2014, p. 151). In conflict, all three aspects are engaged. Looking at this theory, conflict can serve as a trigger to learning that would have an impact on the cognitive, emotional, and social dimension leading to deep change in the identity of an individual or an institution. This can potentially offer "self-actualisation experiences" (Gaggioli 2016, p. 97); that is, a transformational opportunity. But how can museums facilitate this process?

In this chapter, I want to investigate how exhibiting conflict can become a transformative strategy. To do so, in Sect. 8.2, I will explore the working process, the collection process and the tools used to display multiple narratives in the case of the MHM. In Sect. 8.3, I will pay particular attention to the transformative impact

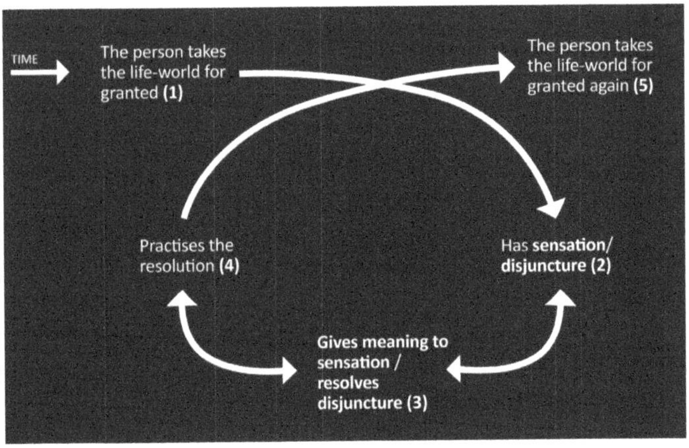

Fig. 8.2 Learning according to Peter Jarvis, design Bullitt identity

of such a practice on the institution itself, and I will also discuss its impact on the participants and on audiences.

8.2 Conflict in the Museum in Practice

Conflicts are not equal in terms of their transformational potential. Conflict can only become a learning opportunity if it is perceived as a disjuncture, if it questions the frames, the life-world order of the learner and it leads them to practising a resolution. In the case of the rue d'Aubagne, the conflict between the inhabitants and the municipality was impactful as it called into question the cognitive, social, and emotional order of the inhabitants. Indeed, and as noted above, to protect the population, 4500 inhabitants were made homeless by the Marseille municipal authority. The social security that the municipality was expected to provide inhabitants with disappeared behind what was felt to be unjust and police-driven actions to keep the inhabitants away from their (albeit dangerous) homes. The inhabitants' sense that "the city has a duty to protect us" clashed with the actions of the municipality: the inhabitant's cognitive knowledge about the municipality's role, their sense of social security, and their emotional stability were all destabilised. At all three levels, the conflict with the municipality destabilised the life-world the inhabitants took for granted. The disjuncture was further complicated as the conflict was also not (solely) individual; rather, it was between a group of individuals in a tight-knit neighbourhood and the municipality. Yet, as often in Marseille, as the sense of injustice spread, other inhabitants also mobilised in solidarity.

This sense of injustice was coupled with a duty of remembrance. As the director of the Museum, Fabrice Denise, remembers, the inhabitants were collectively animated by:

> the fear of forgetting, the fear that there would be a collective amnesia and that in 50 years' time there would be no more talk of 5 November 2018. Because in fact, when they were consulting archives, they came across building collapses in the 19th century, structural collapses that killed people and that nobody is talking about today. It was a traumatic shock for them to say to themselves: "For God's sake, if we don't talk about this thing that happened in 1868, we won't be talking about what happened in 2018, once the media has had its day and four or five mayors of Marseille have come and gone, we won't be talking about it anymore. So how do we ensure that it is remembered?" Well, we have to do something with a museum. You see, the process is pragmatic.[1]

With this joint decision to collaborate to memorialise the events (which is a form of giving meaning to the disjuncture/conflict), the dialogue between the inhabitants, the MHM, and the municipal authorities could begin. The following considers this

---

[1] Unless otherwise noted, all quotes are taken from an interview between the author and the MHM director, Fabrice Denise, held on 19 January 2024. While the events described started in 2018, the participatory process with the museum took place over a longer period of time. This process finished with a participatory de-installation of the exhibition in January 2024. The interview was done at this point to be able to consider the process in its entirety.

history and its transformative potential from the point of view of the processes and people, the objects and the exhibition strategies.

8.2.1 Working with Conflict: Processes, People, and Transformation

The Musée d'histoire de la ville de Marseille was chosen for a number of reasons but certainly the fact that it is financed by the municipality itself played a role. The museum was then seen as a symbolic space to take over, to call the municipality, to start a process of acknowledgment and repair memory, to give meaning to the events, and to some measure resolve the conflict.

At the beginning of the process, the inhabitants' collective[2] was accompanied by museum expert Christine Breton. She was already in contact with the local population and was experienced with participatory practice and was asked to help by the collective. According to the director Denise, Breton acted as mediator between the population and the institution. As Denise reports, Breton

> told them, if you want to talk to museums, if you want museums to build collections, you can't just go at it in any old way. Because the museum is a system, it's an administrative, cultural and scientific system [...]. And there's a particular language you have to speak to the museum, if you want to be understood by the museum. If you attack them [...] in a brutal way, that is of no interest to them, by being purely vindictive, it won't work. On the other hand, if you go about it in a more skilful, constructive and co-constructive way, it will work.

The collective then decided to work with a democratic selection process and voted to select the object to be brought to the museum. They then organised a symbolic walk from the neighbourhood "rue du musée" (Museum Street) to the museum to bring the memorial object, the chains, to the museum during the 2019 European Heritage Days. The object was received by the director of the museum as a gift.

The museum director also played an important role as he accepted the gift and participated in the symbolic process that went with it. He de-escalated the situation with the municipality by emphasising that the process of the local population gifting objects to the museum was nothing new and was part of the usual collection policy of the museum—even though he was very aware that such an object had a different political, emotional, and symbolic charge. Also, when the local government of the municipality changed following the 2020 elections, the director saw the opportunity to expand and anchor the project in the institution and let the museum play its

---

[2] The inhabitants' collective started as a group of local individuals that wanted the memory of what happened in the neighbourhood to be memorialised. They worked with Manifesta, the European Nomadic Biennal (https://manifesta13.org/index.html) as a catalyst of local voices by organising the selection of the symbolic object brought to the museum in the "rue du musée" event (see below). In 2020, they became a formal 'association' so they could work more fluidly with the city's institutions. Their main goal is to promote cultural production, heritage creation, and inhabitants' participation in urban policymaking.

role of repair. In the cycle of transformative learning, this symbolic process can be understood as "giving meaning" to the disjuncture/conflict.

The inhabitants' collective also changed shape over the course of the exhibition and its planning. It started as a resident's collective and was then transformed into a traditional association with a single charismatic head. The association then shifted to a new form of governance with multiple vice-heads to ensure shared power/visibility.[3]

An agreement was signed between the new municipality and the association, anchoring the partnership between them, the museum, and the new municipality, thereby giving the project an administrative structure and (limited but welcome) financial means. More importantly, however, the agreement's text contains an acknowledgement from the municipality of the trauma rendered by the collapse and the following conflict with the municipality. To some extent, this text can be seen as the municipality taking responsibility for the conflict and looking for a solution to mend the relationship with the population and acknowledging the role of the association in creating collective resilience. In the cycle of transformative learning, this partnership can be understood as "practising resolution" both on the part of the municipality and on the part of the inhabitants. The agreement text mentions explicitly that:

> The tragedy of the collapse of the buildings at 63 and 65 rue d'Aubagne on 5 November 2018 is an event that will forever mark the history of the city and the memories of the residents of Noailles, a district in the historic heart of Marseille.
>
> The disaster was a traumatic event on a collective scale, highlighting the humanitarian crisis facing residents of substandard housing in Marseille. Among the many citizen initiatives that sprang up in reaction and response to this trauma, there was one that quickly caught the attention of the Musée d'Histoire de Marseille. This is the "Rue du Musée/Musée de la rue" project led by the Noailles Debout Association, which since the collapses of 5 November 2018 has been developing an approach aimed at questioning the place and role of local residents in the construction of their city: a citizens' initiative, the popular naming of the Place du 5-Novembre, exhibitions, publications, collections, urban events, etc. These initiatives are based on the need to organise a process of collective resilience among residents, enabling them to:
>
> - overcome the trauma by writing it into a recognised collective history;
> - maintain links and cohesion within the community and with the outside world;
> - anticipate risks and organise innovative responses.[4]

---

[3] They were also supported in that work by other more experienced associations, such as the association Hotel du Nord.

[4] A copy of the convention Convention de Partenariat entre la ville de Marseille et l'association Noailles Debout! pour le project «rue du musée/Musée de la rue» (2023), unpublished, was kindly provided by the MHM. Extract translation by the author:
«Le drame des effondrements des immeubles des 63 et 65 de la rue d'Aubagne, le 5 novembre 2018, est un événement qui marquera à jamais l'histoire de la ville et la mémoire des habitants de Noailles, quartier du cœur historique de Marseille. Cette catastrophe a constitué un événement traumatique d'une ampleur collective mettant en exergue la crise humanitaire que vivent les habitants de logements indignes marseillais.
Parmi les très nombreuses initiatives citoyennes qui sont nées en réaction et en réponse â ce traumatisme, il en est une qui a rapidement concerné le Musée d'Histoire de Marseille. Il s'agit du projet «Rue du Musée/Musée de la rue» porté par l'Association Noailles Debout qui développe

What we see here are transformative processes rather than output. The conflict and trauma triggered processes of memorialisation on the part of the inhabitants (meaning-making), who were transformed from complainants into active memory builders. The intervention of key bridge people (Breton between the inhabitants' collective and the museum, and Denise as a bridge between the inhabitants' collective and the municipality) smoothed the process. The museum was transformed from a place of memory to a place for grieving and reconciliation (also a process of meaning-making). The municipality was also transformed from an antagonist to an enabler of memorialisation. The agreement and the work with the museum "writing history" finalises the transformative learning process by "practising resolution." In all these processes, we see the cognitive, emotional, and social weaved together and mobilised through symbolic events, objects, and texts. We see here Illeris' multidimensional conceptualisation of transformative learning (2014) in action and strong links become visible between transformative learning and matters of identity.

8.2.2 Collecting Conflict: Object, Collection, and Balancing Voices

In such a context, the importance of the representativity of the object exhibited is paramount as it becomes a symbol for the conflict. It is interesting that in our case the first object to be brought to the museum originated from a vote. As Denise explained, this means that it's an object "that already comes from a jury. It's already a jury, just as we, the regional scientific acquisition commissions, have gone through exactly the same procedure of objects, arguments, ballots, and the result of a vote that democratically designates an object." This collective aspect is important, with the chain and lock holding significance (cognitive, emotional, and social) for all the inhabitants. Participants were very attached to participatory democracy principles and in the event of disagreements there was, according to Denise, an agreed principle that "all objects, as long as that object was inscribed in a value chain and in the narration of one inhabitant, any object had its place in the exhibition."

For this collecting of objects aspect, the director also insisted throughout the process on the long-term partnership and the uneven pace of the collection of objects,

---

depuis les effondrements du 5 novembre 2018 une démarche visant à interroger la place et le rôle des habitants dans la construction de leur ville: dynamique citoyenne, baptême populaire de la place du 5-Novembre, expositions, publications, collectes, animations urbaines etc. Ces démarches reposent sur la nécessité d'organiser un processus de résilience collective des habitants permettant de:

- *dépasser le traumatisme par son inscription narrative dans une histoire collective reconnue;*
- *maintenir les liens et la cohésion au sein de la communauté avec l'extérieur;*
- *anticiper les risques et organiser des réponses innovantes.»*

which was undertaken over the project's three-year duration, without pressure on the part of the museum. There was an awareness from the museum that

> if we had roughed up our colleagues, our partners, a little by saying to them, well, listen, every three months there has to be one more object, […] there's got to be documentation. […] I think we would have lost them, quite clearly. So we understood that the timeframe was different. So here we had a space for research, [which is] long. And it's a time with periods of doubt, periods of retreat, periods of acceleration.

Finally, the balance between the collective and the personal was an important part of the process of object selection. The objects were complemented by personal accounts, drawings, oral testimonies, objects that have been lent or donated or artistic projects carried out in the city at the time (Fig. 8.3).

This variety demonstrates the importance of polyvocality in the exhibition. It recognised that while having a collective aspect, the experience nevertheless stayed deeply individual. In particular, the recording of witness accounts (2 h of narration by the inhabitants that could be consulted in the exhibition space) created an individualised emotional framework for the objects themselves. Similarly, labels written from the perspective of a specific inhabitant created a direct link to the individuals in the community. This insistence on repeated long-term collection of objects and multiple events around the exhibition link to Duerden and Rossman's (2019) stance on the importance of repetition to anchor the transformative learning results.

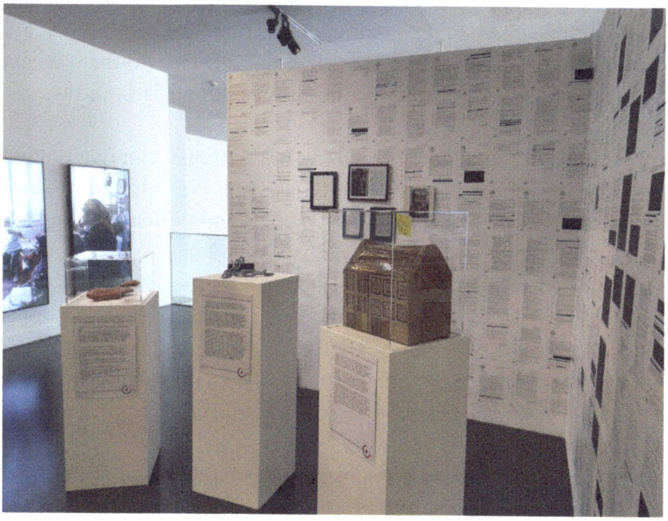

Fig. 8.3 Exhibition installation shot containing the chains, roof tiles, and a cardboard house (and accompanying story from inhabitants on the labels) as well as interview extracts and documentation at the Musée de la ville de Marseille. Photo Emilie Sitzia

8.2.3 Exhibiting Conflict: Space, Time, and Dispositives[5]

The first dimension that comes into play in the transformative experience of the MHM's exhibition is the museum space. The museum is located in a shopping centre, which already gives it a peculiar status inside the city. Unlike other Marseille institutions, it is weaved in the daily life of the city.

Furthermore, the museum has a specific section dedicated to participatory projects (section 13), which the director identifies as a strength, as the museum "had the intuition and ingenious idea of reserving a space that would be filled and emptied according to the participatory projects with local residents." Denise further explains that by keeping this space available, "there's a little empty shell that fills up, depending on opportunities for collaboration, either from the museum to the city, or from the city to the museum." This space, a sort of dialogue box with the city, allows the institution to give space to the local communities inside the museum.

Moreover, there is further porosity between the museum and the rest of the city that was particularly acute throughout the project. For example, the chain and lock were first exhibited during Manifesta in another city-owned building.[6] Similarly, another flagship object, the model of the neighbourhood created in 2019 by students at the Marseille School of Architecture (Fig. 8.4), who had been affected by what had happened on rue d'Aubagne, was presented around the city and in bars and in the local town hall before joining the museum's collection.

Finally, at the end of the exhibition period, after a participatory deinstallation of the exhibition, a human chain of the inhabitants carried the objects to the local branch of the city hall where the exhibition will next be shown. This porosity of space makes the narratives accessible and places the museum as holder but not owner of objects or the narrative.

The second dimension that came into play in the transformative potential of this exhibition was the treatment of time. From the start, the exhibition was envisaged as evolutive, like multiple "acts" to a play. The first embodiment of the exhibition—that is, "Act 1 taking place"—was followed by Acts 2 and 3, which relaunched the exhibition every 5 November. It inscribed itself in memorial time (the anniversary of the traumatic event) rather than in museum time (a new exhibition every six months or so). It allowed for micro-experiences of transformation as well as the gradual building and rebalancing of the narrative. This also allowed for the "practice of the resolution," as per Jarvis's model, at different times, reinforcing change and anchoring it in the longer term.

Finally, the exhibition dispositive put in place provided a structured experience for the visitors. While the museum helped and facilitated certain modes of presenting the

---

[5] The term dispositive is used here in reference to Foucault. In an exhibition context, it is understood as the discourse carried by an exhibition explicitly (through text in labels, audio material, videos, etc.) but also non-explicitly (exhibition design choices, juxtaposition of objects, architecture, unsaid rules, etc.). It allows for a holistic examination of an exhibition and its impact on visitors.

[6] Manifesta 13, Musée Grobet-Labadié, 2019, https://manifesta13.org/fr/participants/noailles-debout/index.html.

Fig. 8.4 Model of Noailles neighbourhood made by the students of the Marseille School of Architecture and screen with interviews of inhabitants reacting to the chains at the Musée de la ville de Marseille. Photo Emilie Sitzia

material, they didn't overly interfere in the form. Strategies of direct engagement with the individual members of the inhabitants' collective were favoured. Audio tracks, written witness accounts, and video interviews were all designed to foster empathy and individualise the discourse. An emotional form of polyvocality was aimed at. This dispositive structured the experience of the visitors, but because they were quite different from other exhibition strategies in the museum, they also disoriented and surprised them. Indeed, the museum otherwise presents a relatively classical historical collection of objects in a relatively classical didactic manner (even if an effort is made to use technology to enhance a relatively academic and monovocal discourse).[7] The kinds of objects, the scenography and the polyvocality of the "rue d'Aubagne" part of the museum certainly stand out.

8.3 Transformative Impact of Conflict in Museum

In the previous section, I have established how conflict can act as a trigger to transformative learning and play a role in the process, the collection of objects, and the display dispositive. The following part will also now focus on the transformation experiences, looking at the long-term view of the stakeholders. The exhibition of conflict at the Musee d'histoire de la ville de Marseille led to a change of perspective,

[7] Objects to be found range from Greek and Roman amphoras to remnants of boat or religious sculptures covering 2600 years of history in 13 chronological sequences.

attitude or behaviour for the institution, participants and visitors.[8] In the following, I briefly consider the impact on each of these groups.

8.3.1 The Institution

When engaging in such participatory practices and to some extent in museum activism, literature establishes that institutions often gain relevance, polyvocality and new narratives, and a contribution to social justice (Simon 2016; Golding and Modest 2013; Coffee 2008; Janes and Sandell 2019; Sitzia 2017, 2023). But beyond this, this case study shows that the institution came out of this experience transformed in several other ways.

First, its relationship to time has been modified. This is evidenced by the director, who recounted that we "learned to work with our eyes a little less on the clock," knowing "that this project would have to mature slowly, that it was a project that would find its place." This work process also sometimes required the institution to ignore municipal standard administrative processes that were unsuitable to this timescale.

Second, the institution also gained a new place as a space of negotiation with the political world and as a place of repair for the city government, which also involves accepting emotions as part of its role. The museum director identifies the opening of the exhibition as "a very, very strong time," explaining that when "the families, the victims, started arriving at the museum [...] you really understood what heritage meant. And you see the memorial side of things [...]. That's when you really get to grips with the power of the museum institution and this idea of remembering and of the museum in mourning, you see it for what it means."

Third, ways of working were also permanently changed. The institution's staff learned about participatory practice and working with civil society. As Denise (2024) articulates, "for us, there will be a before and an after, and we'll also have increased our skills in these ways of doing things." Denise also observes, "what really makes us strong at the History Museum is our ability to combine the experimental with things that are a little more traditional and a little more conventional. And we put the same energy into it. The processes are not the same, but the energy, the convictions, the professionalism, and the commitment are the same. After that, it takes very different forms, of course."

[8] There were also changes for the municipality; however, as there was a complete change of government, this is harder to evaluate and therefore not undertaken here.

8.3.2 *The Participants*

For the participants engaged in co-creating an exhibition, the transformation is partly emancipation, partly empowerment through visibility (Sitzia 2017, 2019, 2023). A large part of the transformative learning experience, in that particular case, consisted of learning the language and processes of the museum. Furthermore, the initial conflict with the municipality meant learning to co-construct with the institution rather than taking a combative stance and allowed participants to become makers of institutionalised memory. The participants through this practice therefore understood and accessed the symbolic power of the museum through their own creation and documentation of the collection (Fig. 8.5). Furthermore, participants took an active part in cultural democracy as they became the mediators and tour guides of the exhibition. They became agents of change within and outside the institution.

Fig. 8.5 Post-it calling for new objects to be gifted in the exhibition space of the Musée de la ville de Marseille. Photo Emilie Sitzia

8.3.3 *The Audiences*

While in the design of the exhibition, there was a desire to raise awareness, empathy, and move visitors to action, and the results were more mitigated. Indeed, as the exhibition was placed within a more traditional, overarching history museum narrative, mediation was not always clear and efficient. There was a need to understand what this exhibition was about, regardless of whether visitors were tourists or inhabitants.

Overall, the director identified three main attitudes or audience responses. First, there were visitors that had limited or no awareness of the participatory project, who encountered the exhibition at the end of their visit and were possibly not transformed or intrigued, and thus didn't engage with the content. Second, there were visitors intrigued by the originality of the form/presentation who were then absorbed by the content and whose empathy was triggered by the exhibition dispositive. These visitors certainly had what Duerden and Rossman qualify as a memorable and possibly meaningful experience as they discovered the conflict and the points of view of the inhabitants. The third category were proactive visitors (students, locals coming with associations, experts in participatory practice, such as university or museum professionals) who came to engage with the action research project and understand the participatory process. This category of visitors is most likely engaged in a transformative experience as they came to engage and change their perspective on the dynamic process initiated by the conflict.[9]

8.4 Conclusion

Transformative experiences in the museum can have a significant impact on the institution, the audiences, and the participants themselves. It can help museums be agents of change and contribute to social justice. But it can only do so if it accepts to be a truly agonist space, where conflicts are not necessarily resolved, and consensus is not necessarily found. By being a place for voices to be heard and questions to be asked, for empathy to be triggered and action and change to be initiated, museums can use conflict to trigger change and become transformative learning spaces. This is particularly the case when a museum tackles, as the MHM did, such conflict over a longer period of time and allows the exhibition to evolve to the pace of memory and repair rather than that of a strict exhibition calendar. It allows for all involved for a gradual building of the transformative experience creating culmination events (Gaggioli 2016) but also sustaining the transformation over the longer term and allowing for what Jarvis calls the practice of the resolution (2009). The case study of the MHM has shown that such a process is possible and is also a deeply social activity that necessitates a new level of participants' agency and institutional flexibility.

[9] Further quantitative and qualitative audience research would be necessary to confirm this impression relayed by the museum director and the floor staff.

References

Black G (2005) The engaging museum: developing museums for visitor involvement. Routledge
Borg C, Mayo P (2010) Museums: adult education as cultural politics. New Dir Adult Cont Educ 35–44
Coffee K (2008) Cultural inclusion, exclusion and the formative roles of museums. Mus Manag Curatorsh 23(3):261–279
Denise F (2024) Research interview with the author, unpublished
Duerden M, Rossman JR (2019) Designing experiences. Columbia University Press
Gaggioli A (2016) Transformative experience design. In: Gaggioli A, Ferscha A, Riva G, Dunne S, Viaud-Delmon I (eds) Human computer confluence. De Gruyter, pp 97–124
Golding V, Modest W (eds) (2013) Museums and communities: curators, collections and collaboration. Bloomsbury Academic
Illeris K (2014) Transformative learning and identity. J Transform Educ 12(2):148–163
Janes R, Sandell R (2019) Museum activism. Routledge
Jarvis P (2009) Learning to be a person in society: learning to be me. In: Illeris K (ed) Contemporary theories of learning. Routledge, pp 21–34
Lynch B (2011) Collaboration, contestation, and creative conflict: on the efficacy of museum/community partnerships. In: Marstine J (ed) Redefining museum ethics. Routledge, pp 146–163
Mezirow J (2006) An overview over transformative learning. In: Sutherland P, Crowther J (eds) Lifelong learning: concepts and contexts. Routledge, pp 90–105
Mezirow J (2009) Transformative learning theory. In: Mezirow J, Taylor EW (eds) Transformative learning in practice: insights from community workplace, and higher education. Jossey-Bass, pp 18–32
Mouffe C (2016) An agonistic conception of the museum. ProyectoMuseu, np. http://proyectomuseu.org/an-agonistic-conception-of-the-museum/?ng_wp_cron=1639564257.4222729206085205078125
Sandell R (2003) Social inclusion, the museum and the dynamics of sectoral change. Mus Soc 1:45–62
Sandell R, Nightingale E (eds) (2012) Museums, equality and social justice. Routledge
Schulman S (2017) Conflict is not abuse: overstating harm, community responsibility, and the duty of repair. Arsenal Pulp Press
Simon N (2016) The art of relevance. Museum 2.0
Sitzia E (2017) The ignorant art museum: beyond meaning-making. Int J Lifelong Educ 37(1):73–87
Sitzia E (2019) Public participation and agency in art museums. In: Eriksson B, Stage C, Valtysson B (eds) Cultures of participation. Routledge, pp 185–200
Sitzia E (2023) Multiple narratives and polyvocality as strategies of inclusive public participation: challenges and disruption in the history museum. Museologies 10(2):51–63

Prof. Dr. Emilie Sitzia holds a special chair at the University of Amsterdam and is an associate professor Cultural Education at the University of Maastricht. She specialises in museum participatory practices, the impact of art on audiences and word/image interdisciplinary studies. Emilie's research spans the fields of history, literary studies, art history, museology, cultural education and sociology. She focuses on issues of storytelling, identity and multimodality in space, in text and in images. In 2022 she co-edited the volume *Participatory Practices in Art and Cultural Heritage: Learning Through and from Collaboration*.

Chapter 9
Ochre Painting Workshops as a Tool for Interactive and Sensory Museum Learning

Tammy Hodgskiss

Abstract Ochre is a colourful thread that flows through the Origins Centre—from the earliest known art forms through to its use in rock art paints. Ochre holds significant cultural value and is still widely used around the world for its mineral properties, for ritual, art and in industry. Ochre painting workshops are offered at Origins Centre Museum as part of the larger museum experience. The workshops are interactive and tactile and foster a personal link to our shared human past through sensory and first-hand engagement with the material. They are structured as informal sessions to experiment with ochre and natural pigment, while learning about other medicinal and cosmetic applications of ochre, and why this unassuming rock is important in our human journey. The experience also allows for information sharing about ochre and insight into the publics' understanding of our deep time human journey and allows museum professionals to connect with their public. The workshops highlight our shared human heritage, and our diverse yet inter-linked cultural practices. They also aim to create a personal and memorable learning experience that facilitates direct interaction with museum artefacts and encourages a more contemplative and personal connection with the past.

9.1 Introduction to Origins Centre

Origins Centre is situated on the University of the Witwatersrand (Wits) campus, in Braamfontein, Johannesburg, South Africa. Origins Centre provides visitors with a multi-sensory experience of Africa's complex heritage. The exhibits begin with the origins of humankind in Africa and then move through the development of technology, art, culture and symbolism (Fig. 9.1). The journey continues with an

T. Hodgskiss (✉)
Origins Centre, University of the Witwatersrand, Johannesburg, South Africa
e-mail: tammy.hodgskiss@wits.ac.za

L. Calvi et al. (eds.), *Transformative Museum Experiences*, Springer Series on Cultural Computing, https://doi.org/10.1007/978-3-031-89521-0_9

exploration of the diverse southern African rock art traditions, highlighting the lifeways, art and cultures of the indigenous San and Khoe peoples[1] and their ancestors. These ancient archaeological stories and rock art masterpieces are illustrated and honoured through contemporary art installations by well-known South African artists (Fig. 9.1e, f). The centre is open to the public and is frequented by school groups, students, university staff and local and international tourists. Researchers, teachers, artists and a range of academic stakeholders also visit the museum for research purposes, or to display their work within the space and collaborate on outreach programmes (Wits Origins Centre Strategic Plan 2021).

Origins Centre was opened on 6th March 2006, by Thabo Mbeki, the president of the Republic of South Africa at the time. The name 'Origins Centre' does sometimes result in people assuming the museum is about the origins of humankind, especially since it is situated close to the Cradle of Humankind World Heritage Site. However, a focus of the museum is on southern African rock art, its meaning and the lives and beliefs of the indigenous populations of southern Africa who created it. The museum offers a dynamic mix of art and science—telling the story about the origins of art and of cultural and symbolic expression. The origins not just of how we *became* human, but of what *makes* us human.

Origins Centre was initially formed as a Not-for-Profit Section 21 company (McGhie 2009), but in 2017, it was incorporated into Wits University, within the Faculty of Science. Its incorporation into the Science Faculty resulted in a reframing of the museum offerings with enhanced academic and research outputs (Wits Origins Centre Strategic Plan 2021). Origins Centre now has a broader mission to 'provide a multi-disciplinary space at Wits to display art, fossils and artefacts that tell a scientifically researched narrative about the 'origins' of life, humankind and society' (Wits Origins Centre Strategic Plan 2021). This renewed vision of a space within and beyond the museum facilitates discussion, encourages creative ways to communicate, display, preserve and research the African past and indigenous knowledge systems, ensure ethical and reflective knowledge construction within the field, and actively give voice to the previously unheard in the African past or history books (Esterhuysen 2000). This also includes increased involvement with communities and with researchers; encouraging academic citizenship projects and creating multi-disciplinary science communication and outreach avenues for the university.

With these broader goals in mind, Origins Centre has focussed on implementing ways to captivate the visitor within the stories of the museum—to create and foster

[1] In the museum, the terms 'Khoe' and 'San' are used as inclusive terms for the rich diversity of communities, cultural and language groups which form the indigenous populations of southern Africa. 'San' (or Saan or Bushman) refers generally to indigenous hunter-gatherer populations of southern Africa, while 'Khoe' refers to indigenous pastoralist groups, although the hunter-gatherer and herder groups were not necessarily distinct, separate cultural groups from each other through time. Evidence of this complex mixing of people, shifting identities and ways of life is shown through archaeological and ethnographic material culture, rock art styles and language. For more see Challis and Sinclair-Thomson (2023). These groups spoke many languages (Khoisan languages, colloquially called 'click languages'), which some living descendants still speak, such as |xam, Ju-hoan, N/uu, Nama, Khwe and Khoekhoe.

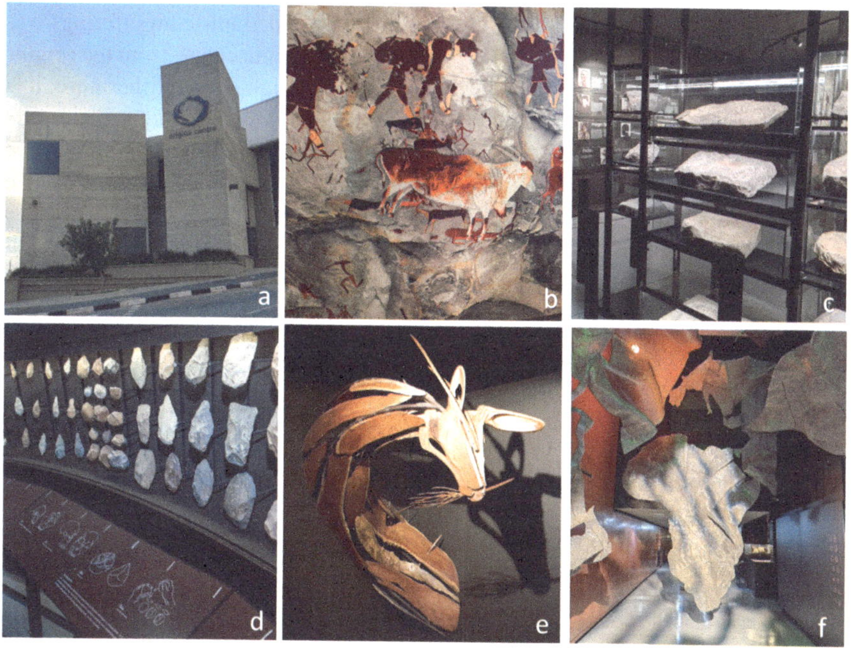

Fig. 9.1 The Wits Origins Centre Museum. **a** The Origins Centre building, **b** print of Ndedema Gorge rock art replica by Harald Pager, **c** original southern African rock art panels on display, **d** original southern African stone tool exhibit, **e** wooden sculpture by Russel Scott, the full sculpture depicts an eland-headed snake weaving in and out of the wall—drawing from such creatures painted in San rock art, **f** aluminium wire sculpture 'World Map' by Walter Oltmann illustrating the movement of humans out of Africa

educational yet personal connections with the past. The museum hosts a range of temporary exhibitions, lecture programmes, workshops and family-focussed events, and various spaces in the museum are popular as unique and heritage-rich venues for private functions. One of the educational offerings—and a way of transforming the museum experience—is the interactive ochre workshops. This chapter will discuss how these workshops are run, what the main aims are, and reflect on the success of the workshops in providing an immersive and interactive learning experience.

9.2 Crafting Narratives: Why Ochre?

In 2017, funding was received from the National Institute of Humanities and Social Sciences (NIHSS) to expand the display on the innovations of the Middle Stone Age in South Africa and the origins of early 'cognitively complex' *Homo sapiens*. This includes some of the earliest evidence of art, such as engraved ochre, ochre paint and engraved ostrich eggshell (Fig. 9.2a; e.g. Henshilwood et al. 2001; Texier et al. 2010). The idea to incorporate ochre into the extended museum offerings was hatched. Ochre is a common thread that runs through the museum—from the origins of human creativity and innovation through to rock art pigments. Furthermore, it is a readily available, perhaps underappreciated, resource, which is still widely used around the world. The initiative makes archaeological and indigenous knowledge more accessible through an interactive and immersive workshop that helps to transform how exhibits and content are received and engaged with. So, what exactly is 'ochre'? The term 'ochre' is an umbrella term that is used to describe a wide range of earth minerals or rocks that have a pigmentatious quality (Fig. 9.2). They are conventionally red, yellow, orange or even purple in hue, and are comprised largely of iron oxides or oxyhydroxides within clays or calcites (Popelka-Filcoff and Zipkin 2022; Velliky et al. 2024), but the term 'ochre' can even include non-iron-containing forms of pigment-rich rocks or sands, of white or blue hues (Huntley 2021; Gustafson 2023). These earth minerals can be called colouring materials, earth pigments, or mineral pigments, or divided by their geological form, such as hematite or shale. Interestingly though, different ochres and the powders produced from these earth minerals were (and are) not used solely as pigments.

The earliest evidence of ochre use dates within the Early Pleistocene at around 500,000 years ago in southern Africa, before we find evidence of anatomically

Fig. 9.2 A range of ochre types and mineral pigments collected around southern Africa. **a** Engraved ochre nodule from Blombos Cave, South Africa, 77,000 years old

modern *Homo sapiens* (Watts et al. 2016). By roughly 160,000 years ago (and more convincingly by 100,000 years ago), ochre—and especially red ochre—was regularly used; and ochre pieces, and processing tools are found at most Middle Stone Age sites around Africa (e.g. Hodgskiss 2020; Dapschauskas et al. 2022). Ochre is an important material in our human journey because it appears at a time of significant technological advances and behavioural innovations for our species. Some ochre applications are potential indicators for the capacity for complex cognition or 'modern' thought, such as intentionally engraved designs on ochre pieces or compound hafting adhesives that include ochre (Henshilwood and Dubreuil 2009; Wadley 2015). The use of ochre from the time we 'became' human and its continued use throughout our human journeys—across time and space—makes this simple rock a special and treasured resource.

Ochre can be processed in many ways and is used for a range of tasks, in both archaeological and contemporary contexts. Ochre powder is used as pigment and paint, in ritual ceremonies, as a beauty product, to tan hides, as skin protection, in hafting adhesives, and as a nutritional supplement (e.g. Rudner 1982; Velo 1984; Lombard 2007; Abrahams 2010; Rifkin 2011). So ochre is not *just* a pigment, and although the workshops focus on pigment production and experimentation, they also offer a way to find out more about how these rocks can be used, how archaeologists study them, and what they might have meant to past societies.

I worked together with Steven Sack, Megan Storme Gathercole and Suramya Bansal to put together the initial plans for the school-oriented ochre workshop offering, curricula-aligned material and marketing materials for schools. The ancient archaeological past of (southern) Africa is not well covered in the South African History Curriculum 2011, and the Middle Stone Age period is largely brushed over. Grade 11 and 12 Human Evolution content focusses on the fossil evidence of becoming *Homo sapiens*, and the Grade 5 material covers the hunter-gatherer lifeways of the ancestors of indigenous San hunter-gatherer groups (Esterhuysen 2000; Gathercole 2020). Aligning the ochre workshop content to the curriculum meant including a broad southern African Stone Age context—from the earliest and innovative uses of rocks, conversations around cognitive complexity of early humans, as well as the use of rock art pigments by indigenous populations.

The workshops were started to encourage and support children's learning and to provide teachers with additional information and tools to inspire students about certain topics through engaging and interactive activities (Andre et al. 2017). By broadening the narratives in the curricula, this platform aims to create an interface between learners, educators, academics and southern African archaeological heritage. After initial planning and advertising with a focus on school groups, the workshop structure developed organically, and grew as more requests for workshops for adult groups, art students and even preschool groups were received. The ochre workshops are now offered as a permanent part of Origins Centre's programming. Workshops are modified slightly per group, depending on the age and interests of the group requesting the workshop, the size of the group or the amount of time they have to spend at Origins Centre.

The museum experience for school groups includes a multi-sensory guided tour, and then groups can choose to do the ochre workshop and/or an interactive lecture on human evolution. The art class–style ochre workshop follows effectively from the tours as it provides an informal and fun way to address any thoughts or (mis)understandings about the museum narratives (Grant 2021); it also offers the opportunity to think and ask about how people lived in the past or about how the past can be interpreted, while also allowing attendees to actively participate in this history. In this way, they have some control over what they are learning and doing (Wickens 2012). This playful experience allows for more conversation, inquiry and discourse that helps facilitate learning and memory formation (Vygotsky 1967; Coffee 2008) and helps to develop an interest in museums and history.

9.3 Interacting with the Museum

Origins Centre views learning in the museum as a sociocultural process and programming offerings are modified to meet the needs of visitors, and to ensure diverse views are incorporated into the museum (Esterhuysen 2000; Weil 2002; Andre et al. 2017). Workshops, public lectures and seminars offer a way to have visitors play a part in the (hi)stories told in the museum—to create the museum as a place where community engagement can happen (Barrett 2011; Henning 2020). This is especially relevant given the importance of storytelling and community in South Africa's diverse cultural practices and histories (Mdlalose 2014). School and student groups who visit Origins come from diverse economic and cultural backgrounds and have a wide range of home languages. The museum therefore needs to convey content in a more inventive and engaging way, to bridge those barriers and assist learning.

The museum underwent upgrades in 2021 and some of the issues that had been observed in the centre's narratives (Kuljian 2016; Grant 2021) were addressed. Importantly, the entrance displays about the earliest technologies and fossil hominid evidence were followed abruptly by a discussion of the descendants of indigenous populations of southern Africa, and rock art traditions. This may have resulted in misconceptions that San people were comparable with hominid fossils mentioned in the corridor just before. The upgraded displays now discuss the earliest art forms and innovative technologies of modern *Homo sapiens* in the Middle Stone Age and the cultural diversity of the later Stone Age in southern Africa. The exhibits now demonstrate the long period of time of our human physical development, as well as our varied cultural expressions and technological, behavioural and social changes through deep time until now. The upgrades also include a new introduction to the (mis)representation and naming of San, Bushmen and Khoe indigenous groups and their descendants and ancestors, to move away from colonial narratives. This helps to contextualise the indigenous lifeways and cultures that are spoken about in the museum. Since the ochre workshops tell this long history of ochre use, these vast timelines and contexts are reiterated to guests during the activities too.

The museum provides interpretations of rock art, hunter-gatherer ways of life, insights into San and Khoe mythology/cosmology, and personal stories from individuals from around southern Africa—dispelling colonial stereotypes that are damaging and untrue (Kuljian 2016; Grant 2021). Engagement with descendant communities has been integral in informing the museum content and is paired with archaeological insight into the belief systems, ritual practices and lifeways of San and Khoe groups and their ancestors around southern Africa (e.g. Vinnicombe 2009; Ndlovu 2012; McGranaghan and Challis 2016; Viestad 2018). The museum is honoured to curate and display original painted and engraved rock art boulders that are South African national heritage items that form part of the Wits Rock Art Research Institute (RARI) collections (Namono 2021) (Fig. 9.3). Many of these items were removed from sites in the early to mid-1900s as a way of protecting and preserving 'endangered' rock art (Lewis-Williams et al. 2000; Grant 2021). This method of preserving (yet partially destroying the remaining) rock art is controversial and is no longer best practice (Lewis-Williams et al. 2000; Namono 2021). Many guests to Origins Centre have never visited a rock art site before, and the original pieces curated in the museum offer a way for guests to have a first-hand experience of the beauty of these spiritually imbued artworks and an appreciation of the people who made them.

Engagement with the art and art-making processes is provided in the rock art displays, which describe some of the meanings and stories behind the painted images, how people interacted with them in the past, and they also reveal different aspects of painting methods, techniques and ingredients (Fig. 9.3). Three of the original painted rock art panels on display at Origins will be described briefly here as they are relevant to the ochre workshops—The Mapote Stone, The Wartrail Panel and The

Fig. 9.3 Select original rock art panels on display at Origins Centre. **a** The Mapote Stone (image: David Pearce, RARI), **b** The Wartrail Panel, **c** The Klipfontein Stone display, **d** engraved (pecked) eland in the rock engraving archive

'Klipfontein' Stone. The Mapote Stone (Fig. 9.3a) was painted by Mapote, a Basotho man living in Quthing in Lesotho in 1930. Mapote had grown up with San friends and remembered the painting methods they had used, so was asked by Marion How (an amateur archaeologist and historian) to paint the way he remembered them painting (How 1962). Mapote spoke of the ritual of communally collecting and preparing pigments and ingredients. He said fresh eland blood was added to make better paint and to make the paint more powerful or supernaturally potent.

The Wartrail Panel (Fig. 9.3b) was removed from a farm in the Eastern Cape of South Africa in the 1940s, as an effort to preserve the rock art. The images of therianthropic figures (half human, half animal) are interpreted in terms of San cosmology, and link to beliefs and experiences during ritual practices of healing and trance (Lewis-Williams et al. 2000; Lewis-Williams 2004; Nguni 2015). The images are intricately painted, with fine lines and are extremely detailed. This display also includes a magnifying glass to view a section of the panel and is presented alongside a redrawing of the paintings. Together they allow for an appreciation of the delicate painting techniques, detail, colours as well as seeing the roughness of the rock surface that was worked on. The so-called 'Klipfontein Stone' display at Origins Centre offers visual insight into the materials possibly used by the original painters (Fig. 9.3c). This painted rock art panel is also called the Walter Battiss panel, as the original panel was removed from the shelter on the request of the artist Walter Battiss in the 1940s (Lewis-Williams et al. 2000). Contemporary South African artist, Stephen Townley Bassett, was commissioned to create a replica artwork of this beautiful panel. Stephen works with natural materials in his artistic practice to create 'documentary paintings' (or near exact replicas) of painted rock art panels from around the country. The panel chosen portrays important imagery found in San rock paintings, such as therianthropes, red lines fringed with white dots and a dying eland. Alongside this display, which also features a video showing Stephen's artistic process, are the paint and painting materials he used, which are resources that were used by San hunter-gatherers in the past, such as ochre, carbonised pigments, animal hair and porcupine quills for painting tools, shells or horns for containers, and binders of animal and plant origin (Townley Bassett 2002; Arocena et al. 2008). These displays appreciate the cultural contexts of the art and help to show the relationship between objects and people, and between the past and the present (Kreps 2003). From the understanding and appreciation gained in the museum on the communal, spiritual and personal processes of paint-making, the workshops offer a practical way to further respect an art form that was practised from as early as 27,500 years ago (Vogelsang et al. 2010) in southern Africa. This allows the visitor to directly engage with the objects and painting process—to create their own images and symbols, thereby increasing engagement and self-exploration (Garner et al. 2016). This aims to enable a more transformative personal and emotional connection with the past—from the first uses of mineral pigments to rock art paint applications, and the histories and people involved therein.

9.4 The Ochre Workshops: Getting Hands Dirty

The workshops are structured as science communication platforms to experiment with ochre and mineral pigment, while learning about its medicinal and cosmetic applications, its past uses, and why this unassuming rock is important in our human story. The workshop processes are easy to change depending on group requests (focus areas, e.g. origins of art, hunter-gatherer lifeways, different paint manufacturing techniques) and the length of time available to the attendees. School educators are looking for hands-on activities to boost learning during the few outings they get to take their groups on in the year, but they often have limited time and so a workshop is packaged into a 30–45 minute session, after a museum tour. Family groups or international visitors often have more time and a workshop can extend to 90 minutes. The tools provided to each group depend on the amount of time and space available. Guests are seated at tables and have all the materials and tools they need in front of them. To start, attendees are invited to look at the different types of ochre on their tables (Fig. 9.4)—touch it, see the colour coming off on their fingers, or even lick it (if they are inspired by being told that ochre can be eaten to help alleviate stomach cramps). The ochre on the tables is collected from around southern Africa, and the museum is situated on the Parktown Shale geological formation so museum staff do not have to go far to collect a range of colours of shales. For older groups, more complex topics, such as the geochemical properties of ochre, can be discussed. Attendees get to try different processing methods—to smash, crush, grind or scrape the ochre pieces—to produce colourful powder. Tools provided for this are small grindstones, stone flakes/tools, rocks and wooden sticks (Fig. 9.4). Archaeological finds from the Stone Age are mentioned—ochre pieces with scratch marks and incisions, or stone tools with residues on them—and what this means to archaeologists. Each person is encouraged to use different techniques to produce a few different colours of powder from the various ochre pieces, and the powder is placed in plastic palettes. Questions around the use of containers in the past are brought up here—what kinds of containers would have been used in the past? Did you know the oldest container known in the world is from South Africa? It is an abalone (perlemoen) shell, and it was used 100,000 years ago to mix an ochre 'paint' (Henshilwood et al. 2011). From this, discussions about access to water are brought up—how did people in the past carry water?

Pigments are then mixed (Fig. 9.4) after explanations of why we do not only use water with the pigment, and why binders are added. While organic binders in rock art paintings are not always preserved, binders that have been detected in rock art paints or documented ethnographically, such as sap, aloe vera, egg, blood, animal fat and milk, are discussed (Arocena et al. 2008). Store-bought honey and egg are the main options used for the workshops, although in the future, we could explore using sap from trees that are in the indigenous garden at the museum, e.g. *Vachellia* species. This would further reiterate the concept of using what nature provides, as people did in the past, and also taking the museum experience outdoors and seeing nature and natural resources from a different perspective. Water for mixing is

Fig. 9.4 Origins Centre ochre workshops: tools and processes

provided in squirt-bottles, and water and the binder are added to the powder in small amounts until a smooth paste is made. During the mixing process, many attendees realise that the powder they thought was fine-grained, actually required more grinding or crushing, and this sparks discussion on the use of lower and upper grindstones in the archaeology, or why soaking, straining and mulling pigment is the norm in contemporary art practices. Attendees have the freedom to try to crush the pigment more or can just paint with a slightly granular paint as an experiment. A range of application tools are supplied, such as paint brushes, sticks, feathers and porcupine quills. These options are drawn from archaeological evidence as well contemporary and ethnographic painting techniques. Attendees are encouraged to experiment with ways of applying the paint to different surfaces, such as using their fingers, using the unmixed powder or splashing or dripping paint onto the surface (Fig. 9.4). If there were no time constraints, many attendees would be interested in creating their own paintbrushes from objects like feathers, leaves, animal hair, etc., using historically known methods. The paintings are made on paper, board, rocks or used as body paint (Fig. 9.5). The goal of the workshop is not the artwork produced at the end, but rather the process. Allowing the attendees to explore ways of expressing themselves with paint and deepen the connection with the materials of the past. This can help to visualise these histories and hopefully create a more personal connection with it. During the workshops, questions are posed to encourage attendees to think about how people lived in the past (both in deep time contexts and more recently); to think about the skills and knowledge required to make a good paint or the human ability

Fig. 9.5 Origins Centre ochre workshop: experiences and outcomes

to use and decipher symbols. Questions such as: How did people in the past make sure their paint was the right colour or that their colours did not mix (especially as some children forget to rinse their paintbrushes)? What are the symbols we use now? Why do we sign our artworks? What does a logo or abstract design mean to us? Can we tell if people were right or left-handed from the handprints? Concepts of the past–present continuum are also challenged—that we are not separate from the past but have come from it and that our experiences now, and interaction with the past, can still contribute to and change interpretations of the past.

9.5 Experiencing Ochre: Outcomes and Feedback

Although simple paint-making techniques and tools are used, the workshops aim to give the attendees a sense of the materials used from nature, the long history of humans using ochre and that processing pigments and making paints is not as simple as it may seem. The visitor gets to use the tools and ingredients in different ways and see that the process requires knowledge, time and energy. The visitor becomes the subject of the narratives, rather than the receiver (Garner et al. 2016). The ochre workshop experience gives the attendee the chance to see how they identify with people and ideas in the past—their ancestors. A wide range of ages and interest groups attend the workshops—from 3-year-olds to students and academics to established artists, and each person brings their own interpretation, ideas and experience. Tasks are structured, but with individual choice in the types of ingredients, colours, and method of application, as well as the type of art or imagery that is produced. This immersive interaction with objects coupled with the choice to contemplate and express oneself artistically aims to provide the visitor with an experience that is unique and individual—one that creates a more personal educational experience within a museum setting (Falk and Storksdieck 2005). The workshops for children are light-hearted and provide a space for them to have fun and make a mess, while learning about our past and the natural world. For adult attendees, the workshops offer a more in-depth dive into past and present ochre uses and paint-making—but also framing the activity as a chance to relax, enjoy and be a part of the history. The informal nature of the workshops encourages social interaction and allows people to ask the instructor questions or discuss with their peers something they saw in the museum or do not understand. The conversations and interactions between the people seated at one table often have a defining part in their final products—producing artwork with a similar theme, for example, or encouraging more creative ways of using the paint. The activities create a shared heritage-related experience that is not restricted to one culture or time-period, mirroring our efforts to *create* a cultural practice within the museum (Coffee 2008)—not *enforcing* a cultural practice. There are complexities in facilitating large groups (over 100 people) due to space, time and resource constraints. A more informal option for large groups was developed, where they still get to have an ochre experience, but they do not do a full workshop. This is done in the garden and parking lot area outside Origins (Fig. 9.5). Groups get to see different types of ochre and use pieces to draw, like chalk, on the ground, and then use ready-made iron-oxide paint to make their mark—their handprint—on a large poster that can be taken back to their classroom. Another hurdle that the workshops have helped to tackle are language barriers, especially with younger children or school groups from rural areas. Ochre and iron-oxide rich clays (commonly called *ibovu/ibomvu* or *sebilo*) are still used by many communities in southern Africa—for cultural rituals such as female coming-of-age rites or marriage rites, for traditional healer training ceremonies, as a sunscreen, or to decorate houses or huts (Russell 1993; Rifkin et al. 2015; Buthelezi-Dube et al. 2022). Using a material that is familiar to some of the attendees, and doing hands-on activities rather than being *told* the story and uses of ochre (in English), does help to break down the language barrier. This interaction can help create a sense of community and connectivity within the group at the museum as well as facilitate engagement between the visitor and guide/instructor on an emotional and intellectual level. Feedback from teachers, lecturers and tour leaders about the workshops has been positive. Teachers like the connection that the activity has with content in the curriculum—that it makes the content tangible—and that this can be redone in the classroom or at home. A few teachers have suggested, or contacted the museum afterwards, to ask where they can collect ochre from so that they can do the activities with their learners again or have wanted some more information on certain aspects. Some groups are there for the fun and hands-on activity (regardless of what facts are being taught), and this interaction is encouraged as well and promotes artistic expression, relaxation and enjoyment within an educational space. Workshop requests have also come from university and secondary school teachers and lecturers as they have expressed a need for further information on the origins of art in Africa, rather than a Western/Euro-focussed narrative, which is not well explored in the current curricula. Attendees can receive (English) worksheets that also include information about ochre and its deep time and historical uses. The initial plan was to use these during workshops, but having this worksheet took away from the informal learning experience (making it feel like work, rather than a fun exploration). Further, completing a worksheet when one's hands are covered in ochre is not practical. The worksheet is now given upon request, and to those who want to know more about ochre or would like to do the activities in their own time.

Attendees are not asked to complete a formal evaluation of content or provide critiques on the workshop, so results and feedback are observational. The comments from participants are valuable in ensuring the product is useful, meaningful and maintained, and that the outcomes are worth the effort. It will be important moving forward with these programmes that we record feedback and results formally so we can further enhance our educational offerings and content (Wickens 2012; Jordaan 2022) and to perhaps secure further funding and expand our programme offerings. We have received more formalised feedback from student groups, as part of the university Teaching and Learning procedures, where a common opinion was that the students appreciated the hands-on element, as opposed to sitting in a lecture hall. Whether this translated to better knowledge retention of the course content is not known. Qualitative results would include feedback, verbal or written notes, participatory observations, comments and pictures. Currently, the workshops and artworks are photographed, and these are kept for our records or to promote workshops and the museum. Video recordings, or photographs showing faces, are not usually taken, as use of them requires that permissions are received from participants (or their parents), which is not feasible for school groups, especially. More formal permission forms for groups could be considered if this content was deemed necessary, and if it is known that the images will be used on a public forum, or for research purposes. The museum is receiving increased numbers of requests for the ochre workshops—by the general public, by preschool groups who have their own public art-making and painting initiatives, and by more schools and university groups that are visiting the museum. Further, judging by the fact that schools are re-booking the ochre workshops as an add-on to their groups' museum visit in following years, the ochre workshops are experienced as beneficial and enjoyable, and valuable added-extra to enhance the museum visit.

9.6 Thoughts and Conclusion

A number of outcomes from the ochre workshop offering at Origins have been achieved: information sharing on the long history and many uses of ochre; a fun and informal experience in a museum to create enthusiasm for history, museums and exploring our natural world; increased immersive engagement with museum content; an educational museum experience that breaks down the boundaries of a static museum space and helps to create a memorable and personal interaction with the past, history and art; an added offering to attract more visitors to the museum; and a way to delve into an exciting aspect of archaeological and rock art research while encouraging community and group engagement and connection. The workshops have offered me, as an ochre researcher, useful insights into different ways to process and use ochre. This community involvement and potential to engage with traditional knowledge systems is an important element in understanding the vast uses of ochre (Velliky et al. 2024). Since some attendees are familiar with ochre, this provides the opportunity to learn about their knowledge and use of the material, such as its use as a jeweller's rouge or abrasive polish agent for beads and jewellery; eating ochre to help fertility; mixing ferric oxide powder bought at a hardware store with water to use as sunscreen; or simply just a story about them finding some ochre on a walk and enjoying crushing it. The ochre workshops have become a personal process (as a museum professional and ochre researcher), to both learn and share information. Costs for the ochre workshops are kept as low as possible so it can be offered to schools with small budgets. Luckily the resources required are mostly either free (ochre) or re-usable (palettes, brushes, etc.) but just need to be collected or cleaned, which can be time-consuming. The main activities of the workshop focus on paint-making in the last few thousand years and so this is the main takeaway from the workshops. Going forward, ways could be found to reiterate the deep time ochre link, perhaps through introducing the scientific process and how archaeological ochre assemblages are analysed. There are many options to expand on the workshops—such as including the sourcing or collecting of ochre (what it looks like in the landscape, where to find it), simple paint-brush making, the introduction of other tools that have been found to be used archaeologically to process or use ochre (e.g. stamps; Rosso et al. 2016) and doing microscopic analysis of ochre pieces to understand the archaeological process of identifying use-wear. All resources for these are available on campus and would offer a collaborative activity with researchers in archaeology, geoscience and fine arts at Wits. The Origins Centre aims to provide greater public access to South Africa's vast archaeological and historical archives, and to create quality educational experiences around them. Multiple voices were involved in creating the displays, content, art installations, multimedia content and education programmes, and the Centre continues to look for ways to have multiple voices contributing to the content and public programming (Esterhuysen and Viestad 2021), such as through new touch screens, virtual reality, an augmented reality experience and Google Arts and Culture virtual exhibitions.[2] The ochre workshop experience offers another way that the museum visit can be transformed—where the museum's role moves to a facilitator and collector of knowledge and the visitor is an active participant in the histories. By giving the visitor the chance to interact with the material, they guide the discovery and interpretation (Garner et al. 2016), which helps to enhance the cultural and historical experience in the museum as

[2] Origins Centre Augmented Reality app—OriginsCentreAR Google Arts and Culture link https://artsandculture.google.com/partner/origins-centre.

the attendees create their own—shared—human experience from it. The ochre workshops also provide an engaging, cost-effective and simple way of learning about an aspect of the way people did things in the past, and embrace a vision of the museum to make histories more tangible and meaningful. This science communication initiative transforms the museum experience from a static, one-sided information giving source, to a more interactive experience that gives voice, opinion and agency to the visitor.

References

Abrahams PW (2010) "Earth eaters": ancient and modern perspectives on human geophagy. In: Landa ER, Feller C (eds) Soil and culture. Springer, pp 369–398

Andre L, Durksen T, Volman ML (2017) Museums as avenues for children: a decade of research. Learn Environ Res 20:4776. https://doi.org/10.1007/s10984-016-9222-9

Arocena JM, Hall K, Meiklejohn I (2008) Minerals provide tints and possible binder/extender in pigments in San rock paintings (South Africa). Geoarchaeology 23(2):293–304. https://doi.org/10.1002/gea.20215

Barrett J (2011) Museums and the public sphere. Wiley-Blackwell

Buthelezi-Dube N, Muchaonyerwa P, Hughes JC, Modi AT, Caister K (2022) Properties and indigenous knowledge of soil materials used for consumption, healing and cosmetics in KwaZulu-Natal, South Africa. Soil Sci Annu 73(4):1–12. https://doi.org/10.37501/soilsa/157408

Challis S, Sinclair-Thomson B (2023) The impact of contact and colonialism on indigenous worldviews, rock art, and the history of southern Africa. Curr Anthropol 63(25):S91–S127. https://doi.org/10.1086/722260

Coffee K (2008) Cultural inclusion, exclusion and the formative roles of museums. Mus Manage Cur 23(3):261–279

Dapschauskas R, Göden MB, Sommer C, Kandel A (2022) The emergence of habitual ochre use in Africa and its significance for the development of ritual behavior during the Middle Stone Age. J World Prehist 35:233–319

Esterhuysen AB (2000) The birth of educational archaeology in South Africa. Antiquity 74:159–165. https://doi.org/10.1017/S0003598X00066291

Esterhuysen A, Viestad V (2021) Re-thinking the curatorial—interrogating old practices and new efforts in colonial collections and archives. Crit Arts 35(4):1–4. https://doi.org/10.1080/02560046.2021.2004434

Falk J, Storksdieck M (2005) Using the contextual model of learning to understand visitor learning from a science center exhibition. Sci Educ 89:744–778. https://doi.org/10.1002/sce.20078

Garner JK, Kaplan A, Pugh K (2016) Museums as contexts for transformative experiences and identity development. J Mus Educ 41(4):341–352

Gathercole MS (2020) The neglected past in the South African history curriculum. Unpublished M.A. thesis, University of the Witwatersrand, Johannesburg

Grant J (2021) The Origins Centre: enlivening the Bushmen. Crit Arts 35(4):5–21. https://doi.org/10.1080/02560046.2021.1952635

Gustafson H (2023) Book of earth. Abrams

Henning E (2020) From colonial curiosity to the community: South African museums as emerging social hubs. S Afr Mus Assoc Bull 42:9–20

Henshilwood CS, Dubreuil B (2009) Reading the artefacts: gleaning language skills from the Middle Stone Age in southern Africa. In: Botha R, Knight C (eds) The cradle of language. Oxford University Press, pp 41–61

Henshilwood CS, Sealy J, Yates R, Cruz-Uribe K, Goldberg R, Grine FE, Klein RG, Poggenpoel C, van Niekerk K, Watts I (2001) Blombos Cave, southern Cape, South Africa: preliminary report on the 1992–1999 excavations of the Middle Stone Age levels. J Archaeol Sci 28:421–448. https://doi.org/10.1006/jasc.2000.0638

Henshilwood CS, d'Errico F, van Niekerk KL, van Coquinot Y, Jacobs Z, Lauritzen S-T, Menu M, García Moreno R (2011) A 100,000-year-old ochre processing workshop at Blombos Cave, South Africa. Science 334:219–222. https://doi.org/10.1126/science.1211535

Hodgskiss T (2020) Ochre use in the Middle Stone Age. In: Oxford research encyclopaedia of anthropology. Oxford University Press. https://doi.org/10.1093/acrefore/9780190854584.013.51

How MW (1962) The mountain Bushmen of Basutoland. Van Schaik

Huntley J (2021) Australian indigenous ochres: use, sourcing, and exchange. In: The Oxford handbook of the archaeology of indigenous Australia and New Guinea. Oxford University Press, pp 743–770. https://doi.org/10.1093/oxfordhb/9780190095611.013.21

Jordaan J (2022) South African centring and museum visitor feedback on the past: reframing opportunities at the Kwazulu-Natal Museum in South Africa. S Afr Mus Assoc Bull 44:22–28

Kreps C (2003) Curatorship as social practice. Curator Mus J 46(3):311–323. https://doi.org/10.1111/j.2151-6952.2003.tb00097.x

Kuljian C (2016) Darwin's hunch. Jacana

Lewis-Williams D (2004) Quanto? The issue of 'many meanings' in southern African San rock art research. S Afr Archaeol Bull 168:86–97

Lewis-Williams D, Blundell G, Challis WM, Hampson J (2000) Threads of light: re-examining a motif in southern African San rock art. S Afr Archaeol Bull 55(172):123–136. https://doi.org/10.2307/3888961

Lombard M (2007) The gripping nature of ochre: the association of ochre with Howiesons Poort adhesives and Later Stone Age mastics from South Africa. J Hum Evol 53:406–419. https://doi.org/10.1016/j.jhevol.2007.05.004

McGhie L-M (2009) Archaeology and authenticity in South African heritage locales and public spaces. Public Archaeol 8(4):351–372. https://doi.org/10.1179/146551809X12537170074211

McGranaghan M, Challis S (2016) Reconfiguring hunting magic: Southern Bushman (San) perspectives on taming and their implications for understanding rock art. Camb Archaeol J 26(4):579–599. https://doi.org/10.1017/S0959774316000408

Mdlalose M (2014) Storytelling at freedom park://hapo interactive space. S Afr Mus Assoc Bull 35:13–16

Namono C (2021) Curation as engagement: Boulder exhibits at the Origins Centre, South Africa. Crit Arts 35(4):22–43. https://doi.org/10.1080/02560046.2021.1995455

Ndlovu N (2012) The presentation of rock art in South Africa: old problems, new challenges. In: Smith B, Helskog K, Morris D (eds) Working with rock art: recording, presenting and understanding rock art using indigenous knowledge. Witwatersrand University Press, Johannesburg, pp 280–291

Nguni S (2015) Termites of the gods: San cosmology in southern African rock art. Wits University Press

Origins Centre Museum Strategic Plan (2021) Origins Centre Museum 2021–2025 (version 3.1). Draft plan. Origins Centre Museum University of the Witwatersrand, Johannesburg

Popelka-Filcoff RS, Zipkin AM (2022) The archaeometry of ochre *sensu lato*: a review. J Archaeol Sci 137:1–13. https://doi.org/10.1016/j.jas.2021.105530

Rifkin R (2011) Assessing the efficacy of red ochre as a prehistoric hide tanning ingredient. J Afr Archaeol 9(2):131–158. https://doi.org/10.3213/2191-5784-10199

Rifkin R, Dayet L, Queffelec A, d'Errico F, Summers B, Lategan M (2015) Evaluating the photoprotective effects of red ochre on human skin by in vivo SPF assessment: implications for human evolution, adaptation and dispersal. PLoS One 10(9):e0136090

Rosso DE, Africa Pitarch M, d'Errico F (2016) Middle Stone Age ochre processing and behavioral complexity in the horn of Africa: evidence from Porc-Epic Cave, Dire Dawa, Ethiopia. PLoS ONE 11(11):e0164793. https://doi.org/10.1371/journal.pone.0164793

Rudner I (1982) Khoisan pigments and paints and their relationship to rock paintings. Ann S Afr Mus 87:1–280

Russell M (1993) Women, children and marriage in Swaziland. Int J Sociol Fam 23(1):43–57

Texier P-J, Porraz G, Parkington J, Rigaud J-P, Poggenpoel C, Miller C, Tribolo C, Cartwright C, Coudenneau A, Klein R, Steele T, Verna C (2010) A Howiesons Poort tradition of engraving ostrich eggshell containers dated to 60,000 years ago at Diepkloof Rock Shelter, South Africa. Proc Natl Acad Sci 107:6180–6185. https://doi.org/10.1073/pnas.0913047107

Townley Bassett S (2002) Rock paintings of South Africa: revealing a legacy. David Philip

Velliky B, Hodgskiss T, Mendoza Straffon L, Gustafson H, Gollifer A, Haaland MM (2024) The framework for ochre experiences (FOES): towards a transdisciplinary perspective on the earth material heritage of ochre. In: Abadía M et al (eds) Deep-time images in the age of globalization; rock art in the 21st century. Springer, pp 109–128. https://doi.org/10.1007/978-3-031-54638-9_8

Velo J (1984) Ochre as medicine: a suggestion for the interpretation of the archaeological record. Curr Anthropol 25(5):674

Viestad VM (2018) Dress as social relations: an interpretation of Bushman dress. Wits University Press

Vinnicombe P (2009 [1976]) People of the eland. Rock paintings of the Drakensberg Bushmen as a reflection of their life and thought. Wits University Press

Vogelsang R, Richter J, Jacobs Z, Eichhorn B, Linseele V, Roberts RG (2010) New excavations of Middle Stone Age deposits at Apollo 11 rock shelter, Namibia: stratigraphy, archaeology, chronology and past environments. J Afr Archaeol 8(2):185–218. https://doi.org/10.3213/1612-1651-10170

Vygotsky L (1967) Play and its role in the mental development of the child. Sov Psychol 5(3):6–18

Wadley L (2015) Those marvellous millennia: the Middle Stone Age of southern Africa. Azania Archaeol Res Afr 50:155–226. https://doi.org/10.1080/0067270X.2015.1039236

Watts I, Chazan M, Wilkins J (2016) Early evidence for brilliant ritualized display: specularite use in the Northern Cape (South Africa) between ~500 and ~300 Ka. Curr Anthropol 57(3):287–310. https://doi.org/10.1086/686484

Weil SE (2002) Making museums matter. Smithsonian Institution Press

Wickens KA (2012) Museums and community: the benefits of working together. J Mus Educ Early Learn Natl Convers 37(1):91–100

Dr Tammy Hodgskiss (married surname Reynard) is the Curator and Acting Head at the Origins Centre Museum, University of the Witwatersrand, South Africa. She was born and bred in Johannesburg, South Africa, and lives there with her husband and two children. Tammy is an archaeologist and received her Ph.D. in 2013 from Wits University. Her research focus is on archaeological and historic ochre and pigment use in Southern Africa. She manages exhibitions and public programming at Origins Centre, and is passionate about creating engaging and inclusive educational experiences.

Part III
Supporting Technologies

Chapter 10
Preserving Immersive Experiences as Transformative Museum Experiences

Lora Markova

Abstract Immersive experiences generated via the use of eXtended Reality (XR), encompassing augmented reality (AR) and virtual reality (VR), form a crucial part of today's creative and digital landscape whose cultural value should be recognized as an emerging heritage to be safeguarded for current and future generations. Museums, especially, have provided a salient context for XR to evolve from an emerging technology into a medium of creative expression within the design of meaningful and transformative museum experiences. Preserving immersive experiences poses challenges for contemporary conservation due to issues of technological obsolescence, forms of collective and distributed ownership, and the interactive, participatory, and performative nature of creative technologies. This chapter addresses two London-based immersive experiences as case studies—*Virtual Veronese* (23 July–5 August 2019) at The National Gallery and *Curious Alice: The VR Experience* (22 May–31 December 2021) at the Victoria and Albert Museum (V&A). The chapter fulfils a three-fold function: first, it explores the transformative potential and socio-cultural dimensions of immersive experiences that call for their cultural preservation; second, it discusses the transformative nature of immersive media content and its technological preservation; and third, it reflects on how both preservation aspects have brought transformations in museum practices, policies, and structures.

10.1 Introduction

Contemporary cultural expressions within the creative industries, cultural organisations, galleries and museums—and increasingly so in the (post-)pandemic context—are being generated through the use of digital, haptic, and spatial computing technologies, such as eXtended Reality (XR), encompassing augmented reality (AR), virtual reality (VR), and mixed reality (MR). Immersive experiences form a crucial part of today's creative and digital landscape whose cultural value and significance should be recognized as emerging heritage in their own right to be safeguarded for current

L. Markova (✉)
Loughborough University, London, UK
e-mail: l.markova@lboro.ac.uk

L. Calvi et al. (eds.), *Transformative Museum Experiences*, Springer Series on Cultural Computing, https://doi.org/10.1007/978-3-031-89521-0_10

and future generations. Museums, especially, have provided a salient context for XR to evolve from an emerging technology into a medium of creative expression within the design of meaningful and transformative experiences that may alter worldviews and self-perceptions (Gaggioli 2016) and potentially contribute to identity exploration (Garner et al. 2016). Simultaneously, ongoing technological innovations have triggered transformations in museum practices and structures, which, in this essay, will be addressed through the scope of the preservation of immersive content.

Preserving immersive experiences and 'born-digital' objects poses challenges for contemporary conservation due to issues of technological obsolescence and intangibility, forms of collective and distributed ownership, and the interactive, participatory, and performative nature of digital and emerging technologies. Unlike traditional artworks and analogue objects, born-digital artefacts are a form of 'dynamic content' as defined by the digital preservation expert Rosenthal (2015). Hence, practices of archiving, collecting, and preserving born-digital objects and experiences have transformed from avoiding to maintaining 'inevitable change' (Depocas et al. 2003).

A range of museum-led initiatives have paved the way to emerging practices of preserving immersive content and immersive experiences; for instance, the preservation strategies and challenges tackled by the Variable Media Initiative (VMI) and the Conserving Computer-Based Art initiative (CCBA) at the Guggenheim Museum, New York, the Time-based Media Art (TBMA) initiative at the Smithsonian American Art Museum, the cross-institutional Matters in Media Art by MOMA, SFMOMA and Tate, the Rhizome online archive of born-digital art, and two recent UK-based research projects—*Preserving Immersive Media* (2018–) by Tate and *Preserving and Sharing Born-digital and Hybrid Objects* (2022) by the V&A within the Towards a National Collection (TaNC) programme on using digital technologies for the creation of a unified virtual national collection across institutions in the UK.

In this context, the Creative Research and Innovation Centre (CRAIC) at Loughborough University London convened a series of collaborative workshops on collecting and archiving immersive experiences in partnership with the V&A Research Institute (VARI). The workshops took place in spring 2022 and were followed up by a roundtable on *Preserving XR* co-organised with the immersive studio OmBeond in February 2023. These collaborative events built on the success of UK's Industrial Strategy Challenge Fund 2017 programmes delivered by UK Research and Innovation (UKRI)—the Creative Industries Clusters Programme (CICP) and Audience of the Future (AotF) as the major investment initiatives into immersive R&D and skills in the UK. The discussions aimed at establishing a dialogue between creative technology (CreaTech) companies, memory institutions, policymakers, and academia by recognising the importance of cross-institution collaboration between museums and external experts within contemporary conservation, as studied by Laurenson et al. (2022). Drawing on a range of case studies and examples related to CICP, AotF, and the V&A, the collaborative workshops addressed a range of questions such as: What strategies are currently available for the preservation of immersive, AR/VR and 360-degree experiences? How could immersive content remain accessible for future generations and audiences? How can heritage institutions and the industry standardise digital preservation formats, practices, and methods? How can CreaTech companies, the heritage sector, policymakers, academics, and user communities develop collaborative methods for digital preservation?

This chapter elaborates on the key issues tackled within the collaborative CRAIC and VARI workshops by addressing two London-based immersive experiences as case studies—*Virtual Veronese* (23 July–5 August 2019) at the National Gallery and *Curious Alice: The VR Experience* (22 May–31 December 2021) at the V&A. Both immersive projects were debated within the workshops from the perspective of their potential future re-installation and called-for preservation. The chapter, hence, engages with processes of museum experience design, presentation, and preservation resonating with Annet Dekker's proposal to rethink the museum into "a 'living space', where presentation, preservation, discussion and active exploration go hand in hand" (Dekker 2015, p. 51).

The first section outlines the conceptual dimensions of immersive experiences as transformative museum experiences in terms of socio-cultural, spatial, and medial transformations. Next, the chapter maps relevant preservation policies and museum-led strategies, as well as documentation approaches towards audience experience and emerging forms of industry-led preservation that signal changes in museum contexts. Finally, the text delves into the selected case studies—*Virtual Veronese* and *Curious Alice: The VR Experience*—to reflect on preserving their dynamic nature and transformative potential, and how immersive experiences are interlinked with transformations in museum practices, relationships, and structures.

In this sense, this chapter aims to fulfil a three-fold function: first, to acknowledge the transformative potential of immersive experiences which calls for their cultural preservation; second, to discuss the transformative nature of immersive media content and its technological preservation; and third, to reflect on how both preservation aspects have brought transformations in the museum sector.

10.2 Immersive Experiences as Transformative Museum Experiences

The rising use of immersive technologies and forms of immersive storytelling in the museum context has triggered the emergence of *enriched* museum experiences (Calvi and Vermeeren 2023), expanding the *participatory museum* paradigm (Simon 2010) into growing opportunities for audience co-creation of museum experiences across real and virtual spaces.

Andrea Gaggioli has defined immersive VR as "an *epistemically transformative technology* since it allows individuals to encounter totally new experiences from a first-person, embodied perspective" (Gaggioli 2016, p. 107). The transformative potential of VR experiences, according to Gaggioli, manifests through manipulating bodily self-consciousness, embodying another person's subjective experiences, and altering the laws of logic and nature, which may bring self-actualization and change in users' worldviews and perceptions (ibid.). These aspects relate to Garner et al.'s definition of transformative experiences in the museum context (beyond their technological realisation) as "experiences in which visitors come to see the world through the lens of new ideas and identity exploration" concerning personal and social identity formation (Garner et al. 2016, p. 342). Similarly, the socio-cultural and political implications of using immersive technologies within museums and heritage sites have been suggested by Bolter et al. (2021) which will be studied further within the analysis of the immersive experience *Virtual Veronese* at The National Gallery, London.

Jenny Kidd and Eva Nieto McAvoy's research on immersive experiences within museums, galleries, and heritage institutions has further shown that institutions create *immersive encounters* with the intention to: "(a) increase visibility and contribute to a culture of innovation, (b) appeal to new audiences, (c) allow for more meaningful participation, (d) facilitate better engagement, and (e) provide additional revenue" (Kidd and McAvoy 2019, p. 4).

Digital and emerging technologies also reshape museums' experiential and spatial dimensions, transforming the museum into a participatory 'content platform' (Simon 2010), a 'distributed network' (Bautista and Balsamo 2011), and a 'deep space' that can be "encountered both inside and outside the museum, constantly renegotiating the visitor's continuous repositioning of their own presence across different temporalities and spatial configurations" (Giannachi 2021, p. 119). Furthermore, building upon Michel de Certeau's conceptualisation of space as a practised place, Gabriella Giannachi has suggested that the space of the digital museum can be defined as *augmented* in terms of overlaying different and possibly remote places "in which visitors re-construct their presence by moving between archival or imaginary spaces;" *performative* in the sense that the visitors activate these spaces as the actual performers of digital works; and *relational* since visitors document and share their experiences with other in-situ visitors as well as through social media (Giannachi 2021, p. 121).

The spatial design of museum experiences, across physical and virtual environments, also relates to transforming visitors' worldviews and perceptions. This process can be understood in terms of *worldbuilding* (McDowell 2019) as suggested further in this chapter within the analysis of *Curious Alice: the VR Experience* and the exhibition *Alice: Curiouser and Curiouser* at the V&A. Design practices of worldbuilding are closely related to forms of multimodal and transmedia storytelling across media platforms and involve novel technologies. In this vein, Kidd (2014) has suggested extending Henry Jenkins' theory of participatory culture and transmedia towards re-conceptualising museum experiences through the notion of the *transmedia museum*. The transmedia museum, according to Kidd, is defined by four central characteristics—*co-location and pervasiveness*, blending online and offline display and activities; *granularity*—suggesting the fragmented, flexible, and portable nature of digitised or born-digital content; *incompletion*—inviting visitors to co-construct museum narratives and *user-created content*; and *immersion and playfulness* that describe the experiential dimensions of a museum visit (Kidd 2014, pp. 33–38). Specifically, in relation to immersive storytelling experiences, Alke Gröppel-Wegener and Jenny

Kidd have proposed a framework encompassing multiple experiential layers with a focus on participants, process, creation, and story (Gröppel-Wegener and Kidd 2019).

Building upon these perspectives, this chapter will explore the transformative potential of the immersive experiences *Virtual Veronese* and *Curious Alice: The VR Experience* in terms of socio-cultural, spatial, and medial dimensions, and how their potential preservation entails transformations in preservation practices and museums.

10.3 Collection and Preservation Policies Context

Digital technologies and ongoing innovations have transformed museum practices which should be reflected in current collection and preservation policies. This section aims to map relevant approaches and existing conceptual gaps that define the policy context for preserving immersive content.

UNESCO's *Charter for the Preservation of Digital Heritage* (2003a) defines digital heritage as the "resources of human knowledge or expression, whether cultural, educational, scientific and administrative, or embracing technical, legal, medical and other kinds of information, increasingly created digitally, or converted into digital form from existing analogue resources. Digital materials include texts, databases, still and moving images, audio, graphics, software, and web pages, among a wide and growing range of formats. They are frequently ephemeral, and require purposeful production, maintenance and management to be retained" (UNESCO 2003a). Digital preservation is then described as the process aimed at ensuring the continued accessibility of digital materials, which requires digital objects to be understood and managed at four levels: as physical phenomena; as logical encodings; as conceptual objects that have meaning to humans; and as sets of essential elements that must be preserved in order to offer future users the essence of the object (UNESCO 2003a). From a practice-led perspective, digital preservation has been defined as "the series of managed activities necessary to ensure continued access to digital materials for as long as necessary" by the Digital Preservation Coalition (2015)—a UK-based non-profit organisation that advocates for digital preservation and long-term access to digital content and services.

UNESCO's conceptualisation of digital heritage and its preservation tends to favour an object-based understanding towards the digitisation of analogue objects and artefacts that do not necessarily grasp the dynamic, interactive, distributed, and experiential nature of digital culture and creativity. The experiential dimensions of technology-induced creativity rather relate to UNESCO's definition of intangible heritage, however, UNESCO's *Convention for the Safeguarding of the Intangible Cultural Heritage* does not acknowledge born-digital cultural and creative expressions (UNESCO 2003b). This internal contradiction has policy implications and leaves conceptual and technological gaps in recognising and preserving innovative creative expressions, and specifically native immersive content and immersive experiences, as potential cultural heritage for future generations.

At a European level, Horizon Europe's second pillar on Global Challenges and Cluster 2 on *Culture, Creativity and Inclusive Society* have provided support for projects rethinking digitised heritage, and heritage in transition facing change with confidence by following the core requirements for projects to provide an in-depth understanding of the changing nature of heritage by involving citizens and applying evidence-based methods already tested on a small scale (European Commission 2023a). Relatedly, the pan-European platform EU Collaborative Cloud for Cultural Heritage focuses on digitised tangible objects. Moreover, whereas the EU's *VR/AR Industrial Coalition* strategic paper (European Commission 2022) and EU's *Strategy on Web 4.0 and virtual worlds to steer the next technological transition* (European Commission 2023b) have committed to major investment in XR technologies for the creation of the Metaverse, there is no allocated funding for the preservation of native immersive content. Hence, to date, there is no EU policy framework for the preservation of immersive content and experiences.

Within the UK's policy context, the Department for Culture, Media and Sport (DCMS) launched the Culture and Heritage Capital Programme in 2021 as a framework for future decision-making with a focus on digitising physical assets, yet acknowledging the importance of preserving performance and digital assets, in terms of digital collections. The related AHRC/DCMS *Scoping Culture and Heritage Capital* report (DCMS 2022) explored the British Film Institute (BFI) National Archive among its case studies. BFI's collection practices recognise the potential preservation of emerging screen sectors such as digital games, born-digital and immersive content—also reflected in BFI's ten-year strategy *Screen Culture/2033* (BFI 2022), which can be understood as an emerging approach towards the potential preservation of immersive experiences.

The V&A also offers a leading example of the acquisition, display, and preservation practices that have been closely related to the creative industries and digital culture, as well as a long-standing practice of collecting performing arts. The V&A's Theatre and Performance Archives, including the National Video Archive of Performance (NVAP), outline relevant directions for documenting the experiential, time-based, and ephemeral features of creative immersive content. Moreover, the V&A's *Collection Development Policy* (2019) and its strategic objectives aim to "focus and deepen the relevance of our collections to the UK creative and knowledge economy"—documenting and making accessible design and creative processes and inspiring the work of practitioners across the creative industries.

As the V&A's recent *Preserving and Sharing Born-digital and Hybrid Objects from and across the National Collection* research report (2022) highlights further, the tech industry becomes the gatekeeper of part of our cultural heritage—raising new questions around the intersections between media and cultural policies. The report signals a number of gaps in current policy and the need to develop more experimental and small-scale pilot initiatives to help understand preservation needs and requirements. These crucial points were also discussed within the CRAIC and VARI collaborative workshops, emphasising the need to standardise practices across the creative industries and heritage institutions.

10.4 Strategies Related to the Preservation of Immersive Experiences

Transformation is integral to the variable and ephemeral nature of born-digital and immersive experiences, which poses challenges for preservation due to technological obsolescence, forms of collective and distributed ownership, and the interactive, participatory, and performative features of digital media and emerging technologies. This section outlines museum-led preservation strategies, documentation methods of audience experience, and emerging forms of industry-led preservation that provide practice-based approaches to the technological preservation of immersive content and entail a shift towards collaborative museum practices.

10.4.1 Preserving Born-Digital and New Media Artworks

An early approach to the preservation of new media art (often born-digital and time-based) lies in the Variable Media Initiative (developed in 1998 by Jon Ippolito, an associate curator at the Guggenheim Museum in New York) and the Variable Media Questionnaire (VMQ), launched in June 2003 by the Daniel Langlois Foundation and the Guggenheim Museum. The VMI paradigm *Permanence Through Change* (2003) uses an interactive questionnaire to map creative intent and proposes artist-approved strategies for the preservation of artworks created in ephemeral and obsolete mediums. VMI employs four preservation strategies: *storage*—defined as preservation of the tangible or material, rather than the interactive or experiential elements of the work; *migration*—transferring the work into contemporary hardware or software; *emulation*—mimicking the original experience as closely as possible with the use of current and emerging technologies; and *reinterpretation*—recreating the behaviour of the work in a completely different medium according to a score or other interpretive instructions.

The Guggenheim also hosts the Conserving Computer-Based Art initiative (CCBA), which is an ongoing, practice-based research project that emerged in an attempt to address issues such as hardware failure, rapid obsolescence, and the lack of established best practices in the preservation of computer-based art. CCBA argues that within documentation, conservators should analyse the vulnerabilities of the work and its reliance on specific software or hardware, and operational systems. "Conservators must understand the technical dependencies of the artwork and must also identify and secure the proper resources for long-term preservation (such as specific hardware and peripherals, source code, executable programs, or media assets like video or audio files). These physical and digital components often vary depending on the technology employed in the artwork" (Guggenheim Museum 2016). In this sense, as defined by Deena Engel, the CCBA initiative aims to respond to the challenges of "ongoing digital innovation and the resulting inherent instability of digital artworks" (Dover 2016).

The V&A's AHRC-funded project *Preserving and Sharing Born-digital and Hybrid Objects* goes beyond the realm of technical obsolescence. The related research report (V&A 2022) discusses the multilayered and complex authorship of many born-digital objects associated with communities or corporate ownership and expands on the potential of collaborative approaches to collection and preservation, suggesting industry and community involvement in the decision-making processes.

10.4.2 Preserving Immersive Content and Related Challenges

Tate's research project *Preserving Immersive Media* is a major investigation into the challenges of preserving immersive artworks and offers pragmatic recommendations to creative practitioners and collecting institutions. It explores the suitability of established digital preservation strategies for securing long-term access to immersive media. The project outlines four groups of strategies for the preservation of artworks employing immersive media such as 360 video, real-time 3D, VR, AR and MR, namely: *stockpiling*, *hardware migration*, *emulation*, and *code migration* (Ensom and McConchie 2021).

Patricia Falcão and Tom Ensom from Tate's Time-based Media Conservation team (a section of Tate's Conservation Department) have previously investigated the main risks faced by digital objects—the loss of the bits of digital information and the loss of the means to access information in the context of ongoing technological change, which they have defined as *content-centric* and *object-centric* preservation challenges. In relation to software-based art and digital objects, Falcão and Ensom emphasise the relevance of *emulation* (and related techniques as *virtualization*) as strategies that can maintain and recreate specific technical features (e.g. lighting and processing of the rendering engine), as well as the 'performative' character of virtual environments—"the idea of integrity of performance runs through all software preservation work and achieving this could be considered one of the conservator's main goals" (Falcão and Ensom 2019, p. 241). Another discussed approach is the focus on the code—"here emphasis shifts from understanding technical environment to understanding what the software *does* and how this might be changed or reimplemented in order to avoid obsolescence" (ibid.).

In the context of VR environments' dynamic content, *migration*—the transformation of an older digital file format into a newer file format—has emerged as a difficult and time-consuming method for cultural heritage institutions that contradicts the mass digitisation efforts embedded in archive workflows, as argued by Rosenthal (2015) and Cranmer (2017). Hence, VR and other interactive content are thought to be "most legibly preserved" within the "interdependent software environments in which they were created," as proposed by Rhizome (2016). Rhizome has begun to develop an open-source software tool and dataset that could automatically connect collections of digital artefacts (including software) with emulation environments for re-enactment of the collection's contents. As Cranmer has observed, "this would shift the focus of emulation from single objects into mass preservation, which would present a welcome change in archival practices" (Cranmer 2017, p. 12).

Experimental approaches of *emulation* and *virtualization* include physical mapping of user interface, interaction modalities, and locomotion, as explored by a recent research project at the University of New South Wales, Sydney that proposes strategies to capture, simulate, and reproduce experiences originally designed for large-scale immersive architectures within VR. The project provides a framework to capture the sense of embodiment, the emotional engagement, and the spatial dimensions which are central to immersion (Kuchelmeister 2018). A comparable approach has been undertaken by the Karlsruhe Institute of Technology proposing a 'synesthetic documentation' method and e-Installation as a virtualization method that reproduces all synaesthesia, interaction, and meaning levels of re-enacted artwork via advanced 3D modelling and telepresence technologies which offers an intermediate and long-term solution to archiving and dissemination (Muñoz Morcillo et al. 2016).

10.4.3 Preserving Audience Experiences

Audience experience has emerged as an important yet under-researched subject in the literature on contemporary conservation. William Real considers that the preservation of technology-based arts as "something that is above all an experience might require conservators to take a more fluid view of what may or may not be changed about a work, challenging conventional notions of accuracy and authenticity" (Real 2001, p. 221). Irvin (2006) suggests that preservation practices should be applied in correspondence with the experience that the author has designed and sanctioned for the audience. Similarly, van Mechelen (2006) discusses the "ideal, intended experience" as a guide for decision-making processes and preservation. Moreover, in relation to the preservation strategies of emulation and virtualisation, Rosenthal (2015) has introduced the notion of *experiential fidelity* to describe how close a recurring user experience can be kept to the original viewer's experience.

Central initiatives on digital preservation, such as the VMI and the Capturing Unstable Media project have also recognized the importance of documenting audience experiences of new media objects. Practice-based approaches involve video recording of audience interactions to capture the experiential, spatial, and performative nature of time-based works. The CloudPad project on documenting MR performance developed tracking of *participant trajectories* as a method to capture audience-generated and audience-facing documentation and introduced an original archiving tool integrating 'cloud computing' into the annotation and synchronisation of mixed media resources (Giannachi et al. 2012). Engel and Wharton (2014) also argue that users' (or viewers') aesthetic experiences must be thoroughly documented and understood both through data models and source code documentation, as well as through non-technical user-point-of-view narrative-style documents. Furthermore, as acknowledged by Annet Dekker and Gabriella Giannachi, forms of audience-generated documentation "challenge the authority of museums and other cultural organisations" (Dekker and Giannachi 2022, p. 12). Hence, it becomes relevant to investigate how heritage institutions and the creative industries can address the collective and distributed ownership of digital objects and the role of end users and user-generated content in informal practices of digital preservation.

10.4.4 Towards Industry-Led Preservation of Immersive Experiences

Recent studies, such as Evanthia Samaras' doctoral project on the preservation of visual effects in the screen industries (2021) propose that archival practices should be adopted to assist the industry in self-archiving their records more effectively and to support industry recordkeeping and business activities that facilitate the formation of archive collections. This can ensure that significant evidence of visual effect production (records about the technologies, artistic process, and working life of practitioners) and its continuing value that extends beyond production outputs is preserved over time for future generations.

A recent example of a collaborative collection and preservation approach is the partnership between BFI National Archive and the UK-based art and design studio Marshmallow Laser Feast in developing a pilot experimental acquisition of the VR project *In the Eyes of the Animal* (2015–). The project "highlights the importance of experimental and research-led collecting practice to understand requirements, build capacity, and redefine expectations for both institutions and creators" (V&A 2022, p. 29).

Another example is the website Findings in the Future of Live Performance. It provides a multidisciplinary archive that documents recorded talks and videos sharing insights from the AotF Demonstrator project *Dream* (Royal Shakespeare Company 2021). It also features learnings from 15 R&D projects run between 2019 and 2021 by the partners of the Audience of the Future Live Performance consortium of specialist organisations, research institutions, and pioneers in immersive technologies (AotF 2021). These examples signal emerging collaborative practices of industry-led documentation and preservation that can inform CreaTech companies to self-archive creative immersive experiences.

10.5 Preserving Immersive Experiences: Case Studies

This part of the essay delves into two London-based immersive experiences—*Virtual Veronese* at the National Gallery and *Curious Alice: The VR Experience* at the V&A. The discussion aims to articulate their transformative potential in terms of socio-cultural, spatial, and medial dimensions. It also tackles the transformative nature of immersive technologies and how the preservation of immersive experiences signals transformations in museum practices towards cross-institution collaborations.

10.5.1 Case Study 1: Virtual Veronese—*The National Gallery, London*

Virtual Veronese (23 July–5 August 2019) was an R&D immersive prototype developed by StoryFutures as part of the Industrial Strategy Challenge Fund's Creative Industries Clusters Programme in collaboration with The National Gallery, London and the CreaTech company Focal Point VR. The immersive experience recreated the original exhibition settings of Paolo Veronese's altarpiece painting *The Consecration of Saint Nicholas* (1562) into VR and AR experiences transporting visitors into San Benedetto al Po church near Mantua in northern Italy by featuring a 3D spatial model of the church's chapel. The prototype aimed to tell the story behind the painting that was commissioned by Bishop Andrea Asola in 1561 as a powerful act to resist Counter-Reformation demands and proclaim loyalty to the Roman Catholic Church in a moment of European schisms. *The Consecration of Saint Nicholas* has been in The National Gallery's permanent collection since 1826 after being looted from its original location during the Napoleonic Wars, and it reached the London art market in 1811 when it was acquisitioned (Gill 2019).

StoryFutures' R&D prototype made use of immersive storytelling integrating a photogrammetric reconstruction of the San Benedetto al Po church's chapel and volumetric video capture performances built in the Unity game engine. The gallery visitors could experience two narrative versions accompanied by a 3D audio soundtrack of choral music—a story-led version using a fictional narrative delivered by virtual actors portraying Veronese's patron, Abbot Asola and a monk living in the church of San Benedetto al Po; and a factual version narrated by a volumetric video avatar of Dr Rebecca Gill, a former Ahmanson Fellow and Curator in Art and Religion at the National Gallery who conducted the research on *The Consecration of Saint Nicholas* painting and its original settings. Both scenarios were presented as a VR experience for Oculus Quest, and AR experiences for two devices—Magic Leap (placing a transparent display between visitors' eyes and the in-situ physical reality) and Mira Prism (using a semi-transparent mirror to reflect content from the screen of an inserted iPhone). In this sense, the VR experience replaced The National Gallery's settings with the photogrammetric reconstruction of San Benedetto al Po church and a computer-generated version of the painting, while the AR experiences blended virtual and physical gallery settings by adding an image layer around the actual painting *The Consecration of Saint Nicholas* visible in-situ.

Audience research conducted by StoryFutures has analysed the similarities and differences between *Virtual Veronese*'s VR and AR experiences with a specific focus on the different user perceptions of presence, engagement, enjoyment, and possible negative side effects. As reported, enjoyment and behavioural engagement were high on all devices, with the Oculus Quest VR version receiving higher scores than both AR headsets, Magic Leap and Mira Prism. Cognitive and emotional engagement were similar between the three devices. With regards to presence (spatial presence, involvement, and sense of being there) Oculus Quest achieved a higher score than both AR devices. In conclusion, it was observed that the VR experience provided a higher level of immersion than the AR versions, to a certain extent related to Oculus Quest and Magic Leaps' higher resolution textures and 6DOF (6 degrees of freedom allowing visitors to view in all directions) than Mira Prism's 3DOF (Verhulst et al. 2021).

10.5.1.1 Preserving *Virtual Veronese* as a Transformative Museum Experience

The immersive dimensions of Paolo Veronese's Renaissance frescos and paintings have been outlined in Olver Grau's book *Virtual Art: From Illusion to Immersion* (2003) that explores immersive experiences from the perspective of media art history. As argued by Grau, Renaissance and Baroque paintings, frescos and panoramas, succeeded by pre-cinematic optical illusion devices, such as magic lanterns (*lanterna magica*) and dioramas, can all be understood as predecessors of today's immersive environments. The transformative potential of *Virtual Veronese* in terms of socio-cultural significance relates to the opportunity to experience displaced artefacts in their original cultural context and settings. As suggested by Jay David Bolter, Maria Engberg, and Blair MacIntyre, overcoming distance through immersive experiences in museums and cultural heritage sites has historical, cultural and political implications—"museums and heritage sites are committed to bridging the gaps between now and then or here and there—bringing the past into the present or bringing what is physically distant into the visitor's presence" (Bolter et al. 2021, p. 108). Moreover, Garner et al. (2016) have defined the transformative potential of museum experiences as a process of *re-framing*, *re-seeing*, and *re-enacting* one's personal and social past towards discovery, critical reappraisal, and identity exploration. In this sense, the transformative value of *Virtual Veronese* emanates from the opportunity to *re-frame*, *re-see*, and *re-enact* Paolo Veronese's original work via forms of immersive storytelling.

The potential for identity exploration and the socio-cultural dimensions of immersive experiences also expand towards emerging attempts to decolonise museum narratives. A recent example is Inter-Lab's *Decolonising the Museum—an AR storytelling to connect and engage visitors with collections* using AR technologies that aims to help the Great North Museum: Hancock, Newcastle to connect with diverse communities and uncover complex stories behind the collection's artefacts. Hence, it can be suggested that immersive storytelling has the transformative potential to display multilayered and multivocal museum narratives and to symbolically 'decolonise' museum collections through generating counter-hegemonic cultural representations.

In this context, StoryFutures Academy, as part of the 2022 *Unboxed: Creativity in the UK* festival, also released the large-scale immersive storytelling project *StoryTrails* that uncovered untold cultural histories through remixing British Film Institute (BFI) and BBC archives into AR and VR experiences touring 15 locations across the UK. *StoryTrails* won the 2023 Museums + Heritage Award in the category Best Use of Digital and within its creative development, the project recruited and upskilled 50 emerging creators from underrepresented communities in the UK. *StoryTrails*'s approach of involving communities and reusing archives to uncover diverse stories resonates with Amalia Sabiescu's conceptualisation that the performative and creative value of living archives relates to "fulfilling the potential of cultural heritage for building collective memory, community and identity" (Sabiescu 2020, p. 506). Additionally, critical and creative practices of remixing archives—as performed by *StoryTrails* within VR experiences and AR trails—could generate inclusive 'third spaces' of cross-cultural interaction and a transcultural imaginary, as argued elsewhere (Markova 2022).

The socio-cultural dimensions and the transformative potential of *Virtual Veronese* entail the value of its preservation and re-installation for future audiences. Restoring the project would be dependent on maintaining the software runtime environment (e.g. keeping the game engine software up to date through code migration) and preserving the hardware specifications. The case study also evokes documentation of visitor interaction, e.g. through video game emulators (Rosenthal 2015) and by capturing user journeys, e.g. with experimental tools such as CloudPad (Giannachi et al. 2012). Within the collaborative CRAIC and VARI workshops specific attention was paid to the financial barriers and technological complexities of scaling up an R&D prototype as *Virtual Veronese* to all acquisitions at a collection level. The discussion problematised that R&D and formal collection policies do not align with each other, outlining the need to rethink collection practices and institutions and integrate preservation processes within R&D funding cycles and experimental and collaborative R&D activities.

10.5.2 *Case Study 2:* Curious Alice: The VR Experience—*Victoria and Albert Museum (V&A)*

Curious Alice: The VR Experience was launched and presented within V&A's *Alice: Curiouser and Curiouser* exhibition (22 May–31 December 2021) that showcased V&A's role both as a collector and a creator of immersive content. The VR experience was created in partnership with HTC Vive Arts, produced by immersive games studio

Preloaded, and incorporating collaged artworks by illustrator Kristjana S. Williams. As a multisensory exhibition *Alice: Curiouser and Curiouser* featured more than 300 objects presented within five thematic sections—*Creating Alice*, *Filming Alice*, *Reimagining Alice*, *Staging Alice* and *Being Alice*—that encompassed film, performance, fashion, art, music, and photography, reflecting the ongoing legacy and impact of Lewis Carroll's book *Alice's Adventures in Wonderland* (1865) and its sequel *Through the Looking Glass and What Alice Found There* (1871) across cultural contexts, creative disciplines, and media formats over 157 years.

The thematic section *Reimagining Alice*, for instance, focused on artistic expressions inspired by Carroll's books, from John Tenniel's illustrations for the first published edition in 1866 to 1970s psychedelic posters by Joseph McHugh and pop art by Peter Blake. In this sense, the V&A's *Alice: Curiouser and Curiouser* bears certain similarities with earlier exhibitions on the subject, such as Tate Liverpool's *Alice in Wonderland* (4 November 2011–29 January 2012) and The Atkinson's *Inspired by Alice* (25 May 2019–7 September 2019). A specific focal point within *Alice: Curiouser and Curiouser* was the Surrealist movement's engagement with Alice's imaginary realities—"Everyone has the power to accompany an ever-more beautiful Alice to Wonderland," as highlighted in a displayed quote by Surrealism's founder, André Breton. Another display was a letter from the British Surrealist Eileen Agar considering Lewis Carroll, and his potential to unleash the unconscious, as the godfather of the Surrealist movement. The exhibition also featured Max Ernst's painting *Alice in 1941* (1941) evoking a portrait of his lover and collaborator, the British-born/Mexican Surrealist, Leonora Carrington. This thread of Surrealist reimaginings also included Salvador Dalí's rare illustrations for a limited edition of *Alice's Adventures in Wonderland* in 1969. The exhibition's experiential dimensions of a surrealist Wonderland were also induced by the *Mad Hatter's Tea Party*—a flying chairs installation with animated projection mapping, designed by the award-winning theatre designer Tom Piper.

In parallel, the *Filming Alice* section assembled multiscreen projections of cinematic adaptations of Lewis Carroll's texts, including moving image fragments from Cecil Hepworth and Percy Stow's silent fantasy film *Alice in Wonderland* (1903), Paramount Productions' 1933 pre-Code feature film, and Walt Disney's 1951 animated musical. The exhibition's film highlights also featured LED screen installations with episodes from Jan Švankmajer's surrealist stop-motion puppet animation *Alice* (1988, original Czech title: *Něco z Alenky/Something from Alice*) and Gavin Millar's imaginative film *Dreamchild* (1985) incorporating puppet characters by the 'Muppets' creator, Jim Henson. Next to posters and ephemera from various motion pictures, the *Filming Alice* section also displayed sketches, costumes, and large-scale projections from Tim Burton's more recent reimagining *Alice in Wonderland* (2010), whose VFX-intensive production design blends live-action, motion-capture and CGI animated characters that have paved the way towards reinterpreting Alice's imaginary world in VR.

Curious Alice: The VR Experience recreated Lewis Carroll's Wonderland as a playful, interactive, and immersive environment, finding a creative conjunction between technology, story, and creative imagination. The VR experience offered an in-situ and a home version with three scenarios of interaction—solving the Caterpillar's mind-bending and psychedelic riddles; racing against the clock to find the White Rabbit's missing glove; and defeating the Queen of Hearts in a curious game of croquet with interactive pink flamingos and hedgehogs, inspired by *The Queen's Croquet-Ground* chapter in *Alice's Adventures in Wonderland*. The experience's 3D world, characters, and interactive assets were created from Victorian engravings cut-outs, as the original source material to be volumized, montaged, and animated in a virtual environment. The use of a parallax technique (layering the image space at different layers' speed to create an illusion of depth) directly borrows from Victorian paper theatres in the V&A's collection that have inspired the project's illustrator Kristjana S. Williams. The use of VR as a creative technology has allowed for the creation of user experiences that play with scale and perception and translate Lewis Carroll's literary imagination into interactive diegetic cues, such as falling down the rabbit hole, stepping through the looking glass, and shrinking when interacting with the 'Drink Me' bottle. In this sense, the VR experience explored the curatorial possibilities of using immersive technologies and designing transformative visitor journeys across physical and virtual spaces, as well as expanding the show's 'deep space' (Giannachi 2021) into post-exhibition visitor experiences through the ongoingly available *Curious Alice* VR Viveport Home version.

10.5.2.1 Preserving *Curious Alice: The VR Experience* as a Transformative Museum Experience

Alice: Curiouser and Curiouser transformed the V&A into a *transmedia museum*—borrowing Jenny Kidd's notion (2014)—where visitor experiences are generated across media texts, technologies, and platforms into a mode of transmedia storytelling. Drawing upon Henry Jenkins' theory of convergence culture and transmedia, Kidd has suggested that Jenkins' conceptualisation of "radical intertextuality and multimodality for the purpose of additive comprehension" has become the norm in designing contemporary museum experiences (Kidd 2014, p. 27). *Alice: Curiouser and Curiouser*'s use of projection mapping for creating a theatrical effect in the physical museum settings, also resonates with Leslie Bedford's perspective that theatricality creates a threshold experience for visitors, or a *liminal space*—"real or metaphorical, between the ordinary and the extraordinary, the known and the unknown—that is the imagined world of an exhibition" (Bedford 2014, p. 123). Overall, it can be observed that the transformative potential of *Alice: Curiouser and Curiouser* lies in altering the laws of logic and nature (Gaggioli 2016), by creating hybrid visitor experiences through practices of *worldbuilding*, defined by Alex McDowell as "a narrative and systems design practice that exists at the intersection of design, technology and storytelling" (McDowell 2019, p. 105)—both within the physical and virtual spaces of the exhibition, across media platforms and creative technologies.

Correspondingly, the preservation of *Curious Alice: The VR Experience* and the re-installation of the *Alice: Curiouser and Curiouser* exhibition and its hybrid and experiential world would depend on both documenting the material installation of physical props and preserving the immaterial technological components. In this context, it is relevant to consider emerging forms of audience-led documentation of immersive experiences through social media platforms (Instagram, TikTok, YouTube vlogs), which can be conceptualised as user-generated forms of transmedia storytelling. V&A's research report *Preserving and Sharing Born-digital and Hybrid Objects from and across the National Collection* has also defined user-generated content via Instagram as an informal preservation activity that can shape polyvocal stories and overcome biases and dominant big tech narratives (V&A 2022, p. 95).

The discussion within the collaborative CRAIC and VARI workshops focused on the *Curious Alice: The VR Experience* and its home version by acknowledging that distribution models are vital for the 'lifecycle' of creative immersive experiences, as argued by Jarvinen (2022). Overall, it was concluded that the potential preservation of *Curious Alice: The VR Experience* would require rebuilding the collaborative relationships between the V&A's team of curators, producers, designers, the CreaTech companies (HTC Vive and Preloaded), and the user communities involved in the experience.

10.6 Conclusions

By studying the immersive experiences *Virtual Veronese* and *Curious Alice: The VR Experience*, this chapter's objective was to explore three interdependent lines of enquiry. First, the discussion articulated the cultural value and significance of immersive experiences as transformative museum experiences, which calls for their cultural preservation as emerging heritage in their own right to be safeguarded for current and future generations. The transformative potential of the two immersive experiences analysed as case studies was addressed through the scope of their socio-cultural, spatial, and medial dimensions. Second, by outlining museum-led initiatives and digital preservation strategies, the essay acknowledged the transformative nature of immersive media content that poses challenges for technological preservation and evokes experimental and informal methods of industry-led and audience-generated forms of archiving and documentation. Third, by engaging with the current policy context and existing policy gaps regarding the preservation of native immersive content as innovative creative expression, the chapter identified and tackled necessary and emerging transformations within museum practices, relationships, and structures. In this vein, the essay also drew on key issues explored within the collaborative CRAIC and VARI workshops that outlined a trajectory towards industry-led and collaborative preservation across the museum and the CreaTech sectors. Ultimately, the analysis of *Virtual Veronese* and *Curious Alice: The VR Experience* revealed the vital role of the creative industries and community involvement in emerging and experimental processes of preserving immersive experiences as potential cultural heritage for future generations.

Acknowledgements The author would like to thank Prof. Andrew Chitty and Prof. Graham Hitchen, co-directors of the Creative Research and Innovation Centre (CRAIC) at Loughborough University London, and all participants in the collaborative CRAIC and VARI workshops.

References

AotF Audience of the Future (2021) Findings in the future of live performance. https://findingsinthefuture.live/. Accessed 10 Feb 2024

Bautista S, Balsamo A (2011) Understanding the distributed museum: mapping the spaces of museology in contemporary culture. In: Trant J, Bearman D (eds) Museums and the web 2011: proceedings. Archives & Museum Informatics, Toronto. http://conference.archimuse.com/mw2011/papers/understanding_distributed_museum. Accessed 15 Sept 2023

Bedford L (2014) The art of museum exhibitions: how story and imagination create aesthetic experiences. Routledge

BFI (2022) Screen culture/2033. Ten-year strategy. https://blog.bfi.org.uk/wp-content/uploads/2022/09/BFI-Screen-Culture-2033_Ten-Year-Strategy.pdf%20Accessed%2010%20February%202024. Accessed 10 Mar 2024

Bolter JD, Engberg M, MacIntyre B (2021) Reality media: augmented and virtual reality. The MIT Press

Calvi L, Vermeeren APOS (2023) Digitally enriched museum experiences—what technology can do. Mus Manag Curatorsh 39(3):335–356. https://doi.org/10.1080/09647775.2023.2235683. Accessed 15 Feb 2024

Cranmer C (2017) Preserving the emerging: 360-degree video and virtual reality. Report. https://publications.beeldengeluid.nl/pub/584/NISV_final_Candice-Krenmer.pdf. Accessed 20 Jan 2022

DCMS (2022) Scoping culture and heritage capital. Research report. https://www.gov.uk/government/publications/scoping-culture-and-heritage-capital-report/scoping-culture-and-heritage-capital-report. Accessed 25 Feb 2023

Dekker A (2015) Curating in progress. Moving between objects and processes. In: Barranha H, Martins S (eds) Uncertain spaces. Virtual configurations in contemporary art and museums. Instituto de História da Arte, FCSH—Universidade Nova de Lisboa

Dekker A, Giannachi G (2022) Documentation as art: expanded digital practices. Routledge

Depocas A, Ippolito J, Jones C (2003) Permanence through change: the variable media approach. Guggenheim Museum Publications

Dover C (2016) How the Guggenheim and NYU are conserving computer-based art. Part 1. https://www.guggenheim.org/articles/checklist/how-the-guggenheim-and-nyu-are-conserving-computer-based-art-part-1. Accessed 25 Feb 2023

Engel D, Wharton G (2014) Reading between the lines: source code documentation as a conservation strategy for software-based art. Stud Conserv 59(6):404–415. https://doi.org/10.1179/2047058413Y.0000000115. Accessed 22 Feb 2023

Ensom T, McConchie J (2021) Preserving virtual reality artworks. https://www.tate.org.uk/file/preserving-virtual-reality-artworks. Accessed 25 Feb 2023

European Commission (2022) The virtual and augmented reality industrial coalition. Strategic paper. https://op.europa.eu/en/publication-detail/-/publication/9aaef6fd-28db-11ed-8fa0-01aa75ed71a1. Accessed 1 Oct 2023

European Commission (2023a) Cultural heritage in transformation—facing change with confidence. In: HORIZON-CL2-2023-HERITAGE-01-04. EU funding & tenders. https://ec.europa.eu/info/funding-tenders/opportunities/portal/screen/opportunities/topic-details/horizon-cl2-2023-heritage-01-04. Accessed 1 Mar 2024

European Commission (2023b) Strategy on web 4.0 and virtual worlds to steer the next technological transition. https://ec.europa.eu/commission/presscorner/api/files/document/print/en/ip_23_3718/IP_23_3718_EN.pdf. Accessed 1 Mar 2024

Falcão P, Ensom T (2019) Conserving digital art. In: Bowen J, Gianichi T (eds) Museums and digital culture. Springer series on cultural computing, pp 231–252

Gaggioli A (2016) Transformative experience design. In: Human computer confluence: transforming human experience through symbiotic technologies. De Gruyter Open Poland, Warsaw, Poland, pp 97–122

Garner JK, Kaplan A, Pugh K (2016) Museums as contexts for transformative experiences and identity development. J. Mus. Educ 41(4):341–352. https://doi.org/10.1080/10598650.2016.1199343. Accessed 12 March 2022

Giannachi G (2021) Into the space of the digital museum. In: Franco S, Giannachi G (eds) Moving spaces. Enacting dance, performance, and the digital in the museum. Ca'Foscari Digital Publishing

Giannachi G, Lowood H, Worthey G, Price D, Rowland D, Benford S (2012) Documenting mixed reality performance: the case of CloudPad. Digit Creat 23(3–4):159–175. https://doi.org/10.1080/14626268.2012.656274. Accessed 15 Mar 2022

Gill R (2019) Art in a time of crisis. In: Paolo Veronese, 'The Consecration of Saint Nicholas' and the church of San Benedetto al Po. https://www.nationalgallery.org.uk/exhibitions/past/virtual-veronese/art-in-a-time-of-crisis-paolo-veronese-the-consecration-of-saint-nicholas-and-the-church-of-san-benedetto-al-po. Accessed 1 Feb 2024

Grau O (2003) Virtual art: from illusion to immersion. The MIT Press

Gröppel-Wegener A, Kidd J (2019) Critical encounters with immersive storytelling: genre, narrative and environments. Routledge

Guggenheim Museum (2016) The conserving computer-based art initiative. https://www.guggenheim.org/conservation/the-conserving-computer-based-art-initiative. Accessed 15 Mar 2022

Irvin S (2006) Museums and the shaping of contemporary artworks. Mus Manag Curatorsh 21(2):143–156. https://doi.org/10.1016/j.musmancur.2006.03.009. Accessed 12 Mar 2022

Jarvinen A (2022) The creative immersive content lifecycle: from distribution to restoration. Digital catapult report. https://www.digicatapult.org.uk/wp-content/uploads/2022/05/DC002_AOTF-REPORT_AW_220421.pdf. Accessed 10 Feb 2023

Kidd J (2014) Museums in the new mediascape: transmedia, participation, ethics. Ashgate Publishing Limited

Kidd J, McAvoy EN (2019) Immersive experiences in museums, galleries and heritage sites: a review of research findings and issues. Discussion paper. Policy and Evidence Centre PEC

Kuchelmeister V (2018) The virtual (reality) museum of immersive experiences. In: Proceedings of electronic visualisation and the arts EVA conference. https://doi.org/10.14236/ewic/EVA2018.39. Accessed 12 Mar 2022

Laurenson P, van Saaze V, van de Vall R (2022) Bridging the gaps between theory and practice through cross-institutional collaboration in the conservation of contemporary art. In: Swinnen A, Kluveld A, van de Vall R (eds) Engaged humanities. Rethinking art, culture, and public life. Amsterdam University Press

Markova L (2022) Remixing transcultural mobilities on screen: remapping Europe, a remix project. In: Trandafoiu R (ed) Border crossings and mobilities on screen. Routledge. https://doi.org/10.4324/9781003127703-12. Accessed 1 Feb 2024

McDowell A (2019) Storytelling shapes the future. J Future Stud 23(3):105–112. https://doi.org/10.6531/JFS.201903_23(3).0009. Accessed 20 Jan 2024

Muñoz Morcillo J, Faion F, Zea A, Hanebeck UD, Robertson-von Trotha CY (2016) E-installation: synesthetic documentation of media art via telepresence technologies. In: Boştenaru Dan M, Crăciun C (eds) Space and time visualisation. Springer. https://doi.org/10.1007/978-3-319-24942-1_11. Accessed 12 Mar 2022

Real WA (2001) Toward guidelines for practice in the preservation and documentation of technology-based installation art. J Am Inst Conserv 40(3):211–231. www.eai.org/user_files/supporting_documents/william_real.pdf. Accessed 10 Mar 2022

Rhizome (2016) IMLS national leadership grants for libraries. Research project proposal. www.imls.gov/sites/default/files/lg-70-16-0079_proposal_narrative.pdf. Accessed 10 Mar 2022

Rosenthal D (2015) Emulation and virtualisation as preservation strategies. LOCKSS program. Stanford University Libraries. https://mellon.org/media/filer_public/0c/3e/0c3eee7d-4166-4ba6-a767-6b42e6a1c2a7/rosenthal-emulation-2015.pdf. Accessed 12 Mar 2022

Sabiescu AG (2020) Living archives and the social transmission of memory. Curator Mus J (4):497–510. https://doi.org/10.1111/cura.12384. Accessed 1 Feb 2024

Samaras E (2021) Safeguarding digital telecinematic history and culture: archiving film and television visual effects records. Ph.D. thesis. https://opus.lib.uts.edu.au/handle/10453/148877. Accessed 12 Mar 2022

Simon N (2010) The participatory museum. https://participatorymuseum.org/read/. Accessed 1 Sept 2023

UNESCO (2003a) Charter for the preservation of digital heritage. https://unesdoc.unesco.org/ark:/48223/pf0000179529.page=2. Accessed 1 Mar 2022

UNESCO (2003b) Convention for the safeguarding of the intangible cultural heritage. https://ich.unesco.org/en/convention#:~:text=The%20%E2%80%9Cintangible%20cultural%20heritage%E2%80%9D%20means,part%20of%20their%20cultural%20heritage. Accessed 1 Mar 2022

Van Mechelen M (2006) Experience and conceptualisation of installation art. Lecture. https://inside-installations.sbmk.nl/OCMT/mydocs/VAN%20MECHELEN%20Experience%20&%20conceptualisaton%20of%20Installation%20Art.pdf. Accessed 3 Mar 2022

V&A (2019) Collections development policy. https://vanda-production-assets.s3.amazonaws.com/2019/08/05/10/18/38/9432e948-aede-479a-bdee-3cb18be965c2/2019%20Collections%20Development%20Policy.pdf. Accessed 10 Mar 2022

V&A (2022) Preserving and sharing born-digital and hybrid objects from and across the national collection. Research report. https://vanda-production-assets.s3.amazonaws.com/2022/01/20/12/49/45/92b733d4-929e-429e-9fd1-82d134405465/VA-ResearchReport-Jan22.pdf. Accessed 3 Mar 2022

Verhulst I, Woods A, Whittaker L, Bennett J, Dalton P (2021) Do VR and AR versions of an immersive cultural experience engender different user experiences? Comput Hum Behav 125(2021):106951. https://doi.org/10.1016/j.chb.2021.106951. Accessed 1 Feb 2024

Lora Markova is a researcher at the Creative Research and Innovation Centre (CRAIC)—Institute for Creative Futures (ICF), Loughborough University London, where she also leads the modules Immersive Experiences and Creative Technologies, and Creative Industries: Contexts and Practices. Her publications focus on immersive experiences, transcultural aesthetics, and media arts. Lora obtained a Ph.D. (Cum Laude) from Deusto University, Bilbao with EU-funded research mobilities at Goldsmiths, University of London, and the University of Birmingham. Her background involves positions at the former Netherlands Media Art Institute NIMk, Netherlands Institute for Cultural Heritage ICN, Greenpeace International, Amsterdam, and the European Commission, Brussels.

Chapter 11
The Phygital Museum Ecosystem: Pushing Comfort Zone Boundaries in the Visitor Museum Experience

Alessandra Miano

Abstract The hybridisation of how we inhabit the world around us, divided between the real and the digital, is pushing towards a reintegration of the two spheres. This trend, known as 'phygital', goes beyond marketing by applying the benefits of our digital and physical worlds to cultural heritage and museums. The ecosystemic dimension created by digital, multichannel, and multi-device configurations impinges on the communicative and experiential aspects of museum exhibits, allowing a fluid connection between what happens inside the museum and the world beyond its walls. In the context of museum experience design, phygital technology enriches the synaesthetic experience by simultaneously exploiting the narrative and interactive capabilities of technology alongside the material and emotional value of the space and artworks on display. This chapter explores how different levels of integration between story-based digital technology, physical space and visitor engagement can be categorised through a taxonomy of phygital museum experiences. This taxonomy will thereafter be used to examine how these experiences can lead visitors to expand their perception and interpret the museum space as a multi-layered experience open to different connections. The taxonomy will be contextualised in relation to a corpus of relevant research and relevant examples and will be compared with recent past and ongoing exhibitions in Dutch museums. Phygital experiences invite visitors to museums to participate actively, transforming their view of the museum from a static, informative place to a dynamic space for exploration and discovery, where culture is reinterpreted and collective meaning is created.

A. Miano (✉)
Department of Architecture and Industrial Design, University of Campania "Luigi Vanvitelli", Aversa, Caserta, Italy
e-mail: alessandramiano2@gmail.com

L. Calvi et al. (eds.), *Transformative Museum Experiences*, Springer Series on Cultural Computing, https://doi.org/10.1007/978-3-031-89521-0_11

11.1 Introduction

Museum experience design is currently trending in two directions: on the one hand, expanding the narrative to allow a re-reading of collections, highlighting multi-voiced stories beyond the physical dimension of the artwork they contain, and, on the other, involving visitors as active and direct participants in the stories. In this context, the advanced integration of digital layers within the physical space of a museum represents a horizon of application that can allow visitors to experience art and culture in new ways, combining the narrative and multimodal potential of digital technology with the material and evocative power of the artworks on display. The concept of 'phygital' (Borsotti 2022; Carella et al. 2019; Debono 2021; Lupo 2019; Nofal et al. 2017) refers to the incorporation of digital technology into physical, forming a subtle layer (Yates and Løvlie 2023) that can tell a story without obscuring it or losing concentration, reinforcing the intimate and emotional relationship between the viewer and the artwork. This approach transforms the ways people have traditionally experienced museums. Rather than taking a more contemplative attitude, where viewers stand in front of a work of art displayed as immutable content and whose unapproachability is decreed as the main act of reverence, this approach catalyses the progressive opening up of the dialectical relationship between the artwork and the visitor, mediated by digital technology.

The digital transformation of museums is not only about technological innovation but also about visitors and what they can do with technology (Parry 2023). This concept suggests that digital technologies are not to be considered simply as a means of digitalising material but rather as tools to reorganise it by filtering and re-reading existing content (Debono 2021). The resulting reorganisation can be activated through the ongoing participation of the visitors themselves, and this transformative aspect of digital technology, capable of generating innovation in both content and use, lies at the core of the phygital experience. In this context, the integration of digital technology in museum spaces can be seen as part of a broader trend towards the real-virtual hybridisation that is a characteristic of everyday life. Moreover, technology assumes an ecosystemic dimension, described by Bollini (2016) as 'systemic-environmental multitasking' (p. 6). Here, technology is not something separate from ordinary activities; rather, it is incorporated into them, blurring the lines that divide them to the point that it becomes indistinguishable, interacting with the environment, and adapting to user needs. These practices can be interpreted through Henry Jenkins's concept of *convergence culture* (2007), wherein cross-media information flows simultaneously across different platforms and through multiple devices and where the users become the active trigger of the cultural circuit.

The chapter aims to construct a taxonomy of phygital experiences through a literature review and an analysis of suitable case studies. These experiences will be categorised on the basis of the interplay between the formal qualities of digital technology, the storytelling of the exhibited artworks from the tangible to the intangible, and, lastly, the physical involvement of visitors. In this context, the taxonomy will elucidate the different ways in which phygital technology acts as an interactive mediator, showing its potential not only for displaying tangible artworks but also for drawing visitors closer to the shadowy, invisible side that triggers visibility through active participation.

To identify relevant categories for our taxonomy, we begin by examining the principal theoretical concepts surrounding 'phygital'. Re-contextualising it from everyday life activities within cultural heritage and museums makes it possible to interpret the dialectical overlapping of the digital and the real in the relationships between devices, physical space, the artwork on display, and the visitor. The literature review, supported by relevant examples, defines the field of application of phygital technologies. We first review the various digital technology tools available and how they are used to engage visitors within the physical space. These range from wearable digital technologies that provide an interactive experience with the artworks and their surroundings, prompting visitor participation, to transparent embedded devices that react to the movement of the visitors in the space. Following this approach, digital technology can be designed to respond through a language based on everyday actions, such as *speaking*, *touching*, and *walking*, referring to the concept of *natural interfaces* (Cirifino et al. 2011), where interacting with technology feels like an extension of natural behaviour. In phygital museum spaces, digital technologies overlay physical space with an experiential-narrative space. This entails a shift where the interplay between physical space (*situativity*) and the capacity for physical interaction (*physical affordance*), as analysed by Nofal et al. (2017), establish two essential criteria for defining the operational framework of visitor experience, triggering spatial dynamics governed by a visitor's movements. The transformation of museum proxemics towards a performative dimension (Trocchianesi 2014) can be understood by considering the growing centrality of visitor movement within a contributive dynamic that draws visitors into an experience of active participation, from a contemplative dimension to an interpretative one.

Starting from the premise that there are, indeed, distinct phygital experiences, we may conclude that there are two approaches to framing the level of visitor engagement. At first, we can say that visitors can identify with protagonists of the stories and contribute to updating the pathways and content present in the exhibition in real-time, setting their multi-voiced and multi-directional components in motion. Or, secondly, their movements and physical participation can manipulate the space, serving to activate the installations and, dynamically overlapping, continuously shaping the reconfiguration of the exhibition.

We can further explore the taxonomy by comparing case studies from recent and past exhibitions in Dutch museums (2022–2023). These studies offer insights into the various themes that phygital museum experiences can offer, albeit within a specific geographic context. Examining these case studies allows us to identify the characteristics of each category and how they relate to each other, as well as the limitations and opportunities that phygital museum experiences can offer.

11.2 The Phygital Museum Ecosystem: Cultural Heritage Between Bits and Atoms

'We live between two realms: our physical environment and cyberspace. Despite our dual citizenship, the absence of seamless couplings between these parallel existences leaves a great divide between the worlds of bits and atoms' (Ishii and Ullmer 1997, p. 1). Since the dawn of the Internet, the world has been witnessing an ever-increasing gap between physical and digital reality in daily life. This raises the question of how to connect these two spheres and prevent digital experiences from becoming disconnected from the changing nature of physical relationships in the real world. The answer to this dilemma proposed by the authors is the integration of 'bits into atoms', through a seamless overlapping of digital technology, embedded in objects and relationships, '[...] onto (i) our skins/bodies, and (ii) into the physical environments we inhabit' (Ishii and Ullmer 1997, p. 2). This incorporation of digital technology into everyday life expresses the potential of using the digital world not as something separate from reality, but as an amplification of reality itself, expanding the sphere of possible interactions.

The hybridisation of how we live represents the main field of application for the phygital, whose gradual expansion stems from its ability to blur the boundaries between the real and the digital, exploiting the interactive potential of both (Lupo 2019; Del Vecchio et al. 2023). Specifically, phygital is a marketing term coined in 2007 by the Australian agency Momentum Worldwide to refer to the convergence of the consumers' physical and digital worlds. The term's spread from the sphere of marketing to everyday life, particularly in the wake of the 2020 pandemic, is due to its ability to capture the convergence between physical interaction and digital experiences. Gaggioli (2017) describes phygital as being characterised by *context awareness*, responsiveness to users' spatial movements, *embeddedness*, miniaturisation via the Internet of Things, and usability through *natural interfaces*. Such behaviours are rooted in everyday life, so much so that we can speak of 'reality as an app'.

How can *phygital* represent a design approach in the field of cultural heritage and, in particular, within the physical museum space?

Re-contextualising the term within cultural heritage, Nofal et al. (2017) speak of phygital heritage, 'by blending the digital empowerment of cultural learning, storytelling and entertainment into the heritage artefact, activity or environment' (p. 221). The integration of digital technology in everyday life, seamlessly blending digital inputs with physical gestures and vice versa, acquires specific connotations in the field of cultural heritage: on the one hand given the capacities of digital technology to offer flexible, immersive and personalised experiences; and on the other, taking into account the intrinsic characteristics of physical reality through *physical affordances*, moving towards reactive physical gestuality and *situativity*, which denote intrinsic connection with the spatial context. By examining the interplay between *physical affordance* and *situativity*, Nofal et al. (2017) construct a model that extrapolates three layers of phygital heritage, positioning relevant digital technologies. These are: (a) the *augmented*, as a visible and recognisable layer of communication superimposed on physical space through the use of devices such as *augmented-virtual reality* or, in broader terms, through wearable devices, which are potentially context-aware through geolocation technologies, establishing direct communication between the physical device and physical space, activated by the user; (b) *integrated*, where interaction takes place between the spatial context and the artworks on display. In this case, it is incorporated in devices such as diffuse projection technologies, sound sensescapes or *tangible interactions*; and (c), *actuated*, using an interface directly manipulated by the user through *shape-changing technologies*, which transform the physical shape of objects based on the user input.

Phygital experiences mainly operate within the realm of *mixed reality* (Milgram and Kishino 1994), as delineated by the 'virtual continuum' diagram. This continuum moves from the real environment to the virtual, envisioning scenarios where physical and digital elements are simultaneously superimposed. *Mixed reality* transitions between *augmented reality*, where reality is enhanced by the digital layer, and *augmented virtuality*, in which it is the physical reality that enhances the virtual scene. Moreover, with *mixed reality*, the integrated visualisation of the real and the digital, and their capacity for simultaneous interaction, are to be considered contextually (Interaction Design Foundation 2022).

Within the category of *mixed reality*, *tangible interactions* are central: Hornecker (2015) speaks of *tangible interactions* in terms of an extremely heterogeneous set of phenomena, such as 'embodied interaction, tangible manipulation and the physical representation (of data), embeddedness in real space and digitally augmenting physical spaces', emphasising the progressive shift of interest from the digital interface to interaction in space and the movement of the user's body. Furthermore, the tangible experience is not strictly limited to tactility; rather, it involves *multisensoriality*, represented by touch as a bodily extension of all the other senses (Merleau-Ponty 1945; Pallasmaa 2012). Duranti et al. (2016) divide *tangible interactions* into two categories: on the one hand, *objects through interaction*, namely *embedded interactions*, incorporating the digital technological level within physical objects; on the other one, *gestures through interaction*, defined as *embodied interactions*, where the focus shifts from the object to the bodily movement of the visitor. In this case, the action triggers, modifies, and becomes part of the narrative embedded in space, which acquires sensorial qualities.

The dialectical real-digital dimension of phygital spaces relies on different terminologies in order to emphasise the possible theoretical and applied structure of the spatial actors. Benford et al. (2009) define visitor experiences in *hybrid spaces* as 'continuous trajectories', creating an interconnection between digital and real devices along coherent paths that unite narrative, space, and time. Here, the trajectory does not imply the construction of a pre-determined sequence, which the visitor must follow, but rather a structured interconnection between the 'canonical trajectory' that is produced by the designer and the experience shaped by the visitor, based on a 'participant trajectory' nourished by the continuous encounter between the planned experience and the meaning it assumes through visitor interaction (Benford et al. 2009). Trocchianesi (2014) defines hybrid experiences as being characterised by a situated use of digital technology, in which the path is oriented by *fragmentation* and *hypertextuality*, given that hypertext triggers a potentially expandable associative mechanism, which breaks linearity. The construction of a hybrid hypertextual space, shaped by the transformation that the relationship between physical and digital devices triggers in exhibition spaces, unfolds through the design of environments where the plurality of multilevel and multidirectional information requires a continuous personal and collective effort of re-composition and re-reading. A space constructed in this manner delegates the creation of the path to the visitors' processes of awareness, allowing associations between data to produce infinite variables through which to experience the space.

In the *Digital Depot*, a project at the Museum Boijmans van Beuningen in Rotterdam, the focus is on the overlap between the digital layer, on the one hand, which can be accessed using a transparent touch screen positioned in front of the artwork to be explored and, on the other hand, the work of art itself. Through this direct connection, visitors not only deepen their knowledge of the exhibit in front of them but are also stimulated to make connections with related works by the same artist or that are displayed in the museum collection. The content on the screens focuses on the details of the corresponding artwork, but, at the same time, it creates connections among the various items in the exhibition, inviting the visitor to take unprecedented trajectories and superimposing a hypertextual layer that uses the digital to prompt non-sequential associations.

Thus, beyond the different terminologies and the possible interpretations of the prevailing approach, the common denominator is the synergy between the real and the digital, with their ability to encourage physical involvement by the visitor. This engagement is not necessarily bound by the logic that the real should take precedence over the digital. Indeed, Debono (2021) proposes five possible phygital scenarios of application, emphasising the variable relationship between the real and the digital. These are: (a) *physical with a token of digital*, referring to a digital presence in the museum using different communication channels (social media, a website), which can offer an overview of the museum, inviting the public to visit it in person; (b) *physical with digital as an extension*, whereby it is possible to 'replicate' the physical visiting experience through, for instance, virtual tours, meant to be a virtual twin of the real space; (c) *digital as a pointer to the physical*, where the digital does not replicate the physical dimension but is used as a stimulus to visit the museum; (d) the *parallel and cross-referenced existence of physical and digital* explores the potential for museums to live in a transmedia dimension, existing simultaneously on more than one autonomous but complementary level; and (e) *digital with a token of physical*, referring to a scenario where a totally digital experience rests on some physical exhibit.

The concept of phygital thus calls for an ambivalent perspective that recognises the importance of the physical museum experience while also challenging the idea of the museum as a necessarily localised physical place. The museum may be an extensive reality thanks to the potential of the digital network. However, in drawing up a taxonomy of phygital experiences, we must ask what the benefits may be of a physical experience created by the superimposition of the digital onto the physical environment, coordinating the interactive potential of the digital with the evocative materiality of the artwork on display.

In the phygital dimension, the role of bodily involvement becomes paramount, starting from the premise that bodily experience serves as the primary cognitive interface (Dewey 1934; Merleau-Ponty 1945; Pallasmaa 2012). The body is stimulated as a 'triggered body' (Daneluzzo et al. 2023, p. 401), sensitive to the input of objects as they react to the movement and action of the visitor, but it is, at the same time, a 'relational trigger' (Borsotti 2022, p. 449), able to engage relationships in space and with other visitors. Corporeal involvement initiates a self-reflexive process, where self-knowledge is mediated by the awareness of one's position in the world in relation to the presence of others, and that 'exteroception is accompanied by proprioception' (Gibson 1979, p. 179). Moreover, the process of making meaning of the outside is mediated by embodiment, which is connected to the phenomenological encounter with the world around us (Witter and Calvi 2018).

In Teamlab Borderless's multi-sensory environments, space is constructed in response to a visitor's actions and movements. The configuration of space continuously changes depending on how the visitors move. For instance, a space filled with inflatable balloons continually changes depending on the movement of the visitors. By pushing or bumping into one of the balls displayed, a visitor not only triggers a reaction in the object but also influences the configuration of the entire environment, transforming the input–output dynamic into a staging of actions and reactions that involves the whole space.

Recognising the body's role in constructing meaning both internally and externally means having to consider dynamic movement as a key element of design. Traditionally, designers focused on creating static artefacts, while 'today designers think about how people interact over time with product and place' (Lupton and Lipps 2018, p. 10). Therefore, the process of meaning-making requires the relationship with the external space to overlap with the mutability of relationships with the objects and people that inhabit the spaces.

11.3 A Taxonomy of Phygital Museum Experiences

Based on the literature review and some relevant examples, in this section we outline a taxonomy of four phygital museum experiences, conceived to illustrate different transformative capabilities in terms of the variable relationship between the formal qualities of the device, storytelling, and visitor involvement (Fig. 11.1). The first is *wearable technologies as a relational trigger of spatial context*, for which physical mediation devices are used. These are intimate, as they are close to the body, connected to the space and the exhibits, which allows visitors to discover both the space and the artworks, navigating the space and superimposing an infinity of possible trajectories upon it. The second is *Let the space talk: diffuse technologies between immersion and storytelling* through video and audio projections integrated within the space itself so that visitors can freely enjoy the experience with no need for a mediating device, as if the space itself is speaking and the visitor can appreciate the impression of being inside it. The third is *interactive machines: technologies integrated into reagent devices*, designed as devices that can be activated when visitors touch them, triggering an incremental sequence of actions which involve visitors in a discovery process, guided by devices that simultaneously use multimodal communication modes, programmed as wonder machines. The last type of experience consists of *technologies incorporated in objects and spaces as embodied gazes of cultural heritage*. Here, the technology represents an invisible layer, integrated through 3D reproduction and sensors, in objects or sensitive environments that are activated through the physical participation of the visitor. In this case, it is not the space that speaks but the visitor who becomes the centre of the narrative, the main actor of the staging constructed through the digital layer.

We move on now to examine the taxonomy in detail, drawing on case studies selected from recent exhibitions in Dutch museums. This focused approach allows us to closely examine the strengths and weaknesses of the different scenarios.

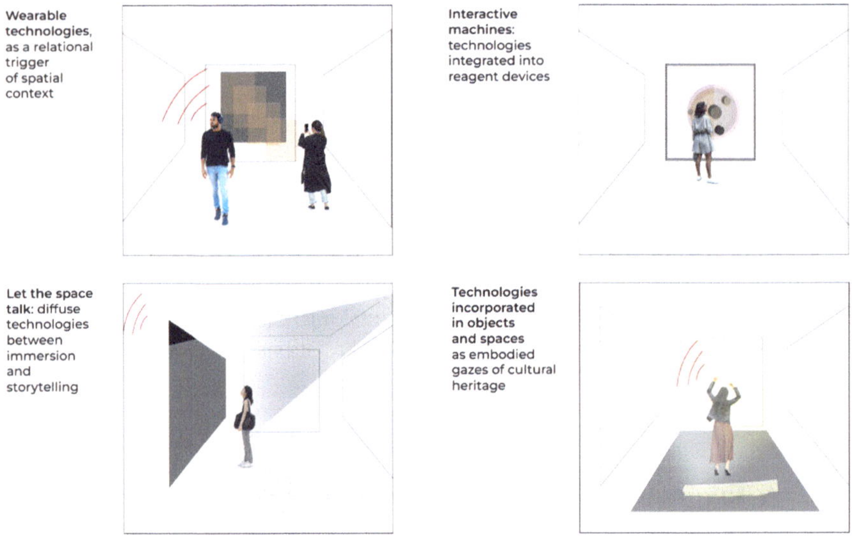

Fig. 11.1 A taxonomy of phygital museum experiences constructed by the author

11.3.1 Wearable Technologies as Relational Triggers of Spatial Context

Central to the discussion is the reference case of the Depot Boijmans Van Beuningen in Rotterdam, designed by MVRDV. This facility serves as an accessible art depository, showcasing the collection of the neighbouring Boijmans Van Beuningen museum.

The mission statement affirms that the Depot is not a traditional museum but a place of work. In this facility, visitors will not find predefined paths or labels; instead, they are free to create their own unique visit experience. This approach is in sympathy with the Depot's identity as a museum of the city, which builds its collection through collaboration and exchange with the local community. In this sense, the *Family of Objects* is a digital programme in which visitors, via an app, can vote for selected items stored in the depot, allowing them to be displayed as 'partners' of selected artworks already on display, sharing the exhibition space, which gives visitors a co-curatorial role.

In this environment, devoid of traditional references, visitors extend their knowledge of the artworks primarily through the use of the app. By framing the QR codes displayed, visitors can access additional information and save their own collection of objects to explore beyond their visit. The app's 'Untold Stories' section provides insights into the artworks on display through a series of 4–5 questions, resembling a quiz format. These stories typically begin with a general description of the artwork's historical period, followed by details of how it came to be housed in the museum, whether through donation, loan, or purchase. Additionally, the app offers insights into the type of inventory number assigned to each artwork, such as the letters 'BRL', indicating a loaned piece. Through this interactive experience, visitors not only learn about the artworks on display but also gain an understanding of the journey each exhibit made before being exhibited at the depot, effectively assuming the role of internal museum staff.

One interesting example is the painting *David with the Head of Goliath*, painted in 1657 by Francesco Barbieri (Fig. 11.2). The app tells an untold story concerning the painting, namely that it was not ascribed to Barbieri until 2016. It had been hanging in an office in a Dutch city hall, its true value unrecognised. The storytelling within the app unfolds in several layers: it explores the painting's relationship with the museum, examines the artist's life, and encourages reflection on various planes. Through audio narration, the painting itself adopts a voice, telling the story of all the years of neglect during which it went unappreciated.

In this case, visitors are invited to feel they are taking an active part in the narration, assuming the point of view not of a passive beneficiary but of the internal dynamics of the museum they are in. They are even able to decide which work from the depot will occupy centre stage (in *Family of Objects*). Certainly, the discovery of an infinite number of stories enriched by the interactive quiz opens up the complexity of an exhibit, both in terms of the present but also with regard to connections with previous events and other artworks. Here, the topic of *fragmentation and hypertext*

Fig. 11.2 Depot: highlights from the graphical interface of the visit app

(Trocchianesi 2014), through the navigation linked to the conscious choice of the visitor, creates a multi-level and multi-directional dynamic, in which it is impossible to determine in advance the infinity of trajectories and perspectives open to the visitor. The dynamic created by the quiz induces incremental interactivity with the visitors, who are invited to discover the artwork through a filter that continually takes them inside and outside of the museum. In this sense, the possibility of saving 'my collection' on the app so as to be able to review the contents later seeks to build a long-term relationship with the museum, inviting visitors to build their own version of the collection on display on-site as well as after the visit.

11.3.2 Let the Space Talk: Diffuse Technologies Between Immersion and Storytelling

The exhibition *Youth*, by artist Anne Imhof, located in the basement of the Stedelijk Museum in Amsterdam, unfolds as a sprawling, labyrinthine installation. Within this space, visitors lose their way, guided by minimal elements: video projections featuring an accompanying avatar, driving music setting the rhythm of their journey, and a setting comprised of familiar elements stripped of their usual context. This route is an entryway into the darker side of society, unsettling visitors to promote a reaction. However, despite the immersive nature of the installation, which heavily relies on spectacle, its lack of a clear narrative prevents visitors from engaging in a transformative experience that extends beyond the sensory stimulation of the moment.

The exhibition *Wey Dey Move: Imagining New Worlds Through Dance and Masquerade* at Het Nieuwe Instituut in Rotterdam presents a different approach, showcasing the social and spiritual role of dance in the culture of Lagos in Nigeria. The immersive environment is constructed on two levels. On the first level, the physical setup recreates an urban and natural space, projecting the visitor into the lagoon metropolis of Lagos. The second is an immersive reconstruction of the world of dance through transparent semi-spheres acting as supports for video projections, putting the visitor at the centre of the story (Fig. 11.3). The space comes alive thanks to the presence of the visitors, who become part of the projection itself, by entering into the narration guided by the voice of the protagonist communities. 'Wey dey move' is a Nigerian term meaning that things are constantly changing and evolving, like a body in motion, inviting the visitor to take in the spirit of this way of life even beyond the museum itself.

Fig. 11.3 Wey dey move, the transparent panels on which the dance is projected allow the visitor to continuously feel part of it

In both cases, the technological component is almost ‘transparent’; visitors walk in and feel as though they are an active part of the installations, amplifying the role of the body as an interface of meaning-making relative to the narrative environment and as continuous triggers of relationships with the outside, the artworks, and the other visitors.

The concept of immersiveness, envisaged as a bilateral relationship between the physical environment enhanced by digital technology and the visitors themselves, emphasises the centrality of storytelling as a filter in an approach that allows for the expansion of the multisensory experience within the space. The reconstruction of the Lagos context triggers a dynamic of *doubled synaesthesia*, ‘the interweaving of natural senses and a new artificial, virtual sensibility’ (Balzola and Rosa 2011, p. 63), stimulating the present and the non-present at the same time. This process takes the visitor right inside Lagos and constructs a narrative in which the visitors themselves play an active part. Conversely, in the case of *Youth*, while the total immersiveness of the installation creates strong sensorial involvement, it does not trigger real internal participation in the narration. The result is that visitors perhaps feel like spectators to a highly personal artist’s tale that one may not enter, separating the sense-creation of the space from the meaning-making, embodying the stories through their own participation.

11.3.3 Interactive Machines: Technologies Integrated in Reagent Devices

The exhibition *Our Colonial Inheritance* at the Tropenmuseum in Amsterdam shows how colonialism has shaped the world today and, through the installation designed by Kossmanndejong, highlights the multi-voiced nature of positions that have often remained in the dark.

The *monument of names* is a digital monument containing the data for hundreds of thousands of enslaved people. Their names are displayed together with their relationships to each other, supplemented by personal stories. The monument consists of two parts: a touchscreen and a large-screen projection. Visitors can search for names through the touchscreen, and, by clicking on a name, additional information about that person is displayed. Lines appear on the projection screen showing the names of known relatives, and the projection grows, revealing a multitude of connections. The monument thus visualises the social ties between enslaved people, making the visitor aware of interwoven relationships that have been obscured for many years (Fig. 11.4).

Interactive machines act as reactive devices, triggering interactions that require a dialectic between the device and the user, creating a participatory dynamic. Visitor involvement proceeds through narrative sequences, which require a visitor to make some movement, causing the participatory outputs to become visible. The devices become interpretive stations, where knowledge of the works is filtered through the

Fig. 11.4 The monument of names, the double layer: the touchscreen and the projection

visitors' digital graphic reworking, displaying the results both in the device itself and through projections in space. It is a narrative circuit fed by the visitor's actions, using the device as a social mediator and, at the same time, a mechanism of incremental discovery. The double level of touch screen and projection highlights the complexity of the artwork, which expands thanks to the repeated searches conducted by the visitors. It is from their active participation that the visualisation of otherwise invisible connections emerges.

In contrast, the installation called *Du Feasts and Tambù*, in the section on slavery, resistance, and resilience presents artefacts associated with the annual Du Feasts celebrations held on Surinamese plantations. During these events, slaves would express opposition to their circumstances, beating African drums and performing dances. Visitors are encouraged to interact with the instruments on display, triggering sounds by pressing buttons, and thus simulating the collective ritual of dance. Narrating artworks through shared sound also means questioning whether a vision-based narrative is the only possible means of fruition. In this case, therefore, it would not be possible to understand the objects of the 'du fest' without experiencing their sound and without the reciprocal interaction of the visitors to elicit a response from the objects, staging the public dimension of the fest. In this instance, it is interesting to note that the way the interactive device filters content is able to offer visitors a response capable of triggering an emotional dimension quite different from what a didactic reading of the objects on display would have triggered.

11.3.4 Technologies Incorporated into Objects and Spaces as Embodied Gazes of Cultural Heritage

The exhibition *Humania*, designed by the Kossmanndejong and hosted at the Nemo Science Centre in Amsterdam, offers a journey of discovery of the human body and its potential. It allows visitors to understand who we are, how we experience interaction with others, and how far we can push our potential through various installations that invite visitors to get involved, both individually and cooperating with others, from testing one's reflexes to checking one's balance by holding a device steady with another visitor, challenging physical motor skills, or learning how to interpret one's gait. These installations have strong performative potential since it is, in fact, the visitor who is on display in an environment that is conducive to exploring aspects of being in the world and collaborating with others. Performance serves as a mechanism for contextualised meaning-making, experienced through the movement of one's body. It is a process of self-awareness, defining one's position through the presence of the other.

At the *Markiezenhof* in Bergen op Zoom, the design of four-period rooms strikes a balance between the need to preserve spaces and objects while maintaining the original layout on the one hand and, on the other hand, telling stories about the court in a way that will involve visitors. The story that is enacted and linked to the palace space is that of the Marquise Marie Anne Van Arenberg. The Marquise is the protagonist of a love story, which later turns out to be tragic. Through twelve points of interest, distributed across four rooms, the developing story of the Marquise is told through the use of smart replicas and sensitive environments that are activated when the visitor moves around the room. Each story requires a gesture by the visitor to activate it as if to establish a personal and intimate connection. Visitors become increasingly involved in the narrative as their visit proceeds. For instance, when they enter the intimacy of the bedroom and touch a lamp, the lights go out, and a screen displays the story of Marquise's love and the resulting tragedy. A family quarrel is enacted in the dining room, and visitors are invited to sit down and ring the bell, activating the voices of the participants. Then, in the next installation, the visitor has to sign in order to decide what the conclusion of the story will be, finding out in the last room how the story really went (Fig. 11.5). According to a study conducted by Calvi et al. (2024) which involved interviews of 30 participants via convenience sampling and then analysed through the tools of the Interpretative Phenomenological Analysis, emerges different perspective: while some participants felt the intimacy of the narrative as an aid to discovering the space, others said that the excessive presence of the digital elements induced a sense of pressure, requiring more moments of reflection (Calvi et al. 2024).

In both exhibitions (*Humania-Markiezenhof*), bodily involvement is central, even if it plays different roles. In the first case, the interactive artefacts are visible as physical devices, activated not through conventional means of interaction with the digital—following the input–output model—but by placing actions in the forefront, as the very subject of the story and the mechanism for transforming the content

Fig. 11.5 The dining room: visitors sit at the table and activate the installation by ringing the bell. The individual dishes light up as each character speaks. Copyright The author

on display. In the second case, however, the technology is completely invisible, integrated into the sensitive environments that require human action, not as mere triggers, but as conduits into the narratives, allowing visitors to identify with the characters and decide how the storyline will develop.

At the core of sensitive environments lies the recognition of visitors' actions as transformative agents in a deliberate choice to incorporate their actions as part of the narrative itself. As Jacucci (2004) observes, participation unfolds in stages. First, visitors agree to participate by starting to move within the space (*circumspection phase*), then they test their movements (*test phase*), and once they become aware of them (or coordinate with other visitors if actions are collective), they can use their bodies as interfaces, understanding their transformative capacity (*play phase*).

11.4 Discussion and Conclusions

This comparison of the four categories within the taxonomy seeks to reveal the potential and limitations of phygital applications. The complexity of the relationships brought into play highlights the impossibility of establishing rigid consequentiality, integrating the various components in different ways, especially in terms of the environmental context and the guided freedom of choice of the visitor. Visitor involvement takes different forms, ranging from the active-interactive to the active-performative, from their ability to manipulate the digital layer through continuous participation to staging their physical participation as the very focus of the storytelling.

The wearable near-device concept (*Depot*) invites us to reflect on how technological devices can capture visitors' movements, becoming both a prosthesis and a narrative-interactive amplifier. The ability to stand in the museum in front of an exhibit and to open up a behind-the-scenes scenario, as well as the history of the painting, inducing the visitor to make totally new associations, makes the narrative potentially open-ended. This potential is further expanded through the possibility of being able to save information and carry it beyond the visit. However, the introduction of a device does not make the relationship with the experience completely free. This theme is surpassed by the immersive approach (*Youth-Wey Dey Move*), which allows visitors to explore the space without any intermediary devices. Yet, it asks to strike a balance between allowing the visitor freedom of movement and empowering them by assigning a new role. Going beyond sensory stimulation, this role confers the ability to become completely immersed in the stories. The amplification of an active research component is primarily achieved through interactive devices (*Our Colonial Inheritage*), which allow data to be re-elaborated based on visitors' filter, accompanying them to fixed stations which respond to their actions, offering data translations in such a way as to be multimodal and potentially participative. The possibility of not only activating the narrative but of being able to directly modify it lies at the heart of the fourth category of embodied technologies (*Humania-Markiezenhof*), where the body becomes the interface with no digital prosthesis, integrating the actions of the body into the narrative itself.

Thus, the frontiers of phygital technology force us to consider how participation can lead to a continual reinterpretation of heritage itself, thereby identifying a level of 'innovativeness' in visitors' direct experiences.

What perspectives emerge from the taxonomy of phygital experiences? The taxonomy demonstrates how with different technological tools mediated in physical space, it is possible to channel multi-voiced narratives constructed from visitors' active participation, which are thus never identical.

The story creates interactive relationships built through digital technology, shifting the focus from the device to actions, from the physical prosthesis to the exploration of experiences otherwise inaccessible in the physical world. The connection between the material dimension of space and the interactive layer is constructed as simultaneous communication between the real and the digital, adapted to the mutability of human relationships. The space becomes the story, constructed as a hypertext guided by the visitor's associations, suggesting multiple connections. The potential of digital multi-modality offers a multi-voiced perspective on the narratives created around the artworks on display.

Digital technology is thus designed to prompt an encounter between the body and the artwork, involving perception, action, and cognition. Here, the act of perception requires the mediation of a physical action to achieve cognitive awareness. While this dynamic finds its most quintessential expression within the museum space and surrounding works of art, it is by its very nature a hybrid destined to transcend the confines of the museum, extending the flow of information beyond the visit, triggering transformative experiences that exploit the ecosystem to amplify and manipulate the interpretation of cultural heritage.

References

Balzola A, Rosa P (2011) L' arte fuori di sé. Un manifesto per l'età post-tecnologica. Feltrinelli

Benford S, Giannachi G, Koleva B, Rodden T (2009) From interaction to trajectories: designing coherent journeys through user experiences. In: Proceedings of the SIGCHI conference on human factors in computing systems (CHI '09). ACM, New York, NY, pp 709–718. https://doi.org/10.1145/1518701.1518812

Bollini L (2016) Large, small, medium. Il design della comunicazione nell'ecosistema digitale. Maggioli Editore, Santarcangelo di Romagna

Borsotti M (2022) Digital practices for generating interaction: exhibits and museums as phygital environments. In: (In)tangible heritage(s): design, culture and technology—past, present, and future; AMPS proceedings series, vol 29, no 2, pp 449–455

Calvi L, Bargeman B, Hover M, van Waalwijk J, Strijbosch W, Mitas O (2024) Storytelling as a tool to design museum experiences: the case of the secret marquise. In: Zanella F, Bosoni G, Di Stefano E, Iannilli GL, Matteucci G, Messori R, Trocchianesi R (eds) Multidisciplinary aspects of design. Objects, processes, experiences and narratives. Springer series in design and innovation, vol 37. Springer, Cham, pp 423–433. https://doi.org/10.1007/978-3-031-49811-4_40

Carella G, Arquilla V, Zurlo F, Tamburello MC (2019) Phygital experiences design. Diid 67:129–135

Cirifino F, Giardina Papa E, Rosa P (2011) Studio Azzurro. Musei di narrazione, percorsi interattivi e affreschi multimediali. Silvana Editoriale

Daneluzzo M, Zannoni M, Dall'Osso G, Gasparotto S (2023) Design and responsive technologies for human well-being. Diid—Disegno Ind Ind Des (DSI 1) 10. https://doi.org/10.30682/diiddsi23t3a

Debono S (2021) Thinking phygital: a museological framework of predictive futures. Mus Int 73:156–167. https://doi.org/10.1080/13500775.2021.2016287

Del Vecchio P, Secundo G, Garzoni A (2023) Phygital technologies and environments for breakthrough innovation in customers' and citizens' journey. A critical literature review and future agenda. Technol Forecast Soc Change 189

Dewey J (2005) Art as experience. Penguin. Original work published 1934

Duranti D, Spallazzo D, Trocchianesi R (2016) Tangible interaction in museums and temporary exhibitions: embedding and embodying the intangible values of cultural heritage. In: Proceedings of the 6th international forum of design as a process. Editorial Universitat Politècnica València, Valencia

Gaggioli A (2017) Phygital spaces: when atoms meet bits. Cyberpsychol Behav Soc Netw 20(12)

Gibson J (1979) The ecological approach of visual perception. Houghton Mifflin, Boston

Hornecker E (2015) Tangible interaction, 5 July 2015. Interaction Design Foundation—IxDF. https://www.interaction-design.org/literature/book/the-glossary-of-human-computer-interaction/tangible-interaction

Interaction Design Foundation—IxDF (2022) What is mixed reality (MR)?, 24 Jan 2022. Interaction Design Foundation—IxDF. https://www.interaction-design.org/literature/topics/mixed-reality-mr

Ishii H, Ullmer B (1997) Tangible bits: towards seamless interfaces between people, bits and atoms. In: Proceedings of the ACM SIGCHI conference on human factors in computing systems (CHI '97). Association for Computing Machinery, New York, pp 234–241. https://doi.org/10.1145/258549.258715

Jacucci G (2004) Interaction and performance. Oulu University Press

Jenkins H (2007) Convergence culture: where old and new media collide. New York University Press, New York

Lupo E (2019) Design e cultural driven innovation. i+Diseño 14:120–132

Lupton E, Lipps A (2018) The senses: design beyond vision. Princeton Architectural Press

Merleau-Ponty M (1945) Phenomenology of perception. Routledge, London

Milgram P, Kishino F (1994) A taxonomy of mixed reality visual displays. IEICE Trans Inf Syst E77-D 12:1321–1329

Nofal E, Reffat RM, Vande Moere A (2017) Phygital heritage—an approach for heritage communication. In: The 3rd annual international conference of the immersive leaming research network, Portugal, 26–29 June 2017, pp 220–229. https://doi.org/10.3217/978-3-85125-530-0-36

Pallasmaa J (2012) The eyes of the skin: architecture and the senses. Wiley, Chichester

Parry R (2023) Staging postdigitality. Interdisciplinary perspectives on museums, digital culture and design research. Presented at Convegno Nazionale Architettura degli Interni e Allestimento, Politecnico di Torino, Sept 2023

Trocchianesi R (2014) Design e narrazioni per il patrimonio culturale. Maggioli Editore, Santarcangelo di Romagna

Witter M, Calvi L (2018) Enabling augmented sense-making (and pure experience) with wearable technology. In: Chisik Y, Holopainen J, Khaled R, Luis Silva J, Alexandra Silva P (eds) Intelligent technologies for interactive entertainment. INTETAIN. Lecture notes of the institute for computer sciences, social informatics and telecommunications engineering, vol 215. Springer, Cham. https://doi.org/10.1007/978-3-319-73062-2_11

Yates M, Løvlie AS (2023) Subtle sound design: designing for experience blend in a historic house museum. J Comput Cult Herit 17:1–15. https://doi.org/10.1145/3633476

Alessandra Miano Designer, Ph.D. at University of Campania Luigi Vanvitelli. Her research is focused on the diffusion of hybrid technologies in cultural spaces, investigating the relationship between technology and storytelling, linked to the bodily engagement of visitors. She conducted research as visiting scholar at Rotterdam University of Applied Sciences and IT University of Copenhagen.

Chapter 12
Seeing Art Through the Eye of the Algorithm: Artificial Intelligence in the Museum

Anders Sundnes Løvlie, Louie Søs Meyer, Christian Sivertsen, Peter Kun, Matthias Freiberger, and Sebastian Risi

Abstract Artificial Intelligence (AI) techniques are currently receiving much attention in art and curatorship—and in museum experience design. This chapter asks: How can AI affect the experience of art in a museum? Can seeing art through the eye of the algorithm show us something new? We present a range of examples of applications of AI in museum experience design and discuss three main approaches: image analysis, generative AI and critiquing AI. Based on insights from testing and evaluation of former designs, we reflect on the ways in which AI can highlight details and interpretations, synthesise the aesthetics of a large collection or even all of art history—and what it might also obscure and distort.

12.1 Introduction

Artificial Intelligence (AI) technologies have made giant strides in recent years in areas such as computer vision, natural language processing, intelligent interfaces, and generative systems such as image generators (Dall-E, Stable Diffusion, Midjourney)

A. Sundnes Løvlie (✉) · L. S. Meyer · C. Sivertsen · P. Kun · S. Risi
IT University of Copenhagen, Copenhagen, Denmark
e-mail: asun@itu.dk

L. S. Meyer
e-mail: lomm@itu.dk

C. Sivertsen
e-mail: csiv@itu.dk

P. Kun
e-mail: peter@peterkun.com

S. Risi
e-mail: sebr@itu.dk

M. Freiberger
University of Copenhagen, Copenhagen, Denmark

L. Calvi et al. (eds.), *Transformative Museum Experiences*, Springer Series on Cultural Computing, https://doi.org/10.1007/978-3-031-89521-0_12

and Large Language Models (LLMs) such as GPT (recently popularised as ChatGPT) and LLAMA. There has already been much debate about the use of these technologies in cultural heritage and museums (Ciecko 2020; Fontanella et al. 2020; Villaespesa and Murphy 2021). While there are obvious challenges and risks—such as misinformation, algorithmic bias, insensitivities in relation to difficult topics, and so on—we believe the technology also offers interesting new opportunities for creating thoughtful and transformative museum experiences.

In this chapter, we will discuss approaches to applying AI techniques in the design of museum experiences. We focus on the type of AI known as Computer Vision—through which computer systems can be used both to recognise and analyse images and to generate new images. We will present examples of designs that illustrate opportunities and challenges with these approaches. The examples are drawn from past research in museum experience design—both our own and that of others—as well as AI art and research.

12.2 Background and Related Work

There is a long history of research in the areas of Design and Human-Computer Interaction (HCI) conducted in collaboration with museums, aiming to create novel experiences with museum collections (Vermeeren et al. 2018; Hornecker and Ciolfi 2019; Waern and Sundnes Løvlie 2022). Such research has explored a variety of technologies and approaches, such as smartphones, virtual reality/mixed reality, tangible and embodied interactions, games—and, more recently, AI. Much of this research has been motivated by the digitisation of museum collections which has been an ongoing effort for several decades, aiming both to secure the contents of the collections for the future and also to increase public access to collections. These efforts have resulted in large databases of art and heritage collections—for instance, the EU-funded Europeana database contains over 30 million images. Facilitating online access to museum collections not only increases the access of citizens who cannot physically travel to visit the museum they are interested in, but it also expands access to the vast number of artefacts in archives that cannot be exhibited physically in the museums. It is commonly suggested that large European museums usually have a very small share of their collections on display in their physical exhibition spaces, both due to limitations in space and other capacity limitations, as well as many artworks being too brittle to exhibit. For instance, the National Gallery of Denmark only has 0.7% of the collection on display ("SMK Open: Setting Art Free" 2018).

This digitalization agenda in the museum and cultural heritage sector has fostered the implementation of AI techniques for such things as collection management, audience predictions, art authentication, and more (Ciecko 2020; Fontanella et al. 2020; Villaespesa and Murphy 2021; Sinatti et al. 2022; Maietti 2024). The EU-funded "Time Machine" project explored the idea of a "Big Data of the Past" to digitise large amounts of cultural heritage data and create visualisations with the use of AI.[1] However, making collections available digitally may not in itself be sufficient to facilitate engagement. In the effort to create novel and engaging experiences with digital collections, many cultural heritage institutions—such as Europeana—have encountered a challenge with *metadata*—the various data associated with an artefact in a collection, such as keywords and other information that enable search, browsing and other forms of exploring the database. Describing and allocating metadata to museum and cultural heritage items is an essential yet labour-intensive task, which often requires highly specialised domain expertise from museum curators and researchers (Meinecke 2022; Giannini and Bowen 2019).

Several museums have experimented with computer vision techniques to enrich their metadata (Tallon 2018; Smith 2019; Stack 2020). Such algorithmic enrichment may be helpful both for museum researchers who frequently need to search their collection, as well as for non-expert audiences. For example, the Harvard Art Museum invites online users to investigate how computers see and process images of artwork, comparing metadata generated by humans to metadata generated by AI technologies developed by Amazon, Clarifai, Imagga, Google, and Microsoft. Another example is the Princeton Art Museum, which has experimented with computer vision for various purposes, including detecting visual similarities in Chinese paintings from different eras (Villaespesa and Murphy 2021). Museums have also explored using computer vision techniques in experiences for visitors to the physical museum exhibition, for instance, through mobile apps which use image recognition to allow visitors to point their camera at an artwork and receive information about it (MacDonough 2018; Sundnes Løvlie et al. 2021). Although AI techniques show great promise for museums, there are potential pitfalls concerning bias. Museums hold a wide selection of artworks in their collections, among them pieces representing controversial, challenging, and painful parts of history and contemporary society. Research has found that AI models are limited by bias, specifically in terms of cultural and gender biases (Villaespesa and Murphy 2021). Ciecko (2020) questions whether museums should withhold some artworks from being classified by computer vision algorithms, highlighting colonization, slavery, and genocide as particularly challenging topics.

In recent years there has been a surge of artists working with generative AI systems to create art, sometimes referred to as "AI Art" (Zylinska 2020; Cetinic and She 2022; Epstein et al. 2023) or "Machine Learning Art" (Audry 2021). However, in this chapter, we will focus on the use of AI and machine learning for *Experience Design* in an art museum context, rather than creating new forms of art.

At the current point in time (2024) much attention is directed at LLMs such as GPT and LLAMA. Some research has been done to explore the application of these systems in museum contexts. In fact, museums have been using a variety of chatbots for a long time—Vidu and colleagues (2021) provide an overview with the earliest example dating back to 2004. However, with the popular success of LLMs, there seems to be a sharp rise in interest in the use of these technologies in museums. Some projects present technical concepts but stop short of applying or testing them in practice (Mann et al. 2022), whereas others (Wang et al. 2024;

[1] https://cordis.europa.eu/project/id/820323.

Trichopoulos et al. 2023a) have experimented with LLMs in the context of "virtual museums", treating the museum more as a virtual exhibition space than an actual museum institution. Trichopoulos and colleagues (2023b) report on an experiment using GPT-4 to create a museum guide tested in an actual museum context, and conclude with a caution that it is currently impossible to ensure that the model always provides "correct, scientifically valid, and evidenced knowledge" to visitors. Spennemann (2023) engaged with ChatGPT to assess whether this could be used as a tool for developing an exhibition concept, concluding that it served well as a "brainstorming tool" but that the contributions of the human curator were "essential". LLMs have also been used in a variety of other tasks relating to visitor insights and museum management and planning (Vidu et al. 2021; Murphy and Villaespesa 2020). However, in the following, we will focus primarily on approaches using computer vision rather than text-based interaction.

12.3 Image Analysis

Perhaps the most frequently discussed strategy for using AI in museums is the idea of employing AI techniques—in particular, computer vision—to analyse digitised museum collections, usually with the purpose of creating richer metadata in order to improve searchability and to make new digital experiences possible.

Enriching metadata is seen as a crucial component to unlock the potential of digitalization to provide richer experiences with museum collections. In order for digital museum collections to be of any use, people must be able to search and find items of interest to them. This can be done with the help of metadata such as keywords that are assigned to an item—for instance, if one searches in the collections of the Norwegian National Museum for 'Hardangerfjord' one will be able to find the famous painting "Bridal Procession in Hardangerfjord"—unsurprisingly, since that precise word is used in the title. However, searching for other objects that feature prominently in the painting such as 'boat', 'mountain', or 'cloud' does not work, since there are no such keywords associated with this item. Even though these objects are immediately visible to the human eye, the digital system needs to rely on keywords (that is, metadata) explicitly describing what can be seen in the image. However, having humans manually analyse and assign a sufficiently detailed list of keywords to each of the numerous items in all the world's cultural heritage databases would be a momentous task. For this reason, there is great interest in the potential for using AI to improve collections metadata.

Some museums have already started applying computer vision to enrich the metadata of their collections—such as The Metropolitan Museum of Art (New York), the Barnes Foundation (Philadelphia), Harvard Art Museums (Cambridge, MA), and the National Gallery of Denmark (Copenhagen). However, the "cross depiction" problem has for many years been a challenge for AI: While algorithms could recognise objects in photographs with impressive accuracy, they would struggle to detect the same objects in other styles of depiction such as paintings and drawings (Hall et al. 2015; Geirhos et al. 2019; Kadish et al. 2021). A few years ago Ciecko and colleagues (2020) reviewed the state of the art in commercially available computer vision systems, applied to images from art museums. The authors applied off-the-shelf systems to suggest keywords relating to images of artwork, and observed a surprising degree of accuracy with a broad variety of images, from classic art to more contemporary and abstract depictions. However, they also observed some weaknesses relating to anachronism, cultural bias, gender bias, and delicate topics (i.e. an image of iron ankle manacles from Australia's convict history was labelled as "Fashion Accessory" and "Jewelry"). Due in part to such weaknesses Villaespesa and Murphy (2021) conclude that the use of computer vision for metadata enrichment mostly remains an experimental effort for museums (see also Villaespesa and Crider 2021).

One particularly interesting strategy for dealing with the weaknesses and errors produced by computer vision systems was proposed by Kevin Bacon from Brighton Museum and Art Gallery (UK), in an experiment that formed part of the EU-funded GIFT project (Bacon 2019). Bacon proposed that rather than directly applying the AI-generated keywords in the museum database, the keywords may be presented to human users—museum staff members—who were asked to review the AI-created tags, both removing incorrect tags as well as adding new tags inspired by the AI keywords. Thus the AI system worked as a "provocation" that helped human users notice features of the digital images that they otherwise might not have thought about documenting in metadata.

While the above examples are all from the last 3–5 years prior to the time of writing, they are already on the verge of being obsolete. Significant progress in artificial intelligence has been achieved in recent years through advances in machine learning (Vaswani et al. 2017; Devlin et al. 2019; Radford et al. 2021) which leverage the enormous collections of annotated images on the World Wide Web, resulting in the advent of powerful multimodal models which are able to classify and describe the contents of images with impressive accuracy and versatility, such as CLIP (Radford et al. 2021), GLIP (Li et al. 2022), ChatGPT (Achiam et al. 2024), and LLAVA (Liu et al. 2023).

As an illustration of this technological leap, consider the analysis of Pablo Picasso's collection of lithographs titled "The Bull", which was reported by Meyer and colleagues (2024). Picasso's lithographs demonstrate a range of depiction styles from lifelike drawings to ever more abstract styles. When the authors first analysed the image in 2021 they used a state-of-the-art image recognition algorithm (Fast R-CNN (Girshick 2015), pretrained on the Common Objects in Context (COCO) (Lin et al. 2014) dataset); however, the algorithm could only classify three of the most lifelike drawings as showing a "cow" (as the COCO dataset had no separate category for bull). In 2023 the authors tested the Grounded Language-Image Pre-Training (GLIP) (Li et al. 2022) algorithm on the same image, and at this point, the algorithm could correctly classify even the most abstract drawings as bulls.

How might this leap in accuracy and versatility in image analysis be used to design novel museum experiences? This was investigated by Meyer and colleagues through the design of a prototype for a web interface that allows museum visitors to explore a digital art collection using the *objects* depicted in paintings as the primary entry point (Meyer et al. 2024). They used GLIP to label objects in all the 6750 paintings in the digital collections of the National Gallery of Denmark (SMK), resulting in a dataset of 109,145 labelled objects. The resulting website, called *SMKExplore*, invited visitors to browse through collections of objects such as 'butterflies', 'skulls', 'guitars', etc.—altogether 120 separate types of objects, which was the maximum number of labels that the technical setup would allow (see Fig. 12.1). Users with an interest in a particular topic—for instance, occultism—could browse through a list of images of objects such as skulls, skeletons, demons and ghosts, and by clicking on any object they would see the entire artwork it appeared in along with links to further information, other objects in the image and more (Fig. 12.2). When this design was tested on 22 visitors at the National Gallery, participants were overwhelmingly positive and many suggested this experience made them see the artworks in new ways. Seeing similar objects depicted by a variety of artists from a variety of time periods and in different styles, offered visitors a new perspective: "*Many motifs are reappearing. It makes sense, but when you see it like this, it is wild*" (Meyer et al. 2024). Some test users also reported that this experience made them pay attention to paintings which they previously had disregarded when passing by them in the physical museum exhibition.

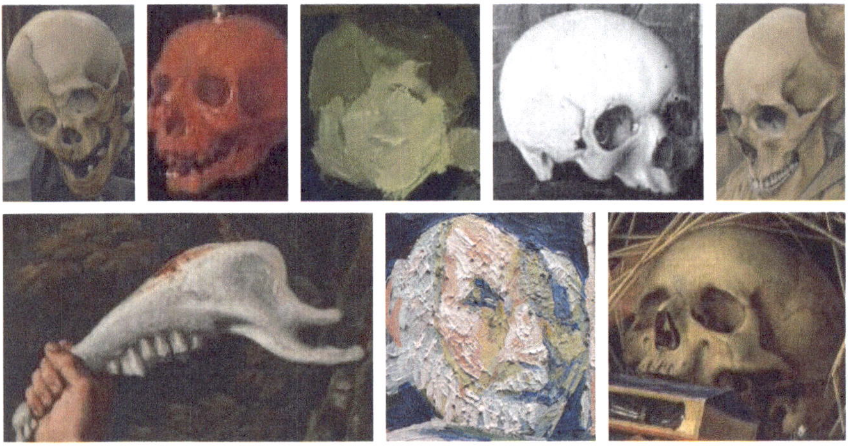

Fig. 12.1 A selection of details labelled by the GLIP model as "skull" in paintings from the collection of the National Gallery of Denmark. Details from the following artworks (from top left): three skulls from Convento dei Cappucini at Palermo, L. A. Ring; A Cabinet with Objects of Art, Georg Hainz; Portrait of a Boy, Edvard Weie; Saint Jerome, unknown artist; three skulls from Convento dei Cappucini at Palermo, L. A. Ring. Bottom, from left: Cain Slaying Abel, Paolo de Matteis; self-portrait, Niels Larsen Stevns; Trompe l'oeil with Studio Wall and Vanitas Still Life, Cornelius Norbertus Gijsbrechts

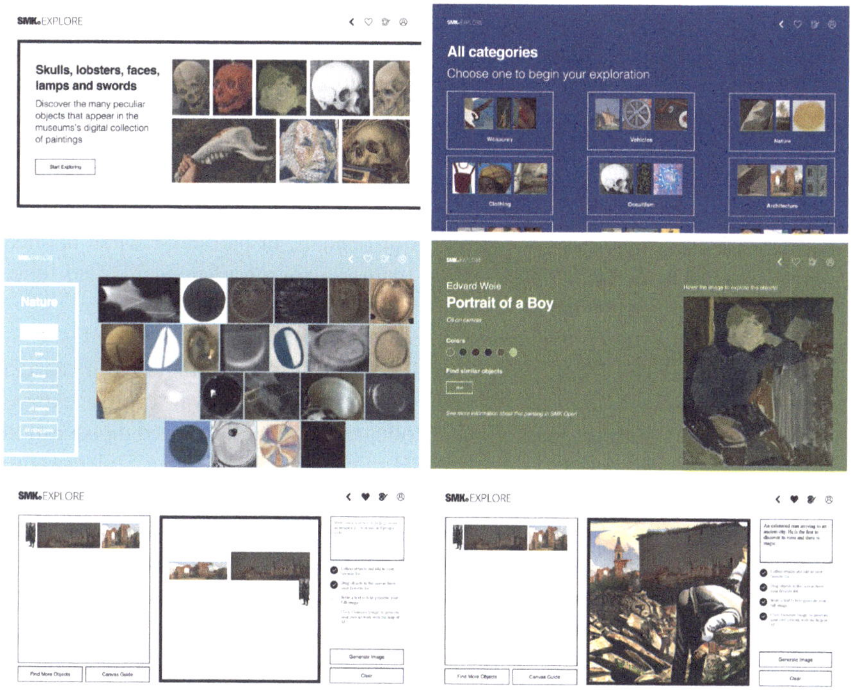

Fig. 12.2 Screenshots from the SMKExplore website presenting the art collection through objects detected in the paintings

12.4 Generative AI

In the last few years, there have been remarkable breakthroughs in generative AI—systems that create high-quality images and text, usually based on text prompts from human users. The implications of this development for art and culture have been the subject of much debate (Epstein et al. 2023). Such technologies have been used to make artworks by artists such as Refik Anadol, Mario Klingemann, Trevor Paglen, Helena Sarin and more, sometimes referred to as "AI Art" (Zylinska 2020; Grba 2022) or Machine Learning Art (Audry 2021). As these technologies have become increasingly easily accessible they have also fostered an extensive amateur culture, with communities forming around using "prompt engineering" to create aesthetic images and sharing them through online forums such as Behance or Discord—or even buying and selling prompts in online marketplaces. These technologies have also been used to create visitor experiences for museums and art galleries. For instance, The Dalí Museum in St. Petersburg, Florida used machine learning to create a lifelike "deepfake" version of Salvador Dalí which would engage visitors in conversation—even taking selfies with them (Billock 2019). AI is also used in the popular genre of "immersive" art shows (Mondloch 2022; Mathias 2022), typically for animating the artworks or creating dynamic visualisations with elements from the artworks. Academic researchers have also started to explore the use of generative AI for museum experiences. For instance, Hettmann and colleagues (2023) used Natural Language Processing (NLP) as well as image analysis to facilitate narration and gameplay in a museum context. Similarly, Wang and colleagues (2024) used a multimodal Large Language Model (LLM) to create guided tours inside a "virtual museum" system. However, the use of generative AI also raises risks about inaccuracy, disinformation and other harmful content, in particular when applied to sensitive historical content such as the memorialization of genocide and other historical atrocities (Makhortykh et al. 2023).

Generative AI has received much attention from media and audiences and is obviously fascinating as a technology that allows people to create rich imagery very easily. However, can it also help us to see art in new ways—and create novel aesthetic experiences in a museum context? Sivertsen and colleagues (2023a) explored this question through a design experiment at the MUNCH museum in Oslo, using StyleGAN to create an installation that offered an immersive experience with Edvard Munch's "green room" paintings. Interestingly, in this project, the model was deliberately "underfitted"—meaning that the training of the model was stopped before it had reached an optimal result—in order to enhance the sense of ambiguity inherent in Munch's artworks (Sivertsen et al. 2024). Thus, in this case, the AI model actually obscured and distorted the view of the original artworks, both in order to avoid creating a digital replica that would compete with the original artwork, but also to facilitate a certain perspective. Sivertsen and colleagues argue that their use of technology could be seen as a form of non-verbal art critique that might facilitate an "education of attention" for the visitors (Sivertsen et al. 2023c).

In another project, Sivertsen and colleagues (2023b) built an "interactive drawing table" that to an even greater degree altered the view of the original art. They used a generative AI model trained on the MUNCH museum's extensive collection of drawings and sketches to give visitors an experience of drawing "together" with Edvard Munch: As visitors draw on the paper, the AI model tries to respond with lines and patterns based on its internal representation of Munch's aesthetics (Fig. 12.3). Here, the generative AI allowed visitors to engage with the Munch's sketching practice as a *process* rather than as a set of static images—and it allowed visitors to consider the synthesised aesthetics of a large collection, rather than a few individual images. While Sivertsen and colleagues focused on the specific art collection of the MUNCH museum, Kun and colleagues (2024a, b) have used the general multimodal model of Stable Diffusion to explore how generative AI can present the visual aesthetics of a variety of art styles and motifs. They present a "generative picture frame" which allows users to interact with an image generation system via an interactive display which mimics the format of a traditional portrait painting with a large ornamental physical frame and a small e-ink display imitating an information plaque (Fig. 12.4). However, the system also includes a panel with knobs and buttons which users can turn to adjust parameters of the generated image such as mood, artistic style and randomisation. Turning the knobs makes the system generate a new image in response to the user's input—thus altering the situation from one passively viewing

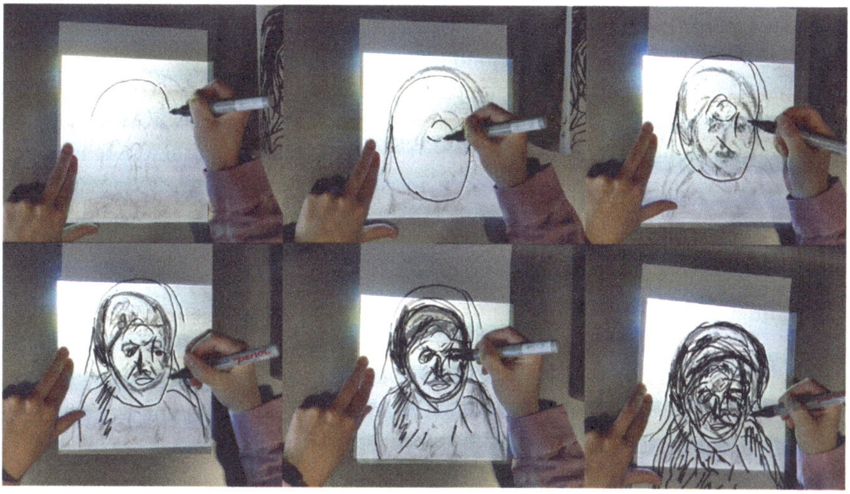

Fig. 12.3 Participant interacting with the *New Snow* interactive drawing table. Illustration from Sivertsen and Sundnes Løvlie (2024)

Fig. 12.4 The generative picture frame. Illustration from Kun et al. (in press)

a preserved, static artwork to instead exploring and playing with a system that can generate a potentially endless series of new images.

12.5 Critiquing AI

While the new opportunities made possible by AI may seem exciting to some, others focus more on problematic aspects with the new technologies. Many artists have created artwork that uses AI technologies to explore and critique the technology itself.

One well-known example is *Imagenet Roulette* by Paglen (2019), an installation which explores the problematic assumptions underlying the Imagenet dataset, one of the main datasets used to train computer vision algorithms. The dataset is built on the assumption that all nouns in language can be tied to images, which can then be used to train computer vision algorithms to detect the objects these nouns denote. For instance, when an algorithm is trained on a vast amount of pictures of dogs and cats and horses, it can "learn" to detect whether there is a dog, cat or horse in a photograph. However, when applied broadly to *any* noun including a variety of characteristics of human beings, some problems with this approach become apparent: How could an algorithm analysing visual patterns in a photograph detect whether someone is a 'kleptomaniac', a 'debtor', a 'swinger', a 'snob' or a 'slav'? *Imagenet Roulette* exposes this problem by presenting an algorithm trained exclusively on images in the "people" subcategory of Imagenet, inviting users to upload a photo of themselves to have the algorithm label them with labels that may sometimes seem arbitrary and sometimes outright offensive.

A number of art projects use similar approaches to explore problematic or interesting aspects with computer vision technologies. For instance, *Machine Bias* by Yazdani (2018) uses an algorithm trained on mugshots of convicted criminals to generate images of "future faces of prisoners"—a provocation which raises questions about predictive policing and the use of AI in the US justice system. In the Instagram art project *in transitu* by Ada Ada Ada (2021), the artist turned the camera on herself as she entered a process of gender transition. For three years she has regularly uploaded a photo of herself, naked from the waist up, along with the outputs from a number of commercial computer vision algorithms attempting to classify her gender. While the photos always showed the same person with only small variations in facial expression, hairstyle and pose, the outputs from the algorithms varied widely, sometimes contradicting each other with high confidence. This artwork demonstrates elegantly how societal norms are embedded in AI algorithms—in this case, the assumption that gender can be treated straightforwardly as a binary variable—while also demonstrating some of the limitations in computer vision analysis of human appearance.

While the above examples are artwork, similar design strategies have been used in non-art contexts. For instance, *Biometric Mirror* is an installation created by a technological research project in order to invite critical reflection on biometric analysis through computer vision. The installation invites people to be photographed and analysed by a psychometric system which classifies them on a range of parameters such as 'aggressiveness', 'weirdness' and 'emotional instability' (Biometric Mirror—Investigating the Ethics of Artificial Intelligence, n.d.).

Critique is central to much art practice, whereas it is perhaps somewhat less prominent in experience design. However, Benford and colleagues (2022) have presented a study called *Sensitive Pictures* which offers a critical exploration of techniques for emotion detection—including computer vision. The study invited art museum visitors to explore an emotionally charged interpretation of selected artworks, while capturing data about their emotions through a range of approaches, including an AI-powered emotion detection algorithm. The study concluded that AI emotion detection was not effective, both due to limitations in the technology and obstacles to applying it in the art museum context. However, the study revealed a surprising tendency for visitors to trust in the technology, even when it contradicted their own accounts of their emotions during the experience. This tendency to overtrust in AI will be discussed further below.

12.6 Discussion

So far, we have presented a number of examples using AI technology to create novel museum experiences. These are still early days, and with the rapid developments in technology, it seems likely that there will be much innovation in this area in years to come. However, based on the examples presented here, what can we say about the experience of AI-based designs in museums at this point in time?

12.6.1 Seeing Art Through the Computer Eye

The science of Computer Vision aims to enable computer systems to understand and interpret visual information—simply put, to *see* in a way similar (or at least analogous) to how humans see. Applying Computer Vision in museum experiences allows us to turn that equation around—inviting visitors to see through the "eyes" of the computer. Seeing through someone else's eyes is a major theme in the understanding of culture, and has also been used as an approach to museum experience design (Spence et al. 2019). But what can we learn from seeing through the computer's eyes?

Until recently, art and visual culture was always experienced through looking at one or a few images at a time. Students of art history might learn about historical epochs, styles and artistic movements which might encompass numerous artists producing large bodies of artistic collections over many years (or even centuries). However, the visual experience of these collections would always be limited to the relatively few examples that could be presented in a specific museum exhibition or catalogue. Learning about an era or movement in art history meant studying some selected few, representative examples from that body of artwork. The advent of the computer, and the Internet, have given us powerful new ways of browsing and searching through large amounts of images—analogous to a great increase in the power and speed of our nervous system, according to McLuhan (1964). However, without the application of computer vision, this is just an improvement in navigation—in how we sort through vast amounts of images—it does not change the way that the images are *seen*. This is where Computer Vision offers a fundamental shift. In the terms of Lev Manovich, Computer Vision allows us to see one billion images at a time: To "study the patterns, trends and dynamics" of visual culture via computational analysis of images (Manovich 2020, 1).

In the study by Meyer and colleagues (2024) this idea was put to the test: Does seeing a large art collection through the lens of Computer Vision—specifically, object detection—allow museum visitors to have a novel experience and a new perspective on the art? According to the test participants in the evaluation, the answer seems to be yes. Seeing similar objects depicted by different artists and in a variety of styles and epochs, allowed visitors to compare: "*It shows how different artists from different parts of the world, during different times have treated that object. Say, an apple would be very different in the Renaissance than today*". However, this view also made them pay attention to details, and see the individual paintings in a new light: "*by going through details that struck me, I also had the chance to pay attention to paintings that maybe I disregarded in the exhibition*". It made visitors pay attention to things they previously wouldn't have thought they would be interested in: "*I didn't think I would be interested in a painting of cows, but that was very surprising and interesting*". Perhaps most interesting of all, some participants noticed that the AI model had mislabelled some details—and this made them reflect not just on the reliability of the Computer Vision technology, but also on their own interpretation of the images: "*it kind of made you question whether it was you or the AI that was making a mistake*". Some visitors noted that the incorrect labelling made them reconsider their own interpretation of the images: "*One of them said it was a guitar, but it was open-heart surgery. It looked like a guitar. It was quite interesting.*"

While Meyer and colleagues thus demonstrate that the lens of object detection could help museum visitors see the artworks in a new way, this setup was still mainly focused on presenting the original artworks, through the particular details detected by the AI model. Sivertsen and colleagues (2023a) take this one step further in the *New Snow* project, where the original artworks are not presented directly—instead, visitors interact with an AI model that represents the collection as a whole, through its training data. The argument presented by the authors is that engaging with the system allows visitors to experience the art in a more active way: The visitor's attempts at drawing are met with a response from the system that represents the aesthetics of Edvard Munch's sketches, thus engaging the visitor in a sort of playful dialogue. The visitor is confronted with the aesthetics and the *practice* of the art sketches as represented through the AI model rather than through looking at individual sketches. From a museum curator's perspective, this may seem like a less respectful way of presenting the art—as the original artworks are obscured by the model, and it is debatable how accurately the system truly is able to represent the way in which Edvard Munch would draw in practice. Test participants also met some challenges in interacting with the system, as the system's responses were confined by the patterns and aesthetics learned through its training data—for instance, drawing an owl would not result in any meaningful response from the system, probably because there are not so many drawings of owls in the sketches of Edvard Munch. Even so, participants reported that interacting with the system did offer them an aesthetic experience which gave them a new perspective on Munch's art. In the words of one participant:

> It was a very interesting way to experience the art, instead of the very static image in the museum, where you can also look at the lines and collect from the different images. It gave a different feeling of the artist when you got to interact with it yourself. There were a lot of

things changing but you could still clearly see that it was from the same artists in the same style.

Compared with *New Snow*, Kun and colleagues (Kun et al. in press) have gone even further with their "generative picture frame" *GenFrame*, which generates images based on prompts to the Stable Diffusion model. In this case, the original artwork is further obscured: The images produced by the model are based on the statistical ways that the model relates the words in the input prompt to the vast body of training data, which includes a broad variety of images collected from the internet—some of which may be high art of the type belonging to art museums and galleries, but much of which is all kinds of other images including amateur art, cartoons, advertisements and so on. Similarly to *New Snow*, the system works through synthesising all the images and styles it has been trained on, allowing users to play with the system to explore the variety of aesthetics and styles it can output. Thus the experience—and perhaps, learning—relies on exploring the patterns and aesthetics output by the model, rather than individual images.

The design works through a quite literal "framing", a physical format that mimics the presentation of art paintings in museums, and thus invites users to consider the question: Is this art? Posing this question directly to test participants resulted in mixed responses—some felt that the AI system lacked unique human qualities such as emotions and creativity, which are necessary to create art; whereas others argued for broader notions of art, questioning whether such a system could be considered as creative. As a study participant formulated it:

> As a human, I have experiences from all my life. When I create traditional art, it is based on my own previous experiences. When I create AI art, it feels more collective, I have access to a lot of data from other humans at once. Maybe AI art feels more collective. It draws from vast data, making it holistic.

However, not all participants agreed that the outputs of the AI system should be considered art: "For me, art involves a person who has related herself to a topic. [...] there should be a human process for me, an emotional and intellectual investment. Without this process, it would be more of an illustration rather than art." Perhaps the most interesting aspect of this discussion is not the specific answer to the question whether the visuals generated by the AI should be considered art, but rather the reflections that were sparked by the design. Arguably, this represents another example in which an AI system inspired museum visitors to see art from a new perspective.

12.6.2 Trust

There is much debate and unease with AI both in society in general, as well as within the cultural sector. Currently, much focus is on the problems and risks associated with generative AI, summarised by Epstein and colleagues (2023). Foka and colleagues (2023) have debated some of the challenges with the use of AI and Machine Learning (ML) in the cultural heritage sector specifically. There is not enough space here to discuss all these challenges, instead, we will focus on one issue that seems particularly pertinent: Trust.

Much effort is being made within the AI industry as well as academic research to develop trustworthy AI systems, under labels such as "explainable AI", "accountable AI", "trustworthy autonomous systems", etc. These efforts reflect the broader unease with the development of AI. One challenge that is often highlighted is the risk of misinformation. Generative AI models are notorious for "hallucinating"—that is, they can generate information that appears authentic but is not. This may happen in ways which are unintended by any human users, such as when a large language model invents facts which are not real (Ye et al. 2023); or it might be used with malicious intent, for instance, to create "deepfake" imagery for the purpose of deceiving others. Considering the deep commitment museums have to education and knowledge dissemination, it is of great importance to ensure that museums do not inadvertently become disseminators of misinformation.

When deploying designs that use AI in museums, we have expected visitors to voice such types of concerns and meet the technology with a great dose of scepticism. However, we have often been surprised in the opposite way, encountering visitors who have tended to place much trust in the technology—sometimes perhaps even a bit too much. For instance, in the *Sensitive Pictures* study (Benford et al. 2022), when visitors were presented with the data output by the system about their emotions after going through the experience, they would often change their descriptions of their own emotions to match what the AI system said they had felt during the experience. In fact, this happened even in cases where we could see that visitors were misinterpreting the data (due to ambiguity in the way it was presented): Visitors who had expressed great enjoyment with the experience saw data that they misinterpreted as saying the AI had detected frustration, and then changed their account to fit better with this reading. In the words of one of the visitors: "*I don't know about frustrated. Yeah I guess frustrated in the way that, you have to grapple with emotions as they come up and sometimes you don't want to*". Some visitors figured the AI must have picked up on their bodily discomfort: "*Very frustrated—that was because I had to pee!*"

Similar observations were made in the study of object detection by Meyer and colleagues (2024), in which the authors noted that participants were surprisingly willing to trust the computer vision system's interpretations of objects in the artworks—even coming up with excuses for the system when the objects seemed to be labelled wrongly. For instance, one visitor commented on seeing a painting of a spear being mislabelled by the algorithm as a 'flute': "*Especially with the flute, he showed a lot of pictures of long, thin objects, which I do understand why he would think is a flute.*"

In the above examples, it seems likely that the visitors' tendency to trust or even overtrust in the AI may have been influenced by the fact that they encountered the technology in a museum, which is a highly renowned and trusted institution. This should perhaps be taken as a warning for museums intending to include AI in their visitor experiences: If the AI is not entirely trustworthy—and as the output from artificial neural networks is probabilistic, no such system can be entirely fool-proof—then the museum may be at risk of lending its authority to AI-generated disinformation, that visitors may take at face value due to their trust in the museum institution. This risk calls for extra vigilance when museums apply AI—perhaps in particular for museums dealing with sensitive topics such as historical trauma. Given that a total degree of trustworthiness in AI is unlikely to be achieved any time soon, museums might want to consider ways of highlighting the limitations of the technology to foster awareness. One way to do this would be through critical design approaches that expose flaws in the technology, similar to the examples discussed above. A possible strategy could be to embrace the uncertainty inherent in AI and highlight the resulting ambiguity as a way to foster critical reflection and invite visitors to interpret with care, as discussed by Sivertsen and colleagues (2024). Another strategy would be to present speculative designs that explore future scenarios involving AI, in order to open up the future use of AI for reflection and critique in the present.

12.6.3 Limitations and Future Work

AI and Computer Vision techniques are in rapid development, and new designs and applications are presented daily. It is likely that this book chapter may have missed some interesting uses of AI already, and many more are likely to come in the near future. In particular, there is much interest currently in the use of large language models as well as multimodal models. Future research should explore in more depth the potentials—and pitfalls—of applying LLMs in museum experiences.

Much concern and debate have been directed at the risk that AI might perpetuate and reinforce cultural biases and stereotypes. However, such biases are characteristics of human thought and are inevitable in all modes of human expression including art practice, curatorship and interpretation. Instead of working to avoid bias in AI, we might consider turning the perspective around, and asking: How can we use AI to expose, explore and critique our biases, prejudice, and all the various stereotypes we might not even be aware of? That would require not only a critical approach to AI but also a productive one, in which AI is actively experimented with and applied in a variety of aesthetic designs and experiences—not just as an effective way to navigate large collections, but also as a new way to *see* art. Not necessarily better, nor worse, but different—and certainly interesting.

Acknowledgements The research reported in this chapter has been supported by the Villum Foundation as well as the MUNCH museum. Additionally, we thank the National Gallery of Denmark for allowing us to test the SMKExplore and Generative Picture Frame prototypes on their premises.

References

Achiam J, Adler S, Agarwal S, Ahmad L, Akkaya I, Leoni Aleman F, Almeida D et al (2024) GPT-4 technical report. arXiv. https://doi.org/10.48550/arXiv.2303.08774

Ada Ada Ada (2021) In transitu. White curtain, JPEG, Instagram profile, gender recognition AI. https://ada-ada-ada.art/projects/in-transitu

Audry S (2021) Art in the age of machine learning. The MIT Press, Cambridge, MA. https://mitpress.mit.edu/9780262046183/art-in-the-age-of-machine-learning/

Bacon K (2019) AI as provocation rather than solution. In: The GIFT box: tools and ways of working to help museums make richer digital experiences for their visitors (blog). https://gifting.digital/brighton-museum/

Benford S, Sundnes Løvlie A, Ryding K, Rajkowska P, Bodiaj E, Paris Darzentas D, Cameron H, Spence J, Egede J, Spanjevic B (2022) Sensitive pictures: emotional interpretation in the museum. In: Proceedings of the 2022 CHI conference on human factors in computing systems. CHI '22. Association for Computing Machinery, New York, NY. https://doi.org/10.1145/3491102.3502080

Billock J (2019) With a little help from A.I., the Dali museum brings the famed surrealist to life. Smithsonian Magazine, 9 May 2019. https://www.smithsonianmag.com/travel/with-little-help-from-ai-dali-museum-brings-famed-surrealist-to-life-180972127/

Biometric Mirror—Investigating the Ethics of Artificial Intelligence (n.d.) Accessed 8 Feb 2023. https://biometricmirror.com/

Cetinic E, She J (2022) Understanding and creating art with AI: review and outlook. ACM Trans Multimed Comput Commun Appl 18(2):66:1–66:22. https://doi.org/10.1145/3475799

Ciecko B (2020) AI sees what? The good, the bad, and the ugly of machine vision for museum collections. Mus Rev 5(1). https://themuseumreviewjournal.wordpress.com/2020/04/23/tmr_vol5no1_ciecko

Devlin J, Chang M-W, Lee K, Toutanova K (2019) BERT: pre-training of deep bidirectional transformers for language understanding. arXiv. https://doi.org/10.48550/arXiv.1810.04805

Epstein Z, Hertzmann A, The Investigators of Human Creativity (2023) Art and the science of generative AI. Science 380(6650):1110–1111. https://doi.org/10.1126/science.adh4451

Foka A, Eklund L, Sundnes Løvlie A, Griffin G (2023) Critically assessing AI/ML for cultural heritage: potentials and challenges. In: Lindgren S (ed) Handbook of critical studies of artificial intelligence. Edward Elgar, Cheltenham, UK, pp 815–825

Fontanella F, Colace F, Molinara M, Scotto Di Freca A, Stanco F (2020) Pattern recognition and artificial intelligence techniques for cultural heritage. Pattern Recogn Lett 138:23–29. https://doi.org/10.1016/j.patrec.2020.06.018

Geirhos R, Rubisch P, Michaelis C, Bethge M, Wichmann FA, Brendel W (2019) ImageNet-trained CNNs are biased towards texture; increasing shape bias improves accuracy and robustness. In: International conference on learning representations (ICLR 2019), New Orleans, Louisiana. https://openreview.net/forum?id=Bygh9j09KX

Giannini T, Bowen JP (eds) (2019) Museums and digital culture: new perspectives and research. In: Springer series on cultural computing. Springer International Publishing, Cham. https://doi.org/10.1007/978-3-319-97457-6

Girshick R (2015) Fast R-CNN. In: Proceedings of the IEEE international conference on computer vision. IEEE, Santiago, Chile, pp 1440–1448. https://doi.org/10.1109/ICCV.2015.169

Grba D (2022) Deep else: a critical framework for AI art. Digital 2(1):1–32. https://doi.org/10.3390/digital2010001

Hall P, Cai H, Wu Q, Corradi T (2015) Cross-depiction problem: recognition and synthesis of photographs and artwork. Comput Vis Media 1(2):91–103. https://doi.org/10.1007/s41095-015-0017-1

Hettmann W, Wölfel M, Butz M, Torner K, Finken J (2023) Engaging museum visitors with AI-generated narration and gameplay. In: Brooks AL (ed) ArtsIT, interactivity and game creation. Lecture notes of the institute for computer sciences, social informatics and telecommunications engineering. Springer Nature Switzerland, Cham, pp 201–214. https://doi.org/10.1007/978-3-031-28993-4_15

Hornecker E, Ciolfi L (2019) Human-computer interactions in museums. In: Synthesis lectures on human-centered informatics, vol 12, no 2, pp 1–171. https://doi.org/10.2200/S00901ED1V01Y201902HCI042

Kadish D, Risi S, Sundnes Løvlie A (2021) Improving object detection in art images using only style transfer. In: The international joint conference on neural networks (IJCNN). Virtual Event: IEEE. https://arxiv.org/abs/2102.06529

Kun P, Anton Freiberger M, Sundnes Løvlie A, Risi S (2024a) GenFrame—embedding generative AI into interactive artifacts. In: Proceedings of the 2024 ACM designing interactive systems conference. DIS '24. Association for Computing Machinery, New York, NY, pp 714–727. https://doi.org/10.1145/3643834.3660750

Kun P, Freiberger M, Sundnes Løvlie A, Risi S (2024b) AI art perceptions with GenFrame—an image generating picture frame. In: DRS2024. Design Research Society, Boston, MA. https://doi.org/10.21606/drs.2024.997

Kun P, Freiberger M, Sundnes Løvlie A, Risi S (in press) AI art perceptions with GenFrame—an image generating picture frame. In: Design research society 2024. Design Research Society, Boston, MA

Li LH, Zhang P, Zhang H, Yang J, Li C, Zhong Y, Wang L et al (2022) Grounded language-image pre-training. In: Proceedings of the IEEE/CVF conference on computer vision and pattern recognition (CVPR), pp 10965–10975

Lin TY, Maire M, Belongie S, Hays J, Perona P, Ramanan D, Dollár P, Lawrence Zitnick C (2014) Microsoft COCO: common objects in context. In: Computer vision—ECCV 2014: 13th European conference, Zurich, Switzerland, 6–12 Sept 2014, proceedings, part V 13. Springer, pp 740–755. https://doi.org/10.1007/978-3-319-10602-1_48

Liu H, Li C, Li Y, Jae Lee Y (2023) Improved baselines with visual instruction tuning. arXiv. https://doi.org/10.48550/arXiv.2310.03744

MacDonough K (2018) Smartify. Multimed Technol Rev. https://doi.org/10.17613/95t4-2t63

Maietti F (2024) Digital heritage documentation. Mapping features through automatic, critical-interpretative procedures. In: Giordano A, Russo M, Spallone R (eds) Beyond digital representation: advanced experiences in AR and AI for cultural heritage and innovative design. Springer Nature Switzerland, Cham, pp 427–442. https://doi.org/10.1007/978-3-031-36155-5_27

Makhortykh M, Zucker EM, Simon DJ, Bultmann D, Ulloa R (2023) Shall androids dream of genocides? How generative AI can change the future of memorialization of mass atrocities. Discov Artif Intell 3(1):28. https://doi.org/10.1007/s44163-023-00072-6

Mann E, Dortheimer J, Sprecher A (2022) Toward a generative pipeline for an AR tour of contested heritage sites. In: 2022 IEEE international conference on artificial intelligence and virtual reality (AIVR), pp 130–134. https://doi.org/10.1109/AIVR56993.2022.00026

Manovich L (2020) Cultural analytics. The MIT Press, Cambridge, MA. https://mitpress.mit.edu/books/cultural-analytics

Mathias N (2022) Meta-artistic immersion in digital exhibitions. history—mobilization—spectatorship. J Aesth Cult 14(1):2129160. https://doi.org/10.1080/20004214.2022.2129160

McLuhan M (1964) Understanding media: the extensions of man. McGraw-Hill, New York, NY. https://mitpress.mit.edu/9780262631594/understanding-media/

Meinecke C (2022) Labeling of cultural heritage collections on the intersection of visual analytics and digital humanities. In: 2022 IEEE 7th workshop on visualization for the digital humanities (VIS4DH), pp 19–24. https://doi.org/10.1109/VIS4DH57440.2022.00009

Meyer LS, Aaen JE, Regitse Tranberg A, Kun P, Freiberger M, Risi S, Sundnes Løvlie A (2024) Algorithmic ways of seeing: using object detection to facilitate art exploration. In: CHI conference on human factors in computing systems. ACM, Honolulu

Mondloch K (2022) The influencers: van Gogh immersive experiences and the attention-experience economy. Arts 11(5):90. https://doi.org/10.3390/arts11050090

Murphy O, Villaespesa E (2020) AI: a museum planning toolkit. Goldsmiths, University of London, London, UK

Paglen T (2019) ImageNet roulette. https://paglen.studio/2020/04/29/imagenet-roulette/

Radford A, Wook Kim J, Hallacy C, Ramesh A, Goh G, Agarwal S, Sastry G et al (2021) Learning transferable visual models from natural language supervision. arXiv. https://doi.org/10.48550/arXiv.2103.00020

Sinatti E, Weckert S, Dobrzalski E (2022) Image garden: curating collections and designing smart exhibitions with AI-based tools. I-Com 21(1):83–94. https://doi.org/10.1515/icom-2022-0010

Sivertsen C, Sundnes Løvlie A (2024) Exploring aesthetic qualities of deep generative models through technological (art) mediation. In: DIS '24: designing interactive systems conference proceedings. ACM, IT University of Copenhagen, Denmark. https://doi.org/10.1145/3643834.3661498

Sivertsen C, Haas R, Hauch Jensen H, Sundnes Løvlie A (2023a) Exploring a digital art collection through drawing interactions with a deep generative model. In: Extended abstracts of the 2023 CHI conference on human factors in computing systems. CHI EA '23. Association for Computing Machinery, New York, NY. https://doi.org/10.1145/3544549.3583902

Sivertsen C, Mathias N, Sundnes Løvlie A (2023b) Educating the attention of museum visitors through non-verbal art mediation. In: IASDR 2023: congress of the international association of societies of design research. Design Research Society, Milan, Italy. https://doi.org/10.21606/iasdr.2023.222

Sivertsen C, Smith M, van der Zwan S (2023c) Art critique by other means. In: Proceedings of the 2023 ACM designing interactive systems conference. DIS '23. Association for Computing Machinery, New York, NY, pp 343–352. https://doi.org/10.1145/3563657.3596069

Sivertsen C, Salimbeni G, Sundnes Løvlie A, Benford S, Zhu J (2024) Machine learning processes as sources of ambiguity: insights from AI art. https://doi.org/10.1145/3613904.3642855

Smith JH (2019) SMK's collection search levels up. Medium (blog), 4 Sept 2019. https://medium.com/smk-open/smks-collection-search-levels-up-cf8e967e9346

"SMK Open: Setting Art Free" (2018) SMK—National Gallery of Denmark in Copenhagen (Statens Museum for Kunst), 21 June 2018. https://www.smk.dk/en/article/smk-open/

Spence J, Bedwell B, Coleman M, Benford S, Koleva BN, Adams M, Row Farr J, Tandavanitj N, Sundnes Løvlie A (2019) Seeing with new eyes: designing for in-the-wild museum gifting. In: Proceedings of ACM CHI conference on human factors in computing systems (CHI 2019). ACM, Glasgow, Scotland. https://doi.org/10.1145/3290605.3300235

Spennemann DHR (2023) Exhibiting the heritage of COVID-19—a conversation with ChatGPT. Heritage 6(8):5732–5749. https://doi.org/10.3390/heritage6080302

Stack J (2020) Computer vision and the science museum group collection. Medium (blog), 4 Apr 2020. https://lab.sciencemuseum.org.uk/computer-vision-and-the-science-museum-group-collection-a6c20efb0ac9

Sundnes Løvlie A, Eklund L, Waern A, Ryding K, Rajkowska P (2021) Designing for interpersonal museum experiences. In: Black G (ed) Museums and the challenge of change: old institutions in a new world. Routledge, London & New York, pp 223–238

Tallon L (2018) Creating access beyond metmuseum.org: the met collection on wikipedia. The Metropolitan Museum of Art (blog), 7 Feb 2018. https://www.metmuseum.org/articles/open-access-at-the-met-year-one

Trichopoulos G, Konstantakis M, Alexandridis G, Caridakis G (2023a) Large language models as recommendation systems in museums. Electronics 12(18):3829. https://doi.org/10.3390/electronics12183829

Trichopoulos G, Konstantakis M, Caridakis G, Katifori A, Koukouli M (2023b) Crafting a museum guide using ChatGPT4. Big Data Cogn Comput 7(3):148. https://doi.org/10.3390/bdcc7030148

Vaswani A, Shazeer N, Parmar N, Uszkoreit J, Jones L, Gomez AD, Kaiser Ł, Polosukhin I (2017) Attention is all you need. In: Advances in neural information processing systems, vol 30. Curran Associates, Inc. https://papers.nips.cc/paper_files/paper/2017/hash/3f5ee243547dee91fbd053c1c4a845aa-Abstract.html

Vermeeren A, Calvi L, Sabiescu A (eds) (2018) Museum experience design: crowds, ecosystems and novel technologies. In: Springer series on cultural computing. Springer International Publishing. https://www.springer.com/gp/book/9783319585499

Vidu C, Zbuchea A, Pinzaru F (2021) Old meets new: integrating artificial intelligence in museums' management practices. https://scholar.google.com/scholar_lookup?title=Old+Meets+New:+Integrating+Artificial+Intelligence+in+Museums%E2%80%99+Management+Practices&author=Vidu,+C.&author=Zbuchea,+A.&author=Pinzaru,+F.&publication_year=2021&journal=Strateg.+Shap.+Future+Bus.+Econ.&pages=830%E2%80%93844

Villaespesa E, Crider S (2021) A critical comparison analysis between human and machine-generated tags for the metropolitan museum of art's collection. J Document 77(4):946–964. https://doi.org/10.1108/JD-04-2020-0060

Villaespesa E, Murphy O (2021) This is not an apple! Benefits and challenges of applying computer vision to museum collections. Mus Manag Curatorsh 36(4):362–383. https://doi.org/10.1080/09647775.2021.1873827

Waern A, Sundnes Løvlie A (eds) (2022) Hybrid museum experiences. In: MediaMatters. Amsterdam University Press, Amsterdam. https://www.aup.nl/en/book/9789048552849/hybrid-museum-experiences

Wang Z, Yuan L, Wang L, Jiang B, Wei Z (2024) VirtuWander: enhancing multi-modal interaction for virtual tour guidance through large language models. arXiv Preprint arXiv:2401.11923

Yazdani NI (2018) Machine bias. https://nushinyazdani.com

Ye H, Liu T, Zhang A, Hua W, Jia W (2023) Cognitive mirage: a review of hallucinations in large language models. arXiv. https://doi.org/10.48550/arXiv.2309.06794

Zylinska J (2020) AI art: machine visions and warped dreams. Open Humanities Press. http://www.openhumanitiespress.org/books/titles/ai-art/

Anders Sundnes Løvlie is Associate Professor at the IT University of Copenhagen and head of the research group for Media, Art and Design. His research interests include humanistic HCI, experience design, artificial intelligence and museums. He was coordinator for the EU-funded research project GIFT, as well as co-PI for the research project "Algorithmic Ways of Seeing", in which many of the examples discussed in this chapter were created.

Louie Søs Meyer is a Ph.D. student at the IT University of Copenhagen in the HCI and Design Section. Their research investigates machine learning as a design material with a focus on art, biodata and wearable technologies. They are particularly interested in crafting alternative and critical ways of interacting with algorithms.

Christian Sivertsen is a Postdoctoral Researcher at the IT University of Copenhagen, specialising in human–computer interaction, interaction design, and experience design. His research aims to develop technology that supports experiences with art and culture. In his Ph.D., Technology-based Mediation in the Art Museum, he explored novel methods of art mediation using generative AI and immersive technologies. Christian's work seeks to create impactful cultural experiences with the help of technology.

Peter Kun is a researcher at the cross-section of interaction design and data-centric practices. His research agenda on meaningful human-AI interactions looks at data and artificial intelligence from a creative computing angle.

Matthias Freiberger was born in Graz, Austria, in 1983. He earned a Master's degree in Information and Computer Engineering from Graz University of Technology in 2016, followed by a Ph.D. in Computer Science Engineering from Ghent University in 2020. He is currently a postdoctoral researcher at the Pioneer Center for Artificial Intelligence in Copenhagen. His research explores adaptive and open-ended approaches to computer vision and artificial intelligence.

Sebastian Risi is a Full Professor at the IT University of Copenhagen, directing the Creative AI Lab and co-directing the REAL Lab. He earned his Ph.D. from the University of Central Florida in 2012. He has received multiple best paper awards, an ERC Consolidator Grant (2022), and research awards from Google (2019) and Amazon (2020). His interdisciplinary work appears in major AI conferences and media like *Science*, *Wired*, and *Fast Company*.

Chapter 13
Artificial Exchange: Chatbots and the Ethics of Museum Experience Design

Kathryn Brown

Abstract Developments in natural language processing, including the advent of ChatGPT, Google's Gemini, Anthropic's Claude, IBM's Watson, and Meta's LlaMA, have fuelled the use of chatbots for the purpose of mediating museum collections to audiences and enhancing the latter's engagement with art. This chapter explores the rhetoric that has developed about the introduction of artificial conversational agents and debates the ethical consequences of creating and promoting human–machine conversations in the heritage industry. Drawing on examples from the US, the UK, and Europe, the discussion explores various myths of 'conversation' that underpin the use of chatbots. What activities do chatbots replace and are the latter a threat to museum education? Is it possible to design museum experiences that successfully combine algorithmic partners with the curatorial expertise of humans? Having regard to the vested interests of companies who sponsor technologies that underpin the functioning of chatbots, does the use of artificial intelligence require museums to rethink their own cultural position and relationships in wider economies? Examining the hype, possibilities, and limitations of human–machine conversation in museums reveals new curatorial and ethical challenges for heritage institutions that design spaces shared by human and non-human agents.

13.1 Introduction

The heritage industries count alongside many others that are exploring the potential of artificial intelligence (AI) to generate new kinds of audience engagement. Museums, in particular, are turning increasingly to AI in their attempts to broaden access to collections, better evaluate the needs of diverse beneficiaries, and develop relationships with a new range of funders (both academic and industry-based). Central to these efforts are experiments with algorithmic conversational agents (henceforth

K. Brown (✉)
Loughborough University, Loughborough, UK
e-mail: K.J.Brown@lboro.ac.uk

L. Calvi et al. (eds.), *Transformative Museum Experiences*, Springer Series on Cultural Computing, https://doi.org/10.1007/978-3-031-89521-0_13

'chatbots') that are designed in the hope of stimulating innovative ways of talking about art.

On the one hand, the use of AI to expand opportunities for audience participation in cultural heritage is a positive development. It may, for example, stimulate the interest of individuals who would not otherwise be keen to explore art. Indeed, one of the main reasons given by researchers seeking to introduce chatbots into heritage settings is to 'empower' visitors (Gustke et al. 2024, p. 263) or to make exhibitions 'more appealing to a larger audience' (Maniscalco et al. 2024, p. 1). Chatbots offer a new experience in the museum that promises to disrupt conventional styles of education where the balance of power has historically been tipped in favour of experts.

On the other hand, new risks arise when replacing humans with machine interlocutors. Having regard to a range of recent examples, this chapter explores ethical dilemmas associated with the rise of museum chatbots and the potential impact of the latter on the ways in which audiences speak about art. I locate the use of chatbots in a lineage of interactive museum practices and debate the extent to which algorithmic speech acts extend or depart from participatory ideals that informed art production and curation of the 1990s. Specifically, I investigate the kind of museum community that is created or eroded when AI is introduced into heritage spaces and what the implications of museum chatbots might be for the ways in which human beings, acting collectively, make sense of cultural artefacts.

As much recent research has pointed out, developments in natural language processing that are based on the creation of ever-larger databases are far from neutral (Lazar 2024). Bender et al. (2021) examine a variety of risks arising from the development and use of large language models (LLMs), including the cost and environmental impact of cloud computing as well as familiar problems derived from the biased content of the databases themselves. The authors outline how, via bias in the training data, LLMs perpetuate various prejudices in society that reflect hegemonic power structures. In the following discussion, I will argue that the integration of chatbots into heritage arenas raises further issues that are central to the development of museum practices in and beyond the twenty-first century. These range from the practical (the scope of activities undertaken by machines) to the conceptual (audiences' empathetic and imaginative relationship to artworks) and the ethical (the extent to which machine conversations engage audience members as moral agents and the replacement of museum educators by machines).

I will argue that probing the uses of chatbots in museums opens pressing questions not just at the intersection of heritage and technology, but at a wider social level that concerns communities of speakers who share linguistic norms and practices (Morgan 2014). The analysis will begin with a brief overview of recent developments in the use of chatbots and will contextualise these against a background of participatory museum practices that rose to prominence in the 1990s. Locating these technological developments in a longer history of audience interaction provides new insight into why heritage institutions are keen to embrace chatbots. This context also provides a basis from which to examine the ethical and museological consequences of encouraging conversations about art between human and non-human agents.

13.2 From Text to Talk

As might be expected in the emergence of a new field that is based on technological innovation, research into the use of chatbots in museums has been largely case based. This means that recent scholarship has focused primarily on developments in AI and robotics, the manner of implementing chatbots, and quantitative assessments of the successful uptake of AI-based interfaces by audiences. A brief review of key examples from the growing body of literature on the subject demonstrates how quickly this field has changed in response to developments in technologies for natural language processing.[1]

Gaia et al. (2019) provide a helpful overview of the development of 'speaking machines' from the seventeenth century to contemporary AI-enabled chatbots, paying particular attention to the introduction of 'gamification' as a means of making encounters with heritage objects more appealing. Throughout this history, language plays different roles, ranging from use of the written word to the creation of machines that make sounds such as laughter or song and, eventually, language.

In the twenty-first century, many early chatbots relied minimally on speech and were based, instead, on image or text prompts from users. In 2017, Philadelphia's Barnes Foundation trialled a computer vision 'curator' that attempted to match paintings on a scale of similarities relating to their visible properties. This would, the museum hoped, help to open hitherto unexplored networks through its collection that visitors could then explore (Barnes Foundation 2017).[2] In a similar vein, San Francisco MoMA ran a programme called 'SendMe' between 2017 and 2020 in the hope of 'generating personal connections between a diverse cross-section of people and the artworks in our collection' (Mollica 2017). In contrast to the Barnes initiative, SendMe relied on texting: using their mobile phones, audience members could text a work, colour or emoji to the museum and would receive an image of an artwork and its accompanying caption in return. Boiano et al. (2018) examine a similar range of primarily image-based 'museum archive' bots that relied on Twitter (now X) or Facebook as interfaces (e.g. the New York Public Library Postcard bot). In contrast to the Barnes initiative, the latter examples can be understood as a 'correspondence' model in two senses: first, the machine searches for connections between prompt and image; secondly, it promotes an act of communicative exchange (texting) that updates a quaint form of talking about art through acts of written correspondence.

Texting swiftly became (and remains) a staple of museums' conversations with their audiences and employs more or less personalised formats. In 2017, the Anne Frank Museum in Amsterdam introduced a text-based chatbot that aimed to tell 'Anne Frank's story to as many people as possible through technology' (Anne Frank House 2017). Having the format of a familiar text conversation, the bot leads audiences through a fairly structured set of menus that provide information about Anne Frank,

[1] For a fuller literature review of museum chatbots and their underlying technologies see Varitimiadis et al. (2021) and Gaia et al. (2019).

[2] A similar interactive web app called MosAIc was developed by Hamilton et al. (2021) to elicit connections between 'semantically related artworks' across time and geography.

her family and histories of the Netherlands during the Second World War. Bouras et al. points out that the bot 'applies learning techniques to discern responses that are considered successful and increase the rate at which they are reused in similar contexts. It can also operate when user input is not complete or contextualised, and arranges for probing the user for extra information to collect missing information or context elements' (2023, p. 1). The result, however, is still a static conversational model that progresses within the parameters of structured questions and answers. Nevertheless, it does involve a reflexive learning technology such that the programme itself can modify its responses based on its past successes and failures.

Text-based encounters have been used in similar ways by Pittsburgh's Carnegie Museums and the Akron Art Museum. In these cases, however, the chatbot is given an identity—a digital version of the museum's founder, the industrialist and philanthropist Andrew Carnegie (Andy CarnegieBot) in the case of the former, and Dot in the latter. Marketing material issued by both museums emphasises the desire to create 'compelling fun interactions' (Faust 2018) and 'a personal connection between people' (Litt 2018). Bouras et al. make the point in their survey of museum chatbots, however, that most of these interfaces require audiences to ask 'proper questions', offer little guidance through museums as a whole, and tend to follow single paths (2023, p. 4). Put another way, AI language models that are based on predictive outcomes about human speech do not fully account for either the messiness of human conversation or the unexpected ways in which people respond to artworks or explore the heritage spaces in which they are housed.

Müller et al. (2024, p. 274) propose a tripartite categorisation of chatbot technologies by dividing conversational agents into goal-based systems, those designed for a conversation on open-ended topics, and others aiming at information retrieval via question and answer. Varitimiadis et al. (2021) suggest a more detailed taxonomy that begins with basic Q&A chatbots and moves through bots with 'predefined routes of conversation', gamification chatbots, conversational bots that try to control conversation by prompting users to ask certain questions, and finally 'human-like conversational chatbots, where the users can freely ask almost anything, without following any rules or predefined routes' (2021, p. 10). Among these options, AI researchers are turning increasingly to the goal of open-ended human–machine conversation as a means of enhancing audience participation. Gustke et al. suggest that chatbots create 'automated but personalised dialogue' (2024, p. 263), while Maniscalco et al. point to 'new ways of interaction' and information sharing 'as naturally and comfortably as possible' (2024, p. 1).

It is important to contextualise these recent developments as the continuation of a theme that emerged in art and curatorial practices of the 1990s. Statements about the potential of chatbots to create new ways of attracting audiences extend a rhetoric of participation that rose to prominence in that decade (Brown 2016). Spurred by Nicolas Bourriaud's conception of 'relational aesthetics' proposed in 1998 (Bourriaud 2009) and developed in response to innovative art installations of the period, many art writers and curators of the 1990s championed the potential of participatory art forms to generate new kinds of sociability and to reorient the relationship of audience members not just to art institutions, but to each other. Having regard to works by artists including Gabriel Orozco, Jens Haaning, and Rirkrit Tiravanija, Bourriaud made the case that 'interactive, user-friendly and relational concepts' defined the art of the 1990s (2009, p. 8). Participation, in this context, was understood as a strategy for audience empowerment and, as I have argued elsewhere, suggested an updated Enlightenment ideal of aesthetic education in which novel kinds of interactivity were posited as a spur to cultural enrichment (Brown 2016, p. 2). The utopian rhetoric of participation in art writing of the 1990s (and, in particular, Bourriaud's account of it) met, however, with criticism (Bishop 2004; Kester 2004) that I will discuss below. The point I want to make at this stage is that contemporary strategies for audience engagement (and their concomitant social goals) through the use of chatbots can be understood as an extension of these familiar artistic and museological strategies that emerged in the 1990s.

Attempts to use chatbots as a means of encouraging closer connections to collections and enhancing social interaction are most clear in interfaces that exploit an element of gaming. In their study of a chatbot created for the House Museums of Milan, Boiano et al. (2018) explore the role of a virtual companion that was designed to help younger audiences solve puzzles about artefacts in the physical museum. According to the authors, the gaming element fostered 'a friendly competitive environment' while encouraging 'actual exploration of the Museum collections' (Boiano et al. 2018, p. 168). Their experiment leaves unresolved, however, whether audiences were more interested in the technology and gaming elements of the experience than in the collection of the heritage site. Whereas participatory artforms of the 1990s used artworks themselves as a means of stimulating new social and aesthetic encounters, chatbot technologies are an accretion to the collections that they are designed to enhance. The extent to which they direct attention to, or divert interest from, those collections remains an open question. The act of gaming need not be competitive, but in these cases it is, and it serves to distract the participants' attention from the collection towards the gaming community of which the individuals form part.[3]

One development that exemplifies the dilemma is the drive to create increasingly anthropomorphic chatbots. A far cry from the texting interfaces discussed above, this strategy has two major facets that I will deal with in turn: the animation of historical figures and the creation of 'social robots'. Recent experiments with the technological 'reincarnation' of figures from the past include the staging of opportunities to chat with avatars of actual people such as veterans of the Second World War (The National WWII Museum 2023) or King Jinheung, 24th Monarch of Silla, Korea (Noh and Hong 2021). They also extend to the possibility of conversing with a selection of historic and mythical *femmes fatales*, including Helen of Troy and Medusa (Fahden and Gebauer 2024).

As Noh and Hong (2021) point out, animating historical figures can be an entertaining approach to history, but it adds to the range of ethical issues with which museums must contend. The authors argue that users tend to 'empathize with the opinion of the people (chatbots) they have spoken with' and that the perspectives of

[3] To counter the reliance on mobile phones in heritage spaces, Trichopoulos et al. (2023) explore the use of 'smart glasses' equipped with an earpiece and a microphone.

historical figures may, therefore, require the addition of balance from the input of a trained docent (Noh and Hong 2021, p. 12). I would add two further points of concern in connection with this technological engagement with heritage. First, a fundamental question arises about which historical figures to animate in a museum context. The problem of bias as to gender, race, and genre of artefact deemed worthy of collecting has been a subject of debate in museum history for many decades (Nochlin 2018; Pollock 2007; Langfeld 2018). The creation of chatbots based on artists or historical figures already selected for canonisation by museums runs the risk of reinforcing biased museum narratives and prioritising the historical or creative roles of certain individuals while occluding the contribution of other equally relevant, but overlooked figures.

This leads to the second point of concern, namely, the risk of giving epistemic authority to voices that have been socially or historically privileged. Simulating a 'conversation' with King Jinheung may be both entertaining and interesting, but it gives precedence to the monarch's perspective and replicates his power over the (voiceless) people over whom he ruled or whom he defeated in battle. This aspect of the discussion raises an issue that is important in acts of everyday conversational exchange, namely, the ways in which individuals pass, receive, and evaluate information.

Miranda Fricker points out that engaging ethically with a person's testimony (including whether one accepts or rejects that testimony) requires a 'socially situated account of human practice' (Fricker 2007, p. 3) which takes account of power relations between speakers. Imbuing historical figures with the power of speech in the absence of social context risks eliding information about the ways in which the relevant individual's testimony was given, received, and evaluated in its historical context. It can be argued further that the ways in which social context operates to make that person's speech intelligible are also lost in a 'reanimated' encounter.

This points to a key problem in the use of museum chatbots, namely the denaturing of historical speech. In the absence of a wider educational framework, chatbots that animate figures from the past decontextualise both speech acts and the social codes that would have been used to understand them. Such efforts face the dilemma that they either create the illusion that we can understand speech from the past, when we do not, or that we make historical actors speak in a contemporary idiom that dispenses with history. This is because the idea of context plays such a key role in interpreting the past, and chatbot 'speech' is essentially context-free. In such cases, the use of a chatbot to unmoor the past from its socio-cultural circumstances seems at odds with the very histories that the museum is tasked with preserving and problematising.

Questions about how to contextualise a chatbot's speech become particularly important in the case of historical figures whose socio-political views may have been contentious in their own day or that are significantly at odds with the perspectives of contemporary audiences. The aesthetically adventurous art that Paul Cézanne, Edgar Degas, and Pierre-Auguste Renoir produced at the end of the nineteenth century, for example, sits uneasily alongside their socially conservative and antisemitic views that came to the fore in the context of the arrest, trial, and conviction of Alfred

Dreyfus for treason.[4] Does this mean that they are not suitable artists for chatbot material or that their reanimated speech should be censored? In this kind of case, the introduction of chatbots into museum spaces raises questions about the way in which institutions approach the histories of their collections and of individuals whose views are ethically problematic or who lived in societies that differ significantly from those of the audience. This strategy inherits all the problems of approaching artworks via the personalities of their creators.

It might be countered that these problems can be eliminated if museum visitors speak not to a historical figure, but to an entity that is itself socially decontextualised—a robot. As technologies for 'animating' machines continue to develop, so too the potential for human interaction with 'social robots' in the museum space has become a more realistic undertaking. Maniscalco et al. (2024) explore and evaluate user experience of a social robot (Pepper) they designed for *Leonardo da Vinci 3D*, an exhibition co-produced by MEDARTEC, the Municipality of Milan, Art Media Studio and the Institute for High-Performance Computing and Networking of the National Research Council of Italy. The authors' study included an evaluation of Pepper's ability to use both verbal and non-verbal communication, to stimulate dialogue with visitors, and to make artworks more intelligible to audiences.

It is beyond the scope of the present discussion to debate the results of the study. The point I want to note is that while the authors suggest optimistic results for the use of their social robot, the ambitions of the project open further ethical questions. Throughout their study, Maniscalco et al. emphasise their aim of creating a robot that implements 'anthropomorphic mechanisms and metaphors to make human interaction as natural as possible' (2024, p. 2). For the authors, this entails the robot engaging 'with humans on a social and emotional level' and, most importantly, attempting to 'preserve the illusion of dealing with a human being' (2024, p. 3).[5]

Maniscalco et al. suggest that social robots are successful because they make artworks 'more appealing to a larger audience' by offering a novel form of interaction (2024, p. 1). While this suggests that the appeal of the robot is greater than that of artworks (with or without the assistance of a human intermediary), the authors stress the importance of the machine's anthropomorphic features. They argue that the social robot—as opposed to a disembodied chatbot—is capable of creating 'a more stable and lasting engagement […] appearing as more trustworthy and credible also thanks to their physical embodiment' (Maniscalco et al. 2024, p. 2). This raises the paradox that if it were possible to create a social robot that is indistinguishable from a human interlocutor, we would seem to have come full circle. If machines and humans look,

[4] For further discussion of artistic responses to the Dreyfus Affair see Kleeblatt (1987).

[5] Interestingly, the goal of human-like conversation remains the ideal even where the relevant partner is not a human avatar. To take another example, the chatbot Máximo the Titanosaur at the Field Museum of Chicago was designed to answer questions 'in a human-like manner' (Varitimiadis et al. 2021, p. 8). The replication of human speech was the goal—despite the fossilised state of the chatbot's actual counterpart—because, as the developer explained, it would not otherwise be 'fun' (Pequignot 2019).

behave, and talk in ways that are indistinguishable, why—from the perspective of the interlocutor—should the robot be a preferable conversation partner to the human?[6]

The idea that the creation of a social robot should be driven by the desire to simulate human behaviour by engineering 'ever more natural human–robot interaction' (Maniscalco et al. 2024, p. 16) is also troubling. AI has, since its inception, navigated versions of the so-called 'Turing test', broadly, a test in which an interrogator is asked to determine whether their conversation partner is a human or a machine (Oppy and Dowe 2021). As chatbot technologies have developed, the ambition of modelling a conversation that is indistinguishable from human speech has been an object of technical challenge and, indeed, competition.[7] While this kind of experimentation might be a staple element of computer science studies, there are ethical questions about whether the simulation of human behaviour by a machine—and the resulting audience deception—should rightly be part of contemporary museum culture. This culture is premised on drawing a distinction between authentic artworks and forgeries or pastiche. In consequence, curation is driven by the general values that are integral to academic work: to take care over one's results and not to lie (Williams 2002). As repositories of audience trust, should heritage institutions mediate their offerings to the public via essentially deceptive means?

I began this discussion by suggesting that the introduction of chatbots (and the utopian rhetoric that surrounds them) could be understood as an extension of participatory art and curatorial practices of the 1990s. While this genealogy holds true for the simple fact of interactivity proposed by chatbots, there are salient differences between the two. First, participatory practices envisaged audience contribution as part of a democratising trend in museum culture. It was thought that participation could function as a strategy for audience empowerment through acts of co-creation. By contrast, interactive chatbots may be said to reinforce a set of elitist background conditions that emerge at the intersection of heritage and technology because they function in an essentially asymmetric way.

Whereas participatory practices emphasise the agency of individuals in recrafting socio-cultural dynamics and responding creatively to challenges faced by a range of different communities, museum chatbots *impose* technologies and patterns of communication on audiences. Museums identify a lack of engagement with their collections as a problem and draw on technology to solve it. Reflecting Katzenbach's concern that 'algorithmic moderation and regulation will become more and more seamlessly integrated into our social lives' (2021, p. 6), museum chatbots prioritise human–machine interaction at the expense of encounters between humans. Participation may remain a goal, but the method of achieving it is delegated to an

[6] Maniscalco et al. (2024) cite various reasons why social robots in heritage settings can offer 'more successful interaction with humans', but the reasons noted (ability to communicate through verbal and non-verbal signs; embodiment; generation of longer encounters by appearing trustworthy) seem to replicate human forms of interaction rather than generating new kinds of engagement (Maniscalco et al. 2024, pp. 1–2).

[7] The Loebner Prize (1990–2019) was an annual competition that awarded prizes to AI programmes that most successfully simulated human speech.

algorithm and its outcomes are, in consequence, less socially focused than speaking with a museum curator, educator, or cultural mediator.[8]

The second divergence from histories of participatory art and curation concerns the presentation of technology itself. The styles of art associated with interactive practices and, indeed, the methods of their presentation to publics were rightly understood in the 1990s as cultural artefacts in their own right. By contrast, the tendency in chatbot technology is to make the conversational interface as seamless as possible by hiding the underlying technology and crafting more 'human-like' machines. Rather than understanding the machine, its method of functioning, and the algorithms and databases that power its 'conversation' as distinctive techno-cultural entities, the status and function of these components are naturalised. By positing the chatbot as a transparent conduit to a museum collection (rather than as a part of that collection), it is placed outside a culturally demarcated space and assumes an epistemic authority in its own right. In consequence, neither the machine nor the technologies that make it function are appreciated by audiences as socially constructed entities that are derived from and embedded in a particular culture. Technological opacity is therefore connected to, and indeed facilitates, the act of conversational deception described above.

By drawing a contrast between participatory practices of the 1990s and the uses of contemporary chatbots, I do not wish to suggest that there is an easy dichotomy between positive and negative features of these two strategies of audience engagement. Rather, my contention is that both the emergence and appeal of chatbots are better understood when contextualised against a history of museum practices that have historically turned to participation as a means of fostering positive social outcomes. As noted above, it is also the case that interactive art and curatorial practices have themselves been the subject of criticism. Bishop famously argued that participatory art was aimed primarily at artworld insiders who shared an identifiable set of interests (2004, pp. 64–65, 67–69). Kester offered a different kind of critique when he argued that participatory practices were themselves part of a universalising discourse that elided political and economic differences between communities and nations (2004, pp. 104–107; 2011, p. 9). Both Bishop and Kester highlighted the need for questions to be raised about the types of experience created by museums (including who their audiences were) and how strategies for participation could be usefully developed at local and specific levels. Similar questions need to be posed about the use of chatbots. Developing this line of thinking, I now want to consider whether or not participation in algorithmic speech acts supports the creation of diverse museum 'communities' and, if they do, what kinds of community they foster.

[8] It should be noted, however, that such sophisticated systems make use of supervised learning that entails reinforcement from human feedback. This is not, however, the involvement of the end user, but is part of the developmental process that fine tunes the model's outputs.

13.3 Conversation and Community

While chatbots are being introduced by museums in an attempt to devise new encounters with their collections, there is a more potent reason why some cultural institutions are turning towards this kind of conversational interface. This concerns a desire to overcome audience embarrassment when faced with the challenge of talking publicly about artworks. In their project on the use of chatbots in museums, Gustke et al. (2024) gathered qualitative feedback that suggested visitors were more confident when asking questions of machines than humans. In similar vein, Rachabatuni et al. (2024) argue that chatbots can create 'a welcoming and non-intimidating space for questions, fostering trust and interaction' (2024, p. 1). Such ideas came to the fore in a project undertaken in 2017 by the Pinacoteca of São Paulo and IBM Watson that attempted to 'animate' paintings in the collection. Titled 'The Voice of Art' ('A Voz da arte'), the project equipped audience members with cellphones and headsets so that they could ask questions about the museums' artworks or, more adventurously, ask questions of characters depicted in those works. When asked to explain whether or not they enjoyed using the technology, one audience member replied in the affirmative, adding 'I didn't feel ashamed' (Connexis 2017).

Visitor comments about the use of technology to avoid embarrassment suggest more than a desire to encounter art in a new way. Rather, they signal an important problem in wider socio-cultural environments. If audiences are reluctant to express their own ideas about art to another human or if heritage institutions are unable to devise ways in which to mediate their collections successfully, this points to the existence of a problematic museum culture rather than evidence of a community's attraction to technology. When 'The Voice of Art' was created, it was estimated that around 72% of Brazilians had never visited a museum (Pasikowska-Schnass and Lim 2023, p. 2). The use of a chatbot to ameliorate this problem can be understood as part of an increasingly familiar attitude to the potential use and supposed social benefits of AI. As Katzenbach has noted, technology is being positioned 'as a necessary and functional solution to social problems and challenges' (2021, p. 2). In the present case, the so-called 'problem' ranges from a lack of audience empowerment to a perceived staleness in the presentation of heritage sites and their collections. Museum chatbots may operate as a tool to deal with such problems, but it is necessary to enquire not simply into what might be gained by using them in museums, but what might be lost in so doing. The significant loss concerns the displacement of human conversation by algorithmic speech.

The idea behind 'The Voice of Art' was interesting because it sought to stimulate exchanges between audience members and artworks. Video footage of audiences using the technology demonstrated, however, the kind of conversational gap that can arise between humans and machines: in response to a question posed to the protagonist of Candido Portinari's *The Mestizo* (1934) 'Do you like to play soccer?', the response was: 'In 1934, soccer was already huge in Brazil, but a field worker like him didn't have time to play'; a question asked of the female character in Almeida Junior's painting *Saudade* (*Longing*) of 1899, 'Who do you miss?' prompted the response: 'The hat shows that a man lived in the house. The letter in her hands and the black dress make us believe this man died' (Connexis 2017). The difference between the affective content of the question and the bland, informational quality of the response is stark. To the extent that the technology was designed to spark an imaginative encounter between visitor and fictional character, it instead diverted the 'conversation' to the kind of result that would be derived from an ordinary internet search.[9]

It might be argued that as chatbots are trained on increasingly large models and 'learn' from the exchanges they have with human speakers, the ensuing conversations are likely to simulate more affective speech. While some computer scientists have the goal of creating models that demonstrate natural language *understanding* (typically through the creation of ever larger models), Bender and Koller point out that LLMs 'do not learn "meaning", but rather reflect meaning into linguistic form that humans then interpret' (2020, p. 19). While the authors call for more precise language in scholarly descriptions of the uses, possibilities, and limitations of LLMs, their concern about the hype of natural language 'understanding' is acute in the context of the heritage industries.

One description of 'The Voice of Art', for example, claimed that the interface answered visitors' questions 'in real time using cognitive chatbots that *understand human language and intent*' (Barth 2017, emphasis added). Similarly, in their search for improved human–machine interaction, Maniscalco et al. suggest that social robots have 'embodied abilities' that enable them 'to communicate and interact with humans on a social and emotional level' (2024, p. 3). Such descriptions not only encourage the view that machines can (or will one day) act and think like humans, but also imply that algorithmic speech is an adequate substitute for human conversation. This leads to a further ethical issue that arises in the case of museum chatbots, namely, the kind of linguistic community that is created from 'conversations' between humans and machines.

In his discussion of the limitations of 'cyborg speech', Seargeant points out that language is 'intimately tied up with our identity, with the way we manage our relationships and with how we engage with the world' (2024, pp. 115–116). The ways in which audiences interact with artworks can be understood as part of that engagement. Building on arguments about language use proposed by Searle (1980), Bender and Koller defend the view that because humans use language not merely in formal ways, but to communicate ideas about the speaker's 'actual (physical, social, and mental) world', so too responses 'must connect the meanings of perceived inputs to information about that world' (2020, p. 2). While chatbots may simulate human speech to increasingly impressive degrees, their use of algorithms to manipulate formal linguistic elements as a predictive response to keywords and structures proposed by a conversation partner does not—and cannot—function in the same way as human

[9] Trichopoulos et al. (2023) and Rachabatuni et al. (2024) debate potential ways in which to enhance the quality and degree of accurate contextual information provided by chatbots in heritage settings. While such improvements are important, they do not, however, address the affective and ethical qualities of conversation addressed in the present chapter.

speech. While discussions about the design and use of museum chatbots focus on how AI learns from speakers, the better question is how speakers learn from AI. To the extent that 'cyborg speech' does not (and cannot) reflect a human encounter with the world, the risk is that human speakers will modify their own language and conversational structures to better facilitate an exchange with the machine. Speakers are drawn into a form of linguistic interaction that has the structure of gamification while attempting to mimic human speech.

As will be seen from the preceding discussion, the use of chatbots in museum settings is also part of a wider discourse about what people learn from art. I would argue that this misses a crucial aspect of conversational encounters in the museum space. This concerns the use of language not simply to learn about—or even from—art, but rather what speakers might learn about or from each other. Literature about chatbots focuses on engagement and learning but omits consideration of the ethical consequences of conversation between humans.

In an article published in 1994, feminist educator and philosopher Nel Noddings explored the idea of conversation as a form of 'moral education' (Noddings 1994). She focused, in particular, on language exchange between adults and humans, proposing that many children and adolescents 'lack opportunities to engage in real conversation with adults' (1994, p. 114). Noddings debates the qualities of ordinary conversation, including the extent to which it is capable of generating a valuable ethical encounter. For a conversation to function in an ethical way, Noddings argues that the participants need to be aware that their conversation partners 'are more important than the topic' (Noddings 1994, p. 115). The kind of conversational encounter that Noddings envisages is not one that is possible in a chatbot exchange. Not only does participation in algorithmic speech exchange lack the element of empathy, but it also fails to involve the museum visitor in an ethical encounter. This not only means that chatbots fail to produce a community of speakers, but that individuals are trained not to have regard for their conversational partner precisely because it is a machine (even if it is a robot with anthropomorphic features). While chatbots may be able to provide increasingly sophisticated information about heritage objects, they fail to offer the social and ethical encounters that museums have traditionally fostered through simple acts of human conversation.

The final point to make in this context concerns the impact of chatbots on the roles played by museum educators, cultural mediators, and curators. It is worth noting that attempts to improve the responses of chatbots require expert human input. Trichopoulos et al. suggest, for example, that for the purposes of building their chatbot 'Expert curators and domain specialists should work in collaboration with ChatGPT4, reviewing and verifying the information generated by the model to ensure its accuracy and scientific integrity' (2023, p. 2). This is, however, a fundamental change in the role of the heritage expert who no longer actively produces information or creatively associates with a human audience but, instead, verifies information scraped from sources such as Wikipedia for the purpose of fine-tuning the range of responses offered by a machine. As in many other AI contexts, human labour is vital to building an efficient language model, yet it remains invisible and undervalued.[10]

Inevitably, one of the attractions of replacing human museum workers with technologies relates to cost savings. Krantz and Downey (2021) have examined the loss of museum educators in the wake of the COVID-19 pandemic and the ensuing impact of this on the wider social role of the museum. They point out that museum educators have historically been 'the name and face of the museum to local communities' (2021, p. 425) and that the kinds of relationships they build are derived from trust rather than transactional exchange. While museum educators form a bridge between institutions and communities, they also play an important role in fostering open—often productively chaotic—conversations about art, contesting histories, and co-creating knowledge with audiences (as opposed to delivering information to them). This makes their role fundamentally inconsistent with the conversational encounters afforded by chatbots.

13.4 Conclusion

The above discussion has expressed some sceptical views about the uses of chatbots in heritage settings, but this is not to undermine either the computer science or the museum aspirations that underlie the design and implementation of these technologies. Rather, my aim has been to problematise the use of chatbots against a background of museum histories and ethical issues relating to conversation. Understanding the drive to use chatbots in the context of discourses about participatory art and interactive practices provides insight into the ambitions of museums to attract audiences and the risks of using machines as a substitute for humans. Although the aim of integrating chatbots into museum contexts is to stimulate ideas about and responses to art, there is ultimately no shared sense-making between audience and machine because AI does not connect to the world in a way that facilitates such a project. For this reason, the responsible use of chatbots in heritage settings remains a challenge to both museum professionals and researchers.

In his discussion of LLMs, Lazar (2024) makes the point that generative agents 'are excellent *simulations* of human agency' and that, as such, they test our commitment to 'the value of the real'. This idea has potent ramifications in a heritage context where transparency about the difference between fake and authentic artefacts is crucial to the academic and social mission of museums. The introduction of chatbots into museums interposes a fake conversational encounter between audiences and collections that seems, therefore, inconsistent with the overall aim of the institution.

[10] A corollary is the anonymous labour of so-called 'MTurkers' for Amazon's Mechanical Turk platform. Stephens (2022) both contextualises and examines the social implications of 'Human Intelligence Tasks' (e.g. captioning, tagging data, describing audio or video) performed by such workers in conditions of new systems of data capitalism.

In debating the consequences of the technological developments I have examined, one could usefully address and extend the point urged by Leopoldina and Autumn Edwards to 'resist the simple fascination that machines exert on humans and assume the standpoint of critical witness to the socio-cultural changes taking place under our gaze' (Fortunati and Edwards 2022, p. 7). The integration of AI into heritage contexts is one of the major socio-cultural changes that museums have witnessed in decades, but publics and researchers need to do more than assume the stance of a 'critical witness' to such developments. Understanding and actively interrogating the evolution of human–machine conversation in heritage settings entails reflection not just on technology, but on the ways in which the latter's uses appeal to or confound social relations. The use of chatbots can, at the very least, function as a lens through which to better examine the legacies of participatory practices in museum settings and the challenges such traditions present for the future.

References

Anne Frank House (2017) Anne Frank House launches bot for Messenger, 21 Mar 2017. Accessed 24 Jan 2024. https://www.annefrank.org/en/about-us/news-and-press/news/2017/3/21/anne-frank-house-launches-bot-messenger/

Barnes Foundation (2017) Barnes Foundation announces launch of new framework for searching collection online, 6 Nov 2017. Accessed 16 Feb 2024. https://www.barnesfoundation.org/press/press-releases/launch-of-new-framework-for-searching-collection-online

Barth F (2017) Some technical details and challenges of project: the voice of art—IBM | Watson, 3 June 2017. Accessed 9 Mar 2024. https://www.linkedin.com/pulse/some-technical-details-challenges-project-voice-art-ibm-barth/

Bender EM, Koller A (2020) Climbing towards NLU: on meaning, form, and understanding in the age of data. In: Proceedings of the 58th annual meeting of the association for computational linguistics. Association for Computational Linguistics, pp 5185–5198. https://doi.org/10.18653/v1/2020.acl-main.463

Bender EM, Gebru T, McMillan-Major A, Schmitchell S (2021) On the dangers of stochastic parrots: can language models be too big? In: FAccT 21, proceedings of the 2021 ACM conference on fairness, accountability, and transparency, 3–10 Mar 2021, pp 610–623. https://doi.org/10.1145/3442188.3445922

Bishop C (2004) Antagonism and relational aesthetics. October 110:55–79

Boiano S, Borda A, Gaia G, Rossi S, Cuomo P (2018) Chatbots and new audience opportunities for museums and heritage organisations. In: Conference paper: electronic visualisation and the arts, July 2018, pp 9–13. https://doi.org/10.14236/ewic/EVA2018.33

Bouras V, Spiliopoulos D, Margaris D, Vassilakis C, Kotis K, Antonious A, Lepouras G, Wallace M, Poulopoulos V (2023) Chatbots for cultural venues: a topic-based approach. Algorithms 16(339):1–28. https://doi.org/10.3390/a16070339

Bourriaud N (2009) Relational aesthetics. Translated by Pleasance S, Woods F with the participation of Copeland M. Les Presses du réel

Brown K (ed) (2016) Interactive contemporary art: participation in practice. IB Tauris

Connexis Digital Mentors (2017) The voice of art with Watson. [Video]. Accessed 22 Jan 2024. https://www.youtube.com/watch?v=ogpv984_60A

Fahden M, Gebauer A (2024) With AI to art! Chatting with Helen of Troy and Co. through IBM Watson. In: Thiel S, Bernhardt JC (eds) AI in museums: reflections, perspectives and applications. Transcript Verlag, pp 265–272

Faust J (2018) Virtual Andrew Carnegie makes for memorable visit to the museum. Pittsburgh Magazine, 24 July 2018. Accessed 22 Jan 2024. https://www.pittsburghmagazine.com/virtual-andrew-carnegie-makes-for-memorable-visit-to-the-museum/
Fortunati L, Edwards A (2022) Framing the psycho-social and cultural aspects of human-machine communication. Hum-Mach Commun 4(3):7–26. https://doi.org/10.30658/hmc.4.1
Fricker M (2007) Epistemic injustice: power and the ethics of knowledge. Oxford University Press
Gaia G, Boiano S, Borda A (2019) Engaging museum visitors with AI: the case of chatbots. In: Giannini T, Bowen JP (eds) Museums and digital culture: new perspectives and research. Springer, pp 309–329. https://doi.org/10.1007/978-3-319-97457-6_15
Gustke O, Schaffer S, Ruß A (2024) Exploring and explaining museum objects with speech-based AI. In: Thiel S, Bernhardt JC (eds) AI in museums: reflections, perspectives and applications. Transcript Verlag, pp 357–364
Hamilton M, Fu S, Ly M, Bui J, Bopp D, Chen Z, Tran F, Wang M, Rogers MN, Zhang L, Hoder C, Freeman WT (2021) MosAIc: finding artistic connections across culture with conditional image retrieval. Proc Mach Learn Res 1:1–23. https://doi.org/10.48550/arXiv.2007.07177
Katzenbach C (2021) "AI will fix this"—the technical, discursive, and political turn in governing communication. Big Data Soc 1–8. https://doi.org/10.1177/20539517211046182
Kester G (2004) Conversation pieces: community and communication in modern art. University of California Press
Kester G (2011) The one and the many: contemporary collaborative art in a global context. Duke University Press
Kleeblatt NL (ed) (1987) The Dreyfus affair: art, truth, and justice, exh. cat. The Jewish Museum, University of California Press, New York
Krantz A, Downey S (2021) The significant loss of museum educators in 2020: a data story. J Mus Educ 46(4):417–429
Langfeld G (2018) The canon in art history: concepts and approaches. J Art Historiogr 19:1–18
Lazar S (2024) Frontier AI ethics. Aeon, 17 Feb 2024. https://aeon.co/essays/can-philosophy-help-us-get-a-grip-on-the-consequences-of-ai
Litt S (2018) Dot, the new Akron Art Museum chatbot, wants to get you talking about art and life. Cleveland.com (arts), 5 Aug 2018. Accessed 22 Jan 2024. https://www.cleveland.com/arts/2018/08/dot_the_new_akron_art_museum_c.html
Maniscalco U, Minutolo A, Storniolo P, Esposito M (2024) Towards a more anthropomorphic interaction with robots in museum settings: an experimental study. Robot Auton Syst 171:1–17. https://doi.org/10.1016/j.robot.2023.104561
Mollica J (2017) Send me SFMOMA, June 2017. Accessed 22 Jan 2024. https://www.sfmoma.org/read/send-me-sfmoma/
Morgan M (2014) Speech communities. Cambridge University Press
Müller A, Schiffmann M, Neumeister A, Richert A (2024) Exploring beyond exhibits: creating knowledge for social robots in public spaces. In: Thiel S, Bernhardt JC (eds), AI in museums: reflections, perspectives and applications. Transcript Verlag, pp 273–286
Nochlin L (2018) Why have there been no great women artists [1971]. In: Nochlin L (ed) Women, art, and power and other essays. Routledge, pp 145–178
Noddings N (1994) Conversation as moral education. J Moral Educ 23(2):107–118. https://doi.org/10.1080/0305724940230201
Noh Y-G, Hong J-H (2021) Designing reenacted chatbots to enhance museum experience. Appl Sci 11(16):7420, 1–15. https://doi.org/10.3390/app11167420
Oppy G, Dowe D (2021) The turing test. In: Zalta EN (ed) The Stanford encyclopedia of philosophy (winter 2021 edition). https://plato.stanford.edu/archives/win2021/entries/turing-test/
Pasikowska-Schnass M, Lim Y-S (2023) Artificial intelligence in the context of cultural heritage and museums. In: European Parliament briefing, members' research service PE747.120, May, pp 1–11
Pequignot C (2019) Teaching a titanosaur to talk: conversational UX design for field museum. Accessed May 2024. https://purplerockscissors.com/blog/teaching-a-titanosaur-to-talk

Pollock G (2007) Encounters in the virtual feminist museum: time, space and the archive. Routledge

Rachabatuni PK, Principi F, Mazzanti P, Bertini M (2024) Context-aware chatbot using MLLMs for cultural heritage. In: ACM multimedia systems conference 2024, Bari, Italy, 15–18 Apr 2024. ACM, New York, NY, USA. https://doi.org/10.1145/3625468.3652193

Seargeant P (2024) The future of language: how technology, politics and utopianism are transforming the way we communicate. Bloomsbury

Searle J (1980) Minds, brains, and programs. Behav Brain Sci 3(3):417–424

Stephens E (2022) The Mechanical Turk: a short history of 'artificial artificial intelligence.' Cult Stud 37:1. https://doi.org/10.1080/09502386.2022.2042580

The National WWII Museum (2023) The national WWII museum to unveil new interactive oral history experience voices from the front. Press release, 5 Oct 2024. Accessed 19 Feb 2024. https://www.nationalww2museum.org/media/press-releases/national-wwii-museum-unveil-new-interactive-oral-history-experience-voices

Trichopoulos G, Konstantakis M, Caridakis G, Katifori A, Koukouli M (2023) Crafting a museum guide using ChatGPT4. Big Data Cogn Comput 7(3):148, 1–15. https://doi.org/10.3390/bdcc7030148

Varitimiadis S, Kotis K, Pittou D, Konstantakis G (2021) Graph-based conversational AI: towards a distributed and collaborative multi-chatbot approach for museums. Appl Sci 11:9160. https://doi.org/10.3390/app11199160

Williams B (2002) Truth and truthfulness: an essay in genealogy. Princeton University Press

Kathryn Brown is Reader in Art Histories, Markets and Digital Heritage at Loughborough University. Her books include *Women Readers in French Painting 1870–1890* (2012), (ed.) *Interactive Contemporary Art: Participation in Practice* (2014), (ed.) *Perspectives on Degas* (2016), *Matisse's Poets: Critical Performance in the Artist's Book* (2017), (ed.) *The Routledge Companion to Digital Humanities and Art History* (2020), *Henri Matisse* (2021), *Dialogues with Degas: Influence and Antagonism in Contemporary Art* (2023) and *Art Auctions: Spectacle and Value in the 21st Century* (2024). She is the series editor of Contextualising Art Markets for Bloomsbury Academic.

The manufacturer's authorised representative in the EU is Springer Nature Customer Service Centre GmbH, Europaplatz 3, 69115 Heidelberg, Germany. If you have any concerns regarding our products, please contact ProductSafety@springernature.com

Printed and bound by CPI Group (UK) Ltd, Croydon, CR0 4YY
01/10/2026
02225966-0009